The Rise and Fall of the Mounted Knight

The Rise and Fall of the Mounted Knight

Clive Hart

First published in Great Britain in 2022 by
Pen & Sword History
An imprint of
Pen & Sword Books Ltd
Yorkshire – Philadelphia

Copyright © Clive Hart 2022

ISBN 978 1 39908 204 4

The right of Clive Hart to be identified as Author of this work has been asserted by him in accordance with the Copyright, Designs and Patents Act 1988.

A CIP catalogue record for this book is
available from the British Library.

All rights reserved. No part of this book may be reproduced or transmitted in any form or by any means, electronic or mechanical including photocopying, recording or by any information storage and retrieval system, without permission from the Publisher in writing.

Typeset by Mac Style
Printed in the UK by CPI Group (UK) Ltd, Croydon, CR0 4YY.

Pen & Sword Books Limited incorporates the imprints of Atlas, Archaeology, Aviation, Discovery, Family History, Fiction, History, Maritime, Military, Military Classics, Politics, Select, Transport, True Crime, Air World, Frontline Publishing, Leo Cooper, Remember When, Seaforth Publishing, The Praetorian Press, Wharncliffe Local History, Wharncliffe Transport, Wharncliffe True Crime and White Owl.

For a complete list of Pen & Sword titles please contact

PEN & SWORD BOOKS LIMITED
47 Church Street, Barnsley, South Yorkshire, S70 2AS, England
E-mail: enquiries@pen-and-sword.co.uk
Website: www.pen-and-sword.co.uk

Or

PEN AND SWORD BOOKS
1950 Lawrence Rd, Havertown, PA 19083, USA
E-mail: Uspen-and-sword@casematepublishers.com
Website: www.penandswordbooks.com

Contents

Acknowledgements		vi
Introduction		vii
Chapter 1	Dawn of Knighthood	1
Chapter 2	The Norman Era	21
Chapter 3	The Crusades	39
Chapter 4	The Mounted Knight	68
Chapter 5	The Knight's Horse	94
Chapter 6	Age of Chivalry	127
Chapter 7	The Rise of Infantry	164
Chapter 8	Dusk of Knighthood	189
Chapter 9	Rebirth of the Mounted Knight	219
Notes		234
Bibliography		258
Index		272

Acknowledgements

This book was only ever possible because of the owner of Historic Equitation, Dominic Sewell, who first put a lance into my hand, and then, unbelievably, gave me a horse. If that wasn't enough, he also gave me my first opportunity to joust, one I was sure I wasn't good enough for, but one I nevertheless was not going to turn down. The rest, as they say, is history, and further thanks must be made to Dominic for giving me access to his well-stocked knightly-themed library, which enriched the following work immensely. Thanks must also be given to Sam Gostner, who has a rare skill with a camera, and made the effort to photograph me and my equipment for this book. Another thank you is due to all those who read any part of the draft for me, and any errors still remaining are my own. The final thanks must go to the horses which have taught innumerable lessons, but especially to Charlie who has kept me alive when others might not have.

Introduction

When thinking of the medieval period the most enduring image that springs to mind is that of the knight clad in armour, mounted on a warhorse, brandishing a sword or lance. Alongside the stories of King Arthur and Robin Hood, the concept of the knight is one of the few still in the collective consciousness. This image is often supplemented by ideas of rescuing damsels, slaying dragons or brutally suppressing peasants, which is hardly surprising given that one of the most common sources of information on knights is Hollywood movies. By picking up this book, you as the reader are looking for something more, and together we will delve into the world of the European mounted knight. This was a world of human and equine complexity, often misunderstood in modern times. Indeed, the main aim of this book is to correct the many misconceptions surrounding the horses that knights rode. It has been said that civilisation was carried on the back of the horse, and during every important historical moment of the middle ages, a horse can always be found nearby. We shall deal with the size and types of medieval horses, as well as how they were treated and used in combat. This is an area which is not purely theoretical or academic, as there is a contemporary international community seeking to recreate the horses, saddlery, armour and riding techniques of history. This knowledge lends a different dynamic to the historical record and helps bring it to life. For example, taking part in an eight person joust has given me a living window into the world of the mounted knight fighting in a tournament: all of us competing at the same time, in only a small 20m by 20m field, in a whirling and chaotic dogfight filled with broken lances and flashing steel swords.

Before we can understand the rise and eventual decline of the mounted knight in western Europe, the mounted knight firstly needs to be defined. Firstly, of course, a mounted knight needs to be mounted. More specifically, he is mounted on a horse to fight, specifically in hand-to-hand combat. He may occasionally employ missile weapons from horseback, but the mounted knight as discussed here is primarily a close combat warrior. Secondly, he must be a knight. The word itself comes from the Old English *cniht*[1] and the Germanic *Knecht*[2] which both have a common meaning of boy or servant. The meaning in Saxon England over time became that of a household retainer in a manner which begins to reflect the nature of a truly medieval household knight. These retainers and warriors evolved into a separate social class who owned, or at least had the income rights to, land which existed in the main to equip and support the knight with what he needed to go to war. There is continual evolution of the term from the Norman period right through the medieval age, and as a result the actual meaning of the word 'knight' is never constant for very long at all. The noble knight could often be found fighting alongside the non-noble man-at-arms, or the nobleman who was not yet knighted. The non-noble men-at-arms were equipped in the same way as their social betters, suffered the same hardships and fought equally effectively. While our primary focus is those who were actually knighted, men-at-arms were always to be found alongside them so should not be forgotten. The final ingredient required to define the mounted knight for our purpose is chivalry. This was a set of guidelines on a range of subjects, be they practical or aspirational, and are the final part of our definition. Being as transient as the definition of 'knight', we will follow how layers of chivalry were slowly folded into knighthood over time, and how closely the reality matched the ideal. The battlefield nemesis of the mounted knight will also be studied; that is, the increasingly professional infantry within Europe that sometimes managed to overthrow their social superiors. The relationship between the knight and famous infantry such as the Swiss will be explored and we will see how, in what was an arms race, neither group ever had total dominance over the other. The decline of the mounted knight will then be explained through a combination of factors, political, financial and technological, and also why the mounted knight continued to be decisive even 250 years after gunpowder appeared on the battlefield.

To conduct any analysis on events hundreds of years ago, however, we must consider how we know about them in the first place. The amazing thing about the medieval world is that it was increasingly literate and we can look at the words written by knights themselves, as well as their enemies.³ In the first half of the fifteenth century, Gutierre Diaz De Gamez wrote a biography of his master, Don Pero Nino. De Gamez was his standard bearer and fought alongside Pero Nino from the North African Coast to the South of England. The deeds of his master are elevated to glorious heights, even when occasionally he is not particularly sensible. De Gamez is perhaps the true chivalric hero of the tale, barely mentioning himself and serving his master with his pen as faithfully as he had with his banner. In his Prologue he also tells us what a knight should be by explaining to us the four virtues that a fifteenth-century Spanish knight should emulate, namely Prudence, Justice, Temperance and Fortitude. He writes that Justice is, 'human fellowship, not to do evil to a neighbour, but to do him service'. Prudence, he explains, is to follow the path of good, and Temperance is resisting evil and disorder. Fortitude, De Gamez writes, is not to bow beneath adversity, 'nor be lifted up by prosperity … fortitude is humility without pride'.⁴ This knightly ideal that De Gamez clearly holds very dearly is recognisable to modern eyes as part of chivalry. The idea of a human fellowship in the middle ages had a narrower scope of inclusion than it would now, but the urge to do good deeds, persevere through troubles and avoid pride are all qualities generally seen as good today. Throughout this book we will steer a course between such lofty ideals and the dirtier realities of being a mounted knight. A glimpse into the murkier side of medieval military life is given in a poem written by Thomas Hoccleve around 1420, which is just after De Gamez and Pero Nino were active. The following extract implores young men to treat war veterans with compassion:

> How many gentlemen may men now see,
> Who before in the old wars of France,
> Honoured were, and held most fondly,
>
> …
>
> Alas, their fellowship is crooked and lame,
> Now age, decrepit, shuts away favour,
> Now forgotten is their manly labour,
>
> …

> Now these worthy men [are] beaten with the rod,
>
> ...
>
> And since those men who were in arms,
> Are into poverty fallen,
> You men of arms ought especially,
> To help them: alas! Have you no piteous blood
> That might stir you to do for them some good?[5]

Homeless, poor, crooked and crippled veterans would have been a feature throughout medieval Europe.[6] Men without eyes, arms, legs and hands would be visible on town streets, not to mention the hidden masses with deep mental health issues caused by the extreme brutality of medieval warfare. How many lonely old soldiers jumped into a dirty water-filled ditch when they heard the thundering sound of hooves approaching, only to remember they were at home and not on campaign? The reality of medieval warfare lies somewhere between De Gamez's glory and the aching suffering of Hoccleve's neglected veterans. Although the ideals of knighthood as written at the time can be seen as worthy, the reality of the world in which they were forged was unpleasant. If as some have suggested, chivalry evolved in part to mitigate the horrors of war, even if only for the privileged, it had to have been worth a try. We shall chart the merging of mounted fighting ability, piety and finally chivalry as they combined into a new social class, the noble mounted knight.

Chapter One

Dawn of Knighthood

The Ancient World

Horses were first domesticated for food many thousands of years ago,[1] but for war they were first employed as chariot pullers rather than as mounted cavalry.[2] Chariot horses were small compared to modern horses, but by using the technology of the wheel and often being used in pairs, they were able to form an effective fighting system. One of the earliest surviving written works on any subject at all is a manual for the care of chariot horses, written for a Hittite king around 1360 BC.[3,4] Horse breeding, care, training and use all required skilled people to facilitate and maintain so it should come as no surprise that this knowledge was written down. This required a specialisation of professions which meant a society had to exist that could support a body of men so that they did not have to work in the fields to feed themselves. This happened on grand scale, demonstrated by the fact that the great empires of the Hittites and Egyptians reputedly put at least 4,000 chariots into action between them at the Battle of Kadesh in 1274 BC.[5] This suggests that sophisticated systems were in place in both empires to maintain the horses as well as the chariots and other weaponry that went along with them. The sheer cost of having this many chariots was possible because the small ruling class of the population was fantastically rich. This inequality was a feedback loop where only the rich could afford horses, and those that could afford horses became richer due to the power and influence that owning horses tended to convey. The military power didn't hurt either, and it has been argued that the harnessing of the horse was the foundation of a class division that lasts until the present.[6] However some things did change, and the days of the charioteer waned as the ancient world learnt to ride their horses instead. They found that a mounted warrior could not only dodge a chariot while offering more attacking capability, but was also cheaper because no one had to build and look after the chariots themselves. Horses unencumbered by pulling a wheeled vehicle were also more able to traverse difficult ground, not to mention being significantly more manoeuvrable in combat. By the eighth century BC the Assyrians were depicting themselves in art as riding horses into battle instead of chariots, and the mounted warrior was born.[7]

The Greeks

This ability was first notably recorded in Europe in the Greek world, although many other cultures were by this time accomplished horsemen. Indeed Aristotle described a type of government that was made up of citizens taken from the warrior class, 'represented at first by cavalry'.[8] There was a property requirement to be in this class and in this way the Greek aristocrats do hazily resemble later medieval knights. The Greek most famous for his horsemanship works was Xenophon, who wrote on the care and training of horses, and offered such eminently sensible advice as to never approach a horse in anger, and never to use violent punishment when training an animal. He also wrote that reins should be held loosely to avoid hurting the mouth of the animal, and that the utmost attention to be paid to avoid damaging the back of the horse.

Another of Xenophon's work, *The Cavalry General*, is more of a military manual in the use of cavalry. He recommends the use of mounted scouts and patrols and also learning over which types of ground infantry are quicker than horses. More sophisticated advice included ruses such as giving all the mounted grooms staves to hold, which from a distance will look like lances to the enemy. This sixth-century BC manual made much of the need for constant practice for war because, 'when it comes to charging and retiring, the onward-dashing gallop, the well-skilled timely retreat, expert knowledge of the ground and scenery will assert superiority over inexpertness like that of eyesight over blindness.'[9] It is not clear if all Greek states employed cavalry as well drilled as Xenophon described however, or rather if he was writing with the aim of improving the mounted forces of his state. One interesting comment is that he suggests cavalry horses can be part funded from the money paid by those wishing to avoid cavalry service. This sounds a lot like the later medieval system that allowed knights to pay their king an amount of money so that they did not have muster themselves to his service. He also mentioned hiring foreign cavalry to bolster numbers, another practice that is common throughout history. This is probably more apt for the Greeks however, due to the often mountainous terrain of their states, where it is harder to raise and maintain quantities of horses. The grasslands of northern Greece were the most conducive to the rearing of horses, and it is no accident that the greatest Greek cavalry commander was Alexander the Great, a Macedonian.

Before Alexander most Greek cavalry was used in a supporting role, that is to attack skirmishers and pursue defeated enemies, although they probably would have been effective in throwing javelins at heavy infantry too. Alexander inherited his cavalry army from his father, who is said to have had several thousand elite Companion cavalry serving him. These Companions were landowners and rich men whose purpose was to fight on horseback and can be seen as another ancestor of the European medieval knight. They rode in complicated formations including the wedge, and were used to charge at the enemy to engage in hand-to-hand combat. The Companions were no mere skirmishers and were the battle-winning arm of Alexander's great conquests in the east. He used them expertly to create and attack flanks of enemy formations, as he famously did at the Battle of Gaugamela in 331 BC.[10] It is not however just the date of this tactic which is impressive, but the equipment with which the Companions achieved it. The Greeks did not use saddles and therefore had no stirrups, and still were able to wield long lances with, impressively, two hands. Their training and horsemanship meant that they did not fall off the horse when their charge impacted the enemy, and nor did they require reins to steer. These soldiers were not always of noble birth, at least later on, but were elite and drilled themselves to hone their combat performance. Even if they had no code comparable to chivalry and therefore cannot be considered knights, this made them at least equal to the medieval knight in combat and riding skills, if not more so.

The Romans

The *equites*, or equestrian class, in the Early Roman Republic provided themselves and their horses for mounted military service. The *equites* did not have a duty to bring other soldiers with them on campaign, but they did own their own land.[11] There was a wide range of wealth contained in this social class, from relatively small landowners right up to the senators who ran the great Republic. In early Rome the *equites* would form small light cavalry units on the battlefield, although they were far from the primary component of the Roman army, which was their famous legionary infantry. After the Marian Reforms in 107 BC, the army was professionalised and land-based entry requirements removed.[12] This changed the nature of the army and the *equites* shifted to becoming an officer class rather than a cavalry formation. Coupled with this, the spoils of Rome's unending wars brought a flow of wealth into the city, and the vast majority went to those at the top of the social pyramid. These super rich nobles invested their money back into farming and buying up all land they could lay their hands on. The result was that the small landowning *equites* were pushed out of business, and the numbers within the *equite* class shrank. Along with other causes, this process removed this warrior class of mounted landowners from the Republic, and is an example of financial encroachment that foreshadows the decline of the medieval knight over a thousand years later. What Rome did not have was a knightly class with any notion approaching chivalry, and additionally during the period of the Roman Empire most of its mounted forces were foreign auxiliaries. What Rome did provide to those who came after them, was a memory of an organised military system and a blueprint for rule that medieval rulers were keen to emulate.

Eastern Knights

It is worth briefly considering the idea that European knighthood was a unique phenomenon that grew out of Christian areas and doctrine. Within the Sassanid Empire that centred around modern Iran in the seventh century, there were a group of mounted warriors who appear to have parallels with chivalry. In an academic area that has room for development in the West, it is shown that there was a class of landowning lower nobility who collected taxes from villages and provided mounted cavalry to the empire's army. There are a number of different terms for these warriors depending on the language chosen, but to keep one name we shall use the term *azat*. *Azat* primarily means 'free', as in a free man.[13] Secondly it also has ancillary meanings of brave, active, efficient, quick, helpful and magnanimous. In a parallel with the English *cnight*, the word for these men in another language means bachelor, or boy. These free men were sometimes grouped up into units, and are recorded as serving as bodyguards for the Sassanid ruler. These men wore armour, rode armoured horses and were proficient with the use of the lance from horseback.

After the Muslim conquest of the Sassanid Empire, these men were still used and became known to Arabic writers for their generosity, courage and fortitude. This is not a dissimilar list to the one which we have already seen used to describe Christian knights by de Gamez in fifteenth-century Spain (Prudence, Justice, Temperance and Fortitude). The Arabic term *futuwwa* covers the ethos of the later *azats* and the concept has been touted as an eastern chivalry, and there are certainly striking parallels, but as with the European term, *futuwwa* meant different things to different people at different times.[14] One difference from the European knight is that in the East the lower nobility did not take part in the actual business of running the land itself, they just collected the taxes from it. The territories themselves were often subject to a lack of water compared to the West, so wealth ended up being concentrated in the towns instead. Indeed it is the towns where the military were housed in the Sassanid Empire, rather than across the countryside as was normal in most of northern Europe. This means a direct parallel in social structures does not exist, but the *azats* were certainly similar in concept to the European mounted knight.[15] An example of this is that as the Christian knights practised for war in the very warlike tournament, in the East warriors played a sport known in Iran as *chovgan*.[16] Here, in what later became polo, two sides would compete against each other in a sport that was played by kings, queens and nobles, and there were sometimes a hundred horsemen (or horsewomen) on each side. Like the tournament, polo was training for war, just without the ransoms and destruction of civilian property that was part and parcel of the Western game. Although not as realistic a battle experience as the tournament was in Europe, polo was good training and somewhat more civilised. Another more surprising commonality is that of heraldry. Moses Kalankatli, writing in the seventh century, said that, 'noblemen raised their banners with images of animals',[17] which shows that image-based heraldry in some form was invented independently from Europe. It should be noted that this is several hundred years before evidence of it appears in the West, where at first plain colours were used without images.

Merovingian France

After Rome fell at the end of the fifth century a power vacuum opened up in a western Europe filled with warring tribes and those clinging on to the Roman legacy. One collection of tribes vying for power were the Franks, a Germanic people who sometimes fought for the Romans, and often against them. One particular Frank named Clovis,[18] starting with only 500 warriors,[19] managed to unite the Frankish tribes and push out the last vestiges of Roman political influence in Gaul. This was a phenomenal achievement and largely filled the post-Roman vacuum, but critically, he also converted to Christianity. As Clovis conquered territory he gave it out to his loyal followers, while still expecting them to continue fighting with him, thus creating a chief-vassal relationship between land and service.

By his death in AD 511 there was a region roughly covering modern France that could be called the Frankish Kingdom. The Frankish dynasty that Clovis propelled to power are known as the Merovingians, after his grandfather Merovech, and ruled for over 200 years. They were not unsophisticated barbarians and, in Gaul, inherited more than just a memory of Roman infrastructure and rule, if not the actual institutions themselves. Naming their period the Dark Ages does the Franks and their contemporaries a disservice,[20] but as the trade from Roman globalisation ebbed away, the economy of the Franks became ever more agricultural and rural, and farming estates became both self sufficient and self contained. This allowed nobles to rule their own lands directly, and is often regarded as the beginnings of the feudal system, although perhaps more accurately described as the beginnings of a partly manorial society. These nobles were responsible for supplying soldiers, often their own personal retinue, to the Frankish army when war was agreed upon by national assemblies. The Frankish military strategy revolved around defending well-protected former Roman cities, which were often fortified by formidable late Roman walls. All adult males were expected to serve in a militia in their cities and defend the walls when attacked. They could also be summoned to serve outside the city, but only within 300 miles and for a maximum duration of three months, so while the nobles had power, so did the people. The Franks operated a defence in-depth approach which was lifted directly from the grand strategy of Late Imperial Rome.[21] This meant that when attacked, the urban militias would man the strong walls and bog attacking enemies down. The Frankish military machine would then be able to muster a quick reaction force, and crush besieging forces under the very walls they were trying to take. An example of a specific Imperial legacy that we can glimpse was that the Romans had settled military colonists from Sarmatia within Gaul. Under the Merovingians a militia unit of these Sarmatians was still a coherent force under a Frankish commander, meaning that they had not dispersed after the fall of Rome. This shows how the transition from Roman to Frankish was not clear-cut, everything was not purely Roman one day, and purely Frankish the next.[22] The long list of Roman inheritances also included effective battlefield tactics and reasoned strategic thinking.

The sixth-century Bishop Gregory of Tours described the Franks as choosing favourable ground for battles, thinking about logistics, concentrating their forces, fortifying areas and withdrawing when appropriate.[23] On top of this, their social structure was complex enough that several cities at a time could be put under the control of a *dux*, or duke. All in all, the Merovingian state more closely resembled Roman Gaul than a horde of barbarian tribes. These post-Roman Franks existed in the time known as the Migration Period where Goths, Huns, Vandals and others swept across Europe and the Mediterranean. Many of these vast migrations were made by peoples whose way of life was based around the horse, and although most fought as horse archers, some rode fully armoured horses and charged into the enemy ranks. These various peoples had enough skill that one Roman described the Huns as being almost glued to their saddles.[24] The Franks then had fought against mounted warriors, both horse archers and heavily armoured shock cavalry, from their very beginning.

There is a theory that the heavily armoured mounted shock warrior was born 200 years after the Merovingian period, but it existed in the Roman Empire and within the migrating tribes who had contact with the Franks. Did the Merovingians just not bother with heavy cavalry or did they not need it? It seems likely that a people who knew about armoured cavalry, and picked up other historical Roman traditions would have kept on using them, even if in limited numbers. However, their focus was on defending large fortified settlements, or besieging others to add them to their empire, so their priority was their urban militia. Nevertheless, because they used field armies as a hammer to batter enemies who were stuck in sieges, cavalry would have been a valuable military force for them. Due to the financial pressures the Franks were under in the centuries following the collapse of the Roman Empire, it probably meant that well armed and armoured cavalry was in short supply, but this does not mean it didn't exist.

The nobles who maintained armed retinues probably armed them as best they could and these professional warriors would have had time to train, and although evidence is hard to find, it seems likely that there were at least small numbers of well armed cavalry available to the Merovingians. For example, there is a reference in AD 507 to the Franks deploying a mounted unit in battle,[25] and also King Clovis published an edict regulating fodder and water for his men's horses (of some sort), suggesting they were widespread enough to warrant mentioning. In an order given regarding plundering in Aquitaine, Clovis also only allowed his men to take wood, water and grass,[26] the latter of which is of little use in feeding men. More convincingly, in AD 531 Agathias in his *Histories* wrote that the Thuringians dug pits to use as traps for Frankish horsemen. He wrote that the 'charge was slowed by these pits and almost turned back'.[27] This suggests that the knightly charge of the high middle ages was perhaps already a Frankish tactic in the sixth century, and one the enemy was expecting. The word 'almost' also infers that the charge went on successfully despite the pits. Agathias also wrote that at the Battle of Rimini in AD 553, half of the Frankish army of 2,000 were on horseback.[28] If true, this means that the Franks deployed 1,000 cavalry of some sort in one place. This battle was against Byzantium who had a dominant cavalry arm, and given their proven strategic competence, perhaps the Franks deployed more of their own cavalry to match their enemy? Given that Rimini is in Italy which had regions famed for heavy cavalry, it could have been these troops that the Franks brought in to bolster their mounted contingent. To muddy the waters though, the Byzantines also wrote of an entirely infantry Frankish army in Italy, which they defeated. Conversely Gregory of Tours declared the presence of men with mounted fighting skills in his sixth-century work *History of the Franks*, 'Dracolen then meets Gunthram Boso, fights him on horseback and is killed', as well as, 'the men who took away the blessed Martin's horses got into a quarrel and pierced one another with lances'.[29] Gregory also mentioned lances being hurled from horseback, and it is worth noting that the word 'lance' in Latin translates to the English lance, but also to spear. These small pieces of evidence suggest that some Franks rode as missile cavalry, and at least some others could use lances or spears on horseback as close combat weapons. Although specific written evidence supporting the use of shock cavalry is extremely limited, the Merovingians certainly rode horses on raids and campaigns. They hunted from horseback too and had regular contact with horse cultures ranging from the Huns to the Byzantine Empire, as well having peoples from a multitude of cultures living within their territories. Whether or not the Merovingians had actual heavy cavalry units remains to be proven, but they exhibited all the other signs of later medieval societies that did. The historian Bernard S. Bachrach has also stated that the use of mounted warriors increased in the sixth century, rather than in the eighth century as is elsewhere assumed.

Whoever the Merovingian cavalry were, they were not our mounted knights. Those serving a noble lord were generally unfree, and in an age where the Franks were fighting for survival, there was no chivalric concept of mercy to adhere to. The noblemen themselves were free men, and as power decentralised following the decline of Rome they represent the beginning of the social structures seen in the later middle ages. This important development, where groups of professional fighting men congregated at the residences of lords is the start of a recognisably medieval system. These mounted warriors owed allegiance to their lord, and this emphasis on service and loyalty is the basis from which the mounted knight originated.

Carolingian France

In the middle of the eighth century the Merovingian dynasty was overthrown and was replaced by other Franks known as the Carolingians, and it is the Carolingians who had generally been credited with the creation of a cavalry-based army. The now more common alternative view is that the volume of heavy cavalry in the Frankish area simply increased during their period, rather than being created from scratch. The Frankish machinery of state improved throughout the Merovingian and Carolingian periods and as they became richer they could afford more horses, more armour and to train more men. It is probably this increase in economic prosperity that led to a certain tipping point. This point was when there were enough heavily armoured mounted warriors available to mass together into big enough units to charge home, and critically, do so in incidents significant enough to be recorded. Ten mounted warriors could destroy an enemy raiding party thirty strong, but an event of such size is unlikely to make its way into a contemporary chronicle which survives today.

In these chronicles, references to mounted warriors start to increase in frequency as they progress through the eighth and ninth centuries. In AD 755, the time of year where troops were mustered for campaigning season was changed from March to May,[30] which tentatively points to fully mounted armies because they need less time to muster and then reach the war zone. Allowing horses time to gain condition, normally lost over winter, from eating the rich spring grass before going on campaign might mean that the Franks were deliberately only setting off once their horses were back in good condition. In AD 806 a mobilisation request was put out detailing a long list of armaments required for the mounted warrior, 'each horseman is to carry shield and spear, long-sword and short-sword, bow, quivers and arrows'.[31] It is unknown if the bows were to be used from the saddle, however, or dismounted. Perhaps they were just for use during the sieges common at the time, but this list of equipment is the same as for certain cavalry units of the Late Roman Empire, and that might not be a coincidence. There were also land requirements for military service and in AD 808 these were amended and this tells us how expensive a fully armoured knight was. For a man to send a fully equipped mounted warrior with horse, baggage and a horse for an assistant, with food for all for three months, he needed to hold at least 300 acres of land.[32] Anyone who held this quantity of land would meet our land-owning criteria to be a mounted knight. The historian Nithard, who incidentally was Charlemagne's grandson, wrote that in AD 842, knights practised pursuing fleeing enemies while on horseback, again emphasising training.[33]

In the Carolingian era *Chronicle*, it is written that in AD 851 the Franks charged the Breton army at speed and in numbers. Their conflict with the Bretons is explained to the reader by contrasting the cavalry tactics of the two sides. The Bretons threw javelins from horseback and then withdrew, sometimes in an effort to tempt the Franks to follow them, but used agility to avoid close combat. The Franks on the other hand held onto their spears and used them for thrusting before drawing swords.[34] At the battle of Andernach in AD 876 the Frankish army evidently included cavalry, since their troops are described as trying to spur their horses into the battle.[35] This is not required if the goal is only to get within missile range. It is also consistent with the contemporary pictorial evidence, since several Carolingian manuscripts depict pitched battles on horseback including the *Stuttgart Psalter*[36] and *San Paolo Bible*.

The search for a mounted knight existing under an ethos of chivalry is not, however, satisfied by the Carolingians. They fulfil the mounted criteria, so could be labelled as men-at-arms, but not yet chivalric knights. Their soldiers are still soldiers, often known by the Latin term *miles*, but are not a separate class of lower nobility. *Miles* translates to 'warrior' and it isn't until the tenth century that it turns into a title. Below the noble class were the servant knights, that is the vast majority of the mounted knights who could not yet be said to be free men. The same structure can be seen in contemporary Saxon England, where the strong state usually prevented any aristocrats becoming so powerful that they could challenge a monarch by raising their own armies. Looking to chivalry, both the Merovingians and the later Carolingians were most often found fighting against peoples unlike themselves. Chivalry appeared partly as a mechanism to lessen the violence of warfare between the same ethnic group under a Christian framework, which had not happened yet in Europe.

West Francia

After the death of the great Charlemagne in AD 814 his empire started to break apart and what followed was dominated by groups of fragmented lesser rulers. The part of the empire that roughly covered modern France went on to be called West Francia, but strong monarchy and central rule was a thing of the past.[37] Through the ninth and into the early tenth century a succession of monarchs fought to keep control against an increasing number of dukes, who often ruled more land than the king himself. The important difference between these conflicts and those up to and including Charlemagne's was that now the Franks were fighting each other. They were all Christian and in a succession of what were effectively civil wars, relatives were found on both sides. Enemies were no longer faceless, and as foreign, alien tribes were no longer the opposition, this is the approximate time that a concept of magnanimity in victory developed.

When raiding and warfare between the Franks erupted, and combined with a strong Christian backdrop, the rules of engagement started to change. It was obviously in the express interest of the Franks in the powerful noble class to refrain from killing each other. The constant and disunited nature of small and constant conflicts meant that if the nobles continued to kill each other, fairly soon there would be none left. This being realised, as an alternative they started to surrender to each other instead. Enslavement had always been a theme of war, but by now the taking of Christian slaves was heavily frowned upon by the influential church. The innovation that the Franks brought to this problem was that of ransoms. It was enabled by the rise of a money culture, which in the second half of the tenth century was making a comeback, much aided by the opening of new silver mines in Germany.[38] A new influx of silver gave the Frankish nobility the means with which to ransom each other, in addition to the motive. The resulting emphasis on honourable surrender in defeat instead of honourable death in defeat is a major shift, which began in France and only appeared in England when the Normans imported it. Honourable surrender is one of the great building blocks of chivalry and most of the other components fall into place over the next two centuries. It should be added that ransoms initially only happened for high nobility, the servant knights would not have been so lucky as their aristocratic lords if captured. As power devolved from the monarchy, large and small lords both continued to attract armed followers who became loyal to that lord above anyone else. This was an important development because it enabled factions within the Franks to fight each if they wanted to, because the king could not restrain them through loyalty alone. These lords started to meet the definition of knights, especially by the reign of Charles the Simple[39] which began in AD 898. He was a potential king, seen as so bad that he was passed over a number of times before someone eventually put him on the throne, which did not make for strong centralised rule.

It is within this climate that in AD 911 an attack on Paris was made by a Viking later known as Rollo. A tenth-century biographer labels him as Danish, but he would soon become something new entirely. His attack on Paris was actually defeated by the Franks but instead of killing him, they offered him a deal. Rollo would be given lands in Normandy in exchange to aid in the defence of the realm, specifically against other Viking raids down the Seine river which led to Paris. This relationship of service and land was not new, but in this case both sides had very different ideas of what it meant. Rollo took his Northmen to his new capital of Rouen and started the process by which his descendants expanded their control across the region.[40] When King Charles, who had made the grant to Rollo, was no longer in power, Rollo decided his obligations to the Franks were null and void. He went about raiding Frankish regions until the new king granted him more land, behaviour which certainly cannot be called chivalric. From these ruthless beginnings though, the Norman dynasty sprouted. Being Viking in origin, in their early days the Normans initially appeared to have very little to do with mounted knights. The Franks, though, did fight on horseback, with the required skill to be called mounted warriors, and this eventually rubbed off on the Normans. It was a mounted Frankish force that had initially defeated Rollo's Vikings and forced him to the negotiating table, so from their very first days they would have been aware of the level of horsemanship that the Franks had managed to attain. What should not be forgotten about the Viking raiders is that they certainly did know how to ride horses.[41] Newly landed Scandinavian raiders in England often acquired for themselves horses as soon as possible, and used them to scout and raid. If a man can ride well enough to scout and raid, then he must at least have a basic grasp of horsemanship. The transition to using horses for direct offensive action was then probably natural for the Vikings who settled in Normandy, especially considering their natural aggressiveness. After all, the horse could serve them on land as the longship had at sea, and coupled with the Viking spirit, formed a partnership that went on to conquer lands from Sicily to Jerusalem.

Saxons

> Then Hrothgar's thegn leaped onto his horse and, brandishing a spear, galloped down to the shore. The protector of earls ordered eight horses With ornamented bridles led into the building... on

one sat a saddle, skilfully tooled, set with gemstones; That was the warseat of the high-king When the son of Healfdene sought to perform his swordplay.

Beowulf[42]

Only a few decades ago it was taken as granted that the Saxons were not overly familiar with the use of horses in combat.[43] Recently this has begun to change, but there is still a cloud lurking over the subject. This shadow is the assumption that the Saxons might have ridden to a battle, but once there they always dismounted and fought on foot. Why then in Beowulf is a saddle called a war-seat for joining in with sword play? The Saxons were originally a people from the north of the main continent of Europe, in modern day Germany.[44] Before their first recorded presence in England in around AD 441, they are noted as waterborne raiders. However even before they crossed the North Sea, there was a Saxon warrior class that was knightly in its function. The *thegns* were a fighting class whose meaning, servant, is the same as the old English *cniht*. This similarity in meaning suggests a similarity in function too.[45] Like the later knights, the social status and properties of the *thegns* changed throughout the Saxon period. Their warrior culture began in the form of roving warbands, much like the later Vikings, before they settled in Britain and changed.

After a period of conquest, and once the English Saxon kingdoms had been established, they shifted towards territorial defence. When the *thegns* were given land to maintain themselves they in many way resembled knights. It is not correct to assume that the Normans brought the entire concept of knighthood to England, because the *thegns* were already doing many of the things seen as required of a knight. They managed areas of land, and King Edgar insisted on a tithe payment for a *thegn's* land,[46] which implies that there were possibly no landless *thegns* so that landowning, or at least land managing, was part of the definition of the role. From this perspective, they are actually more knightly than the later Norman knights, who were frequently not land owning. The *thegns* also dispensed justice and there are even cases of *thegns* presiding in courts in the Danelaw region of England. The military service owed to their king is central to their reason for existence, and stems from a warrior culture that is recorded by Tacitus back in AD 98. He wrote that, 'to survive the leader and retreat from the battlefield is a lifelong disgrace and infamy'.[47]

Loyalty was a famous trait of the Germans and led to them being used to guard Roman emperors, and loyalty was also a central tenet of chivalry. As was common at the time, the continental Saxon tribes rewarded their loyal warriors with weapons, horses and land.[48] This shows that the value system of the Saxons before they settled in Britain was similar to everyone else, specifically for us that horses were at the heart of society and status. Horses could have just been the ultimate status symbol rather than a war machine, but they were certainly a critical mode of transport and that included in times of conflict. The famous Sutton Hoo helmet displays a rider in battle on some of its panels, although the whole image hasn't survived, it is unmistakably a mounted warrior felling an opponent. The shape of the helmet belongs to a class of helmets that derived from a Roman one, but was possibly made in Scandinavia. Although there is mystery around its origin, the helmet is evidence of a complex European network of cultures of which the Saxons were part. Ever-present Roman influences permeated into the shape and form of the helmet, which may have been made in Sweden but ended up in the grave of a king of Germanic descent in England.[49] The fact that the decoration shows mounted combat is not evidence that the king who wore it rode into battle, but it is evidence that he would have been aware of the concept.

Additionally in the 1990s, two Saxon warrior burial mounds were excavated at the Royal Air Force base at Lakenheath in Suffolk.[50] The two sixth-century warriors were buried with the usual grave goods, including weapons, but importantly both graves also contained horses. A gilded bridle was found in one grave and this means that richly dressed horses were ridden. The Sutton Hoo king was also buried near to a horse and this proximity suggests these animals had a prominent position in Saxon society. One Lakenheath warrior's horse was 142cm tall, or just under 14 hands tall in equestrian terminology, and heavyset, the size and approximate build of a modern English native pony. Other burials across the country also include horses alongside their humans, and often with bridles on their heads, as if ready to ride. The presence of bridles does confirm that at least some Saxons were using horses for riding from the very beginning of their time in England. The fact that the legendary (literally, for we do not know if they were real people) Hengist and Horsa were the first Saxon leaders on British soil is very telling regarding the Saxon opinion of the horse. Hengist means stallion and Horsa means horse, and as a pair they probably originate from an ancient Germanic tradition of a pair of divine twins.[51] By ascribing legendary figures to the leadership of their conquest of Briton, it is possible that the Saxons were attempting to legitimise their gains. During their conquest of Britain, the Saxons would have fought against the cavalry as well as infantry forces of the local population. To what extent they countered them with their own mounted forces we do not know, but on a battlefield with a mounted enemy it is preferable to have some mounted troops of your own.

The question remains, while the Saxons clearly venerated the horse, did they ride them into battle and therefore meet our definition of knights? It is relevant that the Carolingians and Saxons were described as fighting a 'cavalry battle'[52] in AD 784 in the *Revised Annals of the Kingdom of the Franks*. The Repton Stone from Derbyshire also shows a mail-clad (also known as chainmail: armour made from tiny interlocking rings) Saxon warrior, possibly a king of Mercia, riding a horse. He appears to be armed with a Saxon *seax*, a single-edged long knife or sword like weapon, and a shield. Intriguingly, the Aberlemno Stone in Scotland is thought to show a battle between the Picts and Northumbrian Saxons that occurred back in AD 685. Both sides are shown fighting each other on horseback, armed with spears and shields. Bede wrote of that battle in the eighth century that, 'The [Picts] feigned flight and lured the [Saxon] king into some … mountains; there he was killed.'[53] This raises the possibility, however, that the Saxons had simply mounted up in order to pursue their fleeing enemy. Refuting this theory though, the vertical order of images on the stone suggests a fully mounted encounter preceded the feigned retreat, so this could be evidence of Saxons fighting on horseback deliberately.

Even at the least, the Saxons were mounted while pursuing an enemy, which is a primary function of light cavalry. One translation of an Old English poem known as *Maxims I* states that, 'an earl belongs on a charger's back; a mounted troop must ride in regular array and the footsoldier stand firm'.[54] A horse described as a charger is clear in meaning if the translation can be trusted, but the distinction between mounted and foot troops is unarguable. It is also possible to interpret parts of the *Saxon Chronicle*[55] as well as the *Laws of Athelstan*[56] from the early tenth century as referring to mounted troops, but as with a number of Saxon written sources the translation is key, and sources can be found to argue for and against the use of Saxon cavalry. Alfred the Great and other Saxon rulers certainly employed mounted infantry to counter the Viking threat throughout the Saxon period, and the position of the horse in society was a very high one, but they were not internationally renowned users of shock cavalry. The battles of Maldon[57] and Hastings are the two famous examples where the Saxons rode to battle then dismounted to fight in the close press of the traditional shieldwall. These battles provide the foundation of the evidence for the belief that the Saxons only fought on foot.

Conversely, in the fourteenth century when the English dismounted at Crécy and Agincourt, no one accuses them of not being able or willing to fight on horseback, because it is simply what they thought they needed to do to win those battles. A visit to the geographical area around Maldon reveals a tidal marshy area even more unsuited to cavalry manoeuvres than the muddy fields at Agincourt. All the Saxons had to do at Maldon was block the Viking advance to the mainland, and the shieldwall is the ultimate blocking formation. In the poem that gives us our source for the battle, it is stated that all the Saxon horses were released before the fighting began.[58] This was tactical and symbolic. By releasing their horses, the Saxons were showing that they meant to stand and fight, as they then did, to the bitter end. The story at Hastings was similar in that King Harold was blocking the road to London, and that road was flanked with marshy ground that an army would have great difficulty getting through. Again the deployment of a shieldwall was the most sensible plan when contrasted to the riskier strategy of a cavalry or infantry charge. Harold was trying to contain the Normans as he could not surprise them as he had the Vikings at Stamford Bridge, so again employed the tactic most likely to achieve his objective. As at Maldon, Harold also probably wanted to ensure that his men would be committed to a fight to the death, and again in a repeat of Maldon, they did.

If the Saxons are to be labelled as being unable to fight on horseback because of the fact that they fought certain battles dismounted, then for fairness a comparison needs to be made with the English several centuries later. What we do have for the fourteenth century, however, is examples of English cavalry actions, for example at Poitiers, but if only the battles of Crécy and Agincourt were considered the conclusion would be different. Before he became king, Harold spent time in Normandy with

Duke William and indeed fought for him and rescued some of his men from danger, as shown in the Bayeux Tapestry. William knighted Harold after this and there is a tantalising possibility that while in Normandy, he fought for William on a horse alongside Norman knights. Would Harold, who was part of the very highest social level of England, have been happy to fight on foot while all the Norman men of note rode around fighting on horseback ahead of him? One rather suspects Harold would not have been happy at being left behind. At the most, Harold knew how to fight mounted, which would indicate the knowledge existed in England to teach him. Furthermore, on the Bayeux Tapestry Harold can actually be seen mounted on a horse while in full battle gear just before the Battle of Hastings, but the question of equestrian proficiency remains open. At the very least though, he would have seen first hand how the Norman cavalry operated in some detail during his time in Normandy. As the Norman cavalry formed up below Senlac Hill in England in 1066, no one can possibly suggest that Harold was caught unaware by their capabilities.

Author's Note

Medieval history is normally studied from a chair and usually by a different sort of personality than those who made the history itself. The history of the mounted knight is the history of athletic men who trained often and used their abilities to hurt and kill people. The vast gulf between those of us interested in history today, and those who lived it is so big that it is incredibly difficult to understand them as humans. To make an attempt at it is one reason I started to learn to ride and fight from horseback myself. The experiences this has given me will be used to help our understanding of the mounted knight, but in a tentative manner. This is partly because I started riding in my twenties so I will never reach a fraction of the competence of a medieval knight, and partly because our world is so far removed from the medieval one that all conclusions can only be provisional. Just because we can ride a certain exercise in full armour today does not prove that it was done a thousand years ago. I will endeavour to comment when my experience backs up original sources, improves on the understanding of horses, or dispels myths and misconceptions.

The first myth is that of the stirrup. A lot has been made of the stirrup and its contribution to the evolution of the mounted knight and some of it is problematic. In 1962 a professor of medieval history at Princeton, Lynn Townsend White, suggested that the stirrup is what created heavy cavalry and their famously irresistible shock charge.[59] The idea was that by being able to wedge their feet into stirrups, the force of impact through the rider and lance was increased by so much that a new form of warfare effectively emerged, and as a direct result of this power, feudalism came into existence. Setting aside the debate over the term feudalism itself, this view has proved to be greatly influential and has also been deployed to explain why the Normans defeated the Saxons at Hastings. Objections have been raised against this view academically, questioning if the stirrup can be solely responsible for the structure of medieval society, and surely it has to be too much of a simplification to be followed. Detractors have also noticed that peoples from the east had been riding in heavy cavalry shock formations before the Greeks encountered them in the fifth century BC. These *cataphracts*[60] rode in full armour with no stirrups and wielded long lances with both hands just as the Greek Companions had. Their horsemanship was such that they did not need to hold the reins while in combat, a trait they shared with the Greeks. A misunderstanding of horsemanship has also led to the claim that the lance must have been used as a quarterstaff because there is no way a *cataphract* could have stayed on his horse during impact without stirrups. Revealingly, Roman writers stated that these fearful weapons could transfix two men at once so they were clearly used as lances. Indeed the Romans were impressed enough by the *cataphracts* that they eventually employed their own versions, yet another ancestor of our medieval knights. Having spent a modest amount of time riding in a reproduction Roman saddle myself, which has strong horns at each of its corners to keep the rider's body locked in, I can attest that they keep you very securely on top of the horse indeed. When striking with a lance, the force will categorically not push the attacker out of his saddle. A study[61] was undertaken by the jousting community on impact forces while jousting, and the rider going bareback with no saddle at all, let alone stirrups, actually managed to achieve the highest impact measurement. He also did not fall off the horse while doing it, and one has to have ridden to appreciate how this feels.

When I was trying to work out how to mount the Roman saddle, however, which involves lifting yourself up and over the four horns and then down into it, I decided that stirrups were probably for getting onto the horse in the first place (at least if you are not as fit as a Roman cavalryman, which I am not). When you attempt to dismount from these saddles, you have to lift yourself back up and over the horns again, while trying not to catch your mail armour on it. If you don't get clear of the horns you will snag your armour on them and potentially end up dangling helplessly from the saddle. At that point you just have to hope your horse is sensible and does not take offence to it. This experience was backed up when I later learnt that the word stirrup itself comes from the Old English[62] *stirap* or *stigrap*, where *stigan* means to mount or climb, and *rap* means rope. Therefore for the English, a stirrup had always been a *mounting rope*, so perhaps instead of their adoption of the stirrup being because they couldn't ride very well and needed help to balance, it is because they were technological innovators.

Chapter Two

The Norman Era

From Northmen to Norman

The early Normans carved out a territory for themselves in Northern France during the tenth century, spreading out from their initial Frankish land grant around Rouen and the mouth of the Seine river. They were not the first to settle in the area however, there were existing Norse communities[1] around Cherbourg, Caen and Rouen, but these new Norsemen would have a very different impact. Rollo's Scandinavians were originally settled there to act as a barrier to other Norse raiders sailing down the Seine and attacking the Franks, but within a generation they bullied their way into becoming the rulers of Normandy as a whole.[2] They may have started off as Norse raiders, but they soon adopted many Frankish ways, including speaking Old French and, crucially, mounted cavalry. Always ready to learn, it is possible that the Norman doctrine of mounted warfare started while they were still more Northmen than Norman. This fascinating mix of Viking and Frank is probably best summed up by the eleventh-century monk Geoffrey Malaterra, who was possibly Norman himself and described them as a, 'most astute people, eager to avenge injuries, looking ... to enrich themselves from others rather than from their native fields. Unless they are held in thrall by the yoke of justice, they are a most unbridled people.'[3] This description could easily be ascribed to a ninth-century Viking, perhaps written by a Saxon cleric in England. However, Malaterra wasn't finished, and continued his description with more recognisably Norman traits, 'they can bear hard work, hunger and cold; they are addicted to hunting and hawking, and take great pleasure in luxurious clothes and elaborate trappings for their horses'.[4] The Viking legacy is telling as this was written at a time when the Normans were their own distinct entity, and had already left France to conquer Sicily.[5]

In addition to this and a certain journey across the English channel in 1066, the Normans also managed to get to Iberia, briefly kept vassal cities in North Africa, and fought the Byzantines across Italy and the Balkans.[6] They were so precocious that in 1053 they had no qualms in taking the field against a papal army in Italy, which they defeated despite the presumably outraged Pope himself watching from the sidelines.[7] Back in their homeland of Normandy they formed a ruling class over the top of the local population they had been brought in to rule. This separation from the masses, even if there were already Scandinavian settlers there, mixed with the natural Norman tendency for strong leadership, and led to centralised power under the Duke of Normandy.[8] That being said, the Normans suffered their fair share of revolts and dynastic squabbles, so should not be regarded as being better rulers than their Frankish neighbours. Indeed Saxon England was also historically a more stable state than Normandy was.[9] The Normans, however became particularly effective proponents of mounted warfare and were responsible for exporting the fame of the mounted knight, as well as the shock charge beyond the area of Europe where it originated. Along with cunning diplomacy, their considerable conquests were carried by swift hooves and made at the point of the mounted knight's lance.

Castles

One of the features usually ascribed to the Normans is that of castle building. A castle is a separate concept to a walled town or fortified city, both of which existed long before the Norman period. Indeed humans have always tried to fortify their homes, firstly to protect small family groups against wild animals, and eventually from other people. A castle is specifically a fortified private dwelling, with multifunctional contents. That is, it is not a purely militaristic building such as a Roman marching fort. Castles also served other functions such as law and order, and contained a household whose members were not all soldiers. As the monarchy of the West Franks diminished and lower lords took up the responsibilities of ruling their own areas, they started to build castles for themselves.[10] This can be considered a privatisation of government and these lords intended to protect their property and make a statement about their position by their building works. William Duke of Normandy appears to have seen motte and bailey castles in Anjou,[11] which borders Normandy, and proceeded to copy them before exporting them to

England. By constructing a castle on newly conquered land, the Franks and Normans gave themselves a focal point to gather taxes, dispense justice, display their authority and fall back to in times of trouble.

Another reason for the rise of the castle was the mounted warrior himself. A body of professional mounted soldiers, even if only small in number, could defeat far larger forces of amateur warriors. This meant that in order to confront another group of professional warriors with a chance of winning, a lord would need their own force of professionals. When such small private armies met outside of fortifications, the engagements were pitched battles, ambushes and skirmishes, the result of which was so unpredictable it was a fact of the time that these encounters were decided by God.[12] When lords didn't want to trust their futures to God, they built castles. These were invulnerable to mounted troops and put the defending side in a vastly more advantageous position. It also meant a lord could take more of his own troops away from his home base and confidently leave relatively few men behind to defend his interests. A walled town still needed a decent number of men to hold its walls, but castles, especially smaller ones, could be defended by mere handfuls of troops.[13] This ability meant that early medieval warfare often took the form of sieges and counter sieges, but the potential for mounted troops to move quickly between castles was still critical. Although these castles started off small and wooden, they evolved into stone and became the castle as we tend to think of them today. For the mounted knight, the castle provided a safe place to live and, importantly, store valuable horses. They also provided an occupation for men-at-arms, who were often employed in garrisoning them. Of course knights also had to learn how to attack them, which meant dismounting. One exception to this is of a case where French men-at-arms rode up to their saddles in water through the moat of Pont-Audemer at the end of the Hundred Years War in order to take the town from the English.[14] They were successful apparently because it had only wooden palisades, although how they got through those defences is not mentioned. Usually, however, the methods to take a castle by force included scaling ladders, battering rams and catapults, as well as the devastatingly effective but slow process of undermining the walls to cause their collapse by tunnelling. Probably the best method though was to target the human element of the garrison, because bribes and betrayals meant fewer causalities and the chance to come into the possession of an intact castle rather than a ruin. These strategies left the mounted warriors a less glamorous but still vital role. They were often employed to intercept supplies or reinforcements trying to sneak into castles, and also to forage for their own side's provisions.

Without these jobs being performed castles were harder to take, so to suggest that the mounted knight was useless in a siege is very much an over simplification. Christine de Pizan, remarkable for being a female fifteenth-century author on military strategy, devoted a chapter to this and explained that hundreds of mounted men-at-arms were required along with archers to take care of logistics, including stopping travelling merchants from being robbed.[15] Siege work was the central core of medieval warfare, which is largely because castles were much more common that we might tend to think. In England there are thought to be well over a thousand castles, which is one every seventy square miles, which in practice meant that no place in the country was ever more than a day's ride away from one.[16] The Normans were aggressive military strategists and used castles as part of their offensives too, striking out from safe bases. Sometimes a force might not aim to actually take a castle, just pin its occupants down and stop them getting involved in a second action elsewhere. Alternatively a castle placed on a strategic route of travel could deny an enemy the use of a certain road or river, making besieging those castles unavoidable. The potential nuisance a mounted force could make when sallying out from a castle is what made them a threat to passing armies, especially those a long way from home.

It is perhaps because of the castle that Duke William thought he could leave Normandy with his entire army in 1066, and still feel that his homeland was secure. The invading Norman army actually took a prefab wooden castle with them across the Channel to England,[17] and as they spread across the country wooden castles sprouted up behind them. These started in the south east and spread north and west and were constructed for both military, social and political reasons. William had destroyed much of the Saxon nobility at the Battle of Hastings and although revolts and rebellions did flare up, there was never a Saxon military response to Norman rule that was mortally dangerous. The castles further away from the borders of England were primarily there as administration centres and visible statements to the native population of whom it was now in charge. That said, the use of the castle meant that a relatively small number of foreign overlords could exert power over a large population, and there is an argument that the occupation that followed the initial invasion would not have been possible without them. This is despite the fact that many castles were very small.

Most Norman castles that remain today form only the core of latterly enlarged fortifications, for example the central White Tower at the Tower of London was the totality of the original Norman castle. It makes it easier to imagine how the Normans managed to build so many when their relatively modest size is taken into account. They were still proof against insurgent attacks however, because any disgruntled Saxons who wanted to take a castle did not have the luxury of siege engines. For the first few years of the occupation, a military parallel can be drawn with the use of Forward Operating Bases in Afghanistan in the twenty-first century. Therefore the Norman army became an occupying force with castles as a symbol of their invincibility and overwhelming power, as well as using them for their own physical security. The message being broadcast to the locals by the castles in their midst was clear, and many of the first wave of castles were built on top of Saxon buildings, the symbolism of which probably didn't need explaining to the natives.

The Bayeux Tapestry

The Norman victory at the Battle of Hastings in 1066 is sometimes ascribed to their use of cavalry, and specifically the couched lance. It is a challenge to identify when European warriors first started to couch spears or lances, and some have pointed to the Bayeux Tapestry as pictorial evidence of it. However, the majority of mounted warriors on the tapestry are throwing lances or wielding them in overhead stabbing motions. It is hard to tell the difference between a Norman preparing to throw a lance, and one preparing to stab downwards, because these movements look the same until they are unleashed. Stabbing downwards in this fashion is not a hugely accurate method of attack, although if it does connect, the momentum added by the horse will increase the damage done. There are also a number of images where the lance is held lower, running along the right forearm of the knight. This technique uses the right arm to steady the weapon, which in turn increases the accuracy of the strike. Unlike an overhead attack, the knight can put some of his body behind the blow, which makes it a much more likely to do critical damage to the target. However, running the lance along the right up is not the same as bringing it right up into the armpit. This is what couching means, and it is the way in which the medieval knight made his attacks. The act of jamming the lance up and into the armpit solidifies the lance, locking it in to the body of the knight. This method gives the rider the most control over his weapon, and the best possible chance to hit his target. Most importantly of all, when the lance does impact, the force travels into the body of the rider rather than into just the wrist. Thus couching protects the wrist, and at the same times imparts the full force of man and horse into the target.

Against the Saxons at Hastings, the ability to split a shield or mail coat may have been the difference between life and death. As the tapestry depicts many methods of lance use, it does suggest that those varying methods were all employed. If not due to the embroiderers lack of understanding, this subtle difference between a partial couch and full couch is important because of the difference in effectiveness. Both allow a Norman knight to kill an opponent, but one is knightly in the medieval sense, and one is not. It is certainly possible that the difference is down to the various artists involved not being as interested in the detail as we might be, and perhaps they always mean a full couch. However, and inconclusively for us, in the panel where Harold's brother Gyrth is killed, it appears that a Norman knight is indeed fully couching. The accuracy of the tapestry is boosted by the fact that almost everyone in 1066 would have seen war, and been to some level familiar with how it was conducted. For example, manuscript images are usually created by monks, who quite often were younger sons of relatively high-born families and in many cases will have spent a youth training in war before they were sent to the church.[18] This means we at least cannot discount images drawn by monks as inaccurate due to an unfamiliarity with warfare, but this does leave the Tapestry ambiguous because the identity of its makers are not known for sure.

The Battle

William of Poitiers wrote that at the start of the Battle of Hastings, 'the knights came after the chief, being in the rearmost rank, and all disdaining to fight at long range were eager to use their swords.'[19] This is interesting because firstly it suggests they would have been expecting to start the battle by throwing spears. Secondly, they attacked with swords in close combat and not spears, so they potentially did not charge with lances at all, at least according to William of Poitiers. This first all out attack failed to break the Saxons and when a cry rose up that Duke William was dead, a part of his army composed of his Breton allies started to flee down the hill away from the Saxons. A significant part of the Saxon army chased them and so left the safety of King Harold's shieldwall. The Norman cavalry was able to rally, and then surround and destroy this now exposed force.[20] After seeing so many Saxons fall, the Normans proceeded to create several feigned retreats to draw more English down from their previously impregnable position. This worked, and repeatedly groups of Saxons chased their enemies down the hill, and each time the Norman cavalry wheeled around and cut them off. On every occurrence these pockets of English were destroyed, an achievement made possible by horsemanship as well as discipline. These actions fatally reduced the size of the Saxon shieldwall, and with a prolonged combined arms attack of infantry, cavalry and archery, the Normans engaged in a battle of attrition that they knew they could win.

Eventually, and after King Harold had been killed, the Saxons broke and fled. The presumably exhausted Norman cavalry then switched to pursuit, and caused great damage in the fading October light. This switch of function shows the tactical flexibility of the Norman knights as well as their stamina. Cutting down a fleeing army turned a narrow victory into a crushing one, while being disciplined and fast enough to use a feigned rout to divide and conquer created that victory in the first place. The evidence of William of Poitiers and the Bayeux Tapestry shows that the Norman use of cavalry was sophisticated and experienced. However they do not fit the definition of heavy shock cavalry, which is charging home with the couched lance as their primary tactic. The Norman cavalry of 1066 seems to be more of a transitional force that could be better described as medium cavalry. Orderic Vitalis, writing seventy years after Hastings, claimed that to be effective as a warrior meant knowing the skill of throwing spears from horseback, and practising that skill.[21] Finding pictorial evidence of couched lances is fraught with difficulties but there is the possibility of a fully couched lance depicted in the *Stavelot Triptych*,[22] which is from 1156–8. Even earlier than this, and again only a possibility, there is maybe an early example on the Morgan Manuscript M.736 *Miscellany on the life of St. Edmund*[23] which is from 1130.

If some Norman knights tucked their spears right into their armpits during the Battle of Hastings, then they were on the cutting edge of tactical innovation. Military innovation, however, was a Norman trait, so it is entirely possible. Regardless of whether or not they couched lances to charge in 1066, the Norman cavalry had still played a tremendous part in the victory at Hastings and afterwards in the Conquest in general. Against a Saxon enemy that was mounted at least to travel, the Normans needed to be mobile themselves, and they certainly were. This need for mounted men-at-arms resulted in William, now king, spending vast sums of money to ship them over from Europe and pay them to serve him.[24] These were effectively mercenary soldiers from Brittany, Maine and Anjou, and they were a large part of the force that conducted the infamous Harrying of the North in 1069–70. The mercenary knights went with William through England and Wales to put down rebellions until they reached Salisbury, where he was able to reward them financially for their service. These were not feudal soldiers and they did not owe William service, which shows us that even in 1069 armies were being paid for. This distinction between paid and non-paid troops was made in *The Penitential Code of Ermenfrid* in 1070. This was the church's reaction to the devastation the Normans had caused during the Conquest, and lists the penances certain Normans needed to do to make up for their actions during it. It was the medieval equivalent of a war crimes tribunal and also tells us something about the types of soldiers William used. Most of the penances applied to those, 'who gave military service as their duty'.[25] However, there is a specific clause for mercenaries, 'those who fought merely for gain are to know that they owe a penance as for homicide'.[26] It is interesting to note that the church saw paid soldiers as worse than those who fought from duty, but most interesting is that William had enough paid soldiers to warrant the clause being included in the first place. The Normans therefore were not a martial society based solely on feudal terms, plenty of mounted knights were paid to fight.

Consequences of the Conquest

From the perspective of the mounted knight, a consequence of the Norman Conquest of England was not the sudden creation of the knights as a distinct social class. The granting of English lands to some Norman knights as a reward for their service did create a landowning group in a short time, but it was certainly not the case that all men who were knights were granted land. Although compiled at least twenty years after William was crowned, the Domesday Book shows that a small number of Normans, Frenchmen and Bretons made up of just 200 barons,[27] were landowners on a vast scale. There are over 8,000 subtenants recorded in the 1086 survey,[28] and some of them are men who could be called Norman knights. Before the Conquest Norman knights often belonged to their lord, they were in a way just peasants with training and weapons.[29] A knight who lost his weapons and armour was not considered to be a knight again until he got his hands on some more. If a young man's family, however low born, had amassed enough wealth to equip him with horse, armour and weaponry, and he found time to learn how to use them, he could become a knight. This is how Geoffrey Chaucer, more famed for his writing skills, managed it, as well as John Hawkwood, who went from an Essex thug, to the terror of Italy. This suggests that at this time, being a knight was more of an occupation than a social class.[30] When Duke William knights Harold Godwinson in the Bayeux Tapestry, he gives him weapons and armour to make him a knight. Norman knights could be transferred between lords which made their status little different to the serfs that farmed the land, albeit serfs with swords. However, because a knight was usually given arms only by his lord and did not own them himself, the Tapestry is making a very clear point that Harold is William's man. This was not an unusual arrangement in Europe in the eleventh century, and indeed the later idea of a knight ruling his own lands from his manor casts a shadow over this period, because the reality is far more nuanced.

It is a good time to recall that the English word *cniht* means servant. When considering how the English viewed the Norman cavalrymen now riding around their country, the fact that they used a word for servant to describe these men, not nobility, landowner, or even soldier, is an important one. Obviously some knights *were* landowners although they were the nobility first and fighting knights second. There were some genuinely free knights; that is, they provided their own armour, weapons and horses, but they did not yet run their lands in a manorial system as they later would. This kernel of free knights were the start of the real thing however, and their numbers grew. Another large class in the eleventh century were the unfree knights who were serfs to their lord, and sometimes literally farming serfs themselves. These farming knights could spend most of their lives in their lord's fields, only donning the panoply of war when ordered to.[31] There were also other knights living in a state that was a combination or shade of these types, and as such the picture of post-Conquest knighthood is much more complicated than it initially looks. At the more professional end, this picture included the household knights who were a feature of later times and were already a Norman practice, forming the elite fighting core of armies. There were other professional knights who were in some senses free, and that is the mercenary knights who both accompanied William on the invasion of England, and frequently were called in to help out afterwards.

The very loose definition of a knight that seems to have existed at the time makes measuring them extremely problematic. As many of them were knights only when they were needed to be, this does also raise the question of how proficient they were. If these agricultural knights[32] had to work the land for most of their lives, they might be strong, but how much time could they spend riding and training? Perhaps these knights should be described as semi-professional at best. Indeed, when deciding which knights to bring overseas with him, Henry II of England left the farming knights at home so as not trouble them with a 'long and difficult journey'.[33] In other words, if the king was going to shoulder the expense of travel for knights, he wanted only to send the ones worth the cost. This probable lack of training was reflected in the lack of equipment the lords were keeping in stock a century after the Conquest. The *Assize of Arms* in 1181[34] was, among other things, an attempt to force anyone who had vassal knights to keep enough military equipment for them to use. The fact it was needed suggests that already lords were trying to get around their military obligations and were more focused on their own domestic affairs than the king's international wars. This was probably because most of these wars happened in France, and England itself was relatively peaceful, which did eventually serve to degrade the fighting abilities of the knights on the English side of the Channel. This is not to say that their abilities were fatally eroded, just that their numbers decreased. The household knights of the king and magnates remained strong, and these professionals were the elite nucleus of Anglo-Norman armies.[35]

Anglo-Norman Knighthood

This then shows that the Conquest of England was not as flourishing in the fortunes or numbers of Norman or English Knights. In the hundred years following 1066 it appears instead that knights, or at least men-at-arms, reduced in number and quality.[36] Ironically, this was because of the success of the Norman invasion, and the fact that after 1100 the English were not fighting back which meant that fewer fighting men were needed to contain them. That said, certain lords still maintained their martial capacity by holding on to knights, particularly the barons near the Welsh and Scottish Marches who experienced higher levels of conflict.[37] The Normans then had men-at-arms, and access to hire more, but they and their actual knights both fought in a transitional style, between lightly armoured skirmishing cavalry, and heavily armoured shock cavalry. Importantly for us, what we find with the Normans at the end of the eleventh century are knights in the military sense. By occasionally couching their lance and charging, they have displayed the abilities needed to fight as the typical medieval knight, even if they did not do it all of the time. These men are almost our medieval mounted knights. They do not quite meet our definition because although they lived by codes of honour, it was not yet the full code of chivalry. Instead it seems that chivalry was purely a martial concept during the Norman era. In the immediate wake of 1066 the Normans probably felt that their situation was very much *us and them*, with the newcomers and their allies living in their castles and manors with potentially hostile natives all around them.[38] However, it wasn't long before the Normans started participating in the dynastic and baronial conflicts that rumbled on constantly across Europe at this time.

After William's death his two sons, William Rufus and Robert Curthose, inherited England and Normandy respectively. They fought between each other and this was by no means an isolated incident. From their war onwards however, the practice of ransoming knights flourished. William Rufus was the king in England, but it was the French side in the war that seemed to have the upper hand in the financial war of ransoms.[39] The knights of William Rufus, upon capture, immediately agreed to high ransoms because they wanted to get back to continue earning their notoriously high wages. The French captives, perhaps naively, were only asked to swear homage to William Rufus to be released. This imbalance shows that ransoms were starting to happen in numbers large enough to be recorded in chronicles, and also that the English king was paying large wages to his knights rather than relying on their duty to serve. The Normans were not pioneers of the ransoming concept but in the early twelfth century they were certainly employing it. Perhaps surprisingly, high-ranking rebels could occasionally be forgiven their treason too,[40] and the royal court did start to show other signs of growing into the chivalric epicentre it would later become.

William the Conqueror's court was made up of his family, leading church figures and the wealthiest landowners in England. This was a group with strong ties linked through blood, marriage, conquest, land and money, and its cohesion made it a close knit, functional court.[41] However that was the limit of the courtesy that became integral to chivalry; there was, for example, no emphasis on storytellers or musicians. In contrast, after William Rufus has ascended the throne his court was repeatedly attacked for being evil. Orderic Vitalis and William of Malmesbury both wrote waspishly when they listed its failings, including sodomy, growing long hair and wearing shoes that curled at the end.[42] While not seemingly all so terrible, the impression at the time was that the Norman court was neither morally nor artistically sophisticated.

Comparison to France

While the Normans and Saxons were fighting over England, in France the Frankish Capetian dynasty had been ruling for over a hundred years. They still held the Duke of Normandy as a vassal, along with other significant major landowning dukes. William the Conqueror had, probably, performed the act of homage to the king of France in 1060, but the evidence is unspecific[43] and the Normans had always had a more equal relationship to the crown than other dukes. Before he crossed the English Channel, William had often acted as though he owed no service or loyalty to the French king whatsoever, despite the fact that the French had supported him in his difficult minority. The other dukedoms were not as independent as Normandy and the Capetian king was involved deeply in their affairs, whereas the Normans enjoyed total freedom to do whatever they wished. The other territorial principalities such as Anjou,

Aquitaine and Flanders also were ruled by dukes who were sometimes richer than the Capetian king, and almost as powerful.[44] This was not a true feudal hierarchy because the monarch was not all powerful and land ownership outside of his personal lands around Paris did not flow from him personally.

After William the Conqueror had died the French maintained this situation, at least until when Louis VI came to the throne in 1108. King Henry of England (who was also still the Duke of Normandy) found that Louis wanted all of the French dukes to pay homage to him and play the part of genuine vassals. This resulted in two wars over five years, in which Henry was successful enough for Louis to recognise Henry's right to receive homage from counts of Anjou and Maine.[45] This effectively marked the point, at least from the Anglo-Norman perspective, that Normandy started to become part of England rather than France, and the intermittent Anglo-French warfare that lasted throughout the medieval period had begun. Over the years, however, the Capetians continued to regard Normandy as another duchy alongside the others and only increased their attempts to assert themselves over all of them. This was, in the end, successful, and that centralisation of power led to a more defined hierarchical system and more productive economy,[46] and that paved the way for an explosion in the numbers of knightly lower nobility. Additionally, as the Franks started the long process of uniting themselves, their culture was able to flourish and the seeds of chivalry, long since planted,[47] started to sprout.

Comparison to Germany

When West Francia emerged from the Carolingian lands in the early tenth century, the eastern part of the empire became its own entity, that eventually took on the name of the Holy Roman Empire. During the eleventh century it covered roughly the area of modern Germany as well as parts of northern Italy, Austria and various other lands. This was a vast collection of territories of very different natures and this affected the mounted knight in different ways. The Germanic lands to the east of the old Roman frontier did not have centuries of Roman traditions to draw from, but that is not to say in any way that they lacked organisation or civilisation. The eastern half of the Carolingian Empire was still part of that organised state, although rebellions in Saxony and central Germany were frequent throughout the early middle ages. This constant warfare created a demand for warriors and thus a job description was created, which by the eleventh century had acquired the job title of *Ministeriales*. This fighting job was taken by those unfree men who were up to it, and was no different to the situation of many knights elsewhere in Europe.[48] The memory of the unfree status of the German knights has remained to the modern day though, whereas in England the unfree status of the early knights is less well known. Indeed by the thirteenth century the status of the *ministeriales* was losing its meaning of servitude, and the German knights were merging into the lower nobility and becoming hereditary, as was happening elsewhere. They were an effective fighting force from early on, and it was a purely mounted army that finally repulsed the Magyars in ad 955 at the Battle of Lechfeld in central Germany.[49] The lightly armoured Magyar horse archers were pushed into close combat by knights from across Germany and were resoundingly defeated. This victory is an important moment for the mounted knight as it is possibly the first solely cavalry encounter of the early middle ages in Europe. Here, in ad 955, the (still unchivalrous) mounted knight had most certainly arrived, and he had done so with a bang.

Comparison to Italy

From the tenth century German influence spread southwards into Italy under the banner of the Holy Roman Empire, but the Italians eventually pushed them out and by the twelfth century Italy was a patchwork of self governing city states. These states, such as Venice, Florence, Milan and Genoa, did not owe allegiance to any king and were ruled by their own urban elites. An indication of the immense size of these cities is that by 1300 London had a population of at most 60,000,[50] whereas Florence, Venice and Milan all housed more than 100,000 people within their walls.[51] This was a hangover of the Roman legacy of large cities, which focused Italian life much more into urban areas than the countries to their north, and as a result different systems emerged to produce fighting men. Although some Italian rural noblemen could raise large forces, the lower proportion of countryside nobles compared to their city dwelling counterparts made it a very different landscape to northern France or

England.⁵² Troop recruitment practices varied between the city states too. In some, combat duties were reserved for the upper classes, whereas in others the middle classes also got involved. For example, lawyers might be expected to maintain a full harness of armour and a warhorse, whereas an artist might be expected to own a crossbow. Another method that could be used was recruiting from the working people, to produce troops called sarjeants,⁵³ or more unusually, a lottery was used for the Venetian navy.⁵⁴ These methods were enough to line the walls of a city or an important town, but when an Italian city state wanted to put an army of mounted knights into the field from the thirteenth century onwards, they just paid for it. Capitalism had become so advanced in Italy that cities would even rent out their urban militias to other cities, usually under the pretence of an alliance. With fewer members of the elite having a purely agricultural base, aristocrats went into finance in the time when banking was being created.⁵⁵ Merchants proliferated, capitalism spread and a money economy meant there was cash around to pay for mercenaries. These knights and men-at-arms were known as condottieri,⁵⁶ literally meaning contractor, and operated in companies of mostly Italian soldiers but also included plenty of foreigners. The condottieri companies had the armoured mounted knight as their core troop type, and knights from France, Germany and even England went to Italy when wars paused in their home countries.⁵⁷ They fought in the same way as knights everywhere else but they served no king, instead fighting for whichever Italian city offered them the best contract. The condottieri companies were certainly not feudal armies, rather they were private enterprise operations.

Comparison to Spain

The Spanish evolution of horseback combat was very different to the rest of the continent and this stemmed from its geography. Spain was more sparsely populated than countries to its north, and the terrain generally rougher. It had always been unsuitable for chariots, and this led to a different mode of ancient warfare to evolve. Infantry also played a smaller than normal role in medieval Spain and mounted combat was therefore important to the Spanish. Archery was undeveloped and so what evolved was a close combat mode of fighting that resembled the aerial dogfights of the First World War. Two opposing warriors on strong, agile and intelligent horses[58] would duel together in a dance to get behind and to the left of each other in order to strike. They wore shields on their left side and attacked with spears, constantly manoeuvring and circling to gain advantage. The best horses for this had short backs and could twist and turn, and importantly, excessive size was considered a hindrance. The same equine movements and skills used in this highly sophisticated warfare are still in use in Iberia today in the bullfighting arena, although in modern times the enemy is less able to fight back. The horse was key for this style of riding and the Spanish horse developed into one of the preferred warhorse breeds throughout the whole of medieval Europe.[59] In the Norman period the separate Spanish kingdoms were in the process of reconquering Spain from the Muslims. This process started to speed up in the eleventh century when the nobility started to fight in the style of the Franks, that is with mail clad knights charging with lances. By 1085 they had roughly half of the peninsular under Christian control and by the end of the century this had increased to two thirds.[60] For example, in 1094 the warrior known as El Cid, whose name comes from the Arabic for Lord (sidi) conquered Valencia, although for a time he could have been found attacking the Christian kingdom of Aragon while serving a Muslim ruler.[61] Indeed medieval Spain was not a country explainable just in terms of Christianity versus Islam. Militarily, the Muslims employed mostly light cavalry and the Spanish Christians found that their relatively limited numbers of knights could successfully charge home when deployed properly. Spanish knights could be noble in the way they were in the rest of Europe, but they could also be non-noble, but without the unfree status of many Norman knights.[62] These non-noble Spanish knights lived rurally and over time became a ruling class, but their numbers were smaller than in the countries to the north.

Author's Note

The line of mounted Norman knights stood still at the bottom of Senlac Hill, watching their infantry begin their march up the slope. Ahead and above them was the long line of the Saxon shieldwall, towards which the Norman infantry advanced under the cover of an archery volley. The Saxons were banging their weapons against their shields and shouting their war cry, 'ut, ut ut', which meant, 'out, out, out', and this echoed out across the battlefield. Some of the cavalrymen looking on licked their lips, and many felt their throats drying as they shifted in their high wooden saddles. Their eyes made a note of the ditch that ran along the battlefield and tried to make a mental recording of where the worst ground for their horses was. Others looked up at the shieldwall and wondered if their horses were going to engage it or not. A few of the knights were laughing and joking, but then this was just a re-enactment of the Battle of Hastings, 950 years after the real event, and it was probable that no one was actually going to get killed. This annual event sees a unit of Norman cavalry, on one occasion made up of one hundred horses, charging up and down the battlefield to recreate the order of events that happened on that fateful day in October 1066.

Riders once brought their horses from across Europe to take part, and although a core of riders are accomplished horsemen, the majority are only occasional riders. Despite this, the double line formation of horses can wheel up the hill, across it and down again with near perfect discipline. The ground includes a ditch as mentioned in contemporary accounts, and some moles have made another small ridge quite treacherous for horses, but still the part-time riders manage to keep in formation. The thing that impresses me each year is that with effectively no training they are able to look the part. Indeed they can ride close enough to throw javelins at the enemy, and that was half of the job of the cavalry. When we charge the Saxon shieldwall head on, we have to turn at the last moment to avoid actually steamrollering it, and it is clear that if we did not turn, the riders would be capable enough to hold the charge together. In a cavalry against cavalry encounter they would not survive, but against the infantry the re-enactors show enough skills to succeed without a fraction of the training time the historic Norman knights would have had.

As with the human component, the horses are remarkably effective, although in order to be on the battlefield in the first place they have all had a certain level of training and education. That being said, this particular re-enactment is one of the biggest tests that a horse can undergo. My partner's horse, a gypsy cob stallion called Sparks, had done everything possible in the equestrian world when he arrived at his first Hastings. He had show-jumped, done dressage, cross country, and pulled carriages, as well as been a resolute jousting horse, sensible even when jousting without a tilt barrier. He also managed one day of battle without putting a foot wrong, but on Sunday the tension and excitement got a bit much for him and when the rest of our line cantered off to charge, he planted himself to the spot and reared vertically. Once he had got that out of his system he was fine, but it showed that even the most level-headed of horses will reach a point where their environment is more complex than their brain can deal with. It should be considered that medieval Normandy was a much quieter place than modern England, so modern horses will be naturally more desensitised to the loud shouting and metallic noises of the battlefield than their eleventh-century ancestors. In this area the modern horse trainer has an advantage, but the historic Norman cavalry was nonetheless powerful.

The most obvious demonstration of this power is when we recreate one of the feigned retreats that pulled the Saxons out of their line. Our cavalry unit charges up to the Saxons and engages them in a brief bout of hand-to-hand combat before slowly backing away down the hill. The Saxons are teased into following, at which point we canter down the hill and the now committed Saxons run after us. The Norman cavalry has a second unit, and once the Saxons are a little detached from their comrades still in the shieldwall, this unit charges in between both groups of Saxons and cuts off those pursuing our retreating cavalry. This charge goes from standing still to cantering around the now isolated Saxons in around five seconds. Even if they see the Normans start the manoeuvre, the Saxons do not have time to do anything other than maybe call themselves to a halt. The Normans encircle the Saxons and cut them down before my unit has even reformed at the bottom of the hill, and we usually find no Saxons left to fight by the time we've charged back up to join in. The sources we have of the battle emphasise the feigned retreats drawing the Saxons off the hill, and our attempt to recreate this really does drive home how quickly this tactic works once the Saxons have moved even a short way from the security of their starting point. The mobility of the cavalry is so rapid that they change the nature of the battle situation in mere seconds. Indeed, even if the first Norman rout was a real one as is suggested, then a committed cavalry reserve that was high in self belief could still cut off, surround and overwhelm the pursuing Saxons as if from out of nowhere. If this incident occurred as described then it was probably the critical moment of the battle, a success made possible by the warhorse.

Chapter Three

The Crusades

The Pope on 27 November 1095 was Urban II, and he was standing in a field outside of Clermont in France making a speech. By the time he had finished he had changed the course of history. On that day, Pope Urban II launched a movement that would become known as the First Crusade, but we do not know for sure what he actually said. The five differing accounts we have focus on the false accusation of the terrible treatment of Christians in the Holy Lands, the problems of inter-Christian warfare at home and a reward in heaven linked to penance. Motivated by various combinations of all of these, the First Crusade managed to recapture Jerusalem from the Muslims and carve out Christian territory in what became known as the Crusader States. Throughout a number of further Crusades to the east, mounted knights defeated Muslim forces, were defeated by them, and even fought other Christians. They forged a reputation as the sword arm of God and the defenders of the faithful, and many of the attributes we now ascribe to the knight have their origins in these ventures. We also find Christian knights fighting a Jihad alongside Muslims in North Africa, and forming a Christian Crusader State in the Baltic. Famous reputations were made by individuals and also the knightly orders such as the Knights Templar and Hospitallers, and legends such as Richard the Lionheart were forged. The First Crusade was the event that catapulted the mounted knight to the pinnacle of their reputation, completing their rise. We shall now consider how and why this happened.

The First Crusade

In effect the First Crusade was a solution to two problems faced by the church in the late eleventh century. Firstly, there had been powerful Muslim forces to the south of Christian territories since the eighth century. In Spain the Christians had reconquered two thirds of the country by

1095, but this was very much a live conflict zone. In 1091 the Normans had taken Sicily, but four years later this conquest was not certain to be successful or long lasting. Most ominously, however, were the gains being made by the Turks in modern day Turkey, which had almost entirely fallen to their advances. A few years earlier Constantinople had been under siege, and the Byzantine Emperor Alexius I Comnenus had been requesting help from the Catholic Pope ever since. What remained of the once great Roman Empire was 'on its knees',[1] and in 1095 he had again asked for Christian soldiers to help liberate Byzantine lands, likely expecting a small Christian expeditionary force. Finding an army to go and help the Byzantines was the first problem the Pope had. The second problem was that the Christian knights in Europe were spending far too much time fighting among themselves.[2] The strategic master-stroke of Urban II was to find a way to make one of his problems the solution to the other. It may have been Byzantine decline that opened the door for the First Crusade to happen, but it was the mounted knight who walked through it.

Motivation

What can the motivations behind those who answered the call tell us about the mindset of the mounted knight? One of the sources for Urban II's speech, Fulcher of Chartres, wrote that,

> All who die by the way ... shall have immediate remission of sins... Let those who have been accustomed unjustly to wage private warfare against the faithful now go against the infidels and end with victory this war which should have been begun long ago. Let those who for a long time, have been robbers, now become knights. Let those who have been fighting against their brothers and relatives now fight in a proper way against the barbarian.[3]

Being given in France, the audience of the speech was French, and it was primarily the warfare within that region that Urban II was probably trying to stop. The knights of this time were pious, and religion was not just one part of life, it was the very fabric of it.[4] A Pope's request to march east would therefore be a hard call to ignore, yet earlier calls had been ignored. On this occasion, however, while we cannot know the many and diverse motivations that drove individual knights, we can be sure that they did certainly go. Many knights and men-at-arms went because their lords went and they did not have a choice to do anything else. Some certainly went of their own accord, and their reasons are lost to time. Were these men touched by Christian motives to cease killing others of the same faith? Did some believe that it was their holy duty to protect Christians already in the east? Or were some looking to conquer part of the Holy Land for personal gain? One important fact is that it was perfectly possible for Christian pilgrims to get to Jerusalem and back again in the eleventh century with a reasonable degree of security, indeed in 1026 the Abbot of Saint-Vanne was able to joyfully visit the Holy sites without trouble.[5]

Perhaps a clue lies in one of the very few maps that existed at the time. The English made *Mappa Mundi* dates from a few decades before the First Crusade, and has Jerusalem as the centre of the world on a map oriented to the East. That map, and others, tell us that Jerusalem was literally the centre of the universe for those living in western Europe. Modern cynicism might lean us towards assuming that more materialistic reasons were the driving force behind crusader recruitment, but to understand the genuine piety of the knights of the First Crusade we can look at the People's Crusade. A few months before the heavily armed First Crusade started on its way in August 1096, a mass of impatient peasants had already left for the Holy Land. This fanatical group had no real chance of making it to the Holy Land, let alone doing anything useful there, not without genuine divine intervention. Yet they went anyway, on their own, instead of waiting a few months for military backup. In order to put aside the surely obvious problem of entering enemy territory without an armed escort, it is therefore likely that a genuine religious conviction existed within those who went. The People's Crusade was destroyed in minutes by the Turks, but however misguided the venture had been, they must have been full of real religious zeal. With this level of devoutness being demonstrated, genuine ideological reasons for at least some of the knights who joined the First Crusade cannot be entirely ruled out. This factor is mentioned by Albert of Aachen who spoke of the, 'spirit of penance',[6] that pervaded the venture, and within the medieval culture of sin this was beyond important.

The church had spent a few hundred years telling fighting men that by killing, particularly Christians, they were going to hell. For those thoughtful knights who comprehended the compassionate nature of Christianity, this must have been a profoundly confusing state to find themselves in. They would have seen no alternative to bearing arms in combat, but at the same time the unavoidable consequence was eternal damnation. What the Pope offered in 1095 was a solution to this unsolvable equation, and it explains why taking the cross became so prominent among kings and the nobility over the following few hundred years. If you were convinced you were going to spend an eternity in hell, would you not jump at the chance to avoid that by going on a single military campaign? On top of this, there was an urge to restore balance to the world by retaking the Holy Land, even though its loss was not recent.[7] Order had to be restored, and the fact that it would have to be done at the point of a sword probably gave the knightly ranks a sense of divine self importance. How, then, could a knight ignore a call to save the world as well as his soul, when it came from the man on earth who was closest to God?

A hundred years later, Richard I of England took the cross even before Saladin had recaptured Jerusalem, and proceeded to empty his kingdom of wealth in order to pay for his venture. This was unpopular in England, and he must have been aware that it was a risk to leave it just after he had extorted and squeezed it dry. On top of this, he and King Philip of France had to agree to go on crusade at the same time, because neither trusted the other to keep the peace in Europe in the other's absence. Richard was therefore going on crusade at a great dynastical as well as personal risk, which could mean his piety was genuine. Additionally, a motivation for Richard was penance. He had warred against his father Henry II and probably felt responsible for driving him to his death. A modern view might be cynical of the righteous causes that some crusaders must have held, but this cynicism should be employed warily.[8]

Both Richard I and later Edward I were obsessed with improving the crown's rights and lands, but they both went on crusade when that venture was a direct risk to that goal. William the Conqueror's son, Robert Curthose, even pawned Normandy to his brother William Rufus in order to afford to go on crusade, in effect forsaking his chance at dynastic power in the physical world in order to find spiritual salvation in the next.

The Knights of 1095

Looking at the knights themselves as the First Crusade kicked off, we find in the written accounts some clues as to the increasingly separate space in society that they were occupying. In these sources the term *miles*, meaning knight in Latin, definitely meant a specifically mounted soldier. Guibert of Nogent and Albert of Aachen both used the term *milites* (plural) or *miles* (singular) as a distinct social class, and Guibert spoke of a middle rank of knights during the First Crusade.[9] Albert did not describe kings or princes as *miles*, which suggests that a *miles* was not just a description of the function of fighting from horseback. Albert also described some *miles* as being from a particular castle, for example we have a knight called Folbertus who is written as being, 'a *miles* ... by birth from the castle Bouillon'.[10] Along with other examples this suggests that at the very end of the eleventh century, it may be possible to inherit the status of being a knight and that the status has elevated them above that of an unfree serf. It also shows the link between knights and castles. The process by which knights became truly separated from the peasants was a gradual one, but by the Crusades it was a feature. A few centuries after the First Crusade, Jean de Bueil wrote that 'arms ennoble the man',[11] and although he probably meant those bearing arms professionally only, it encapsulates the sentiment that was forming during the Crusades.

God's Battering Ram

Christendom gave the mounted knight salvation as well as a purpose via the crusades. In turn, the mounted knight gained fame as saviour of the Holy Land, and reputation as the most effective military force in the world. To see if this fame and reputation was deserved we can look in depth at their combat record. First contact by the crusaders with the enemy was made at Nicaea in 1097 as they started their journey east from Constantinople. The knights immediately dismounted and started to attack the walls of the city, but to no avail. They took losses against the well positioned defences of Nicaea, but the mounted knights did manage to wipe out a Turkish relief force.[12] The heads of the fallen Turks were tied to the ends of spears and paraded around in full view of the city, for chivalry did not extend to the infidel.

The Byzantine allies of the crusaders negotiated with the Turks and thereafter secured the surrender of the town, but in a way designed to make the crusaders think it had been won by force, as they had not been party to the talks. This infuriated the crusaders who found out and felt betrayed by their allies. To their outrage they were not allowed to plunder the city, or even enter it in groups larger than ten. This set the scene for the First Crusade; it would be complicated and bloody but eventually successful. Before the Battle of Dorylaeum, which followed the capture of Nicaea, the crusaders had split into two groups, divided into Normans and French. The Norman contingent had made camp at Dorylaeum and faced a surprise attack while still encamped; Turkish horse archers loosed arrows into the camp, causing casualties and confusion. The knights within mounted their horses and attacked the Turks, but being lightly armed they managed to evade the Christian charges. Those left behind within the camp eventually formed a defensive position, but this gave the superior mobility of the Turks the space with which to pepper them with arrows. The expert horsemanship and marksmanship of the Turkish horse archers was a stern introduction to war in the East. The Norman defensive formation was pushed to a river, where soft ground at least discouraged the enemy from getting too close. However, they could do little damage to the horse archers and the situation soon became desperate. Occasionally groups of knights would break out of the formation against orders to charge the Turks, only to be cut down. Other mounted knights chased the horse archers around the countryside but could not get close enough to engage, all the while their numbers thinning as their horses were shot from under them. The armour of the Christian warriors was largely arrow-proof, but there were gaps, and their horses were not armoured.

After seven or eight hours of grinding battle the Normans were near defeat, a steady stream of reinforcements from the French column started to arrive to bolster them. The Turks were pressed by these mounted attacks but held firm until one group of knights found the Turkish camp and set it alight. Seeing the smoke rise behind them the Turks broke off their attack to retreat, and the exhausted crusaders could take stock of what had happened. Although this battle is seen as a costly Christian victory, it cannot be ruled out that after more than eight hours of fighting the Turks had simply run out of arrows. The knights had been partly ineffectual against the mounted horse archers, indeed their horses were painfully vulnerable to the missile-fire they received. The only real positive that could be taken from the encounter was that the mail defences worn by many combatants was able to keep arrows out relatively well. The small links of the mail armour would be unlikely to break at anything other than very close range, meaning the actual point of the arrow wouldn't be able to penetrate and get stuck into a body. This does not mean the concussion from impacts was not felt, or that armour could not fail, or that there were no uncovered areas, just that their armour was beneficial. Although the mounted knights had not been able to bring their lances and swords to bear enough to force a full victory, their mobility had enabled them to reach the Turkish camp and recover the day.

The next action was the Siege of Antioch, which dragged on for nearly eight months before a traitor inside the city opened the gates and the crusaders flooded in. Shortly afterwards a huge Muslim army arrived to turn the tables and started to besiege the now crusader-held city. With no supplies, the Christian's chances of survival looked bleak, and indeed they tried to negotiate a surrender but were refused. On 28 June 1098, they marched out of the city and formed up in open battle array in a last ditch attempt to save themselves. Possibly spurred on by the convenient discovery in Antioch of the Holy Lance, which had pierced Christ's side on the Cross, they attacked.[13] At first it looked like another storm of arrows was going to wear down the crusaders as it had at Dorylaeum, but this time the Franks had more horses and the Turks were not as disciplined. It was also later claimed that a number of Christian warrior saints were riding into battle alongside the living knights, and this miracle is the reason given at the time as to why the attack proved successful. The Muslims were pushed back before breaking and fleeing away from the thundering charge of the mounted knights. They swept all before them, and in this battle the crusading knights proved not only that a knightly charge could be decisive, but also that they could defeat the Muslims in open battle, and their victory became legendary across the Christian world. Composed to celebrate this earth shattering event was the *Chanson d'Antioche*, or *Song of Antioch* which was many thousands of lines long and immortalised the battle.[14] Here, alongside the warrior saints, knights on horseback had fought, died, and been victorious for their religion, and everyone in Europe was going to hear about it. The fame of the crusaders was only to increase when finally, after years of hardship, the exhausted Christians reached Jerusalem.

The heavily reduced force of crusaders, probably now with less than 2,000 mounted knights left, was now largely on foot. Unlike Nicea, which had fallen to negotiation, and Antioch, which had taken several months to take, Jerusalem was successfully assaulted in just over a month. The city had not one, but two walls around it, so the Christians built siege engines and ladders, including two huge wheeled towers that allowed attackers to attack the defenders on the outer wall on a near even footing. Once a foothold was gained on the walls, the defenders panicked and resistance collapsed. Crusaders opened the gates and the ecstatic army flooded into Jerusalem to complete their four year ordeal. Giddy on victory – and probably the confirmation that they were now all certainly going to heaven – the city was subjected to a terrible bloodletting. Indeed some accounts say the blood in the streets was so deep it was up to the horse's bridles. This is an exaggeration, and other sources mention blood running up to knees and ankles, but either way there was a massacre inside the Holy City.[15] This frenzied end to the First Crusade possibly saw the killing of thousands of Muslims, although luckily for the Christian inhabitants of the city they had been expelled as the crusaders approached. The chronicles of the event all mention the killing of people sheltering in the Temple of Solomon, an act we might assume would have been seen as ungodly. This act is horrific to modern eyes, but to the crusaders it was sacred because they were cleansing their Holy City and rebalancing the world. Those who wrote about it did so frankly and with no remorse or shame, indeed the chroniclers seem to be purposely inflating the numbers killed. This has to be one of the very few times in history that an atrocity is publicised by the perpetrators, but it should be remembered that a city that resisted a siege was expected to suffer badly if it fell. Regardless of ethical wrangling, a wave of optimism swept through Christian lands, and knights were the heroes of the hour. They had stormed walls, survived hunger, just about beat off the infidels in combat, frequently lost their horses and generally suffered in a multitude of ways. In other words, they had done their religious duty through their ordeal, and by granting them victory God had shown his favour. The mounted knight had risen.

Cultural Exchange

One reward for this service during the First Crusade was the granting of certain castles and cities to some of the surviving knights. Guibert of Nogent wrote of new men who, by virtue of their arms, had been able to rise in society, indeed social status was fluid in the eleventh century.[16] It was not just land and loot that the crusaders gained from the East, there was an exchange of cultures and ideas that flowed in both directions too. Knights noticed a few things very quickly about the Muslim opponents they had faced, and first – perhaps unsurprisingly – were their horses. The type of horses known as the Oriental Horse includes modern breeds such as the Arab, and their DNA is one of the reasons the modern thoroughbred is fast and slender. The crusaders had been plagued by archers riding sleek, fast and agile horses, and immediately they saw something they liked.[17]

At Antioch they were also astounded when Muslim warriors who wore iron scale armour on themselves and their horses appeared. These *Ghulam* cavalry units were just as heavily armoured as the Christians were, but the crusaders did not generally armour their horses and seeing a large contingent of armoured *Ghulams* must have made an impression. Arriving to fight the supposedly barbarian infidels of the East, a few of the knights who watched them approach must have questioned to themselves why their enemy was actually better armed. In addition to metal horse armour, the use of fabric horse coverings known as *caparisons* eventually made its way back to Europe. Knights saw the advantages of these coverings, including that they kept biting and stinging insects away from a horse's skin which helped to keep them healthy. The Holy Land was also a land of extreme temperatures, and a linen or silk caparison will actually help regulate a horse's temperature too. If this is counter intuitive, think of the Bedouin who live in the harshest desert, and that they do not walk around in shorts and t-shirts. Thirdly, if designed for it, a caparison will provide some protection from arrows, an issue close to home for many knights throughout the crusading period. While on crusade during the 1240s, the Holy Roman Emperor had a treatise of an Arab falconer translated to Latin, and practices and breeds of birds of prey also flowed West.[18] Even the concept of carrier pigeons originated from the Turks. The techniques of warfare that the crusaders took with them to the Holy Land also had to adapt. Once Jerusalem had fallen, new crusaders made their way East to defend it, and had to learn the same lessons their predecessors had. Unfortunately, during the minor Crusade of 1101, three new Latin armies of Lombards, Franks and Bavarians all found themselves either surrounded or ambushed by the Turks and summarily wiped out.

Fatimid Egypt

Before Saladin took control of Egypt, the Fatimid dynasty cultivated an unenviable military reputation among the crusaders. At the Battle of Ramla in 1101, a Fatimid army that was numerically superior lined up against a small Christian army. Three divisions of crusader cavalry charged directly into the middle of the Egyptian army, and although they made a heavy impact they were quickly flanked by the much larger force and nearly entirely destroyed. Further groups of knights charged into the melee and met similar fates. The Egyptian army swallowed up the knights but they could not kill them quickly enough. Skill, armour and faith, presumably along with desperation, meant that the knights made their enemies pay a steep price to overcome them. However the Fatamids never quite managed it, and that was their downfall, for although it probably wasn't obvious through the dust of war, their centre had been badly weakened by the knightly attack.[19]

Looking on, King Baldwin of Jerusalem is described in dramatic terms by the chronicler Fulcher of Chartres, who was there watching, as making a last confession. He then committed his final reserves to the battle instead of withdrawing to safety. This final charge succeeded in killing the Fatimid general, named aptly in some Muslim sources as 'General Disastrous', and triggered a retreat. Having started with a significant advantage in numbers, the Fatimid army should have been able to surround and wipe out the smaller Christian army, but it was not able to due to the resilience of the mounted knights. The following year the tables were turned when King Baldwin incorrectly believed that another Fatimid invasion was just a scouting party. This led him to opposing it with only 200 mounted knights, and no infantry back up whatsoever. Infantry were used as a safe place where knights could regroup, rest or pick up new lances, and by leaving them behind the king was possibly under the impression that a quick charge would easily decide the day. By the time Baldwin noticed he was very wrong, he was already surrounded. Fulcher of Chartres remarked that the 200 knights were enveloped and overwhelmed, 'in the space of less than an hour'.[20] His tone makes this sound like a disappointing effort, but a small surrounded force surviving for even *nearly* an hour shows how hard it was to take a Christian mounted knight out of a fight. King Baldwin took himself out of the fight however, and managed to survive by hiding in a tower and escaping at night under the cover of darkness. He left the shattered remains of his small force to defend the tower, which they did valiantly, before ultimately launching a suicidal charge to the death. One Conrad of Germany fought on alone at the end so fiercely that the impressed Fatimids actually offered to spare his life. Conrad, who happened to be the Constable of Germany, wisely accepted their offer and made himself the only survivor of a disastrous encounter. Mounted knights might have been effective, but this battle showed that unlike at Antioch, they were not always miracle workers.

In 1105, again at Ramla, a Turkish contingent joined with the Fatimids together for the first time against the Franks. This time the Fatimids withstood the usual Latin cavalry charge, and the subsequent battle raged for most of the day. King Baldwin was able to use his troops to see off the Turks attacking his rear and then led another charge, which this time did rout the Egyptians. Baldwin's use of cavalry was again important and decisive. As with the first battle of Ramla, his force was at most half the size of the enemy, and only 500 knights proved to be a battle-winning force against an enemy between 5,000 and 15,000 strong. To further demonstrate the effectiveness of the mounted knight against the Fatimids we need look no further than the Battle of Yibneh in 1123. An entire Fatimid army from Egypt was destroyed by a single Frankish cavalry charge. According to Fulcher of Chartres the Muslim cavalry, 'took flight immediately as if completely bewitched, going into a panic'.[21] The infantry they left behind suffered badly and 6,000 of them were killed for only minor crusader losses, it seems as if the crusaders had the measure of the Fatamids.

Seljuk Turks

The Seljuk Turks were a very different adversary. Their conquest of Anatolia had started in the 1020s and by the time of the First Crusade they had pushed both the Armenians and the Byzantines out of the area of and around modern day Turkey. The Byzantines had worked out that to survive the torrent of incoming arrows that was the primary tactics of the Seljuks, they had to stay in formation and just keep marching. Effectively, they had implemented a defensive march in formation, which the crusaders would later adopt themselves. However, in 1071 at the Battle of Manzikert the Byzantines suffered a decisive defeat when the Turks deployed classic horse archer tactics against them.[22] The Byzantines marched towards the Seljuks, who gave way in the centre to draw them in – and then enveloped them. Amid confusion, possible betrayals and then a final Turkish attack, the Byzantines fell apart and routed, although a few elite units fought to the bitter end. The Seljuks also employed feigned retreats with ambushes to pull units, especially cavalry, out of the Byzantine lines. These cavalry units were sometimes armoured, but as with the crusaders later, their horses generally were not. Critically, by pulling enemy horsemen out of a line and into an ambush, the Seljuks could shoot at them from the side. This presented a much larger horse-shaped target to hit than a front-on shot. From the front, a horse's legs are a very thin target and an archer is left to aim only at the front of the head and possibly part of the horse's chest. This explains why the Turks preferred to cause the disintegration of enemy mounted units before they fully attacked them. Being aware of this, the Seljuks themselves rode directly at an enemy, turned and rode directly away again while firing, so as to never expose the flanks of their horses to incoming missile fire.

These tactics were those deployed against the crusaders when they came up against the Turks throughout the crusading period. One example was the Battle of Harran in 1104[23] when a crusader army besieging the city faced an army of Turkish horse archers who arrived to relieve it. The Seljuks feigned a retreat and for some reason the crusaders followed, even though their own plan had been to conduct a feigned retreat themselves. They reached a plain near Raqqa when the Turks suddenly turned to fight and were joined by the rest of their army. Many Latin leaders were captured and heavy causalities were inflicted by horse archery in what was a total defeat. William of Tyre wrote that there was no battle as disastrous as this, and it marked the start of a decline of the Principality of Antioch, which was the northern Crusader State. At the Battle of al-Sannabra in 1113, the crusaders again fell for the Turkish feigned retreat. They ran into the main Turkish army which doled out another rain of arrows and caused heavy casualties. Survivors rallied and stood fast in a fortified camp where they remained safe but rooted to the spot. The Seljuks couldn't defeat this entrenched foe, but with it pinned down they were free to raid all around the local area and caused immense damage doing so.

These encounters should not be seen as painting a picture purely of Frankish military incompetence however. Indeed, at the Battle of Artah in 1105, while the Franks laid siege to castle of Artah, a large Muslim relief force arrived to break the siege. The crusaders feigned a retreat of their own this time, pulling the Muslims into their camp before wiping out nearly the entire enemy force. The Franks also employed the formation march tactic that the Byzantines had used in the previous century. As early as 1111 at Shaizar, the crusaders stayed in marching formation under incessant horse archer attack, and in what was really a long harassment rather than a battle, fought them off. Mounted knights marched inside a square of infantry to keep them away from arrows, and when the Turks got too close for comfort they charged them to either push them back or actually engage them. Eventually the Muslims lost interest and gave up with only light casualties inflicted on both sides. This early engagement showed that disciplined crusaders could effectively ignore horse archer armies if they brought enough of their own missile troops and, most importantly, maintained good order.

The modern image of the impetuous knight has a foundation in truth, but when their leaders showed tactical sense and self restraint, they could be a controlled force. As the Crusader States started to mature, their leaders and soldiers started to learn about the conditions they fought in and the enemies they fought against. In major battles between 1111 and 1186 the tally of victories and defeats could be said to have left honours even in the Holy Land, which was no mean feat for the undermanned newcomers. Among the Frankish victories we have the Battle of Sarmin in 1114, where Roger of Salerno[24] managed to find a large Turkish army as it was making camp, charged it and destroyed it. He only had 700 knights and a couple of thousand infantry, but the surprise attack led by a knightly charge resulted in thousands of Turks being killed. If deployed correctly, it seems that relatively few knights could cause utter devastation.

In stark contrast, however, Roger of Salerno lost his luck five years later at what became known as the Battle of the Field of Blood. A large force of crusaders, with perhaps 10,000 infantry and 700 knights came up against a force double their size. The Frank's right flank was successful with a cavalry charge, but on the left flank they were heavily defeated, so much so that only two knights escaped and Roger of Salerno was killed by a sword blow. This was the first time a Muslim army with no Turkish component had beaten the Franks. They still employed a high number of archers, so much so that it was said that the slain crusaders and their horses looked like hedgehogs strewn across the field. A few weeks later at Hab, King Balwin II of Jerusalem engaged the victorious Muslim army. The battle did not start well when many of the 700 knights in Baldwin's army were tempted away from the infantry and made their own attacks. The abandoned infantry suffered heavy losses but stoically held their ground. One group of knights wandered off rather bizarrely to retake a nearby castle, and the second scattered after heavy fighting. The third, along with Baldwin's mounted reserve, went from crisis area to crisis area, and through rapid manoeuvring and sharp attacks beat off the Turks. Both sides claimed victory, and while the Franks were recorded as having sustained heavy losses, they must have inflicted many on the Muslims too. This brilliant use of knights again demonstrated their battle-winning ability, even in relatively small numbers.

As we have already seen, King Baldwin was an effective user of his knights, and at the Battle of Azaz in 1125, he feigned retreat against a Seljuk army and with 1,100 knights, tricked his enemy into giving him a target to charge, and killed several thousand Turks in an effective attack.[25] The Franks further demonstrated that they could maintain tight order and discipline under fire during an onwards march known as the Battle of Bosra in 1147. The knights were specifically forbidden to leave formation except to save a Christian from being killed. After an extended period of harassment from horse archers, a Turkish knight fighting for the Christians broke rank, and killed an opponent in single combat. The Seljuks lost heart at this, and combined with the fact they had been unable to draw the crusader knights out of formation, abandoned their attack. The plucky Turkish knight was eventually excused punishment for breaching the formation order seeing as he'd scared off the whole enemy army. Again it can be seen that when disciplined, even the unarmoured horses of the knights could be fairly safe from arrow attacks.

However, the Second Crusade in the middle of the twelfth century shows that these lessons did not always spread very far. The new crusaders entered Turkey disorganised and ill disciplined, and Turkish horse archers wore them down and defeated them. In the see-saw of victories and defeats in the Holy Land the next battle was at Harim, and was a crushing defeat for experienced Franks. Their knights lost discipline and once again, when their forces fragmented, they were destroyed. One of the most famous battles was that of the Battle of Montgisard in 1177, where Saladin approached Jerusalem from Egypt with an army of at least 18,000 men.[26] King Baldwin IV of Jerusalem only had 375 secular knights and eighty Knights Templar with him. These were bolstered by probably several thousand infantry and *turcopole* Turkish mercenary horse archers. Saladin dismissed this crusader force as insignificant, possibly because of the lack of mounted knights. As a result it appears that no attempt was made to keep his army's defensive discipline together. Due to this, Saladin's army and baggage train got strung out while marching, some of which became stuck at a river crossing. When Saladin saw the Franks appear in front of him, he attempted to organise the troops around him to present a front to the Christians, but it was too late. With this element of surprise, the Latin knights attacked while this reorganisation was taking place and stormed the fragmented Muslim army. The seemingly small number of mounted knights charged directly at them at exactly the right moment. This was so irresistible that only 10 per cent of Saladin's army made it back home; it was a truly stunning success for the crusader knights. Saladin's Mamluk troops, who were heavily armed mounted knights, fought to the death, mirroring their Christian counterpart's willingness to die in a lost cause.

Horns of Hattin

The watershed moment of the twelfth century was the campaign that culminated at the Horns of Hattin. Saladin had formed a fragile alliance under Sunni Islam and declared a Holy War, which swung into action after a Muslim caravan had been attacked during a truce. Saladin sent his son with 7,000 Turks to take revenge on Reynald of Chatillon who had commended the caravan attack.[27] They encountered a small force of Christian knights and their skirmish became known as the Battle of Cresson. The crusaders only had 130 knights, including a number of Templars and Hospitallers. If anything, this army was more of a group of grandees, and included both Grand Masters of the orders and many of their senior staff. They were supported by around 400 infantry, but the knights were lured into charging too far from them. As a result they were mostly surrounded and killed before the footsoldiers were similarly wiped out. Only three knights escaped the carnage, including Gerard de Ridefort, the Grand Master of the Knights Templars.

Losing 130 knights does not seem like a particularly high number, but among them were so many high ranking knights of the Holy Orders that it was a considerable blow to the crusader states as a whole. A small number of knights had also proven themselves able to do a disproportionate amount of damage in previous battles, and their absence in the army that would march towards the Horns of Hattin would be sorely felt. After Cresson, Saladin tempted the crusaders to come and seek him out by laying siege to the castle of Tiberias, which stands on the bank of the Sea of Galilee. In response, the full force of the Crusader States was mustered, including armies from the Principality of Antioch, Tripoli and a number of Holy Orders. This army was up to 20,000 strong, including 1,200 knights and 3,000 other mounted troops. It is worth nothing that the 130 knights who died at Cresson would have increased the knightly strength by 10 per cent. This army, more or less the totality of Christian power, marched from Jerusalem towards Tiberias, and over the white hot plains of the Holy Land. Feuding among the Christian nobility clouded their decision making and hampered their every move, to the point where voices spoke out against moving to relieve the besieged Tiberias in the first place.

These voices turned out to be tragically correct. The Christian army reached the village of Tur'an, less than 18km from Tiberias, but found the springs there unable to supply the large army with enough water. Realising that fresh water was required before the imminent battle, the crusaders resolved to take a northerly route towards Tiberias via the springs at Hattin. As the army marched towards the springs they saw to their horror that Saladin had deployed his army in their way and blocked their path. Indeed, Saladin had ensured that the crusaders would have to endure constant horse archer attacks, and all the while they were growing more and more thirsty. As night was falling the Franks made camp, knowing that they would not have access to water that night. The Muslim army surrounded the camp and deployed psychological warfare techniques on the inhabitants, including playing drums and singing loudly all night. Saladin also set fire to the grass around the camp in the morning to cover it in smoke, which must have made those in the camp think the end of days had truly arrived. In a contrasted logical situation, the Muslim army was supplied with water by seventy camels from the Sea of Galilee, who also brought up supplies of arrows for the horse archers throughout the battle. It is telling that at no point did the bowmen seem to run out of ammunition. The Franks were weary and parched in the morning when the resupplied horse archers resumed their onslaught.

The Christians formed for battle into three groups and made a column to march in formation towards the spring. Previously, when these marching formations had held discipline they had succeeded in shrugging off attack, however this army was in a piteous state under the burning sun, that was growing only hotter as the morning wore on. Eventually, Saladin thought his enemy was on the verge of collapse and ordered a full assault. His secretary, Imad ad-Din al-Isfahani, described this moment, 'the sultan had a slave named Mankurus, fighting at the very front. His horse, being rather headstrong, dashed off with him far away from his companions. As his friends were unable to keep up, he found himself isolated among the Franks.'[28] Mankurus fought bravely but alone and in the middle of his enemies he was killed. It sounds rather like Mankurus was unable to control his horse and was an unwilling martyr, but his example spurred on his comrades as the two sides clashed. In response to Saladin's attack, the mounted Christian knights counter-charged their assailants, and successfully repelled the attacks on their flanks.

Considering their thirst, this successful action was impressive and it opened a gap back towards Jerusalem. Balian of Ibelin and a section of the rearguard took the opportunity to retreat and left the battle to save themselves.[29] At the same time, the hard pressed infantry of the centre made their own decision to march in the direction of Lake Tiberias rather than the springs of Hattin. As the crusader forces spread out, this large infantry unit was funnelled by Saladin onto the twin peaks of an old volcano known as the Horns of Hattin. The rest of the army, under constant attack from horse archers, joined them and made an attempt to block the Muslim mounted troops by putting their tents up around the Horns. This might sound rather pointless, but horses will generally not charge through a tent, and the guy ropes can make effective trip ropes if a horse is pushed onto them. While most of the army tried to form a defensive perimeter around the Horns of Hattin, the mounted vanguard launched a charge northwards, but the swift horse archers simply moved out of the way, let them pass, and moved back in behind them. Seeing themselves separated from their comrades on the Horns, the vanguard left the battlefield and the rest of the army to its fate. This act was seen as shameful afterwards and, critically, it removed a large number of knights from the battle. Now abandoned, the King of Jerusalem ordered his infantry off the Horns, but they refused, so he was forced to join them in a desperate last stand. With the royal tent now erected, the crusaders saw the Muslim army regroup and fully encircle them. The attack that followed was a bitter fight to the death and after a prolonged battle the static Christian defenders were annihilated. Apart from the fleeing rearguard only 200 knights with some other mounted troops escaped the carnage. The loss of 20,000 fighting men was cataclysmic for the Crusader States and within four months Jerusalem was lost, along with a string of other towns and castles. Pope Urban III is said to have taken the news of the defeat so badly that he died of shock. This was a turning point for the Crusader States because in the West such a defeat could only mean that God was damning in his displeasure of the crusading cause, and new European knights were less inclined to journey to the Holy Land as a result. The disaster at Hattin marked the point from which the Crusader States were in terminal decline. It also marked a problem for the mounted knight. Although much of the blame was laid on the Knights Templars in particular, the secular knightly warriors had not been able to stave off defeat either. Indeed the retreat of the vanguard was seen as cowardly and questions started to be asked concerning how much of God's approval the crusader knights really had.

Lionheart

Richard of England arrived in the Holy Land in 1191 as the important coastal city of Acre was suffering under siege by a Christian army. A third army was also present in the area, and it was led by Saladin. His army was besieging the Christians outside Acre, making it a siege within a siege, and the Muslims noted on Richard's arrival that he was, 'a great man and respected leader'.[30] After some effective siege work the city fell to the Christians and King Louis of France went home. He had been in joint command with Richard and his departure, which was widely condemned, left the Englishman in sole command.

After shoring up his political position and executing some prisoners,[31] Richard led a 15,000 strong force south. In response, Saladin was obliged to split his forces because it wasn't clear where the crusaders were going. Richard displayed his military prowess by being one of the few crusaders to appear in the East and straight away comprehend the environment. Either he was remarkably quick at understanding the territory and enemy, or he was wise enough to listen to some of the experienced local noblemen around him. His march along the coast was matched by his navy to keep him supplied, and crept along at between five and ten miles a day. This kept his army in one piece and also allowed his European troops to acclimatise to the heat. Saladin eventually started to shadow his march with his own army, and made an attack to pick off stragglers in the rearguard, which Richard drove away with a knightly charge. He continued the march with Templar and Hospitaller knights at the front and back of his marching formation, and infantry screened the army on the side not protected by the sea.

When the Christians had to march slightly inland for a brief time, Saladin attacked with horse archers, but the crusaders held both their nerve and their formation. Unfortunately for Richard, he was struck in the side by a crossbow bolt and wounded, although his mail armour saved it from being fatal. Mail armour of the time was strong enough to keep out a contemporary crossbow bolt, as modern tests have shown, and Richard's survival is evidence of that. Richard shrugged it off and the crusaders continued their coastal march past the forest of Arsuf, after which they pitched their camp.

The following day Richard deployed his marching formation as if he was ready for a battle facing inland, as a crab walking sideways with his front facing the enemy to his landward side. This meant he would not have to halt the march and spend time redeploying for battle if Saladin's army attacked. Saladin did indeed plan to attack the rear third of the crusaders, and hoped the rest of the Latin army kept moving long enough to open up a gap which could be exploited. A mass of foot and mounted skirmishers duly attacked the Christian infantry screen but made little impression. Saladin's planned attack continued on the rear contingent of the marching formation, and pressed the Knights Hospitallers, who found themselves under relentless arrow fire. The Hospitaller crossbowmen were said to have had to fire and reload while walking backwards as the Muslims unloaded arrow upon arrow into their ranks. Eventually their patience wore out, and despite Richard repeatedly refusing permission to attack, one Hospitaller knight turned and charged. Regardless of whether or not this lone knight had lost his mind, the rest of the Hospitallers were duty bound to follow, which they did, and in turn were followed by nearby French knights. Richard had been aiming to reach camp rather than join a battle, but the charge of his rearguard had narrowed his options down to one. He signalled a full cavalry attack, which was timely because his rearguard would not survive for long unsupported.

The Muslim Beha al-Din wrote that the sudden change from marching to all out attack was disconcerting, and looked like a preconceived plan. Which of course it was. The Christian infantry stepped aside to form channels that the knights could ride through, and with over a thousand of them it isn't surprising it made quite an impact on the Muslims watching. The Hospitaller charge had the accidental effect of pinning down the whole right wing of Saladin's army, and Richard's force was able to charge straight in and destroy this whole formation. Seeing this, the rest of the army turned and fled. Richard's discipline was so great that he was able to recall the pursuit after only one mile and regroup. A unit of rallied heavy Muslim cavalry made an attack on Richard's right flank, but fresh English and Norman knights were able to counter charge and put them to flight. This was repeated one last time before Richard knew the battlefield was his. The Christians claimed to have killed 7,000 Muslims for the loss of only 700 of their own, but regardless of numbers this was a famous victory for the mounted knight. They had withstood a hail of arrows and their own temptations in order to triumph by force of their charge. The mounted knight as a fighting force had reached another highpoint where it would stay for over 200 years, seemingly invincible if well led.

Templars, Hospitallers and Teutons

While their secular military prowess was being demonstrated across the Holy Land, the concept of the mounted knight fused with Christianity in a new and revolutionary way. In 1119 a group of knights decided they wanted to stay in the East permanently and formed themselves into a group with the aim of protecting pilgrims making their way from Europe to Jerusalem. At the start of 1120 it was realised that these Brother of the Temple were busy drinking and wasting time, so they were expressly sent out to guard pilgrims. Around 1126, King Baldwin II of Jerusalem wrote to Bernard, the Abbot of a monastery in Clairvaux, and asked him to set down some rules for the Brothers of the Temple to live by. Bernard of Clairvaux was a Cistercian, a monastic order based around poverty and physical service to God. His vision was specifically for a new knighthood, one that would focus its military abilities for the benefit of the church. It should be removed of pride, vanity and never again be allowed to unleash violence on fellow Christians. Their dress was limited to white, brown or black depending on rank, and finery, trimmings or furs were unacceptable. This degradation of the status of the mounted knight extended to their horses, for no gold or silver bridles, spurs, stirrups or decorated saddles were permitted. It goes without saying that no women were to be welcomed into the order, and relations with them were strictly forbidden. Indeed the rooms where the brother knights slept were supposed to stay lit at night in order to avoid them being led to 'wickedness'.[32]

The Knights Hospitaller were formed six years before the Templars, although it took eighty years for military matters to be mentioned in their regulations. However, both envisaged a new form of knighthood, one that was predicated on faith rather than birth. In a world where Christianity was supreme and enjoying a resurgence throughout Europe, the changes the military orders tried to make to the secular knight were a logical progression. Unless you were not Christian, and on the receiving end that is, because the Templars and Hospitallers both proved to be truly elite fighting forces. Their training kept them fit and sharp, and their faith made them quite willing to fight lost causes and attack in hopeless situations. Additionally, the discipline of their daily lives translated to the battlefield which made the knights of the orders more effective and reliable than their secular counterparts. The fact that anyone could join their ranks meant that they formed fully self-sufficient private armies, and were eventually allowed to rule their own lands. They became private enterprise operations, foreshadowing the East India Company by half a millennium.

Their first real large scale military venture, however, was the ill-fated Second Crusade. It ended in failure, but the Templars did their very best to avoid it, including a huge effort to train the new crusaders how to fight the Turks, and this had some effect. The fact that any of the crusaders made it to the Kingdom of Jerusalem at all is probably down to Templar training and fighting abilities.[33] One story has it that while the whole army had been starving, the Templars had kept feeding their horses and fasted themselves to maintain their fighting ability. This paid off when the Turks decided against further attacks because there seemed to be too many strong horses ready to counter them. The Templars had also nearly bankrupted themselves to pay for the French contingent of the crusade to make it as far as they did. Unfortunately, the greatest achievement of the Second Crusade was only that they made it to Jerusalem. After that their efforts petered away and eventually most of the new crusaders went home, having conquered no new territory whatsoever. Despite this, the Templars had shown that a mounted knighthood based on service to Christianity was a force to be reckoned with, a kind of special forces unit capable both of fighting or training up other armies. The downside of the huge investment they made in the Second Crusade was that when it went wrong, the blame was lodged squarely with them.

That said, a glorious defeat could still do much for one's image, as the Templars had found after the Battle of Cresson. When an army of 140 knights, roughly ninety of which were Templars, spotted a Muslim force of 7,000 ahead of it, the Grand Master Gerard of Ridefort ordered an attack. The Hospitallers with him, and indeed his entire senior staff too, all counselled the opposite, but they had vowed to obey the Grand Master, and his mind was made up. Did Gerard think a victory was possible, or was he following the Templar duty that told them death was their reward? Either way, his knights followed him, and so did the Hospitallers and secular knights. They probably felt that not to was at this point cowardly, unknightly. It is a testament to the courage of the religious and non-religious knights that they attacked with total conviction. They were obviously utterly defeated; ironically, Gerard of Ridefort was one of only three knights to escape, which could be seen as a little unfair on everyone else. They made quite an impression on the Muslims they faced however, fighting on and on until overwhelmed. It is interesting to note that only up to sixty of them were actually killed fighting, the remaining seventy were captured. What this could show is that even when surrounded on all sides, the mounted knight was so protected by his armour and ability that his body's energy could fail before the opposition could take him down.

At some point every knight would become too tired to be able to continue to lift their sword arms. For trained and fit Templars this could potentially take a long time, but fighting continuously would eventually leave them unable to defend themselves and be vulnerable to being taken prisoner. Those Templars and Hospitallers who were captured were executed by the Muslims, who deemed them too dangerous to release. Knowing that this was the fate of surrendering, it suggests that those who ended up prisoners were captured exhausted rather than having willingly surrendered. This battle, however, took on a legendary veneer and helped shape the Templar myth. It was a temporary fillip however, for very soon after this the defeat at the Battle of Hattin occurred and the propaganda outcome of that was terrible for the knightly orders. The Templars had deployed a third of their full knightly force, around 200 mounted knights, into the Christian army that chased Saladin towards the twin peaks of Hattin. The fateful decision to embark after Saladin was made largely because of the insistence of Gerard of Ridefort, who apparently had learnt nothing at all from the disaster of Cresson. Once the ultimate battle had begun, it was a Templar charge that broke apart the Muslim attack and allowed the Christian army some space to manoeuvre. Saladin himself wrote of the hard-fought battle, 'The horses' hooves massed dust clouds for them; showers of arrows, shooting out sparks were sent down on them, merged together by the thunder of neighing horses, with the lightning of polished swords flashing alongside them.'[34] A group of Templars fought their way through the melee, but instead of going back to help their comrades, they instead saved themselves – a sore point for the order's reputation for years to follow. Those left behind formed up on the Horns of Hattin with what was left of the Latin army. In a last ditch attempt to win the battle they charged towards Saladin's banner, reportedly turning the sultan pale with anxiety. The Templars never made it of course, and fought on until overwhelmed. Once again Gerard of Ridefort managed to survive, this time with a few hundred Templars and Hospitallers. Saladin, however, was not going to allow members of the knightly orders to fight him in the future so he had them all executed. Except, that is, for Gerard, who once again evaded death. In a continuation of his ill-deserved run of luck, Gerard was eventually ransomed back to the order. Presumably this was because he was the one Templar that Saladin was quite happy to face again.

With the Christian resistance between Saladin and Jerusalem largely now dead, the sultan easily took the Holy city, and then the moral high ground by not massacring everyone inside.[35] The Templars lost the Temple of Solomon, which was their spiritual and literal home, and this hammer blow to the Christian cause reverberated throughout the world. With a third of their knights dead, their home and numerous other castles in enemy hands, the Templars started to look like God might not be with them any more.

After Gerard of Ridefort was released from captivity, the Templars took part in the attempt to retake Acre in 1189. When the Christians started to siege the city, Saladin's army arrived and encamped to the east of the crusader siege lines. An attack was launched, with the Templars leading the way, and they easily overran the camp and caused mass causalities among the Muslim ranks. However the Templars continued their pursuit too far, and found themselves completely surrounded by Saladin's rallied troops. Their perilous situation could be very easily blamed on Gerard's previous history of over doing it, and the outcome was familiar. The Templars were cut down in a ferocious attack, and once again Gerard of Ridefort was captured alive. Saladin was not in a mood to be generous to the grand master this time however, and Gerard's uncanny ability to survive left him in the plain around Acre where he was put to death along with the rest of his Templar knights.

Once Richard the Lionheart arrived, he used the Templars as a reliable elite unit along with the Hospitallers, and they served him well up to and including the Battle of Arsuf. The Lionheart's international reputation was made partly on their backs, and as a result they recovered some of the shine they had lost after the disaster at Hattin. Richard agreed a three-year truce with Saladin and left the Holy Land, bringing some Templars back home with him. The order already had a wide network of lands and banks across Europe and it continued to grow. They got involved with the Holy War against the Muslims in Spain, and bought the island of Cyprus from King Richard. It got to the point that there were more Templar brothers outside of the Holy Land than in it. The Templars and Hospitallers joined the Fifth Crusade against Damietta in Egypt in 1218 where they were joined by the third large knightly order, the Teutonic Knights. This order was German in origin, was based in Acre and enthusiastically took part in the new crusade. After a costly siege they took the port of Damietta and made a march south to Cairo, which was a mistake. They were corralled into a place where the floodgates were literally opened and the crusader army was caught in a torrent of water. They had no option but to surrender, without unleashing a single cavalry charge. In 1250 another crusade did pretty much the same thing with the same outcome, and more knights died for no gain.[36]

Things changed for the worse in 1265 when a new enemy attacked the Crusader States. Sultan Baybars had taken power among the Mamluks in Egypt and steadily built up influence and control over the lands to the east of the Latin Kingdoms. He had also beaten off the Mongols, so finally had enough free time to turn his attention towards the Christians. He quickly took Caesaera, Haifa and Arsuf with ease and neither the Templars nor anyone else could offer any resistance. The following year Baybars returned, but this time to the north of Jerusalem where he targeted the County of Tripoli and promptly killed everyone garrisoning the Templar castle of Safad, including eighty knights. He did this by making a deal with them to leave with their lives, but sent in a lookalike instead. The Templars duly left their castle, unaware that they had not actually made a deal with Baybars at all. Once out in the open, they were rounded up and beheaded one at a time. Baybars was not in the Holy Land to make deals with the Templars. Safad was one of the best Templar castles and the whole region was shocked by its loss. Such was the darkness of the mood that the Templar Ricaut Bonomel wrote that from what he could see, God was now supporting the infidels.

As Baybars continued to take crusader towns and fortifications, so the eastern power base of the Holy Orders diminished. When he took Antioch, the Templars had to withdraw from many castles in the Principality, and the future started to look very bleak indeed. The only thing that kept a crusader toehold was the arrival of the future Edward I of England, whose ten year peace deal was the only thing that kept Baybars from taking Acre. However, in 1291 Baybars appeared outside Acre and the Mamluk victory was inevitable. The Templars and Hospitallers inside the city mounted cavalry charges at the Muslims who had breached the walls but they were far too few and the result was a forgone conclusion. When the leader of the Templars was wounded he retreated on his horse and was followed by his retinue and banner. The other defenders saw the banner falling back and panic swept across the last bastion of Christianity. As the climax of the Eastern crusade came to a bloody end, Baybars showed that he did not share the late Saladin's capacity for mercy, and all inside were killed. The Templars and Hospitallers were ejected from the Holy Land by this defeat and as a result became more bankers and diplomats than warriors.

The Hospitallers indeed survive to today, but the Templars proved to be too good at the banking part of their operation, and that was their downfall. No longer under the ideological protection of being the guardians of the Holy Land, they were fair game for a king of France who needed hard cash and didn't care who he had to take it from. Once he'd emptied the pockets of everyone else in his Kingdom that he could find, including the long-suffering Jews, he did the same to the Templars. It is the completely fabricated but scandalous allegations dreamt up by the king that mean we remember the Templars at all in modern times.[37] Without this extra layer of drama they would have faded into the relative obscurity of the other Holy orders. Another knightly order, the Teutonic Order, moved away from the Holy Land and went north into the cold and wet Baltic. There they carved out a kingdom of their own and ruled over a fully fledged military and religious state. Mounted Knights fought against various pagan tribes in insect-infested swamps during the summer, and across frozen lakes in winter. Only in winter on hard ground could they ever deploy their powerful charge, but the pagans soon learnt to simply stay out of their way. Eventually the Teutonic Knights came up against more organised opposition in the form of the Lithuanians and Russians, who were just as well armed, and by the fifteenth century they had begun to lose ground. Dense woodland and soft boggy marshes it is clear, are not the natural home of the mounted knight. Much as modern armies have found that tanks are not war winning weapons against guerrilla insurgencies, the Teutonic Knights likewise were unable to use cavalry to reach an ultimate victory.[38]

Crusading Legacy

The crusades provided an international platform for the mounted knight to display his military prowess and devotion to the Christian cause. By putting the two problems of unruly knights at home and a pagan enemy abroad together, Pope Urban II pulled off a strategic master-stroke. The creation of a cloud of expectation and possible salvation swirled over mounted knights across Europe; even if they never went on crusade, the idea was always there above them. This accelerated Christianisation of knighthood elevated them from purely secular local rulers and servant warriors, and injected into their ethos many of the elements of chivalry that they had lacked in the tenth century. The First Crusade did not make European knights religious, what it did was burn that piety into the fabric of the knight, and therefore also into the code by which he lived. The righteousness that the success of the crusade created pervades through later chivalric literature, and means that in whatever state the mounted knight went into that crusade, he came out of it meeting our definition of a chivalric mounted knight. His chivalry was still a predominately martial one, but with such an injection of religious zeal, the First Crusade was the first step in the gentling of the knight.

The church may have thus influenced knightly behaviour, but less obvious though was the influence going in the other direction. St Augustine's Just War concept had been accepted across Europe and it allowed violence to be deployed in the cause of justice because the world was imperfect. This idea had served to normalise violence within church circles, and it merged with the existential threats that faced Christendom in the ninth and tenth centuries. Vikings raiding from the north, Muslims from the south, and Magyars from the east all squeezed the church and it really must have felt like the walls were closing in. This fear combined with the concept of Just War, and perhaps the church became a bit less interested in peace and forgiveness than we might think. The knights and men-at-arms who fought off the external threats had been all that stood in the way of the foreign invaders, reinforcing their elevated status. This emphasis on warfare served to militarise the church, and this came to its fruition when the First Crusade was called. The sign of the cross became a symbol of war and crusading across Europe and the Mediterranean, and in the space of a few years the fighting man had found a respectable place in society.

This is in contrast to the fact that prior to Urban II's call to arms, the knights of the ninth and tenth centuries were effectively living under the shadow that they were certainly going to hell. Their religion spoke of peace but their way of life was that of killing, and the First Crusade squared that round hole. Fighting men could suddenly avoid an eternity of suffering, all they had to do was go east and fight the enemies of the church. The Pope had found a way to welcome warriors into the church, and those very pious warriors jumped at the chance of salvation. Not only that, but their deeds on the burning plains of the Holy Land had set in stone their place in history and myth in equal measure. They had defeated the Fatimid armies through classic knightly charges as well as doing the impossible and capturing Jerusalem. Probably more impressively, they had even managed to rein in their impetuosity to counter the armies of horse archers that did everything possible to unsettle them. Their armour had allowed them to become walking pincushions of arrows, and their horses had been swift enough to sometimes catch the Turks on their famously agile and fast steeds. However, they had also proved to be occasionally rash and frequently failed to present a united front to their enemies.

In general then, the mounted knight had adapted slowly but effectively to warfare against the Muslims; the problem was that Christians were not the only ones capable of learning from their enemy. A two-way exchange of ideas and technology flowed between both sides, and that included on the subject of chivalry. The Arabic equivalent, *furusiyya*, was a lifestyle that involved combat training for Mamluk warriors, including horsemanship. Their horses were reportedly so well trained that they could pick up weapons dropped by their masters. This might seem far fetched, but we are training a horse to do this, and he will indeed pick up objects on command. The gifting of ceremonial trousers to Mamluk warriors was akin to a knighting ceremony with its belt, spurs and chivalry, and heavily armoured Mamluk mounted knights were the equal of their Christian counterparts in the charge with the lance.[39]

Author's Note

The first question regarding knights on crusade that pops into people's minds is to wonder how they coped in all that armour. The classic image of a mounted knight probably involves him riding into battle encased in full plate armour, and indeed this is a challenging undertaking in hot weather. However, for the entire period of the crusades, plate armour was not used to fully cover any knight at all. The knights of the First Crusade wore mail armour only, apart from helmets made from solid pieces of metal. Mail armour, by its very nature, is full of holes and heat is capable of going through it and slowly escaping the body of the knight. Thick padding was not generally worn underneath this armour, the under garments were wool or linen and both of those are capable of wicking away sweat. Monumental effigies from the time show armour that followed the shape of the muscles of knights, and this slender look is backed up by a multitude of manuscripts images right through the crusading era. This all meant that the crusaders were not riding around inside ovens as is sometimes imagined. They will have undoubtedly felt the extreme heat and had to learn more acutely about the importance of taking on water, but these factors existed in the West already, especially in southern France, Spain and Italy. On even the hottest days in England horses can cope with relatively hard exercise as long as they have access to water. We have a temperature ceiling above which we will not ride, but in the Holy Land they could keep going if routes could be planned that went from water source to water source. For the knights on horseback, while they were sat upon those horses they would usually be able to limit how much they would sweat. A Muslim custom picked up by the crusaders and exported east was the surcoat. This sleeveless fabric over-tunic sat on top of mail armour and kept the sun off it, which stops the metal absorbing heat. It also acts to catch and disrupt the flight of arrows, as well as keeping water from the body of a knight's mail armour for a while when it is raining. Wearing a surcoat made from two layers of linen has certainly saved my own mail from rusting on more than one occasion. The same principle applies to horses in the form of the caparison, and we use these at home when riding in our fields in the evenings because they stop horseflies and other insects from getting to the horses. The old methods are sometimes the best.

Chapter Four

The Mounted Knight

Medieval knights were individuals whose lives centred around one aim, one expectation, and one gauge of worth, and that was prowess in combat. They knew it too, and a famous knight, the flower of French chivalry that was Geoffrey de Charny, extolled its virtues.[1] So widespread was the knowledge that the lives of Christian knights revolved around their ability to fight, that even their enemies wrote about it. Usama ibn Munqidh was roughly the Muslim equivalent of a knight, and he left a colourful record of combat with the Franks, writing of them that, 'no quality is more highly esteemed in a man than military prowess… They are the ones who give counsel, pass judgement and command armies.'[2] Usama's impression of the Frankish knights he came across in the twelfth century was accurate. By this time, mounted knights had cemented a place of power in the world, having so famously conquered Jerusalem. Knights had already proved themselves able to simultaneously take on the roles of members of parliament, army captains, landowners and judges, as well something like the modern international footballer and celebrity. In this chapter we shall investigate the person of the knight, their education and psychology. We shall try to understand something of their armour and weapons, in order to see how these items of metal lifted up the mounted knight and allowed him to cut his way into the history books. We will also look at their training, and some of their exploits, but first we will start with how young prospective knights were prepared for their martial future.

Preparing a Knight

The moulding of a future knight began more or less from birth. Warrior elites had historically enjoyed a position in most societies that gave them access to the best food and healthcare available,[3] but increasingly in the early medieval period this also extended to education. As a noble-born boy grew up, he had access to an ever-growing list of works designed to teach him of the world, give him a moral compass, and give him examples of behaviour to follow. The quality of this education started to increase substantially from Charlemagne's time, during which the great man himself could read but not actually write.[4] By the fifteenth century there was a huge list of reading material available to educate the next generation, and knights were even writing some of it themselves.

The author who was probably at the top of the education bestseller list was the Roman writer Vegetius,[5] who wrote the widely available *Concerning Military Matters*. A long list of other writers such as Honoré Bovet,[6] Geoffrey de Charny and Christine de Pizan also had works that spread across Europe, which together with others, formed what could very loosely be described as a curriculum. One indication of how widespread these books became, is that Bovet's work still survives in Scottish.[7] The aspiring medieval knight therefore had access to Roman and Greek masterpieces, as well as the progress built on top of that classical knowledge base. Knightly topics included the laws of war, the ethics of taking prisoners, paying troops, and battle formations, although the splitting of loot was often a detailed subject. In addition to academic study, future knights sometimes received on the job training, because they could be taken on campaign with a knight to serve as a page from very young ages. The act of taking enemy children under fourteen prisoner was banned by Henry V in 1417, but this excluded those of the nobility, which suggests enough French boys were ending up in harm's way to warrant the rule in the first place.[8]

The application of knightly knowledge could be applied very young then, and one Hugh Latimer could buckle on his father's harness of armour before he was even six years old in 1497.[9] The effect of their education was to create young men who could be genuinely well read, polite, pious and capable of applying reasoning to problems.[10] When combined with the chivalric fictional literature we shall cover later, their upbringing produced men who understood their place in the world, and firmly believed in themselves. Even knights who had started life as the son of a tradesman and worked their way up, both knew the stories, and knew how they were expected to behave. These stories functioned like Hollywood blockbusters, portraying knights as supercharged versions of reality and proclaiming loudly to the world what was expected of them. The effectiveness of this partly accidental propaganda was so extraordinary that it is still the most common source of knowledge on the theme of knighthood today. One can only imagine the power imparted onto boys when they received their first practice swords, or began their physical training. We still see it each time we first place a training sword into someone's hands today. This preparation of the body for a lifetime of combat started young because it had to, else a knight would be no stronger than a peasant, whose physical strength should not be overestimated.[11]

It wasn't just strength that separated knights from the common man however, the range of martial arts required to be an effective knightly warrior ranged from wrestling with no weapons, to duelling with swords, as well as the small matter of doing it all from horseback. One of the best ways that knights gained a familiarity with these animals, as well as learning to avoid falling off them, was through hunting, which was dangerous enough to impart critical lessons on horsemanship. This was the favourite pastime of many medieval noblemen, for example the esteemed Count of Foix[12] who wrote four works on hunting in the fourteenth century: *On the Nature and Care of Dogs*, *On Instructions of Hunting with Dogs*, *On Hunting with Traps, Snares, and Crossbow* and *On Gentle and Wild Beasts*. That the count wrote two volumes just on hounds is unsurprising, considering he is thought to have owned a staggering 800 dogs himself.[13] His cousin was the English Duke of York, who actually translated these works into English before he was unluckily killed at Agincourt, probably stunting a promising literary career.

Hunting with hounds at this time was very common, and involved both types of hunting dog, that is scent and sight hounds, to track down prey. These hunts could take all day and were sometimes meticulously planned with groups of fresh dogs placed along the expected route of the chase. The skills the future mounted knights learnt here included understanding different terrain, being out all day in all weathers, as well as being on horseback for hours.[14] Deer were a popular noble quarry and hunting them was neither crude nor simple, indeed there were rules for not taking a stag with less than a certain number of tines on their antlers because they were too young. This apparent conservationism came from an intimate understanding of nature that one might be surprised to see in professional fighting men, and those instincts would have been generated while young. Although these principles came from the need to maintain animals to hunt, it nevertheless meant that the nobility of England wanted to keep large tracks of land as unpopulated and despoiled as possible. Spending time away from castles and manors also accustomed knights to sometimes sleeping roughly outdoors, being active without food, and often putting much effort into something while coming home empty handed. All these experiences were essential parts of a knight's training, which included the final butchering of successful kills, hopefully resulting in them being quite at ease with blood and gore.

We should remember that the medieval world was very different to our own, and children would have grown up witnessing a variety of bloodsports. As part of his job, a knight absolutely needed to be able to kill a human, and not baulk at the physical sight of it because this put himself and his companions in danger. A demonstration of this comes from the French knight Jean II Le Meingre, known as Boucicaut, who fought in his first battle when he was only sixteen. Whereas his first enemy hesitated to kill him due to his young age, Boucicaut never considered thanking him for his mercy, instead he showed nothing but ruthlessness and simply stabbed him with a knife.[15] Whatever the spiritual reaction to causing a human death may have been, thanks to the hunt, a new knight on campaign was unlikely to faint at the sight of blood. Interestingly, hunting was the only martial arena in which women were able to play a full part. Indeed, Henry VIII's sister, Margaret, is recorded as having killed a young buck with a bow,[16] and women can frequently be seen riding in hunting parties in Medieval art.

The Tournament

The final step in the education of a knight was the tournament – the ultimate finishing school; the prevalence of, and importance attached to, mounted tournaments and jousting suggests that they were a primary focus of the knightly class throughout the whole medieval period.[17] The tournament, as opposed to the joust, was a distinctly more warlike endeavour. Originating in the age of mail armour, the tournament was originally a training ground for real war, and involved two equal sides who engaged in a battle with each other with sharp weapons. Sometimes each side consisted of hundreds, or even thousands, of knights, and these clashes had little to distinguish them from actual battles. The two sides would line up and charge at each other with lances, and accidents most certainly did happen. However, fatalities were unusual enough that the deceased were often mentioned by name in chronicles, with common causes of death including lances piercing necks and falls from horses. Gilbert Marshal, the son of England's so called greatest knight William Marshal, was killed in a thirteenth-century tournament when he fell from his horse, but he had originally been educated more for the church pew than the war saddle.[18] When the two sides had charged each other once and exchanged lance strikes, they turned around and charged a second time. This manoeuvre was known as the turn, or *tour*, the act which gave its name to the tournament. The emphasis on this part of the event may be because it separated the men from the boys in terms of horsemanship. After the first charge, those horses who were out of control, or simply too excited to turn quickly, would scatter to the wind, causing great embarrassment to their riders.

Generally, after the turn, the battle would fragment with groups breaking off and pursuing combats with each other with whatever weapons they had. The aim was to batter a knight enough that he surrendered, after which the victor would ransom his freedom back, for a price which often included the victim's armour and horse. For this reason horses were off limits to attack, although in one tournament in France in 1503, the Spanish team killed the horses of their French opponents in order to claim victory.[19] The chronicler Pierrede Bourdeille who recorded it was not impressed, and it is likely that no one else was either because the spectators wanted to see a longer contest, and that required the horses being alive. Essentially, the groups that fragmented were playing a team game to try to overpower other knights and extort wealth from them. Which may sound slightly odd, but that is also what happened in most encounters in times of war. In tournaments, participants would beat each other with swords, and although these were often sharp, mail armour and greathelms meant that this didn't particularly matter. A method favoured by William Marshal was to cut or take the reins of a knight, and ride off with his horse at speed.[20] This act would render the knight unable to control his own horse, or stop William dragging him over to a group of his friends, which would have been enough to obtain their surrender. We have experimented with this technique, and have concluded that it requires a team of two to actually steal the reins from a single knight, because the victim is usually able to spot it coming and defend themselves.[21] This reinforces the team aspect of the tournament, which really was about executing cavalry actions as a unit, reading terrain and outwitting opponents. Another outcome was the training of warhorses, who needed to be worked with large numbers of other horses near them to prepare them for the battlefield.

For the knights themselves however, the tournament was something they looked forward to. As with modern soldiers, the medieval knight would have wanted the opportunity to put his training into practice and measure himself against his peers. Being a professional warrior was a time-consuming skill to maintain, and especially the younger knights would have been chomping at the bit to get into the action. Great reputations could also be built upon tournament success, indeed William Marshal's fame would not have been possible without them, and knights would have been eager to display their prowess to the crowds that spectated. Of course greed cannot be discounted as a motivation for attending tournaments, for the financial reward for a successful knight could be life changing. The flip side of this was that being defeated could cost a knight his horse and armour, and lead to his ruin, but it seems to have been a risk that the supremely self-confident knights were willing to run.

On the morning of the tournament itself, however, this self-confidence might have been tempered by a steaming hangover. The festivities that preceded the event itself could be elaborate, expensive and exuberant.[22] Feasting and dancing featured heavily and of course many knights would have had the opportunity to overindulge with wine. As they lined their horses up the next morning for the charge, it has to be possible that some of those knights were feeling quite ill. The other effect of this is that a slight delay in reaction time caused by being hungover, or indeed still drunk, could mean failing to block an attack, or stay on a horse that spooked. Alcohol and horses do not mix at the best of times, let alone in a fight. Staying sober was one way to mitigate the risks of a tournament, but another was to stay away from sharp weaponry. During the thirteenth century, there are records of tournaments sensibly taking place with leather armour and blunted weapons. For example, the future Edward I's first tournament at Blyth, held near his seventeenth birthday, was explicitly conducted without lances or sharp weaponry.[23] Despite this a number of participants were killed or suffered life changing injuries, reinforcing the fact that there were more ways to be killed in combat than by being hit by a sharp weapon.

During tournaments young knights had sometimes jousted against each other before the main event, and as the fourteenth century wore on these preliminary activities increased in importance. Technically, a joust is a one-on-one combat and does not have to be on horseback, but into the fifteenth century mounted tournaments and jousts were still incredibly popular. De Gamez wrote of Pero Nino's jousting in France, which was without a barrier and used sharp war lances, 'it often happens that one horse runs against another, and one horse falls or that they both fall'.[24] This tournament consisted of around thirty men who all jousted together in a free-for-all at the same time, and there were no teams. This was unsurprisingly the type of jousting that was considered the most dangerous, and not all knights dared take part.[25] One reason for caution was that in such swirling chaos, three knights could accidentally all charge each other at the same time without seeing one of the others, and the results could be fatal. I have taken part in jousts with similar rules, and indeed in an eight horse free-for-all, have had two knights attack me at once.[26] The medieval jouster could do little more than trust his horse, his armour, and his God, but this is exactly what his upbringing was supposed to prepare him to do. De Gamez added that those who took part, 'should be practised therein, and should be strong and most skilful horsemen'.[27] The horse was central to this type of competition, and those without the required skills would be shown up, and of course that was part of the point.

The one versus one joust however became more prominent as the fifteenth century progressed, and once the tilt-rail was introduced around 1420,[28] it also became much safer. In 1434, the Spaniard Suero de Quinones and ten companions pledged to break 300 lances against anyone who would face them.[29] Their epic month-long joust is useful for us because every jousting course that was run had its results written down. The first conclusion drawn from these is the newfound safety of jousting; indeed, in 747 courses there was only one death. This was despite the fact that proceedings were being undertaken in only war armour, and with sharp war lances. Hand injuries, however, were common, and there were a few armour failures, but largely the participants survived mostly intact; 79 per cent of the courses were total misses, which gives an indication of how difficult real jousting is. As jousting took over from the tournament, and became safer and more of a social or court event, it started to lose its function as a training ground for warriors.[30] Despite the loss of the team element of the tournament, however, the joust continued to provide training in the wearing and use of armour, taking injuries and horsemanship, although it could never match the tournament as a breeding ground for prowess.

Ceremony & Symbolism

Even if a burgeoning nobleman was accomplished in all these required areas, he was nevertheless not obliged to become a knight at a certain age, or in fact at all. However, unless he was knighted on the battlefield, a new knight would have to undergo a knighting ceremony. As early as 1098, Guy of Ponthieu wrote to the Bishop of Arras that he, 'must decorate and honour Louis, son of the king with military arms and promote and ordain him to *militia*'.[31] *Militia* here has been translated as service-in-arms, and by using the word 'ordain', it suggests that Guy is indicating a ceremony is required to enter the service of the king. Within thirty years this ceremony had become a complex one, for according to an admittedly later writer in 1128, when Geoffrey of Anjou was knighted by Henry I, there were many steps, the first of which was that he had to undergo a bath. Then, wearing a cloth of gold tunic, he was taken to the king who gave him a pair of golden spurs and girded him with a sword belt.[32] He also gave him a horse and arms, an echo of the older and simpler ceremony Harold Godwinson had undergone in Normandy.

By the thirteenth century the ceremonies had become varied and elaborate, as was famously explained fictitiously to Saladin by his captive, Hugh of Tiberias.[33] Hugh explained the use of a bath to wash away sins, the wearing of a red cloak representing the blood to be shed for the church, brown stockings to represent the earth where all knights ended up, a white belt for chastity and also golden spurs. The spurs represented the knight's willingness to obey God's commands as the horse obeys the spur. A sword belt was then tied onto the knight, for these were not yet buckled, containing a sword. The two edges of this sword represented justice and loyalty, the latter of which was one of the foremost ideals of chivalry. The sword is also rather obviously symbolic of knightly prowess in battle, but also of their duty to defend the defenceless. The defenceless, it must be noted, only included those above a certain social status, and obviously the right religion. Lastly, Hugh thought it wise to leave out applying the final step to Saladin, which was a slap across the face. This was known as the *colée* or accolade.[34] This slap is recorded in the eleventh century, and William Marshall recalls receiving it himself,[35] and by then it had already been downgraded from the face to the shoulder. While possibly unrelated, it is worth noting the Roman practice of slapping a slave when freeing them, which was called the *alapa*.

The elaborate knighting ceremony as described to Saladin by Hugh is found in a poem called the *Ordene de Chevalerie*,[36] and is one of a variety of ceremonies found in documentary sources, as well as the Romances. There are differences between them and they change over time, but they all overflow with symbolism. The thirteenth-century polymath Ramon Llull wrote a work, *The Book of the Order of Chivalry*, which lists no less than thirty-two descriptions of the meanings of the various pieces of a knight's equipment, a task which takes Ramon nearly 2,000 words to complete. To list a few of them: the lance represented truth because it is straight; the helmet was the fear of shame; armour symbolised the knight's castle; and spurs both diligence and swiftness. To Llull, the knight's horse symbolised the nobility of courage, and he noted that if the knight failed to uphold chivalry, 'his horse keeps the law of chivalry better than he does'.[37] Llull's book was printed by William Caxton, and in its Epilogue, Caxton added that he was giving the book to, 'King Richard III, King of England',[38] so that all men in his realm could read it.

Despite these symbolisms undoubtedly being familiar to Richard III, he and many others did not always live by them. Richard III had been made a Knight of the Garter when he was just nine years old,[39] but presumably had undergone an elaborate knighting ceremony before that. I have had the privilege to witness a recreated fifteenth-century knighting ceremony in France of a young man coming of age in the jousting community, in an atmospheric little chapel within a castle in Anjou. The new knight had held a vigil overnight in a cold room lit by candles, and despite not personally understanding the French words being solemnly uttered, the ceremony itself meant something to everyone in the chapel. The Medieval knights going through it themselves would have felt the same, a brotherhood of men who had been through the same traumas and hardships. They would have shared the same concerns and worries in life, and had to rely on each other at times of death. Ceremonies like this served to knit groups of mounted knights into better fighting units, building a spirit that led to them being more committed to engaging in fighting as well as building an identity around them.

An example of the level of expectation that this all generated occurred during the Battle of Crécy in 1346, when Edward, the Black Prince, was being hard pressed by the French. The beleaguered prince sent word to his father, King Edward III, for much needed reinforcements. The king refused to send help, and told him that he should, 'suffer hym this day to wynne his spurres',[40] which is usually modernised to, 'let the boy win his spurs'. This famous quotation is interesting because the king did not tell his son to win his sword. Another king knighted a group of men on a battlefield in Spain, and promptly put them in the front rank of an attack so that their, 'spurs will become them'.[41] These tiny pieces of metal tied to the heels of a knight had a meaning greater than their size. Such was their importance that some manuscripts show that while the belt is being girded, the spurs are being attached, and these could be extremely ornate. The Royal Armouries in England has a twelfth-century prick spur that is decorated with many small golden dots, which would have been added only at a fair expense. The spurs were usually intended to be used just before the moment of impact in a cavalry engagement,[42] and so they are associated with the very concept of a mounted knight. In this sense they are the trigger that launches a weapon made out of horse, man and metal. They were also used to enable the knight to communicate to his horse through his legs without having to overly move them, and their correct use is an art form. They are also the only item worn by a knight that linked him to his horse when he was not on it, and when a knight disgraced himself enough for his knighthood to be removed from him, it was his spurs that were symbolically hacked off.[43]

Superheroes

To the people working the land, the time and effort that went into producing knights must have made them seem to be a superhuman ruling class. Their own farming lives were incredibly tough in their own right, but most of them must have been hugely intimidated any time they found themselves up close and personal to a knight. In an age of superstition, the very metal worn by a knight was part of this representation of power. The metal items of knighthood could be at the same time brutal instruments of violence and beautiful works of art; indeed, armour was a living 'expressive sculpture'.[44] This blend of psychological and physical power stayed with the sword in particular throughout history, and is still with us today.

As the mounted knight rose to prominence before the twelfth century, their enemies were not always other knights wearing metal armour. An unarmoured opponent cut by a sword would suffer a grievous wound, and when wielded from horseback, the extra reach, height and momentum enhanced the effect further. It was this terrifying cutting power that led to the need for metal armour in the first place. Before metal armour became commonplace, the sword was the most devastating close-quarters weapon, as well as a symbol of wealth and status. Like all military technologies, swords were expensive to begin with, but over time became more widespread and affordable. The single handed double edged sword, usually with a straight crossguard, remained much the same for the first few hundred years of the mounted knight's lifespan. As metalworking improved, the blades became longer and more able to stab as well as cut, allowing knight's to stab their way into gaps in the armour of their enemies.

They are also more tactically flexible than television would have us believe; for example, in the Uccello painting of the Battle of San Romano which occurred in 1432, a couched sword, rather than a lance, can be seen being used to attack a fully armoured rider. This seemingly unconventional use of a weapon was not isolated, and from the fifteenth century onwards we can find fighting manuals being written, which illustrate through pictures a bewildering array of different techniques.[45] The experts who wrote them travelled around Europe teaching whoever could afford to pay them, meaning that these works could in reality be closer to a *curriculum vitae* than instruction manual. Real conflicts could become rougher and less nuanced than these manuals sometimes suggest, which is often because the manuals we have specifically relate to judicial duels.

In the rough and tumble of desperate combat, swords could snap or fail, but the better ones could see their owners through. One vivid example is after a heavy battle where Pero Nino's sword 'was like a saw, toothed in great notches, the hilt twisted'.[46] In what comes across nowadays as juvenile showing off, Nino then bizarrely sent the battered sword to his lover in France. Continuing the obsession to the present day, the power of the sword in the human imagination remains all consuming, after all who has not heard of Excalibur? The allure of King Arthur's sword is so powerful that, depending on the version of the story, it decided who was the rightful king, or lived in a sacred lake.[47] On top of this, swords also happen to be the same shape as the Christian cross, a happy coincidence for both crusading knights and the church itself. Most importantly though, these weapons represented legitimate power over those who did not have them, putting the knights literally a cut above those below them on the social ladder.

The primary early medieval defence against swords was mail armour, as can be seen on the Bayeux Tapestry, and as early as approximately 1100 'triple mail'[48] is described as being used in Europe. Additionally, in around 1138 in the Holy Land, an Islamic knight wrote specifically how he put one coat of mail over a second.[49] Two layers of mail armour, let alone three, would probably have kept out almost anything short of a catapult stone. The result of this was that by the thirteenth century, where tournaments were taking place on a large scale with sharp war lances, deaths were not too common. Indeed 'deaths were regretted and exceptional'.[50] An analogy to Formula 1 racing in the 1950s is appropriate, where the deaths of around fifteen drivers in that decade did not halt the racing, providing us with an understandable recent parallel.

One difference between a joust of peace and actual war was the wood used to make the lances. Dried pine wood makes lances that will break on a strong impact, and these are ideal for jousts of peace, where the aim is to break the lance rather than to break the opponent. For war, however, the wood from ash trees is stronger and much less likely to break on impact, which means an ash lance has a greater armour-penetrating ability than pine, and is why ash was one of the woods used for war lances. Luis Zapata de Chaves tells us that for jousting the, 'lances must be made of pine, because using lances made of ash or beech… among friends would be a cruel game indeed; and lances made of those woods are for enemies'.[51] When the lance did not break during an impact, something else had to give. Either the target would be pushed backwards in their saddle, or more commonly, the hand of the attacker could dislocate before that happened. Thus the hand to hold the lance became the weak part in the equation, but ever ingenious medieval minds had a solution. An *arrêt de lance*, which in English is a 'lance stop', was a solid bar of metal sticking out from the right hand side of the breastplate, in front of the armpit. It stuck out far enough that a lance could be placed on top of it when couched. This new feature was part of a new weapons' system where the lance was also augmented. A band of leather was attached around the lance just behind where the knight would grip it when couching. This leather band was thick enough that it pressed backwards into the *arrêt*, locking the lance and breastplate together. When couching with an *arrêt*, the mounted knight could actually release his hand and the lance would still stay locked in place. The leather wrapped around the lance evolved into a metal collar, and these attachments were called *grappers*. The genius of this invention was that when the lance hit a target, the energy no longer went through the comparatively weak hand or arm of the knight, but into the hard metal of the breastplate. A strike which previously would have broken the hand of the knight holding the lance, could now be withstood by the *arrêt* system, allowing the extra force to be transferred into the target instead. Even modern breastplates made of hardened-steel have been punctured by this weapons' system in real use, although even then the air pocket between the steel plate and the jouster's chest has prevented the steel lance-heads from reaching flesh. The skill of the mounted knight in war when presented with effective armour, was to aim the lance at extraordinarily small target areas on their opponents. In the thirteenth century, the best way to kill another knight was to aim below his helm and strike his neck. This threat was recognised, and knights are seen and described as wearing some extra protection there, often in the form of whalebone collars or multiple layers of mail.

The next best way to incapacitate the enemy was to aim for the right armpit, or at least the upper arm, partly because the upper body and left arm were almost always protected by a shield. A strong lance hit could potentially slide off a shield and across into the right armpit, or up and under the helm. However there was a worse way to be hurt by a lance, and very occasionally knights were killed by splinters coming in through the vision slits of their helms. This was a horrific thing to happen, but it was not overly common, and would have been considered an occupational hazard. This runs counter to the modern idea that a jouster raises his eyes just before the moment of impact, as to avoid the risk of eye injuries. This a view stated in sources as varied as the film *A Knight's Tale*, and the esteemed historian Maurice Keen (although he got the idea from someone else).[52] Relating specifically to frogmouth helms, that is a large heavy helm with no liftable visor, this is an example of an honest misconception borne from the lack of practical experience in riding in armour. The frogmouth, and some other types of helmets, are angled out beneath the vision slits like the prow of a ship, which means a lance strike that grips on the eye slit is taken up and away from the vulnerable area of the eyes. This incredibly simple design feature relies on the knowledge that *all* lance strikes come from below the eyeline, which means that all lances are approaching the vision slit from underneath. The result is that a jouster wearing a helmet can keep his eyes on the target, and his opponent's lance will almost certainly deflect up and over his own eyes. Anyone who thinks turning eyes away at the moment of impact is a good idea, should try to take a golf swing without looking at the ball. This all being said, accidents can happen and vision slits can end up being entered. This hazard exists today, and in modern jousting it is a risk that every jouster has to be comfortable with before they take up the discipline.

Even historically though, getting hit squarely by a lance might not have been fatal. Usamah Ibn Munqidh described in his memoirs how he skewed a Frankish knight with his lance, the impact of which was so hard that the Frank's shield and helm fell off but, 'having had linked mail under his tunic, my lance did not wound him'.[53] It may be surprising that even from this attack, which was hard enough to nearly unhorse the Christian, his mail armour managed to keep the lance out. The more reliable feature of a mail shirt, however, was its ability to completely nullify edged weapons. The metal rings would stop almost any cut, and the importance of that cannot be overstated. In 1214 at the Battle of Bouvines, William of Breton stated that, 'iron cannot reach them unless their bodies are first dispossessed of the armour'.[54] Several layers of iron were employed by some of Bouvines combatants, meaning they used either multiple layers of mail, or supplemented mail with early coats of metal or leather plates, but either way the armour was seen as extremely effective. William continued that when one soldier tried to attack with a 'knife in at the place where the body armour is joined to the leggings,...

the armour sowed into the leggings will not separate and open up to the knife'.[55] Here we find that mail leg armour was attached to the mail body armour to leave no gap whatsoever for a knife to exploit, as well as a very visual description of the brutality of hand-to-hand combat.

The weights of these mail defensive items varied hugely, but a thirteenth-century knight's mailed shirt and leg armour could weigh anything between 10kg and 20kg. Wearing two layers of mail or extra leather pieces would further increase the weight, but it is not necessarily hugely problematic for the wearer if he is sitting on a horse. Nevertheless, training is required to build up the muscles of the right arm so it can fight as dexterously with the hindrance of the armour as without. A weak knight in full mail armour is a very different opponent to a fully trained and primed warrior, and this helped define the knight as a social class distinct from the peasantry below them. To become used to wearing the armour, a knight had to wear it often and regularly, and as a result would stand above anyone not as physically conditioned. While their weapons allowed knights to deal out punishment on the battlefield, it was their armour that truly elevated them above everyone else. Armour was expensive, took a long time to make, and kept the wearer alive, all of which served to make it a key part of the identity of the fighting knight. Armour was also an expression of the man within it, with different styles indicating where the knight may be from and what sort of status he had. Armour as an art form is an unappreciated area, but first and foremost it was functional. Knights put up with the discomfort and restriction of it because it worked, it kept them going when they were getting hit, and added another shining layer to their myth.

One surprisingly sophisticated example of this is the thirteenth-century greathelm, which is a helmet that can resemble a rather crude and angular upturned metal bucket. One example is the Dargen greathelm, dated between 1250 and 1300 and weighing just 2.3kg, it is made from medium carbon steel. I use a reproduction of this helm, and even with eye slits only 4mm to 6mm wide, I can see everything that happens further than two metres away from me. The breath holes punched into the bottom of it on the right side mean that I can see down through them to my reins, and see a bit of what my horse is doing. Breath holes were often not cut into the left side of helms because this was the side where they were more likely be hit by a lance, and each hole is a weakness that a pointed lance-head could exploit. Under my mail head protection, which sits beneath the greathelm, I wear a metal skull cap called a *cerveliere*. A thirteenth-century knight could therefore have three layers of metal over his head, the result of which meant he could be hit in the face by a solid lance and his brain might not suffer a fatal injury. I have taken a few strong hits, and although my ears rang loudly, I have not been unduly troubled by them. However, the simple cerveliere is a large piece of this protective system and should not be neglected because of its simplicity. My partner does not have a cerveliere under her greathelm, and when I hit her in the head in a similar way, she has on occasion seen stars and been somewhat discomforted by the blows.

It is the willingness, and even eagerness, to receive these blows that differentiates the knightly attitude from those without it. Regardless of the ability to protect the brain and face, the greathelm does have one major weakness, and that is whiplash. The greathelm does not prevent the head being bent back violently on impact, and the neck and spine can be severely damaged by lances hitting the head straight on. For this risk to be mitigated, helms had to be fully buckled down, something which required solid body armour to buckle to. During the thirteenth century, plate metal started to protect the body of the knight as well as the head, in the form of coats of plates. This armour consists of many plates attached in some way together, to give a knight something which looks very much like a modern bullet proof vest.[56] Breastplates made of metal and of a construction that makes them different to a coat of plates do not appear until well after the Battle of Crécy in 1346, and those who fought there did so with coats of plates of various types and sizes.

The Churburg breastplate, designated CHS13 and dated to 1380, consists of a number of vertical plates riveted together to form a single entity to protect the front and sides of the upper body. It is decorated with beautiful borders containing letters in a distinctly medieval font. The edges at the neck and armpits are slightly raised, or rolled outwards, which acts as a breakpoint for weapons sliding along the plate and stops them getting into the vulnerable arms joints. There is a large V-shaped metal bar attached to the front under the neck which also acts to catch weapons and push them away from the neck area, especially useful against arrows or lances. This piece of technology is sophisticated and well thought out, as well as being undeniably a genuine work of art. The knight who strapped it on will have been aware that he was turning his body into a living sculpture, allowing the work of the armourer(s) to speak to onlookers for him.

The evocative image presented to the world would have been deliberate; pieces of high-end armour were trying to make a point, and were designed to put across certain ideas. Status and wealth being the most obvious of these, but also the ever important concepts of prowess and piety. The scripts adorning medieval armour, saddles and other war equipment often invoked the Lord, and were sometimes written prayers asking for protection. One only needs to look at the artwork on Second World War aircraft and tanks to see that some of this spirit lives on into the modern age. The final feature of this breastplate was the *arrêt de lance* affixed to the right hand side in front of the armpit. As we have already discussed, this metal bar (in this case 8cm long) was the innovation that up-gunned the mounted knight and maintained his position as the hardest hitting non-gunpowder weapon on the battlefield.

These full plate harnesses arguably also pushed the image of the knight to an even more otherworldly level. In a world that was quieter than today, the knight whose armour clanked and scraped with every movement would have seemed distinctly unnatural, certainly inhuman. It wasn't just the unnatural protection of their armour that made the knight such a formidable foe, it was his ability to endure it. Wearing a harness itself was lauded by a poem written by Eustache Deschamps in the fourteenth century, 'And those who bear harness a long time, these shall have praise and fair looks.'[57] This does not by implication mean that armour was expected to be overly heavy or cumbersome. In Spain armour was just as developed, and it was written that it should 'be made strong, light and elegant'.[58] It was specifically recognised that it would be 'very absurd if he who wears armour… should be killed or taken prisoner by reason of his being hindered by [it]'.[59] Regardless of good design, fitness or training levels, wearing between 20kg and 40kg of plate armour changed how warfare was conducted, at least on foot. The English learnt very quickly – or more precisely, had known since at least the eleventh century that the side who let the enemy come to them had a huge advantage. It was not just the English who knew this, the French Count of Sancerre was aware that an army, 'should always wait for its enemy'.[60] It is a shame for his compatriots at the battle of Agincourt that they did not heed his advice.

Armour however, was not an invincible forcefield that kept everything out all of the time. Some armour was cheap, some badly made, some didn't fit, and some just was not quite as good as that worn by the richest knights. The dismounted French knights at Agincourt were an example of this when they marched across a muddy field into a barrage of arrows from the English longbowmen. Having allowed themselves to fight on a battlefield where neither the attacking cavalry nor infantry actually had much of a chance of winning, the knights at the front of the formation would have been hit dozens of times before they reached the English line. Some arrows would have glanced off one knight and found gaps in a neighbouring knight's armour, sometimes a thin piece of armour might have been penetrated, and sometimes a thick piece would have failed. Only a small proportion of arrows might actually disable a knight, but the cumulative effect of taking heavy hits on both morale and energy, along with the minor injuries sustained, meant that the knights who made it to the English army were very much the underdogs. The very best French knights were in the front ranks too, and were the ones who were taking these hits. The English men-at-arms were therefore likely to be able to remove the best of their opponents with relative ease – a fact that would serve to unsettle the lesser French men-at-arms behind them. The English men-at-arms and knights who took on the French were experts in close combat skills, and with their backs against a wall, they were also highly motivated to fight hard. As a result, and working within retinues that included a high proportion of archers, they made short work of the French. The heavily armoured knights and lightly armoured archers also complemented each other perfectly, one could be the eyes and ears while the other provided the heavy hitting power. The French lacked lighter troops to support them, and like tanks unsupported by infantry, they paid the ultimate price.

For every Agincourt, however, there was another battle that tells a different story. At the Battle of Patay only fourteen years later, the French outflanked the wooden stakes defending the longbowmen and utterly destroyed them. This was done by a mounted force the same size as the one intended to have been used at Agincourt, but this time to devastating success. As the English commanders were almost all dismounted at Patay, they were likewise almost all captured, revealing an often ignored downside to the English tactic. Even after the victory at Crécy, English longbowmen could be found being defeated in France, for example at the Battle of Mauron in 1352.[61] An interesting aside is the Battle of Morlaix in 1342, where the French in part dismounted their knights to attack the English,[62] a tactic the French have usually been accused of being too arrogant or stupid to attempt. They did it here though, and although it didn't work for them, ten years later at the lesser spoken of Battle of Ardres, it did.[63] This shows us that any stereotyping of French tactical incompetence during the Hundred Years War should be challenged. These examples should show the problems of the temptation to simplify reality too far and suggest one troop type was better than another, or that any particular weapon won a particular battle on its own.

One final important example is that of Verneuil in 1424, where the French employed 2,000 Italian mounted men-at-arms, hired explicitly for their fully armoured horses and riders, and these rode straight through the English archers and their stakes, flattening everyone in their way. Agincourt had been a bloody nose for the mounted knight, but this revenge was bloody and unarguable. It should be noted that at Verneuil, the Italian cavalry then occupied itself with raiding the baggage train instead of winning the battle. That meant that the English dismounted knights actually had a window to defeat the French in close combat, which remarkably they then did. Protected by their own armour they won a famous victory after their archers had been foiled, showing that knights both on or off their horses were still very much relevant as a fighting force.[64] A great deal of this relevance was because of the physical effort put into keeping it that way. As we have seen, richer knights could bring in fencing masters and other specialists to improve their martial skills, and one of the most famous of these, Hans Talhoffer advised them to, 'take great pains in your knightly practices; throwing and pushing stones, dancing and jumping, fencing and wrestling'.[65] What this tells us is that there was an awareness in the medieval period that physical condition could be lost, and therefore had to be maintained. Knights knew that they had to keep using their muscles, and without modern gyms they found their own ways to exercise, although of course some knights are likely to have put a lot more effort in than others.

The knight often touted as the most active in training was Boucicaut, who would 'go for long runs on foot, to increase his strength and resistance',[66] as well as sometimes running in his armour. Putting off training in armour is easy and tempting, but those who persevere are rewarded by a much more comfortable life when they have to wear it in anger. Boucicaut clearly knew this, and would train in armour with poleaxes and other weapons, 'so that he could easily raise his arms when fully armed'.[67] He also followed the maxim of training hard and fighting easy by practising wielding over-weight weapons, which from personal experience is both effective and exhausting. Other training activities including picking up and throwing stones while wearing armour, a full-body workout that has strong echoes in the strongman competitions of today. Unlike modern military regimes however, training was not organised or universal, and standards would inevitably vary, but it is certain that knights could keep themselves physically fit on their own initiative. The full benefits of training were therefore not lost on the medieval warrior, and in the words of one Spanish knight, 'new things are mastered through practice and perseverance – as they say: Practice makes Perfect.'[68]

The End Result

The result of decent education, that is physical, mental and spiritual, created a class of men who were much better at fighting that anyone else in their society. This simple equation of power through force made them the ruling elite of medieval Europe, a position only really contested by the church.[69] The mounted knight was also well equipped, and tough enough to stand firm against the various non-Christian peoples who threatened the continent, before launching the successful First Crusade. Their training, including participation in tournaments and frequent wars, meant that the knights were able, just about, to succeed in the hostile conditions of the Holy Land. In a world of dynastic rather than national politics, knights were also able to rule, sometimes very well, thanks to their worldly knowledge and education. Everything they achieved was built upon their prowess, and maintaining that was a full time occupation, for the ever-present risk of relying on martial skill is that someone more proficient will arrive to take your place.

There was, however, a particularly personal undertaking knights could made in order to mitigate this risk, and it reveals a small piece of the humanity that lived under the armour, and that was the concept of brothers-in-arms. One such contract between unknighted squires Nicholas

Molyneux and John Wynter, signed in 1421,[70] made an allowance that if one died the survivor would feed the other's children and pay for their schooling. Probably most pressingly, however, if one was captured, the other would secure their ransom, and even take their place if appropriate, to allow the other to collect money for their own release. This spreading of risk seems to be a very sensible arrangement to enter in to, but there was also a less contractual way to become brothers-in-arms. During a siege, if an attacking underground mine was met by countermining from the defenders, two knights could fight each other in a dark and dirty duel, and afterwards would become brothers-in-arms because of the extreme nature of the conditions they had shared. Henry V himself is said to have fought in one of these combats in 1420 at Melun, where the tunnel was so large that both combatants could actually joust together on horseback.[71] The sight and experience of two knights charging each other underground, presumably lit by torchlight, is one of the most remarkable of the whole middle ages. A few months later when Melun surrendered, Henry was extremely angry at its defiance, and wanted to execute his underground opponent as a traitor for defying his royal authority. However, when this opponent reminded the king that they were now brother-in-arms, Henry, always a stickler for knightly rules, accepted the argument and relented.

When between knights or squires on the same side though, these relationships could provide the edge in the harsh world of combat, but what was that actually like? The fifteenth-century knight de Gamez described his master Pero Nino in battle with an opponent who 'gave each other such sword blows upon the head… that sparks flew from his eyes'.[72] Nino is also struck by a crossbow bolt in the nose during the same battle, where he continued fighting with it hanging out of his face, and no amount of adrenaline could have stopped him from noticing it. Shortly after, while climbing a siege ladder, he did, 'receive many sword blows on the head and shoulder'.[73] At one point a shield is also pushed into Nino's face, and it drove the crossbow bolt even deeper into his head. By the end his sword is almost broken and the 'blade was toothed like a saw and dyed with blood'.[74] The armour available in this battle in only 1397 was good enough to reduce Nino and his opponent to battering each other in the head until one of them was knocked unconscious, or their helmets finally gave in. That is exactly what happened when Nino's sword finally broke his enemy's helmet and killed him. This description invokes a brutal and primal battlefield where brute strength mixed with aggression and pain tolerance to determine who survived. When reading these tales of carnage and bloodlust, one can be tempted by the stereotypical image of the violent knight misusing his power.

Of course they were not all made in this mould, and not all were cynical oppressors of ordinary people – the reality was intensely more complicated. Any particular knight could be placed anywhere on a number of scales:

Free – Unfree
Christian – Secular
Rich – Poor
Dutiful – Mercenary
Educated – Illiterate
Chivalric – Pragmatic

The possible combinations of these scales represent the unlimited different circumstances a knight could find himself in. The only window we have to view them through now however, is from written records. One recorded case that illustrates the complexity of this is that of Niccolò of Verona. In 1452 in Italy, he was accused of a crime which resulted in all of his belongings being confiscated by the authorities. Who, luckily for us, promptly catalogued them. As a man-at-arms for the rich Duke of Milan, Niccolò was a man who managed to be both rich and poor at the same time. His list of possessions included a large quantity of armour, enough pieces, indeed, to arm three men in full plate armour, and the horses and equipment to go with them. The value of this military equipment was astronomical, however the remainder of his worldly goods was almost non-existent. Niccolò owned a wooden chair, a basket, a saucepan, a bowl, some bedding, one pair of boots and lastly, a hat to sleep in.[75] That Niccolò had six horses and then such a paltry selection of personal items is the mark of a military man always on the move. There are no comforts, indeed he owned nothing to slow him down, and absolutely nothing that was not essential for the business of making war. Niccolò was not a vassal serving the Duke of Milan from a sense of obligation however, but instead a mercenary working for him as a condottieri.

Mercenaries were rarely described in positive terms, but one final demonstration of the complexity of medieval knighthood is that sometimes these Christian warriors were paid by Muslims to fight against other Muslims. In his Canterbury Tales, Chaucer's knight serves one Turkish ruler, 'agayn another hethen in Turkeye'.[76] At first, serving a non-Christian master seems contrary to the very Christian ideals of the knights, but it was a relatively common occurrence as we have previously encountered with El Cid. The church specifically allowed knights to serve under a Muslim banner as long as the enemy was also Muslim, and that the war itself was deemed to be a 'just' one. Such service was usually undertaken for money, but as these knights were spilling Muslim blood it was more or less socially acceptable back home. It is also worth considering why the Muslims employed foreign troops who clearly had no loyalty to them in the first place. One answer is given by the great fourteenth-century Arab historian and philosopher Ibn Khaldun, who wrote that Christians were employed to teach Islamic armies the 'line formation'[77] technique. Although on some occasions they were certainly employed to fight, it does appear that at other times Christian knights were used as military advisors. Khaldun adds explicitly that Christians were not employed in conflicts against other Christians, for rather obvious reasons.

The point, however, is that nothing, including who was good or bad, was ever clear-cut. Knights could be many shades of right and wrong, constructive and destructive, and certainly sometimes they did things that people at the time baulked at. William the Conqueror's Harrying of the North was frowned upon at the time as a needlessly devastating act,[78] and on a smaller scale we find a knight called Jean le Gastelier declaring that it was his job to rough up prisoners in order to encourage them to pay a bigger ransom.[79] The fact that le Gastelier was employing himself with torture tells us that not every knight was sticking to a high-minded code of values, despite efforts from people such as Christine de Pizan. It would seem that her wish that men-at-arms, 'must take every precaution not to destroy the poor and simple folk',[80] was made because such behaviour was a genuine problem. Even the vaunted loyalty of knights was questionable in the fifteenth century, as hinted at by de Pizan again when writing of how she wondered that men dared to make use of safe conducts because of the lack of loyalty in evidence in the world. Good or bad though, the knight was a product of that world, a world based on conflict and full of violence that to our sensibilities often seems to have been casual and excessive. This environment bred tough men, some of whom enjoyed war such as much as Jean de Bueil, who wrote that, 'war is a joyful thing',[81] even after losing his father at Agincourt.

During that very battle, there was a controversial episode where Henry V executed a large number of French prisoners, fearing a counter-attack was incoming. The reasoning goes that he could not spare men to guard captives if the French launched another assault, and had to therefore kill the Frenchmen in his case to free up his troops. However, the killing of prisoners goes against every chivalric principle, making this a reprehensible act. Or is it? Henry V has been accused of acting badly in this episode by some historians, but it is telling that at the time, even the French did not complain about the decision to kill them.[82] For the medieval knight, and in this case king, success was the measure of prowess, that core tenet of chivalry which stood above the others. Killing the prisoners saved his army, and although no new French attack was made, the blame was laid at whoever caused Henry to think there could be one. This complexity around the intent behind an act, and the act itself, tells us that the medieval mind was as complicated as our own, and that knights could apply reason to justify doing something that, given a different scenario, they would not. The medieval knight was, however, progressively softened as the centuries wore on, and it is this softening, usually codified in the form of chivalry, that is what draws us to them today. The contradiction between men who on one day could order the killing of woman and children, and then on another compose beautiful music or poetry, is a source of everlasting fascination because it digs deep into the root of the human condition itself. Perhaps it is this fusing of the extremes of humanity in medieval individuals that allowed the mounted knight to rise to prominence in the first place.

Author's Note

A full fifteenth-century harness of plate armour comes in at least a dozen separate metal pieces, from greaves for the shins, to arm sections and helmets. The foundation for the system is the fabric jacket known as an arming doublet. This is a sturdy item of clothing made from a few layers of material with laces, known as points, hanging off it that the armour will be tied to. The arming doublet is as tight fitting as possible, and designed in such a way that lifting ones arms does not move the doublet around the torso. The torso area is very snugly fitted, and is similar in concept to a corset, although fortunately not quite as tight. This tightness is firstly because the upper leg armour is laced into the bottom of the arming doublet and acts as a weight pulling it down, so the doublet needs to be so tight it does not fall below the hips. The main body armour, the *cuirass*, is also very tight for the same reason, that is to sit on the hips, allowing the weight of the body armour to sit there and not on the shoulders.

This is exactly how large modern backpacks are designed when they have straps that hug the walker's hips. This spreading of weight was deliberate and gives the wearer more freedom of movement and better stamina than if the whole weight of his *cuirass* was on his shoulders. With more laces and buckles the rest of the armour goes on, starting from the bottom and working up, until a helm is placed on the wearer's head. At least half of the process cannot be done without an assistant, and likewise once a helm has been buckled down, it isn't coming off unless an assistant is around to help. The arming process can be managed very quickly if the helpers know the armour – in fact with two helpers, five minutes is an easy target. The arming doublet acts efficiently to spread the weight around the body so that a 25kg harness feels much lighter than a 25kg rucksack, and mobility is reasonably good. Getting on and off horses is possible unaided, as are varied activities such as performing star jumps or climbing ladders. Of course, strength is sapped much quicker in armour than without, but constantly wearing it increases both strength and stamina, and if there is a horse to do the walking, then wearing armour is only a hardship if it isn't done regularly.

The real downsides start with the weather. When the sun comes out, armour is an oven. We have placed a thermometer inside armour on hot days while wearing it, and if it is thirty degrees outside, the temperature inside can be more than forty degrees. To the other extreme, I have been snowed on in armour, and fingers and toes start to lose their feeling much quicker than you'd like, especially when riding a horse in walk where your body isn't moving a great deal. The biggest handicap of armour though is probably reduced vision. With a visor down, or indeed in a helm with no visor at all, a knight on a horse has a terrible view of things happening close to him. He may be able to see his horse's ears, but quite possibly not. He may also not know where his reins are if he drops them, and will sometimes struggle to find them, especially if the horse is bolting or something else has gone wrong. Similarly, a knight could have no idea that an assistant on foot is standing next to his horse, and could run them over without ever knowing an accident was happening. This is just one reason why visors were sometimes unpopular among knights, and in images of combat it is often seen that knights open their visors. The drawback was it meant having to expose the most vulnerable part of themselves in exchange for that full vision. The importance given to vision, and the resulting trend of knights fighting with exposed faces, goes a long way to explaining why swords were still used by mounted knights. In close combat, the sword is a fantastic weapon to slash or thrust into eyes, nose, and mouth. It is no accident that many fifteenth-century fencing techniques employed efficient and brutally effective movements with the sole aim of getting a knight's sword into his opponent's face. The success of such methods can be found in numerous accounts of knights receiving terrible head wounds. For example, during the Battle of Fornovo in 1495, it is explicitly mentioned that the prominent Italian *conditorrei* Rodolfo Gonzaga was killed after he opened his helmet.[83]

The second problem that armour causes its user is a lack of hearing, and some helmets surround the ears in so much padding that they render the wearer close to deaf. The consequences of this on a battlefield are obvious, and is another reason why knights fought in groups and retinues, and not as lone warriors cutting their own path through a fight. Military communication was often done by banners as a remedy to this, as they are tall and colourful and therefore rise above formations of men to make themselves visible at distances. Knights would have known the banners at any given battle, often for both sides, and therefore would usually have a pretty good idea of roughly where they needed to be. Knowing the location of your banner was one thing though, giving complex orders over distance was quite another, especially when talking to the knight next to you might be a struggle. In all of my helms I luckily have some hearing, but some of my colleagues cannot hear a single thing once they are inside theirs. However, as with the lack of vision, the heat, and the seemingly never-ending need to oil the armour, accruing time wearing it allows us to acclimatise and grow used to these minor discomforts.

Chapter Five

The Knight's Horse

The Horse

When discussing the mounted knight's horse, we first have to take a step back from modern horse riding in most of its forms. Regarding the horse itself, it takes relatively few generations of selective breeding to significantly change a breed, and over the last hundred or so years a lot of the traits that aided combat performance have been bred out of modern day animals, because, for example, horses of an easy going temperament are now more desirable. The result of this change is that the medieval horse to the modern horse is as the Main Battle Tank is to the family car. These differences extend to the disciplines horses are used in too. Modern horse racing gives the impression that speed is critically important and puts the image of the thoroughbred into mind when the word horse is spoken. The trade-off made to breed increasing speed is mental and physical fragility. Another change has happened with modern dressage, which looks for horses that extend their legs forward flamboyantly and rewards big movements over physically beneficial ones. The horses trained for this can rarely be ridden with one or no hands in life or death situations, because this is no longer what they are bred for.

Modern English hunting certainly has roots stretching back even beyond the middle ages, but no longer do huntsmen put themselves in personal danger from the tusks of a boar or paws of a bear. As a result, their horses require no technique or training for such encounters as their primary skills are jumping and endurance. Similarly, the rise of the tractor has meant that draught horses in the modern era are now used for riding, and it is probably the size of these breeds that above all else is the cause of many of the myths surrounding medieval horses. A modern shire horse stallion has an average height of 178cm (over 17 hands tall in equestrian parlance)[1] at the base of their neck, and they can weigh over 1,000kg. The shire was bred to pull things, not to take a rider, and they are not suitable for being ridden to war because of their 'slow pace, huge size, docility and soft bones'.[2] It might seem sensible that a heavy horse can carry a heavy rider, but this is a simplification and also an irrelevance, because horses in the medieval period topped out at roughly 155cm (just over 15 hands) in height,[3] and horses the size of shires simply didn't exist. This size of horse in the modern world weighs on average 500kg, so half the weight of a plough horse, and this is a significant difference. Draught horses are built with heavy shoulders that make them ideal for pulling ploughs through the earth. The trade off for heavy shoulders is manoeuvrability, and these horses find bending and changing direction harder than thinner animals. Size in itself is not necessarily helpful or harmful, and draught breeds do carry armour today.

Rather than size, it is the confirmation of those horses which decides if they can cope with the job or not. A small horse with an overly long back for its size is more liable to pick up back problems during a riding career than a large horse with a well proportioned back.[4] England's only great Riding Master, William Cavendish, already knew this in the seventeenth century when he wrote, 'all large horses are not strong; nay, for the most part they are not only the weakest horses, but commonly of no spirit or action'.[5] What William was explaining is that the breeds of horse that are used to plough and pull carts are the equivalent of modern lorries, whereas modern armoured fighting vehicles are as compact and manoeuvrable as possible.[6] There are also a number of full medieval horse armours in existence around the world today and these are made of metal, which means we can measure them to see roughly what size of horse they were made for. Famously, the Royal Armouries in Leeds used a model taken from a 157cm (under 16 hands) height horse to place its fifteenth-century horse armour on, and it fits well.[7] It would not fit well on a larger model.

There is ample pictorial evidence of the size and build of medieval horses, we only have to inspect the Bayeux Tapestry to see how low the feet of the Norman knights are below the bellies of their warhorses. Additionally, any of the thousands of medieval manuscripts and pieces of art that contain ridden horses prove the relatively small size and slender build beyond any doubt.[8] Similarly, finds of saddles from the Viking age onwards show much smaller horses than today.[9] The modern Spanish and Arab horse breeds are among those that most resemble historical horses,[10] and it is indeed on Spanish and Portuguese horses that you find the modern discipline which most closely corresponds to anything ancient, and that is horseback bullfighting. Bullfighting continues in Iberia with the same horses and skills that were once used on the battlefield. Their horses are alert, agile, strong, fit, intelligent and sometimes willing to take on the bulls themselves. It must be stated that the practice of actual bullfighting is absolutely not condoned, it is the horsemanship skills involved that are, even if these two concepts are hard to separate. These horses must be able to evade a charging bull by getting out of the way sideways, sometimes by dancing around a bull, but always staying calm and under control. A skilled *matador* can canter his horse sideways, both hands raised with weapons, and remain in total control of what his horse is doing. This is comparable to the skill level of the knight and his primary weapon, his horse.

Types

The concept of a breed of horse was not prevalent in the middle ages; horses were classified instead by type or function. There were ploughing, everyday riding, pack and parade horses, but the types used in combat were the courser and the destrier. The destrier is the most famous medieval horse type, and is usually assumed to be bigger than other horses, although it is uncertain whether this was necessarily always the case. The usual emphasis placed on mighty destriers should be viewed with caution however, because they only ever seem to have existed in small numbers. For an upcoming Scottish campaign in the 1330s, only thirteen out of over 1,200 horses were classified as destriers.[11] Clearly there were more than thirteen knights or men-at-arms involved, but they absolutely were not all riding horses which met the classification of destriers. When they do appear though, they were always highly prized and valued, for example a fourteenth-century destrier, 'would fetch from £20 to £100'.[12] For a perspective on those values, £25 was the annual income that a man needed in order to qualify as a man-at-arms at the time,[13] which put most destriers out of the reach of the average knight. This is backed up by the example of the Falkirk campaign where 90 per cent of warhorses involved were valued at less than £20.[14]

Most medieval knights were therefore unlikely to ever own a destrier, but it is likely that they all aspired to own such a *magnus equus*, or 'great horse'[15] as they were also referred to. This aspiration was driven by the attributes of the great horse, and that did not necessarily just mean height. Size isn't everything, and in battle it was quality and ability that counted, for a few extra inches in height were unlikely to be decisive. Destriers at a horse market are described vividly by the *The Cartulary of Shrewsbury Abbey* as being, 'the expensive warhorses, of elegant form and noble stature, with ears a quiver, necks upright and large buttocks… at a gallop with their forefeet leaving and landing on the ground together, their rear feet also.'[16] This description combines a physical presence that people would notice, with movements that are later described in classical dressage. Many of them probably were animals that wanted to join in with the fighting too, as this early medieval passage shows, 'They exult in battlefields; they sniff the combat; they are excited to fight.'[17] This might sound like hyperbole, but there have been stallions on the international jousting circuit that when in a melee, will box and even mount other horses in order to take them out.

Having this extra offensive weapon at their disposal will have been something knights will have coveted, let alone for the status boost acquiring one likely gave. Once owned, decent warhorses were not something knights let go of lightly. During the horrendous conditions of the First Crusade many horses were lost, and in the *Chanson d'Antioche* we find that when, 'poverty reduced them to eating their everyday horses, while the spirited horses brought from Spain suffered so badly from hunger that they ate their halters.'[18] This explicit reference to top level warhorses reveals both how important they were to warrant the mention, and also that specifically Spanish ones were not considered 'everyday', and that they survived the arduous journey long enough to be alive when things got really bad. That is not to say that other type of horse were not valued, even a palfrey, a 'horse for the march',[19] worth one tenth of a top quality warhorse, was still a valuable possession at perhaps £1.[20]

The warhorses who were not of the destrier grade are an even trickier subject to follow. The classification of 'courser' comes into use only in the fourteenth century,[21] seems to replace the term 'rouncy',[22] and its meaning was not fixed even from then on. We shall use the term as meaning a swift and strong horse frequently used for hunting and suitable for battle. They were lower in quality than a destrier and certainly cheaper, but were the majority of horses used on campaigns. The courser can be imagined as similar to the modern bullfighting horse, and able to perform that same movements to varying levels of proficiency. Thin and sleek, they could change direction extremely quickly, as well as going from standing to flat out gallops in only a few strides. These complicated movements, while natural to the horse, had to be linked to a command given by a rider which meant that training was required to turn a young horse into a war machine. Regarding the business of defining types of medieval horses, it may be best to follow De Gamez's classification of horses as being for war, parading and jousting,[23] rather than being overly pedantic on specific labels.

Training

How did the mounted knight train to ride, and how important was that skill to him? King Duarte of Portugal was an accomplished knight, and wrote a treatise on riding in the early fourteenth century. He tells us that riding skills are the most valuable that a warrior can have, and give their masters great fame and benefit. In an eloquent text he explains that being a skilled horseman increases a rider's courage and affords them great advantages on the battlefield. Regarding horses, Duarte writes, 'maintain them well … cultivate good habits and suppress great faults'.[24] He adds that, 'agreeable mounts greatly please the hearts of their riders'.[25] These statements show us that the middles ages were not an age of universal animal cruelty. Duarte furthers this by imploring men to treat their horses well and to, 'act like men, and not like beasts'.[26] Indeed he declines to write on looking after horses and curing them of ills because those subjects are well covered in detail in (fifteenth-century) veterinary books already. It may be surprising to find other humane instructions such as only using bridles that are made to fit a horse's head, using the reins carefully, to be quiet and at ease in the saddle. This means Duarte did not intend to be too strong when using the reins, which if done roughly or suddenly can pull a horse's mouth painfully.

One result of the gentle approach advocated is a riding style that makes a rider look like he is not doing anything, which is exactly the aim of riding from the following centuries through to today. For balance, this humanistic approach has to be mentioned alongside the medieval use of spurs. In manuscripts containing knights at war, blood is frequently depicted in the area where a spur is used on the belly of a horse. The use of the spur was supposed to happen just before a moment of action, that is, the second before the impact of a joust or contact with an enemy. Regarding the joust, the fifteenth-century Spanish expert Menaguerra said that, 'the horse should not be pricked a lot with the spurs'.[27] Indeed Menaguerra agrees with Duarte that the spurs should be judiciously used, although they did acknowledge that the use of the spur that would wound the horse, something that is now not acceptable. Modern dressage now has a 'no blood' rule, meaning that a use of spurs that draws blood leads to disqualification. The fact the rule is required suggests that even in modern times, and when not even in a combat situation, riders have drawn blood. The medieval mind had no problem with the concept of drawing blood in battles, jousts and hunts, but using the spurs as little as possible does seem to have been desirable. The mounted knight was taught to use the spur to encourage the horse at the critical moment to maintain its bravery, it was stated categorically that using the spurs too much, or at other times, would cause horses to refuse to move forwards or to become badly behaved. This, then, was a skill that had to be learnt along with all the others.

The mounted knight would have learnt to ride in whichever household he grew up, and would have had the required values and attitudes impressed into him from a very early age. As with his academic education, there were no curricula to follow, so the exact training a particular knight would have received would vary widely, although a number of Iberian treaties survive that give sound advice. The core skills required to ride into battle, however, were universal, and that started with spending time in the saddle. The medieval knight rode with his legs straight or nearly straight, sometimes with his feet angled forwards. This long legged approach allowed a knight's centre of gravity to be as low as possible, which makes it easier to stay in the saddle when things go wrong or a hit is taken. The horse is controlled primarily with what is known as the rider's 'seat', that is his buttocks and hip movements. By pushing their hips in the direction they wish to go, they communicate this desire to their horse. Likewise to control speed, the rider can tense his core stomach muscles to slow down, and push forwards to speed up. His legs also communicate speed changes and can be used to turn the horse, indeed they are required to execute the sharp turns and pirouettes that are critical on the battlefield.

Ideally, the reins are not used to steer or brake, although they are certainly an emergency brake, but are intended to be a subtle tool to communicate softly to the horse. In almost all medieval depictions of knightly combat, it can be seen that the reins are hanging loose. Additionally, the knight will turn his shoulders to turn the front shoulders of his horse, which means he can turn his shoulders to the left, and push his hips to the right to create a certain movement that allows him to close in on an enemy diagonally to his right while keeping his horse's head out of harm's way. This movement has become a modern dressage movement,[28] as did many others a knight would have utilised. This is no accident, for modern dressage evolved from the art of 'dressing', or training, a horse for battle.[29] Only once a knight had mastered the art of riding himself could he really apply himself to dressing his horses. In this sense, dressage was a tool used to strengthen and supple a horse, as well as training him for his life's work, differing from the modern day when it is often only an end in itself.

To find literature in the fifteenth century to guide the training of a warhorse was not a difficult task, as material was far more widely available than we might expect. For example, in one manual for training horses, called *The Living Horse*, the Italian author acknowledges his sources as including, 'Xenophon, Absyrtus, Chiron, Hippocrates and Pelagonius and, for the Latins, Cato, Varro, Virgil, Pliny, Columella, Vegetius, Palladius, Calaber, Crescentius, Albert, Abbas and many others.'[30] This long list tells us that training horses was not ad-hoc or basic, but enlightened, disseminated and sophisticated. Insightful suggestions included using old horses to teach younger ones manners, not being harsh with the rider's commands so as to not add additional discomfort in battle, and not to work a horse beyond his age. This final lesson is lost or ignored frequently today, and leads to horses developing problems due to hard work before their physical body has finished maturing.

The author, Leon Battista Alberti, made the observation that a horse kept in a gloomy stable, remaining inactive for a long time, will become lazy and prone to becoming fearful and timid. Medieval knights reading manuals such as this would have discussed their contents between each other and amended their own horse care and training as a result. Some of them will have followed advice to build up the exercise a young horse was given little by little and by rewarding each step of progress. The horse would be slowly accustomed to loud noises as might be heard on campaign, ideally carefully and never put in any real danger. The horses were treated kindly and it is repeatedly stated in the manual that the horse must not be overworked or be allowed to fall ill. When they did, Alberti recommended courses of bloodletting, but this particular folly should be excused as it was also the primary treatment for human ailments. Alberti's advice is so in depth and good that, if the leeches were ignored, it could be published today and be considered more sympathetic to the horse than some modern approaches.

It is no coincidence that horsemanship works of the middle ages usually contain a section on veterinary care, indeed the disciplines of training and veterinary care were part of the overall skill set of medieval horsemanship. With so much of medieval life revolving around horses, a great many people had extensive experience with horse care and healing, and this was an important subject for every knight. On a campaign, and especially on a fast-moving raid, he had to make sure someone in his party, if not himself, had the required knowledge to keep all of their horses healthy. It is tempting to think that this is the purpose of one treatise, a pocket sized book called the *Liber marescalcie equorum*,[31] which contained detailed instructions for treating horses. For example, there are sections on problems with shoulders or legs, which could be very useful to know about when a man-at-arms was away from home and his life possibly depended on having a horse to ride. The fact that manuals such as the *Liber marescalcie equorum* existed does of course not mean that everyone who rode a horse to war followed or knew about them.

It also needs to be said that not every trainer of horses in the age of the knight necessarily treated them as well as these works describe. In the *Hippiatria sive Marescalia*[32] written in the mid-fifteenth century, a suggestion to cure lazy horses who are trying to avoid effort is to press a heated staff made of hazel under the tail of the horse while the rider strongly applies his spurs.[33] While this will almost certainly make the horse go forwards at some speed, it will not create a well behaved and calm animal to ride. The next time it sees a wooden stick behind it, the horse will probably attempt to escape, with little regard for matters such as avoiding trampling over people! We must be careful not to idolise the Medieval knights for loving their horses and training them gently, because this certainly was not always the case. Different humans are capable of treating horses with the utmost respect to the utmost barbarity, and this full spectrum would have been present in the middles ages as much as it is today.

Supply

Warhorses throughout the medieval period were deliberately and selectively bred, for controlled breeding produced better animals. Stud farms were therefore required as a base for this activity, and duly set up in England from Saxon times onwards in order to increase the volume and quality of horses.[34] The male colts that were not up to scratch were gelded before they reached breeding age, and this is sure evidence of selective breeding.[35] References to trained horses exist, and in Saxon wills there are many references to horses and even stud farms being left to people; for example, 'I grant to my staghuntsman the stud which is in Colungahrycg'.[36] Breeding horses was so widespread that even the Saxon church got in on the act; Burton-on-Trent's abbey held seventy horses in its stud farm at the end of the eleventh century.[37] To keep quality breeding going, as well as a secondary source of good horses, knights also imported horses from Europe, often from Spain and Northern Italy. Indeed in 1215 we find a record of a particular man being put in charge of the 'King's Spanish horses'[38] in Northampton, which tells us that King John had enough Spanish horses to warrant the job.

Ten years later the biography of the great knight William Marshal was written, and within it we are told that in England 'you could see horses from Spain, Lombardy and Sicily'.[39] Horses from Lombardy, that is northern Italy, appeared on the London market as early as 1232, but horse dealing on an international scale was a business as old as mounted warfare.[40] This business could be lucrative for the right people, and when in 1282 Edward I sent a mission to Spain with £1,000 to buy horses, the Spanish dealers surely cashed in.[41] Foreign horses were all well and good, but as Edward I could attest, they were a financial headache, which meant local breeding was always important. For example, in 1279 the king of France proclaimed that every baron, abbot, count or duke with enough pasture should have a stud with four to six mares within two years,[42] he was trying to bolster his own horse stocks. Cost wasn't the only issue with importing horses that a knight would have to consider, their own safety could be an issue.

The unfortunate case of the 47-year-old Gilbert Marshal is a cautionary tale on fiery foreign horses. At a tournament in Ware in 1241, the last son of William Marshall felt the need to live up to his family name, mounting an Italian horse that no other would, and took to the field. He had never ridden the horse before, according to the chronicler Matthew Paris, and rode it badly, and the horse responded in kind, for he flung Gilbert from the saddle and bolted off. Gilbert's foot was caught in the stirrup however and he was dragged along the ground until the high spirited horse had given up its flight. Gilbert's caught foot was probably the only part of him not suffering from external bruising and internal bleeding, and he died in considerable pain several days later.[43] To avoid this, a knight had to judge his own abilities and match them to a suitable horse.

The Italian warhorse may well have been the fastest to turn and had the greatest stamina in the whole tournament, but all good qualities come with a price. It is because of the financial price of horses that we have so much information on them available to us today. From 1282 onwards the English started to keep separate accounts for their horses and this allows us to see how many stud farms existed at any given time.[44] Starting with only two in 1282, under Edward I numbers shot up to twenty-two by around 1300, reflecting the need to maintain forces to fight the Welsh and the Scots. Stud numbers peaked during Edward III's reign at around forty at the time of the Battle of Crécy in 1346.[45] This represented a huge investment in warhorses in the country, bolstered by regular imports from Spain, Lombardy and the Low Countries, and demonstrates both the state's focus on war, and the centrality of the mounted knight to that. The Black Death unsurprisingly dented numbers, but the real decline comes straight after the victory at Poitiers in 1356 when the number of studs drops from around thirty to less than five in only a few years.[46] The result of the Battle of Poitiers was the Treaty of Brétigny which ceased hostilities for a number of years, and meant the astronomical cost of maintaining high quantities of horses was less justifiable. The industry was shut down to almost nothing, resulting in a considerable saving to the English Treasury who no longer had to pay out on wages, horse feed and land maintenance. This financial incentive was made worse by raising wages following the Black Death, and mixed with a peace treaty and the fact that English military strategy was leaning towards a combined arms approach which did not rely on the mounted knight, meant that the English mounted knight was becoming an endangered species.[47] The victory won at Poitiers, ironically in large part due to the mounted knight, was the event that inadvertently started his decline in England. This downwards trend started because warhorse numbers dropped too low, not because the English had decided they didn't need them, but either way, the trend was permanent and the English mounted knight was falling.

Gaits & Capabilities

The slowest type of movement of a horse is the walk, which is a four beat gait, meaning that only one foot moves up from the ground at a time. Horses walk very slightly quicker than the average human and when at the head of a column of footsoldiers they will act to keep the pace up.[48] The trot is a two beat pace of diagonal pairs of legs, which means, for example, the front left leg leaves the ground at the same time as the rear right leg. Trotting, quicker than the walk, can be a fast trot or a slow trot and can be used to cover ground quickly without overly tiring a horse out. When the trot becomes faster it becomes a bouncier experience for the rider and would have been avoided by armoured knights. The best gait for travelling was the amble, as covered before, which is another two beat gait, but this time when parallel pairs of legs move together, that is both legs on the right side leave the ground at the same time. This makes for a much more comfortable experience for the rider than trotting, and is less energy consuming than the canter. The canter is the primary battle gait for the mounted knight, being both smoother and faster than the trot. The canter can be done at almost any speed if a horse is well enough trained however, and this ability is what makes it so useful in combat. A skilled rider can collect up the energy of a cantering horse and hold it there, as if on the edge, until he decides to release that energy as a fast turn or a leap forwards into action. This leap is seen in almost every medieval depiction of knights, the two rear legs are propelling the horse forwards from the ground while the two front legs are reaching up and forwards as the horse begins to launch. If a knight could collect his horse into a coiled spring of energy he could manoeuvre it in battle with great precision in direction and speed. The principle of a boxer dancing on his toes is the same. In the equestrian world this ability is known as collection and provides the additional benefits of reducing the chance of a horse slipping on difficult ground, being a more stable platform for the knight to use his weapons from, and making weight more comfortable for the horse to bear. Collected horses also exercise their bodies in a better way because effectively their posture is better.

A key benefit of being able to canter slowly is a small turning circle. In an aerial dogfight, the ability to out turn the opponent is absolutely critical in order to get into a position to attack. This is exactly the same for the mounted knight, in a one on one duel, if one can get behind and to the left of another, he can attack at no risk to himself. Therefore a well trained knight on a well trained horse has the advantage over one who cannot turn as sharply or quickly. There is little written evidence of this sort collection until the sixteenth century, but earlier horses would have been physically capable of it. Unexpectedly, this ability also could have a use in a full knightly charge. Unless there was incoming missile fire, a force of mounted knights could conserve their energy and would not need to build speed in the same way that nineteenth-century cavalry might have. Well trained horses can go into a canter from standing, so a mounted knight could be at charging speed in only a few strides, and needing only a few metres to do it. This would have enabled formations to be maintained until the very last minute and avoided the problems of riders slowing their horses to avoid the clash, which, according to experienced soldier Francois De La Noue in the 1580s, was a problem.[49] He wrote that only a quarter of the cavalry he had seen in the sixteenth century actually reached the enemy when they charge. This cavalry was not the noble-born force of the mounted knights however, but the problem of keeping formation and courage is probably as old as the tactic of the charge itself. Being able to charge in a collected manner would be a solution to the problem, because the horses would be unlikely to suddenly gallop off out of control and disrupt cohesion. Likewise a consistent speed could be maintained rather than having horses break apart from each other, depending on how fast they are. The downside of this ability is the training level required to use it. For a horse to be able to collect itself it needs to be a certain strength, as well as having undergone a certain period of schooling in order to understand and perfect the skill. Once accomplished, a horse is said to be completely dressed, and this process can take years.

The social system of the middle ages was set up for knights above a certain wealth level to maintain their own horses and for them to be trained. This does mean that horses were being trained professionally by trainers who were experienced and specialised in doing so. This large investment in land, horses and human staff was considerable, and frequent mentions of horse shortages[50] attest to the fact that during wartime, horses were often lost at a quicker rate than they were being trained. A warhorse could perform the functions expected of it without the more advanced aspects of training, for example the knightly charge could certainly be conducted at high speed. The natural state of the horse is that more than half of its weight is being carried by its front two legs; it is naturally inclined to forward movement because that is the direction its bodyweight is travelling. When a horse gallops in this state, all its energy is forwards, and a higher top speed can be reached than when collected; however, the horse will need more space and time to get to it. This is the tactic as seen in the Napoleonic wars, for example, where some cavalry regiments would progress from walk to trot to canter, before going into the gallop when they neared the enemy. This tactic is one a moderately trained horse and rider can manage well enough, and is potentially a good idea if the enemy is trying to shoot at them. The downside is that a change of direction is much harder, and once full speed is reached there is very little chance of stopping it, even if cohesion fails. Horses who are not trained to carry more of their weight over their hind legs as they do when collected, are also in a worse posture to carry the extra weight of an armoured rider. Once the charge has impacted, if a combat breaks down into a melee, an uncollected horse is unlikely to be able to stay in a canter and therefore will lose their mobility quickly.

Attacking Archers

The crossbow was probably the most feared weapon a knight could come up against. A mid-fourteenth century crossbow had an effective armour-piercing range of approximately 220m,[51] and a crossbowman might manage three bolts a minute.[52] The other foe of the mounted knight was the longbow, which may have an armour penetrating maximum range of 200m,[53] and a combat rate of fire of at least six arrows a minute.[54] Different experts will come up with variations on all of these numbers, so this exercise is to give us an impression of what the mounted knight was facing when he willingly charged into a storm of missiles. The question is, what was the volume of incoming projectiles they faced? To answer that question we need to know how long a charging formation of knights would be in that killing range before they hit the enemy. The speed of modern horses being ridden by unarmoured riders is well known and varied, indeed a gallop could be anywhere from 20mph to 35mph. However, it is assumed by everyone that the weight of an armoured rider will slow a horse down, and we do not know how fast a medieval horse would have galloped while carrying an armoured rider with a lance. To solve this problem I took a horse of the correct height and build for a medieval warhorse, placed a medieval war saddle on it, and mounted him wearing my full fifteenth-century plate harness. While carrying a full length pine lance with steel lance-head, I then conducted a charge over 110m of grassland, and timed it. The armour, saddle and lance weighed 35kg in total, which is a 30 per cent increase on my unarmoured riding weight. Despite the fact that the ground was relatively uneven, after a number of charges, the horse managed to cover the ground in an average of 12.5 seconds, at 19.7mph. To conduct a control test this was repeated with no armour the following day to give the horse a rest, and unexpectedly we managed an average time of 13 seconds, which was slightly slower than the armoured test.[55] Obviously this sample size means no scientific conclusions can be drawn, but it did reveal that over a short distance at least, the weight of armour might make pretty much no difference to a horse.

The conclusion, therefore, is that this horse carrying me in armour would have covered 200m in under 25 seconds. That would give a crossbowman time to loose two bolts, and a longbowman perhaps four or five arrows depending on how fast they really shot in battle. Once the horses started to get close though, the archers probably would start to take defensive measures like getting out of the way. The mounted knight probably fancied his chances charging crossbowmen, encased in steel and buoyed by confidence, a couple of volleys were unlikely to unduly worry him. Aggressive warriors would back themselves, and I would rather be on one of the charging horses than on the ground with the crossbow. Facing the longbow may have been a different proposition however. If the archers could manage five volleys, it would mean a new volley hitting the knights every few seconds, and due to sheer volume, these would have caused problems. We cannot calculate any concrete figures based on this little experiment, but what we can argue is that when facing a missile attack, it would be far better to be on a horse moving quickly, given good enough ground to do so. A dismounted knight walking at 4mph would take five times as long as his mounted colleague to reach the archers, and that changes the experience of the knights considerably – they were going to get peppered. Moving slowly they would also make for easier targets, and this gives us an idea of why the mounted knight was such a formidable opponent. Being mounted granted a significant level of mobility to the knights, and this speed allowed them to take the initiative, attack, and defeat their enemies.

Saddles

The most important piece of equipment for a knight's horse was the saddle because it was the interface between the man and the animal. The Greeks had been expert enough horseman to ride into battle without saddles, and still have ability to wield two-handed lances, but the saddle was a definite improvement. The earliest saddles were two bags filled with horsehair placed either side of the spine to rise the rider off from the actual skeleton of the horse.[56] This moved the weight of the rider onto parts of the horse which could take it more easily, and resulted in healthier, longer living and less encumbered horses. This basic saddle acquired a girth strap, which is a fabric or leather band that goes under the belly of the horse and holds the saddle in place. Eventually the saddle itself was solidified and a wooden tree was formed to make a base for a saddle, which was much more rigid than two sacks of hair tied together with string or sinew. Leather horns also developed on the four corners of the saddle, these locked the rider in place and added significant force to cavalry attacks and made hand-to-hand combat a much more viable option.[57] By the early medieval period these horns had become solid front and back pieces, that is the pommel and cantle. These wooden panels enclosed the rider and gave support, which further improved the cavalryman's security on his horse.

Stirrups were added to aid mounting and dismounting horses, which became more of a consideration the heavier the rider's armour becomes. The stirrups were attached to the saddles in such a way that the legs of the rider were straighter than in modern times, sometimes even fully straight and sticking out forwards. Straight legs improve communication between rider and horse, as well as helping the rider to avoid being hit out of the saddle by a lance strike. Strong wooden pommels at the front of saddles acted as a first line of defence from frontal attack, they cover the groin and sometimes upper thigh area, both of which are critical to protect. To further increase this protection, in the fifteenth century steel sheets were added to the front and back of some saddles, although adding extra armour made them heavier.[58] The contrast to these war saddles were ceremonial ivory saddles with intricately carved figures, animals and patterns that are works of art on a par with any other craftwork ever done.[59]

Only the richest knights would ever have had the wealth to commission such extravagant pieces, but in a parade or on special occasions such saddles would ensure everyone present would be aware of their status. The shape of these saddles was comparable to the war saddles, and differ significantly from modern saddles. Being made largely of wood, knightly war saddles are initially assumed to be uncomfortable, but that is certainly not the case. A horseman whose body moves in synchronicity with his horse will not bump or be discomforted by a wooden saddle, although in some cases leather and fabric covers were used. The amount of saddle in contact with the horse was also very much more than in modern English saddles. The side panels of the saddles stretch down the horse both in front of and behind the rider's leg, to create a large surface area that touches the horse. This spreads the weight of the rider more and reduces rubbing and pressure on the horse's back. The medieval design also made the saddle more stable on the horse itself, and correctly fitted medieval saddles should not slide off the side of horses, which is a handy safety feature. The saddles almost hug the horse, which leads to another advantage of the medieval saddle, in that the girth strap under the horse can be left much looser than for modern saddles, which is obviously more comfortable for the horse.

Regarding downsides, the high pommel can get in the way of jumping high obstacles, which although not a medieval concern, is why the pommel in modern English saddles is reduced or gone altogether. What was more of a danger, at least for the overweight medieval rider, was if a horse spooked particularly viciously and the rider's stomach was thrown into the pommel. This is potentially how William the Conqueror was killed in 1087, when his horse reared and the pommel caused an internal injury that became infected. Unfortunately for William this happened in the era before plate armour, because a mounted knight wearing a plate breastplate was entirely protected from such injuries.

Horse Equipment & Armour

The armour of the horse itself evolved in parallel with the knight's own protection. In the Bayeux Tapestry, the horses in battle have a thick leather strap going around the front of the horse's body and attached to either side of the saddle. This so-called breastplate acted to stop the saddle slipping back, which added more combat stability for the knight. Similar leather straps were later seen around the rear of the horse, sitting under their tail. These crupper straps became increasingly elaborate and served as an area a knight could decorate to show his wealth and status. The term *barding* refers to the equipment of the horse and this includes these leather straps, as well as the actual armour which came later.

After the early crusaders started to return home, they brought with them the concept of the *caparison*, which is a full fabric covering for the horse that stretches down to the ground. As discussed before, this covering keeps the sun off a horse, the wind and insects out, and in Europe's climate, acted as a layer of insulation in colder weather. The tournament was already well developed when *caparisons* arrived, but the knights soon realised that they presented a perfect solution to the problem of identification. On the tournament field it was important to know who was who, because the name of the game was to capture a knight, and they needed to know who was worth bothering with. The first solution to this problem was to paint shields, and this indeed worked, but only if a knight was close enough to make his shield design out. Shields also got broken and got lost. A *caparison* could be embroidered with patterns much larger than a shield, and had the added benefit of not being in the line of attack in the same way shields were. This also held true on campaign, where identifying enemies was just as important – especially when the nobility of opposing sides tended to know each other. *Caparisons* are very visible in manuscripts and appear in simple forms in the thirteenth century, before becoming more colourful and decorated through the fourteenth and fifteenth centuries. Unfortunately in art they also hide any horse armour that may have been underneath them. There are, however, images of full mail *caparisons*, but we cannot know how common these were because fabric *caparisons* could be worn on top of them, blocking them from view. Using both metal and fabric coverings would give some protection to the metal rings from the weather, but does mean that it is difficult to know how widespread this configuration was.

One account from the Battle of Bouvines in 1214 describes a footsoldier having to lift up the mail mesh that covered the belly of a horse so that he could stab it,[60] suggesting that some knights had mail horse armour in that period. Padded cloth and leather armours are known to have existed, used especially in tournaments, meaning that a knight had a variety of choices to protect his horse if he wished to. As metal plate armour started to be attached to knights in the fourteenth century, it also started to be attached to their horses.

The first place this happened was the front of the horse's head. These pieces of armour are known as *chamfrons*[61] and were originally made from leather. Leaving holes for the eyes they were strapped over the bridle of the horse, and often additionally tied to them with laces. Knights quickly saw the value of metal *chamfrons* because they protected the part of the horse infantry would point their spears at, and also where a wayward lance would do the most damage. It is common to see a knightly horse in battle armed only with a metal *chamfron*, even in the fifteenth century when plate armour prices were coming down.[62] Going into battle with just a *chamfron* was probably due to its ability to keep a horse operational, a horse wounded elsewhere will probably keep fighting for the duration of a battle, but a blow to the head would critically and quickly affect it. Another method to incapacitate a mounted knight was to cut the reins of his bridle or even to pull the bit out of the horses mouth, which was a valid war tactic. To counter this threat bridles sometimes replaced leather with metal to save them from being cut, and sometimes large metal spikes were added to bridles and bits to stop hasty infantrymen from grabbing them.[63]

The next most vulnerable area of the horse, from another mounted combatant, was the top of the neck. Although in a tournament the expectation was that knights would not aim at horses, in a battle there were no such reassurances and metal neck protection was developed. The *crinet* is a remarkable piece of armour consisting of a series of metal plates that line the top of a horse's neck. They are usually attached from the front to the *chamfron* near the horse's ears, and also to the front of the saddle. These two fixed points kept the *crinet* in place, while the interlocking metal plates move in three dimensions with the movement of the horse's neck. The armour takes on a snakelike property and gives the armoured horse the appearance of a dragon, an idea not lost on medieval armourers who started designing horse armours with that theme in mind. The downside of a *crinet*, at least for a modern rider, is that it stops the reins coming into contact with the neck of the horse, which is one method of steering while riding one handed (known unsurprisingly as neck reining). The first time I rode with a *crinet* was (probably unwisely) in a joust, and I realised that I could not neck rein the horse because it couldn't feel the reins on his neck. I had to very quickly find another way to steer the horse, although luckily for me he was a legend in the modern jousting community and didn't really need telling where to go.

The armour available for a horse to be equipped with did not end with the head and neck however. Metal breastplates, known as *peytral* plates, wrapped around the body of the horse under the neck and provided excellent deflection defence against both missile and pole weapons. Along with a *chamfron*, the *peytral* formed a system with which a mounted knight could ride directly at a group of archers and expect his horse to come through it alive. This grade of armour at a unit level started to appear in the early fifteenth century, for example at the Battle of Verneuil in 1424 where 2,000 Italian horsemen on specially armed horses brushed aside the English longbows in a frontal attack explicitly made possible by their armour. These men-at-arms possibly also had armour on the rear of their horses, a *crupper* piece extending from the back of the saddle down the rear flanks of the horses. These large pieces of iron or steel, along with the rest of their armour, turned the mounted knight into a heavy tank. The full weight of this barding was potentially roughly equal to the knight's own full plate armour harness. The full equestrian plate armour in the Wallace Collection weighs 30kg, which a medieval warhorse could carry. As we saw from my galloping test previously, this weight was not necessarily carried at a detriment to speed, and if the horse armour was only applied prior to a battle, then there is no need to assume those horses would be slowed in their attack. However, this metal armour would have been expensive to acquire, require occasional adjustments while being worn, and would possibly have rubbed the horse, and over longer use worn them out. Someone also had to carry it around when not being used, put it on the horse for the knight to use, and replace any straps and rivets that broke. It takes time to arm a horse, and will slow their walk down,[64] so it is unlikely that many knights chose to ride their horses fully covered when marching day to day on campaign.

The difference between the mounted knight and the modern tank, is that the knight could choose from one moment to another if he wanted to be lightly or heavily armoured. One factor more important on the daily march of campaigns was horseshoes. Metal shoes appear in the archaeological record in England as early as the ninth century and increase in frequency as the years wore on.[65] The shoes were nailed on in a similar way to modern horseshoes and they served the same function, that is to protect the feet of horses on journeys. There are also many pictorial cases of shoes with spikes on the bottom which would effectively make them off-road shoes, and in a world with extremely limited paved roads these would have been widely used.[66] Indeed, even today studded shoes are still used, from show jumping to eventing, to help avoid falls on slippery ground.

Psychology

Often the first comment made about knights and their battlefield use, is that horses are not stupid enough to charge into a mass of men pointing sharp sticks at them. I can, however ,assure you that they very much are. The primary mental faculty of a horse is its memory,[67] and this is how they are able to reach extraordinary levels of training. They remember what behaviour got them a reward and eventually it becomes a trained ability without the need for a reward. The problem is that this memory works with bad experiences too, and a horse can pick up a bad habit just as easily as a good one. Once learnt, any behaviour or ability is hard to get rid of, or correct, and it is this difficulty that makes training horses time consuming and therefore expensive.

Horses are naturally prey animals and have evolved to be alert to danger, which adds a layer of work in order to train them for battle. This prey instinct manifests as horses jumping when a cannon goes off near them, or spooking when a bird flies out of a hedgerow in front of them. These natural impulses can be tempered by the careful and unrushed training methods mentioned in medieval manuals, but there were always some horses that were simply too fearful to be used by a knight. It should be noted that mares and stallions are both capable of aggressive responses to danger and will sometimes favour fight rather than flight.[68] Stallions were the favoured horse of the medieval knight, partly because of fertility related symbolism, and partly because on the battlefield they could be more of a weapon than the average gelding. In the wild, stallions will fight to control a herd of mares, but when not in that position they are capable of living in bachelor herds, that is a herd of stallions, in a relatively peaceful manner. The modern concept of all stallions being uncontrollable is not the fault of the stallions. Those who grow up among other, especially older, horses become socialised and able to function as part of the society of the horse.[69]

There will remain the ability to fight however, and there is ample evidence of stallions fighting for the knight who is riding them. In a melee against an opponent riding a stallion, I was quite surprised when the horse turned into me, while still at a canter, and wrapped his jaws around my knee. Had I not been wearing metal plate knee cops, it could have been the end of my knee. Some stallions on the battlefield will use their teeth and front legs on each other, and humans, without being asked to. More troublesomely, while standing still, some will naturally use their back legs to kick at people or horses they do not like who get too close. Geldings and mares will certainly exhibit the same characteristics on occasion, but it is certain that on average, stallions will put the most effort into fighting. Mares are certainly able to make fantastic warhorses too, however, and although they did use stallions and geldings, Usamah Ibn Munqidh's memoirs do more frequently mention him and others riding mares into battle.[70] In a battle, the ability of horses to act as a sentient weapon for a knight could be life saving, in Ucello's painting of the Battle of San Romano, a chestnut coloured horse is kicking out with his back legs so high that they would be able to harm an enemy rider. This makes the horse a partly autonomous offensive weapon, but one that could also damage friendly forces.

Horses know the difference between a human walking over to pat them, or coming over to hurt them,[71] but in order to ride in formation they require training and familiarity so that they both remain in place and under control. The natural herd instinct of horses aids formation riding, and they do learn to stay in line by themselves eventually. There is an (unprovable) story of retired horses who had fought at the Battle of Waterloo, who once home would daily line up in their field and conduct wheels left and right before a final charge, all without a human in sight. That herd instinct of group action is a fundamental part of the charge of the mounted knight. Once several hundred horses have been set in motion at speed, there is not always a great deal anyone riding them can do to stop them. This returns us to the question of horses charging spear infantry, in what would appear to be a suicidal attack. The question can be answered with another, why would so many British soldiers advance into hails of machine-gun fire during the Battle of the Somme in 1916? That prospect seemed suicidal to some troops, yet the overwhelming majority climbed out of their trenches and got on with it. Likewise, the medieval mounted knight would often charge because he thought he would be victorious, or because that was the order that had been given. His horse would do the same, because it had been asked to and it didn't have a reason to refuse. A horse that has undertaken training to push through a block of men at home will not think twice about pushing through a different block of men on a battlefield. The horse does not necessarily know that the second block will try to kill him, and by the time they found that out, he was among the enemy. Furthermore, in a formation a horse in the front rank with others to his sides and rear will be inclined to run towards open space, and the space in front is more open than the sides or rear, at least until it is too late to change his mind. Only the front rank of horses needs to be brave enough to charge at the enemy, the rest will invariably follow.

These are not academic possibilities, there is video footage of re-enactment events where horses plough through infantry, albeit in a single line, and knock them flying. A third of our horses will not charge home, one third will follow the others anywhere, and the final third will either do it, or *actively seek people to run over*. Until pikes became longer than the lances of the knights attacking them, the infantry spear was not a reliable defence against the mounted knight, which is one reason why infantry is sometimes forgotten about in accounts of battles.[72] It is not until the fourteenth century where infantry weapons start to out-range cavalry, and even then there are countless victories for mounted knights over the next two centuries. The other objection to the concept of the charge, is that knights would not want to lose their precious war horses. This is no doubt true and is probably why compensation schemes were set up by commanders, a notable example is Edward III, to effectively pay a knight for a horse lost while on campaign.[73] This reflects the acknowledgement that trained horses were expected to be lost, and horses can therefore be compared to expensive missiles of the modern age.[74] A warhorse must therefore be seen as a weapon that a knight was expecting, at some point, to lose. The records of horse losses shows that the Black Prince's retinue lost 395 horses out of 1,300 in the Rheims campaign of 1359–60, which is neither a small amount, nor abnormal.[75]

Horse Survivability

Horses are both surprisingly easy and difficult to disable, and by its nature this is a graphic section. The most vital part of a horse is its head, and a heavy blow to the top of the head is likely to severely stun or kill a horse. It is for this reason that horse armour started with head pieces, the *chamfrons*, and either leather and metal armour will protect the horse from some impacts there. Of course, sometimes eyes would have been hit, but this didn't necessarily mean the horse would cease to function right away, or in fact continue to be useful. In the thirteenth century a certain Peter de Nutle had a riding horse which was recorded as only having one eye,[76] but of course many horses react badly to being blinded.

In comparison, the lungs and heart of a horse are usually not great targets from the front because often the horse's head itself is in the way, which also applies to the vulnerable bottom of the neck. From the side, the knight's saddle and legs block most attacks, and after their introduction *caparisons* also made this area a harder target to hit. From the side, however, the neck is exposed and was a primary target for missile weapons. The back of the horse, above its hind legs, was a large target but the thick muscle there could take a lot of damage before the horse stops being able to move. It is the ability to continue to move despite taking punishment that is usually not taken into account when discussing the effectiveness of warhorses. Several wounds could be inflicted and they could still be able to continue fighting for the rest of the day. Usamah Ibn Munqidh described how, during the crusades, his mare was wounded three times in one battle but he continued to fight because he, 'did not feel anything unusual in its conduct'.[77] Whether it survived infection or loss of blood is another matter, but heavily injured horses, especially under adrenaline, will continue functioning under control far longer than might be thought. Usamah Ibn Munqidh also mentioned a horse who had its lower neck pierced by a Frankish lance so violently that the lance went through and into the thigh of its rider. Both survived this blow apparently undaunted, and the horse recovered just to be hit again by a Frank, 'who thrust his lance into the frontal bone of the horse and made the whole bone cave in'.[78] As before, the horse survived, although apparently after the wound healed, a fist would still fit in the hole left behind.

The final contribution from the same author is that a horse had its heart cut by a lance thrust and a number of arrows hit its body but, 'nevertheless carried me out of the battle with its two nostrils flowing blood like two bucket spouts, and I felt nothing unusual in its conduct. After having reached my companions, it died'.[78] In a battle against the Moors, De Gamez described Pero Nino's horse taking heavy wounds as Nino rode through the enemy. The horse lost its strength but not its courage, and he got his rider out of danger and home before it rolled dead to the ground. The account is quite graphic but it adds to the phenomenon of badly injured horses dying just after getting their riders to safety. In contrast to horses limping on wounded, the legs are of course one area where an injury does tend to stop a horse quite quickly. This was a fact not lost on the Romans, who employed caltrops to stop horses by crippling their feet, and they were still being used in the medieval period.[80] Knights could wear full mail *caparisons* to render the legs all but invulnerable, but only a few could have afforded such protection, especially after the Black Death when labour costs rose.[81] For everyone else, the very fact that the horse's legs were probably moving, and were a very small target, was enough to not worry too much about it. Taken as a whole then, the knight's horse was most at risk against *concentrated* missile fire and fortified positions rather than any enemy out in the open. Missiles were also more effective when used against the flanks of horses, as the English appear to have done during their famous victories in France, and the Turks certainly did during the crusades.

Formations

One of the oldest forms of warfare was the raid. Stealing livestock from another tribe is a concept as old as society itself, and in the middle ages it was still practised. Border raids between England and Scotland are famous, but raiding was also the most common form of warfare and occurred in nearly every military episode. Raiding one's neighbour makes you richer and them poorer, so consequently you can afford more soldiers than they can, and the balance of power changes. This theory was put into practise commonly in the early medieval period when dukes and knights fought their neighbours, but was nationalised as countries such as England and France consolidated themselves.

When campaigning in each other's territory, both sides were capable of wreaking terrible destruction on the luckless peasants in their path, and unlike pitched battles, these could be a daily occurrence. Raiding, of course, is significantly more successful when it is done on horseback, when mounted soldiers can avoid concentrations of the enemy and attack with surprise. Horses also allow the raiders to make off with heavier goods and live animals, and it must be noted that this could include humans. The horse was therefore critical for raiding and mounted knights played a full part. When they were scaled up to full armies on deliberate raids, notably during the Hundred Years War, they were called *chevauchees*, the *cheval* part of this name relating to the centrality of horses in the concept.[82] To the local population, these fast moving mounted warriors could appear out of nowhere, burn their crops and homes, and killing them if they didn't get out of the way quickly enough. The surprise element of such attacks meant that fighting men in the target area were unlikely to have enough time to arm themselves and organise substantial resistance. There is little benefit in having a full harness of armour if you do not have time to put it on.[83]

Raids on small scales, whether deliberate attempts to degrade the enemy's economic base, or just to supply friendly forces with food, were perhaps the most common form of conflict a mounted knight would be active in. Only a few actual knights might be present in these situations, often being accompanied by non-noble men-at-arms, light cavalry or mounted missile troops. The heavier armour of the knights and men-at-arms would give a shock attack ability if any organised resistance was encountered, but otherwise light cavalry and mounted archers could be unleashed on unarmed population centres. There were occasions when raiding went wrong. In 1423 an English raiding army was busying herding home thousands of cattle they had stolen in the vicinity of Angers in France, when a group of French men-at-arms found them. The English gave chase, presumably in the hope of gaining more money by capturing some of the French. It was, however, a trap. The French infantry were

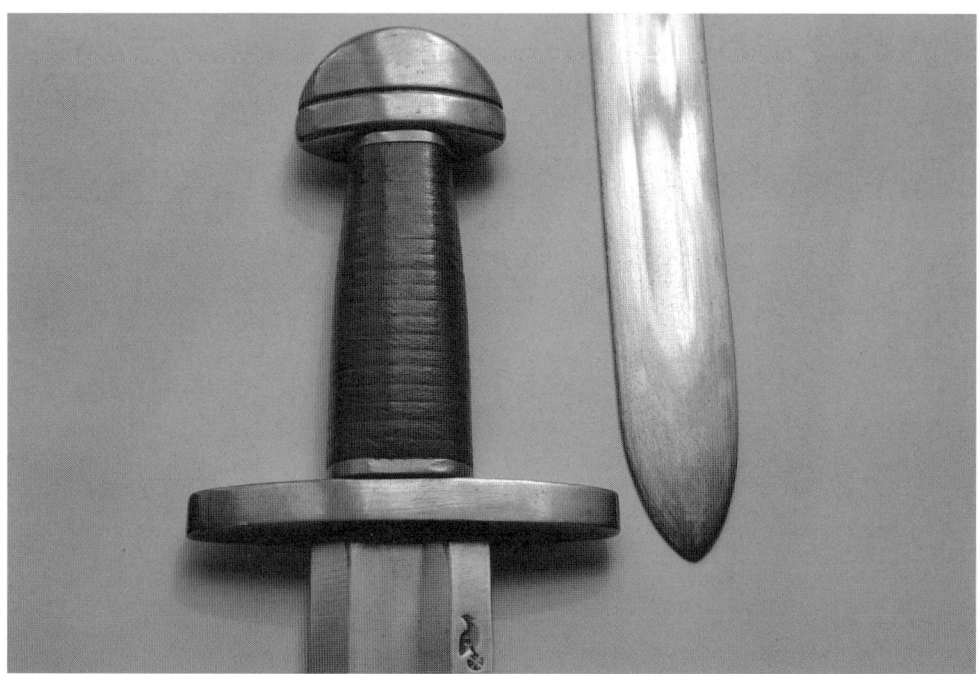

Norman mounted knights, as modelled on the Bayeux Tapestry. The horse on the left is only 13.2 hands (132cm tall), which although smaller than the 15.2 (154cm) horses next to him, is representative of the size of the Norman cavalry horses of the eleventh century. (*Photograph by Sam Gostner Photography*)

Norman swords, weighing only a little over 1kg, these swords are flexible and strong. The blade on the right is fully sharp. Swords of this period were not primarily for thrusting so there is not a stabbing point. (*Photograph by Clive Hart*)

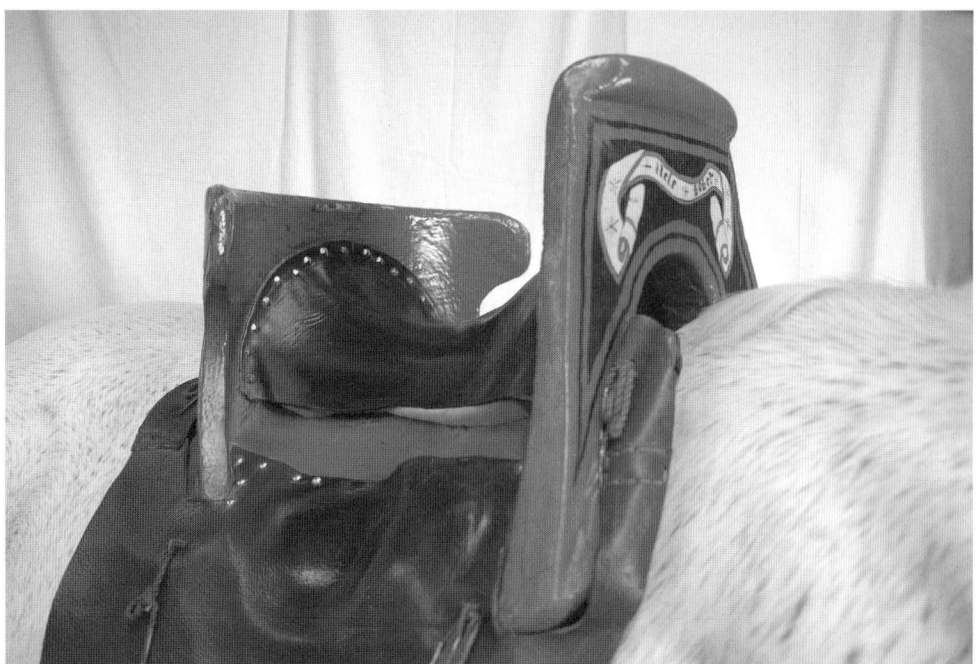

A reproduction thirteenth-century saddle, although not dissimilar to saddles from up to two centuries earlier. Saddles could be elaborately decorated. This saddle is used for jousting, and the medieval Gothic script reads 'aim higher'. (*Photograph by Clive Hart*)

Thirteenth-century tournaments involved jousting with no tilt rail. Here is a double-break between the author on the left, and Mike Canfor. Before the age of plate armour, knights were vulnerable to lances. (*Photograph by Sam Gostner Photography*)

The tournament then proceeded to a melee, the clash of swords. Dominic Sewell and Mike Canfor block each other's attacks. (*Photograph by Sam Gostner Photography*)

High medieval mail armour was sophisticated, leg armour can be seen tightly fitting the leg, making the armour as light and visually pleasing as possible. Knee cops started to appear towards the later parts of the thirteenth century as plate armour evolved. (*Photograph by Sam Gostner Photography*)

By the fifteenth century plate armour fully encased knights as well as parts of their horses. The *chamfron* being worn by the horse, Charlie, is protective and decorative. The green and red canvas tilt rail is visible on the right, introduced to avoid horse collisions. (*Photograph by Ady Jefferies*)

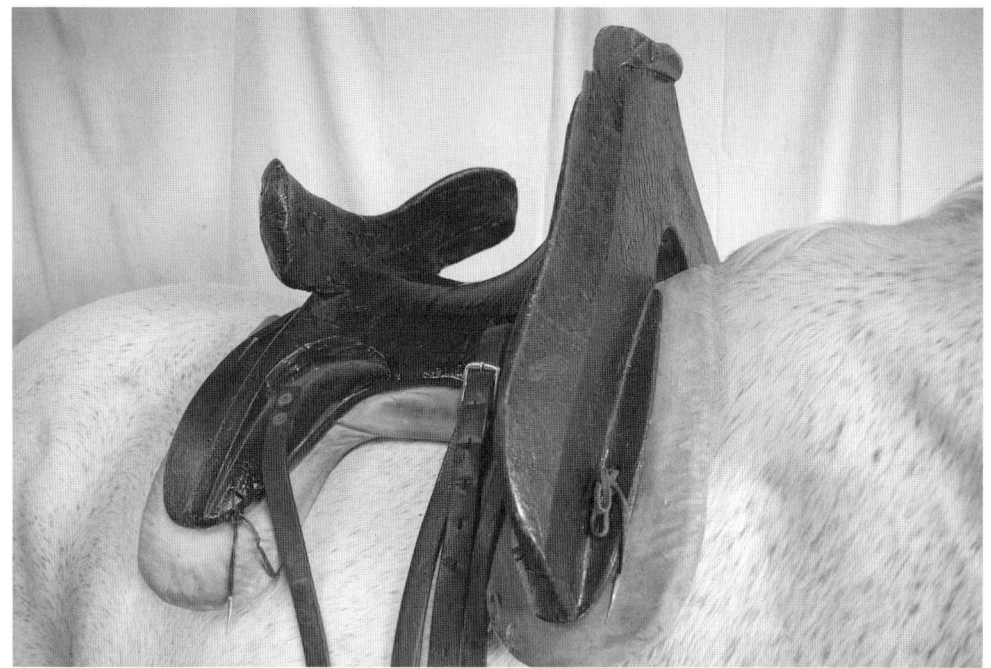

A fifteenth-century war saddle. The high front plate protects the groin and legs of the knight, while the high wings at the back keep him firmly lodged in place. The saddle stretches far down the sides of the horse, spreading the weight of the rider. These can be more comfortable than they look. (*Photograph by Clive Hart*)

A German style right arm, note the large elbow plate which is multi-layered and fluted. The fluting strengthens the armour, and together serves to protect the vulnerable elbow joint. (*Photograph by Sam Gostner Photography*)

The inside of an arm, showing the internal riveting and leather strapping that holds it all together. Sliding rivets can also be seen that in this instance enable the forearm to twist slightly. (*Photograph by Sam Gostner Photography*)

Fifteenth-century mounted knights. The right-most two knights are wearing Italian armour, heavier than German armour but more protective. (*Photograph by Ady Jefferies*)

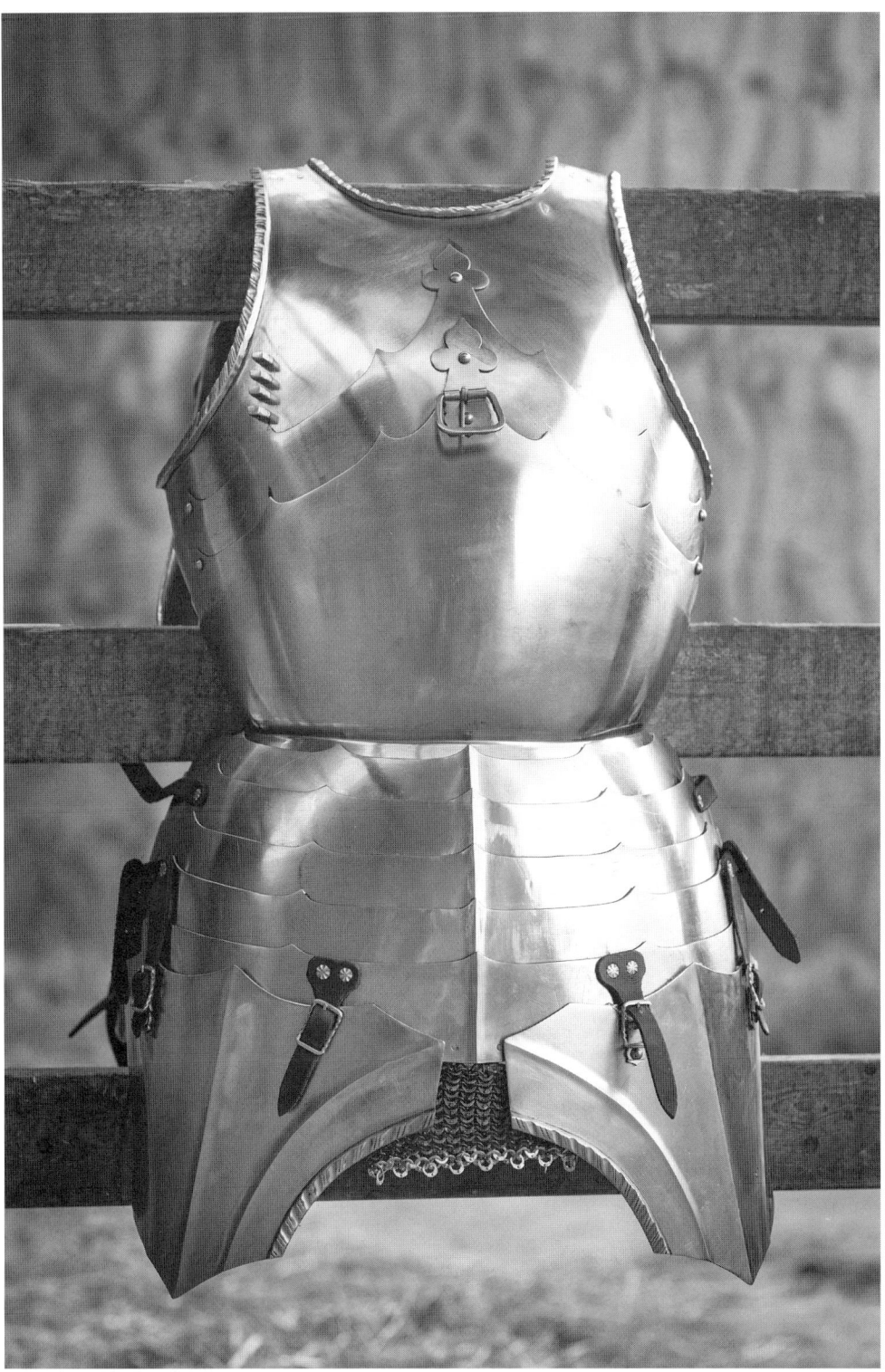

The main body armour, made up of a *cuirass*, and then *tassets* which hang off the bottom of it by leather straps. Three layers of steel cover the vital organs under the ribcage, meaning most weapons of the fifteenth century could not penetrate it. (*Photograph by Sam Gostner Photography*)

The helm on this Italian style armour is a grand-bascinet, a heavy helmet with a frogmouth shaped visor to deflect lances away from the knight's eyes. (*Photograph by Ady Jefferies*)

A lighter form of helm was the *armet*, favoured in war and for jousting, this light helm is easier to wear for long periods than a bascinet, but is not as protective. (*Photograph by Sam Gostner Photography*)

Fifteenth-century arms, gauntlets and shoulder pieces, known as *pauldrons*. These *pauldrons* cover an area frequently hit by lances during mounted combat, and as such are very important to a knight. (*Photograph by Sam Gostner Photography*)

A Germanic style of closehelm, note the long tail of articulated plates that protects the back of the neck. Also visible are the plethora of leather straps that connect the front and back pieces of the main body armour together. (*Photograph by Sam Gostner Photography*)

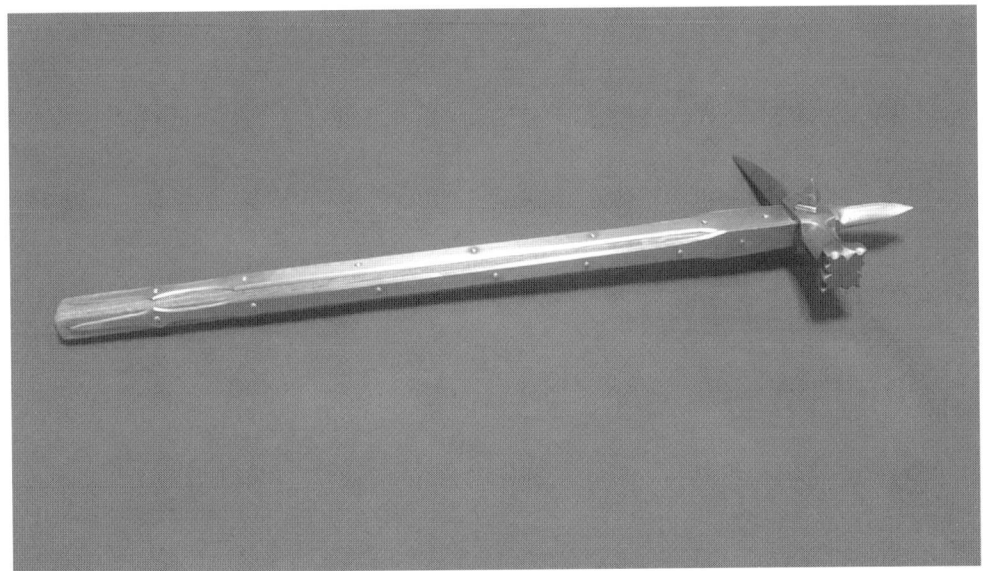

A war hammer, a brutal close combat weapon that could be wielded from horseback. The sharp beak might penetrate lower grade armour, and the hammer could concuss a knight if hit in the head. (*Photograph by Clive Hart from a private collection in Norfolk*)

Gauntlets were vital because hands were often hit in combat, as well as jousting where lances could rip fingers and thumbs off. Articulated small plates try to cover areas that the larger plate cannot. (*Photograph by Sam Gostner Photography*)

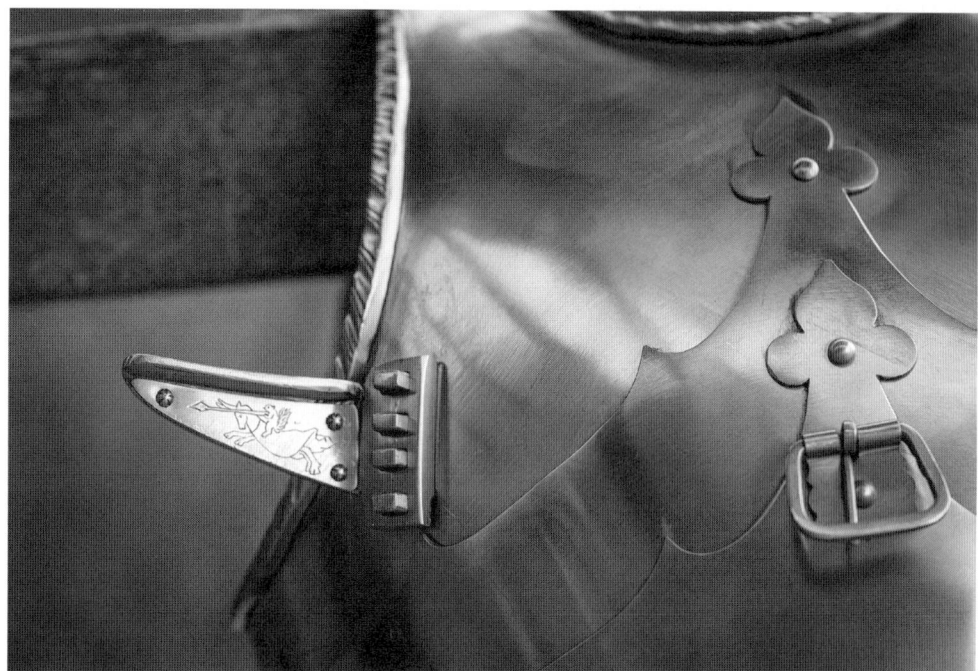

The *arret-de-lance*, projecting out from the right side of the *cuirass* gave the lance something to grab on to. These could be decorated, and turned the knight into a weapon of immense penetrating power. (*Photograph by Sam Gostner Photography*)

The lance, complete with conical metal *vamplate* to protect the knight's right hand. The hand grips the lance between the *vamplate* and the other, smaller piece of metal, called the *grapper*. The knight locks the *grapper* on to the arret so that on impact, the lance is held firm and the knight's wrist does not break from the force. (*Photograph by Sam Gostner Photography*)

A Burgundian man-at-arms with a fully equipped warhorse. The horse armour includes a metal *chamfrom* and demi-*crinet*, neck protection that goes only part way along the neck of the horse. The body of the animal is protected by a full leather bard – while highly decorated it is also light and offers substantial protection for the horse. (*Photograph by Ben van Koert of Kaos Historical Media*)

A knight in a joust might well have preferred a fabric caparison instead of full armour for his horse, and often would have worn elaborate crests on their helms too. (*Photograph by Sam Gostner Photography*)

A full knightly charge would have been a terrifying spectacle to behold. Here it is led by a knight with full German style metal horse armour. A horse equipped in this way would have been unlucky to sustain injuries from bows, crossbows or even sometimes pike weapons. The most armoured horses would ride at the front of an attack in order to screen the less well armoured horses behind them. (*Photograph by Ben van Koert of Kaos Historical Media*)

Despite their armour, the mounted knight was doomed to fade from history, although not because he could no longer fight, or that he could no longer ride his horse. The most ornate part of this armour is the Germanic decoration on the rear of the *cuirass* and *pauldrons*. The wing, or *polyen*, protecting the inside of the knight's knee is also clearly visible. (*Photograph by Sam Gostner Photography*)

waiting in a town and together with their mounted comrades, almost entirely destroyed the English raiders.[84] The key to this, or any raiding action, was the speed and agility of the horses they rode. Whether in raids or large battles, the first tactic of the mounted knights was their charge. The formation used for a charge, as seen in the tournament, was typically a straight line of knights riding abreast. Learnt at home but honed on the tournament field, cantering horses and keeping them in line is not difficult in itself, that is until helms are added and visibility and communication is reduced. In a thirteenth-century greathelm it is possible to see the head of the two horses on either side of you if you are lucky. It is not possible to see the other knights further away from you, unless they surge ahead of you, by which point you have been left behind and might not be able to catch up and reform the line. Wheeling this formation to the left or right therefore requires orders to be relayed down the line by shouting, and is not by any means instantaneous. If the formation is wheeling over rough ground, perhaps with some trees in the way, it is easy to see why they could break up before reaching the enemy.

Groups of knights who knew each other, served the same lord, and perhaps lived together, tended to form up as units within larger knightly formations. These groups were the ones formed up in tournaments, for example the, 'Young King's retinue drove their opponents from the field.'[85] This would mean that there were really several leaders within a large force, which could also mean some groups ended up doing different things to others. If we recall from chapter three the Battle of Hab, where a third of King Baldwin II's knights left a battle to go and lay siege to a castle, we can see that some knightly commanders clearly had minds of their own. Therefore it was not only training that made a line charge possible, but also communication and the relationship between the commanders involved. Communication is also important when wheeling the line, that is turning it left or right. This is a specific skill because the horses on the inside of a wheel need to move far slower than those on the outside to maintain the line. Well socialised horses have no problem riding close to others, but some nervous or dominant horses need to ride next to other horses for a long time before they become comfortable doing so. All these difficulties and challenges mean that charging in a line is not the simple manoeuvre modern films can make it look like.

There was another formation that addressed some of these difficulties, and that was the wedge. This required similar training but meant that a single group could lead it and the knights behind the point of the wedge only had to follow those in front of them. This formation gave mounted knights the ability to punch holes in the middle of enemy armies and cause serious disruption, the panic caused by which could trigger a general rout. One example of the wedge was at the Battle of Tannenburg in 1410, where it was used by the Christians in an attempt to kill the enemy commander.[86] When recounting the Battle of Bouvines in 1214, both the *Marchiennes Account*[87] and Roger of Wendover[88] use the word 'penetrating', when referring to knightly charges into enemy armies and ranks. Roger of Wendover described the Imperial charge as being so forceful that it very nearly reached the King of France. We do not know if wedge formations were used at Bouvines but pre-plate armour knights were able to crunch into opponents in a serious enough way that they burst through enemy armies. Multiple examples of this can be found in the historical record but the most impressive is probably that of the famous French knight Boucicaut, who during the Battle of Nicopolis managed to charge all the way through the Turkish army by himself. Not only that, but having achieved this feat of arms he turned around and ploughed back through them a second time in order to reach his own side.[89]

This series of evidence challenges the theory that a formation of knights would not have charged spear-wielding infantry from an academic perspective. A cantering horse will knock over one man without noticing, as I have seen and can be found online, and only the deepest formations would have actually stopped charging horses. This is why later pike formations had such a great number of ranks, but a medieval army was not always deeper than a few ranks.[90,91] At the Battle of Verneuil, English men-at-arms reportedly threw themselves to the floor to avoid being knocked over by the cavalry attacking them.[92] Consciously choosing to be trampled by horses meant that the prospect of standing and taking the charge must have been even worse.

Knights did not always have to attack in a particular formation to achieve victory however, sometimes it was speed and aggression that won the day. At the Battle of Patay in 1429, less than 200 French knights managed to rout 500 English longbowmen by attacking them so quickly that the archers couldn't fire effectively upon them. They then, through force of action, charged straight at the rest of the English army, and destroyed it.[93] This was a devastating defeat for the English, losing more than 2,000 men, and needs to be balanced against Agincourt when considering the effectiveness of the mounted knight. A few years later, the French leader of this attack, La Hire, used another surprise and highly aggressive cavalry charge to defeat an English army under the Earl of Arundel. In a sign of things to come, Arundel was mortally wounded by an early type cannon, but the encounter had been won by a heavy cavalry charge.[94] Whatever formation was employed in this attack, the successful result was owed to years of training. The best record of training exercises we have come from the ordinance of 1473, written for the armies of Charles the Bold of Burgundy. This ordinance commanded the captains of squadrons to train in part or full armour whenever they could, including to, 'practise charging with the lance, keeping in close formation while charging, to charge briskly'.[95] The men-at-arms also were to train with their missile troops and pikemen, in effect building a combined-arms army that was well drilled. It should be noted that this army was defeated by the Swiss at the Battle of Grandson in 1476, but it does show that by the late fifteenth century training took place in a standardised and logical manner.

Endurance

A horse in the wild can walk anywhere from seven to thirty miles a day grazing,[96] and this walking helps them to build up respectable muscle mass. A horse kept in a paddock will walk considerably less distance per day, but a horse permanently stabled will gain exercise only when humans are working them. This very fundamental difference in how horses could be kept in the middle ages meant that some horses were going to be fitter than others. However, all healthy horses are capable of walking great distances, with or without a rider on them. In 2016 seven horses rode from York to the Hastings Battlefield to commemorate King Harold's fateful march in 1066. These horses were mostly of a medieval size, and ranged from fit to newly backed, and they all completed twenty miles of walking a day for three weeks without a single medical issue, or even muscle soreness.

This rather small experiment can be compared against modern endurance riding where a 100-mile course can be completed in less than fifteen hours. It is interesting that in the early twentieth century, US cavalry units could do the same thing but with a specified payload of 150kg.[97] This is 30kg more than an averagely built man (me) and his full harness of armour weighs, and shows that US cavalry actually expected their horses to carry more weight than a medieval knight did. Interestingly, a set of horse armour could weigh in the region of 30kg and this would bring the weight to equal that of the US cavalry expectation. A fascinating additional point made is that for US cavalry mounts, they 'must not exceed 15.2 in height'.[98] This height is the average height of a traditional Spanish or Arab horse, and shows that in 1917 the requirements for combat horses had not changed since the time of the mounted knight. The American cavalry arrived at a 20 per cent rule for weight to be carried by a horse, that is that a horse can carry 20 per cent of its own weight, although it is acknowledged that this is a rough guide because of the numerous factors involved. This includes the natural strength of the horse, its training and, most importantly, how good the rider is. A rider of average weight that bounces up and down on the saddle will do more damage than a heavy rider who can move smoothly with the horse.

The mounted knights would usually have fallen into the latter category of better riders, and would certainly have tried to have the best horses possible because for them it was a matter of life and death. They explored ways to improve their horses' health and to avoid damaging them in the first place. The ancient development of a saddle to lift a horseman up from the actual spine of the horse was the first step in this, and saddle development improved to spread weight around the horse's back, and avoid overloading the most vulnerable parts of their bodies. The technologically advanced medieval saddles increased the distance knights could ride in one go, and for how many days in a row they could do it. In the event of actual campaigns, however, it was not the speed or range of ridden horses that limited movements, but the baggage or artillery trains. The medieval horse was a beast of burden, and they were not necessarily expected to reach a healthy retirement at the end of their working lives. In archaeological records there are numerous finds of fused vertebrae in horses going back to before the Norman Conquest,[99] and it is likely that some horses were overused. Mounted knights were aware of the abilities of their horses and there are many depictions in art of them riding in less than full armour. Indeed, even those who could afford to fully armour both themselves and their horses would not ride around all the time with it, due to the weight and hassle of attaching, removing and keeping it all clean.

The Horse as a Symbol

The horse was as close to a knight as an animal could possibly be, so close that when someone wanted to embarrass or harm a knight but did not dare to, they sometimes harmed his horse. Cutting the tail off a horse was considered a terrible thing to happen and reflected on its owner.[100] The owner of a fine proud horse was lauded as much as the owner of a horse with a cut tail was whispered about disparagingly. A horse whose tail was cut off in battle was considered damaged enough to have compensation paid for it under a Spanish code,[101] so that the knight did not have to put up with others staring at his horse and knowing how the tail had been lost. This was an attack on the masculinity of a knight but could also be done to make a point.

Thomas Becket, Archbishop of Canterbury, suffered the tails of his horses being cut off in a campaign of terror waged a few days before he was murdered. His assailants also stole his hunting hounds and killed some of the deer on his lands. They were attacking the part of Beckett that was still a warrior in an attempt to emasculate him.[102] Beckett, who had unhorsed many an opponent in battle before he became archbishop, had afterwards maintained many of the pursuits of knighthood, such as riding and hunting. Those who cut the tail off his horse were seeking to make a point that Beckett should change his ways, but Beckett was angry enough about it to excommunicate those involved. The only thing worse than docking the tail of his horse was to hurt Beckett himself, and it is likely that in reality no one was too surprised when this happened fatally a few days later. If a man of the church was affected by the insult of tail docking, one can only imagine the effect on an active knight. The owner of a modern Rolls-Royce car who sees the hood ornament has been snapped off is probably a pretty close analogy. It wasn't just the tail that could be cut off to insult the owner however, the ears of horses could be cut off too. Ears were bizarrely thought to be the source of the powers of procreation, and this insult reflected back onto the knightly owner.[103] Incidentally, this is why criminals often had their ears mutilated during the medieval period.

From these lows, however, come the highs to which a horse can take its rider. If a man can master horsemanship he has learnt the skills to command other men, an army, a country, or indeed an empire. For example, the Duke of Wellington of Waterloo fame went to France to learn Equitation when he was a young man and this taught him many things that would later make him a successful military leader.[104] It is not possible to make a horse obey by lying to it, or pretending that you know what you are doing. Riding horses is an activity that can humble the mightiest of political leaders; indeed there is no hiding behind bluster and pretty words when a horse misbehaves and you cannot do anything about it. The horse of the mounted knight, however, was by definition required in order to raise him up to greatness. The humble horse, an animal which really only needs the company of other horses and a constant supply of food and drink to be content, was harnessed by humanity and turned into a weapon of war. This is both a monumental achievement and a tragedy. That man could pour so much effort into taming, training and maintaining horses for war shows the importance they had in the medieval world. In a time when kings were usually suffering from cash flow issues, such vast expenses would not have been invested had they not worked. Horses carried the Normans to the Conquest of England, and took crusaders to the walls of Jerusalem. The great achievements of the knights were the achievements of their horses too, and the very fact that a prey animal could be convinced to willingly take part in battles is testament to the intelligence and tact of medieval horsemen. The merging of horse and man to the point where they were a single entity was the biggest factor in the rise of the mounted knight. This partnership is what those of us who ride every day are in search of, the horse comes first for us as it did for the medieval knight, one of whom summarised the relationship by writing, 'the knowledgeable knight understands his horse's needs'.[105]

Author's Note

Horses are animals with as great a range of personalities as humans. Within an army of a thousand warhorses, there would have been a myriad of different temperaments, inclinations, likes and dislikes that the humans looking after them would have had to deal with. The nuance of the horse world is lost when we see them on television and at the cinema, where they are usually just there to look pretty, and almost never exhibit any sign of intelligence. They stand still or ride around, but rarely are they part of the story, which of course they were. The character of some horses makes them memorable, and medieval people must have had the same feelings for their horses as we do today.

Horses were not just the backdrop of history, often they were at the forefront. For example, it is a staged horse fight between two men's horses that kicks off the action in the most famous of the medieval Icelandic Sagas, Egils Saga.[106] Likewise, William the Conqueror perished because of a horse related accident, and the death of such a man was quite an important moment in history. Additionally, the philosopher Montaigne mentioned how he chose a good but 'not very strong' horse to ride, a choice he regretted when it was knocked over by another horse and he was sent flying from the saddle.[107]

Montaigne knew the character of his horses, and I cannot help think that this was typical of knights across the medieval period. Each horse has a quirk, and at our stable yard there are some genuine personalities. For example, we have Bento, the shark-horse, who will decide he doesn't like a certain person, and then try every strategy to annoy them. If his chosen victim stands next to him, Bento will look down at their feet, register their position, then look away. Then quickly he will stand on their toes, knowing that by looking away people will think his strike was an accident. His selected victims are always adults, and this shark-horse will happily let children near him and will never acknowledge their existence.

Next we have Coralito, a horse who is very much at the bottom of the herd pecking order, but if another horse is on the other side of a fence line, he suddenly acts the tough guy, and to look at him you would think him the herd stallion. The opposite of him is Perry the Irish Draught, a horse of large stature who will always go over or through an object in front of him, but has never, ever, gone around one. There was one horse even more bullish than Perry, and that was Tejano, who when riding would lock-on to people on the ground near him and try to walk into them, quite a useful trait on a battlefield. Once I was riding him down the road and met my father who was on foot. Tejano puffed his chest out and started to walk – of his own accord – straight at him. My father, with a history in dairy farming, was no stranger to livestock, but he was made to feel intimidated, and was quite sure Tejano wanted to flatten him. A less useful trait belongs to the world's itchiest horse, Neville. His entire life seems to revolve around finding something good to itch his neck on, which is fine if that is a fencepost. It is less fine, however, when it is the cable holding an electricity pylon steady, and he itches it so vigorously that the pylon actually explodes. Needless to say Neville is now kept away from anything his itching can break. His best, literally inseparable, friend is Esteban, a horse who will joust against armoured knights happily, enduring the clanking of armour on top of him as if he didn't notice it. However, if an armoured man walks on foot within half a mile of him, his eyes will widen and he will snort like a dragon, for inexplicably this is different to a knight on his back.

The elder statesman of the group is Charlie, who will do anything you ask him to, except for working with birds of prey, which he does not trust, and being in sight of mules, whose existence he simply cannot comprehend. Lastly there is young Squire, a horse I bought because of his name, who I am quite sure has got himself confused with a dog. He cannot keep his nose out of anything, but if I want to fetch him out of his field, all I need to do is stand by the gate, raise my hand up, and shout his name. From 200 metres away, this giant yellow-coloured horse-dog will bound across the field as fast as his ungainly legs will carry him, slamming to a halt almost on my toes. He will follow you around wherever you go, to the point where it is annoying, but he will never, ever, leave your side.

Chapter Six

Age of Chivalry

Early Martial Chivalry

Early chivalry morphed out of those ancient warrior cultures which prized loyalty and prowess in combat above all else. These characteristics are usually traced back to pre-Roman Germanic peoples, and although this is true, it is also true of almost everyone else who was around at the same time. The mounted knight did emerge from these Germanic origins, via the Germanic Franks, where loyalty was stressed. Prowess is one thing, and stories of it abound, but it is sometimes hard to find strong evidence of loyalty among the top Frankish nobles and royalty during the more turbulent periods of their history. On the other hand, the actual fighting men appear to have remained loyal to their leaders even if those leaders often intrigued between themselves. This legacy of loyalty was cultivated in the groups of young men learning how to fight together that existed from ancient times. Loyalty to them came naturally.[1]

The communal experience of learning to fight and ride as a group, over many years, cemented warriors together, be it in tribes fighting the Romans, or Norman knights invading England. These young men, fuelled by testosterone and a culture of glory and fame, competed to impress each other, to be the strongest, the fastest or the bravest. Encouraged by their elders in this, these youths became fighting men who would not lightly abandon each other in a crisis, thus demonstrating the properties of professional warriors. The social fabric in which these warriors found themselves embedded can be called martial chivalry, at least once the warriors mounted horses. The very word means horsemanship and derives from *chevalerie* which originally meant a body of horsemen.[2] In the beginning then, chivalry could be described as being 'the way of the mounted warrior', in the way that the Japanese *bushido* also means the way of the warrior. This martial chivalry in the early medieval period initially could be seen as a framework for training mounted warriors, in both the physical and mental skills they needed for their occupation. This included attitude, and one of the most important mental attributes required was that of toughness, that is the ability to take physical punishment and suffer discomforts. Constant training and hunting helped to foster these traits, but life on campaign would still offer unique challenges, such as sleeping in armour when attack was feared.[3]

Once a campaign reached the point of action however, a range of attitudes would help the mounted knight to achieve the high prowess that he craved. One helpful attitude was a contempt for their own mortality. The medieval attitude of *Contemptus mundi*, or 'contempt for the world'[4] referred to an ambivalence about secular or religious matters, essentially because life is transitory. Mounted knights who held their own safety in contempt would be much more committed to violent action than others who were not, and therefore more likely to fight their way to success. Importantly, it always paid to avoid contempt for the enemy because, as the British Military Journal in 1804 recognised, that would inevitably lead to underestimation and defeat.[5] However, a certain personal contempt for danger is what a mounted knight needed in order to mount risky direct attacks on horseback. Thus a level of indifference to personal pain, and also suffering in general, was included within chivalric expectations.

Suffering was part and parcel of wearing armour, and it was also part and parcel of being a Christian, a commonality that indirectly sanctified the sword. These expectations and attitudes were communicated to young knights through the powerful medium of narrative. Even in the early days, the myths and legends of the even more distant and dimly lit past were firmly embedded in the cultural fabric of the Franks. This literal backstory was coupled with a set of current expectations placed on them by the whole of society. They were expected to fight, and indeed in the formative years of chivalry, warfare was seen as a good thing.[6] Going to war both maintained society by preserving it from enemies, and brought wealth to it. It had the additional benefit of keeping young men somewhat out of trouble, at least during the summer months which were the main campaigning season. The winter was the time of peace, a time often occupied in the early medieval world by just trying to stay alive. We must then understand that chivalry was forged in an era when to fight was to be good.

The peace movements that came after the year 1000 first challenged, and then influenced, chivalry, but at the beginning, knights certainly thought their way of life was a good one. The men who lived in these groups developed a shared loyalty, partly because they shared a way of life, and this bond was an important part of chivalric culture. The ruling class were a subset of this warrior group and they had extra expectations on top of these, including a certain kind of generosity. This *largesse* is the same as was lauded in the Icelandic Sagas, where chieftains are known as ring-givers, giving expensive arm rings to followers as rewards.[7] A Frankish lord giving money to his followers was doing so in order to increase the loyalty of knights and men-at-arms, something which resulted naturally from the practice of going to war. This fed into the expectation of good rule, and rulers were expected to act in the interest of their people, to protect them.

Old Germanic culture has a history of ejecting leaders who no longer are doing the business; indeed the famous Arminius, who vanquished the Romans at the Battle of Teutoburg Forest, was later assassinated and replaced.[8] Competence was valued more than lineage, which was why leaders were often elected to power rather than born to it. When mounted knights later became landowners themselves, the expectation of good rule was still there, but the penalties of not doing so became much less severe. In this way, the rules of the nobility over time trickled down to the mounted knights throughout the medieval period. These expectations, along with the perennial ones of honouring oaths and being honest (at least superficially) merged together by the twelfth century into the concept of the *preudomme*.[9] Meaning a prudent, wise and independent man, this term is often explained by calling upon the career of William Marshal. Described as the, 'best knight that ever lived,'[10] by a thirteenth-century Archbishop of Canterbury, he became a medieval role model. William was knighted in 1166 and was active until his death in 1219, by which time he had created a legend. His prowess in combat was unparalleled, supposedly once capturing over 100 knights in tournaments in a single year, and even killing the future Richard the Lionheart's horse from under him when the then young prince rebelled against his father's control. He became an exemplar for chivalry because he was even more famed for his loyalty than his military abilities, serving a succession of kings even when their cause was a losing one, or clearly a bad one in the case of King John. By not wavering in his support for King John, and steadfastly remaining loyal to the office of the crown, he created a reputation for unbreakable loyalty.

William's abilities at court, that is his courtliness, might have got off to a shaky start with rumours swirling about accusations of sleeping with Henry II's queen, but William was eventually able to regain his position. By the end of his life he was the most powerful man in the country, the regent of England no less, acting as a guardian for the young Henry III and even fighting off a French invasion at the Battle of Lincoln in 1217. In this battle he led his knights in a charge through the streets of Lincoln to victory, displaying military prowess even when today he would be a pensioner. He was 69 years old. William was not just the ideal mounted knight, but also the ideal *preudomme*, judging by the manner in which he actively pressed his own interests. He secured for himself a colossally rich bride to marry, and created a name for himself that he could pass down to his offspring. This relentless ambition was the driving force behind everything he did, and that was compatible with the image of a *preudomme*.

Acting in a knight's own interest was expected, and indeed sensible. William was active in the time when chivalry was still forming into its true medieval state, and this overt selfishness would start to fall out of favour. For example, he once robbed a runaway clerk on the road,[11] under a very dubious guise of justice, but this event was included in his biography, an account written only to glorify William as a great man. Later chivalry would probably have taken a dimmer view of his actions, and the world had changed even during his lifetime. The courtliness and people skills William deployed in order to progress up the social ladder became more important, for example, more intelligent knights started to be sent off on diplomatic missions to other kingdoms. This diversification of a knight's duties was a sign of things to come, abilities that we would now describe as soft skills were being added to a growing list of things that knights were supposed to be good at. In one sense they were growing up.

Religion

The first Frankish noble warriors who had converted to Christianity merged their new religion with old Germanic traditions, creating a type of religion that was not quite the same as that followed by the monks in their monasteries. The early knights lived dangerous, brutal and sometimes short lives that chimed more with the death and destruction gleefully described in the Old Testament, than the pacifistic New Testament. They were most certainly God fearing Christians, but their experience of the world was such that their Christianity did not turn the other cheek. Before the First Crusade, in the period where warfare was changing from good to bad, the church had employed means to lower the level of violence in the world. In AD 989 the 'Peace of God',[12] was announced which aimed to stop knights in West Francia attacking church property or people, as well as peasants. This attempt to limit the victims of fighting to combatants seems advanced for its time, and indeed it never quite worked. Knights did eventually stop attacking church property, usually, but the peasant class never fully benefited from the Peace of God. Forty years later the 'Truce of God' was proclaimed in order to impose truces between opponents on Sundays and certain other religiously important dates in the calendar. This was more successful and indeed the list of prohibited dates kept being expanded.[13]

One reliable indicator of its impact is that tournaments were scheduled for the middle of the week, which respected the Truce. The extent to which these moderating efforts were adhered to is difficult to know, and was likely mixed at best. With eleventh-century Christian Europe being a very Christian Europe indeed, some knight will have taken notice. Catholicism was not just embedded in culture, it *was* the culture, or at least most of it. On the periphery of life, pushed aside by church teaching, at least for most people for much of the year, was warfare. The peaceful teachings of Christ, and the list of martyrs who had died defending the faith while offering no violent resistance, did not match up with the lifestyle of the knights fighting to keep pagan enemies out of Europe. If they followed pacifist religious dogma to the letter, the knights should have hung their swords up and let pagan outsiders kill them, but in reality neither the knights nor the church wanted that to happen. Despite this, knights remained pious, perhaps sometimes uneasily, and the church exerted an influence in how often, and who, they fought, and those ideas over time infused into chivalry. The worthy (churchmen) and the weak (peasants) should ideally be protected.[14]

This concept was harnessed fully by Pope Urban II when he called for the First Crusade. By giving Christian knights something to do that was compatible with their religion, Urban II managed to ingrain it deeper into the psyche of the knights. Religion was no longer just a thing to be respected, but the very reason the knights should fight in the first place. This revolution thrust Christianity to the forefront of chivalry, a position that it would keep forever. Being a chivalric knight from 1095 onwards meant fighting *for* the church, and until the knight left the battlefield centuries later, he would believe he did so for God. Out of the seemingly miraculous success of the First Crusade, chivalry became forever entwined with the Cross, and the mounted knight became to some extent, a religious warrior. Knightly Orders such as the Templars and Hospitallers took this symbiosis to its extreme, and differentiated themselves from secular knights by their emphasis on poverty, prayer and plainness in all things. This removal of worldly distractions made them better warriors, in the way that religious fanaticism usually makes soldiers fight harder, and their knights were truly elite. However, these orders really fell outside the framework of chivalry and instead lived within the framework of the church. They had no courtly tradition of love, poetry or romance literature, and nor did they enter the tournament field. The Templars and their ilk were mounted knights, and the very best of those, but they were not chivalric at all.[15] Secular knights may have admired their prowess, but at the same time many probably resented their wealth and influence within Europe. The proof of this might be that the religious orders did not leave a lasting mark on chivalry after they had faded away.

Once the Holy Land had been lost for good in 1291, chivalry's religious focus shifted to a characteristically paradoxical mix of warrior saints and the Virgin Mary.[16] As early as the sixth century, Christian doctrine had split womanhood in two, with Mary Magdalene metaphorically representing what the men of the church didn't like about women, namely their sexuality. On the flip side of this, the Virgin Mary was everything a medieval woman was supposed to be, namely pure. Mary's achievement was giving birth, rather than any pious or humane action, and the male medieval church and male society as a whole saw childbirth as the purpose of women.[17] Perhaps surprisingly to us, a cult of the Virgin grew within chivalry, and even kings of England visited out of the way shrines to Mary, such as at Walsingham in Norfolk.[18] What the wives of knights thought as their husbands worshipped a supposedly perfect woman, we can only guess. This devotion was most likely a genuine one, but that does not mean the church and the institution of knighthood were ever on the best of terms. For example, in 1130 the Second Lateran Council banned the tournaments which were the favourite blockbuster events of the knightly calendar, a move many knights will have disapproved of.[19] The church wanted to use the knights to defend Christendom, but at the same time wanted them to stop fighting each other, in a genuine effort to save their souls. They perhaps failed to appreciate the role in the tournament in maintaining fighting ability, and this is just one example of the complicated interplay between chivalry and Christianity. The church also forbade Christian burials to tournament goers, which although must have been concerning for many knights, did not appear to put a dent in tournament activities.

The Pope gave up in 1316,[20] and tournaments became legal again. The legalisation had something to do with the fact that tournaments were fertile ground for crusade recruitment, indeed sometimes whole swathes of participants of certain tournaments had taken the cross en masse. The fact that even during the periods when the church had banned tournaments, the knights participating in them took mass on the morning of the main event and showed their piety, if not their adherence, to the church as a governing body.[21] To Charny, our greatest reference to fourteenth-century chivalry, chivalry and religion were one, a 'specifically chivalric piety.'[22] Generally, however, the Christian faith of the mounted knight gave him the confidence to go into battle knowing his soul would be safe, provided at least that he had led a life that followed Christian and chivalric expectations. The relationship between religion and the warrior class should not be seen as a battle between psalm and sword, rather an intertwining mix of argument and compromise that actually strengthened the institution of knighthood.

Troubadours & The Romances

In a sense, the oldest literature relevant to chivalry is the so called *Matter of Rome*.[23] This term covers a group of works which included the military heroes of Julius Caesar, Alexander the Great and the Trojan Wars of

Greek mythology. Although ancient in setting, the medieval spin on these classical warriors was to turn them into knights who had the same values as their early medieval contemporaries. We have seen how Rome existed as a memory in Frankish Europe, leaving both a legacy in stone as well as in organisation, but it also lingered in the world of fables and legends. Medieval people looked backwards for inspiration because ancient Rome and Greece loomed up behind them as cultural giants to aspire to. Their ideals were those that medieval thinkers tried to live up to; indeed, one of the forces behind chivalry was that of the ancient stories of Alexander, Caesar, and many others. The *Matter of Rome* was widely read from twelfth century onwards, and out of it models of behaviour persisted to the fifteenth century, despite the fact that the heroes were pagans, and therefore couldn't, by Christian definition, be perfect.[24] This religious issue meant that although influential, the *Matter of Rome* was not as important to chivalry as later literature.

Despite that, knights could take from the stories a secular model that they wanted to follow. For example, the focus on constant training and maintaining physical strength can be found from as long ago as Plato and Aristotle. The extreme value placed on this by knights is exemplified by the French hero Boucicaut, who famously boasted he could somersault in his armour and climb up the inside of a ladder using only his hands. Boucicaut may have been at the extreme end of the chivalric fitness fad, but his claims are not all that outlandish considering the time he put into physical training.[25] He was also known as a stern disciplinarian, and saw war as a serious enterprise rather than a display of chivalry. In one of chivalry's contradictions, by putting professionalism above more romantic or egoistical urges, Boucicaut was still being chivalric. The virtue of prowess extended to both leadership and success, as demonstrated by Caesar, who was displaying absolutely no loyalty whatsoever when he crossed the Rubicon, and yet was a person who medieval knights greatly admired. Boucicaut's contemporary, Bertrand de Guesclin, was known for using hit and run tactics, retreating from pitched battles, and generally not leading his men in a normal chivalric manner. However, he managed to recover almost all of the land lost after the French disasters at Crécy and Poitiers by this method, and although it might have been ugly, it was successful.[26,27] We can read into this the continuing importance of prowess above all else within chivalry, regardless of whatever other layers were added in the high middle ages. One rather suspects Caesar would have approved.

Following on from the *Matter of Rome* was the *Matter of France*, which was largely concerned with the great Charlemagne and his Carolingian empire. Charlemagne was seen as the most Christian leader of all, and was held up as the very paragon of chivalry. Indeed his twelve paladins, or knights, are very similar to Arthur's knights, and the adventures that befall them are of the same vein. The most famous of these stories concerns the paladin Roland, who in real life was killed at the Battle of Roncevaux Pass in Spain in the eighth century.[28] This event became a legend in the *Song of Roland*, where the hero leads the rearguard of Charlemagne's army in a heroic and doomed last stand to give the bulk of the army time to escape an ambush. Roland's death immortalised him in French history as well as mythology, and his loyalty and prowess set an example for later medieval knights to follow. The story was so powerful that during the Battle of Hastings, the Norman Taillefer supposedly sang the *Song of Roland* in front of the English to taunt them while, obviously, juggling swords. He killed one English champion sent out to silence him, before channelling his inner Roland by spurring his horse into the enemy in a heroic and obviously fatal bid for everlasting glory. Which, if the story is true, he certainly achieved.[29]

That the *Matter of France* was in every knight's memory and thoughts is clear, and the influence of such stories drove the medieval Frenchman to emulate their heroes, although admittedly most did not go quite as far as Taillefer. Chivalry was already formed as a martial secular concept in these stories, and as usual prowess was a basic requirement of knighthood, alongside the familiar traits of loyalty, courage and honour, which were also held up as ideals to be venerated. Brotherhood, both knightly and Christian, was another theme which was especially potent in stories of a time, when the Frankish empire was battling against non-Christian enemies in almost every direction. The implicit religiosity of the *Matter of France* elevated it in relevance and importance over the *Matter of Rome* and baked Christianity into the DNA of the knight. One consequence of the *Matter of France* of which every mounted knight was probably aware, was that of the magical horse called Bayard. This horse could speak to men and was able to magically stretch his back in order to carry as many riders as he needed to. Bayard gave his name to the term 'bay', which refers to a reddish-brown colour of horse that is still used by equestrians today.

Back in the late eleventh century in southern France, however, a form of song or poetry evolved that became a style known as the troubadour tradition. The two main themes were chivalry and courtly love, which by being mixed together, created a new phenomenon. Some songs were humorous and satirical and therefore became very popular very quickly, eventually spreading from France into Spain, Italy and Germany.[30] Importantly, these songs were performed live at court for entertainment, and played a role in the development of the courtly culture associated with chivalry. The subjects of women and love were examined in these songs, and the idea of love between a man and women eclipsed that of simple sexual desire, transcending into an idealised spiritual perfection. This was a revolutionary concept for a nobility who rarely married for love, and was also heretical to many within the church.[31] The strong sense of individualism that courtly love implies also appealed to knights and served to make them even more individualistic. The idea that a noble woman would only give her love to a man who had to be pure of heart and capable of courtly love, is the one that sits behind the image of chivalry we have today, fuelled by the concept of the wandering knight. For medieval knights this all meant that although they had to be strong, brutal and violent on campaign, at court they needed to be polite, refined and gentle. This is where the later concept of a 'gentleman' began, and the term 'courtesy' evolved slowly to describe it.

Although none of this was put into place in order to temper or civilise knights, it was the unintended long term effect. Alongside these songs and poems was a set of prose works that has left a huge literary impact, the so called romance literature of the middle ages. This genre evolved out of medieval epics such as the *Song of Roland* and added new elements, including the newly fashionable courtly love. Stories often included knights rescuing ladies from monsters, and the adventures of errant knights roaming the world in search of glory and the approval of a certain unattainable woman.[32] These quintessential medieval themes have survived the passing of centuries to provide us with a distorted image of what the medieval world was like, much as would be gained by learning about the modern world solely from Hollywood films. This enduring medieval legacy happened because of the popularity of the romances, and this was in turn because of the language they were written in. This is important because they were not written in Latin, which meant that ordinary people could read them in their own language. As a result, the romances spread to England, Spain, Germany and beyond, and when combined with more serious works such as the biography of William Marshal, made up a broad selection of the material available to the medieval reader. Chivalry and literature formed a potent combination, influencing and inspiring each other in equal measure, and serving to lift the knight above his actions in war.

The historical nature of the stories lodged deep within the medieval mindset, and stuck there. As Johan Huizinga wrote, next to religion it was from the past that sprung, 'the strongest of the ideas that filled the minds and the hearts of those men'.[33] The golden age of chivalric literature in England occurred when the country was riding a wave of triumphant military success following the fourteenth-century victories at Sluys, Crécy, Poitiers and Najera. National pride[34] was a lens through which the knightly class was viewed after winning those victories, and it led to a flourishing of romances and chivalric works. Patronage of literature also increased throughout this period, but not all of that came as might be expected, from wealthy men. They may have been a more hidden driving force, but the patronage of women helped to further spread the popularity of romances. A few noblewomen lived in enough luxury that they could read for hours each day,[35] but what were those women reading? Often they read on religious matters, but probably more often they read the most exciting things they could get their hands on, and that was the romances, the most popular of which were those pertaining to King Arthur.

Arthur

The idea of King Arthur and the knights of the round table are as iconic as any historical story has ever been. Almost anyone knows about the sword in the stone, Merlin or Lancelot the knight, and every now and again somebody publishes a new theory about who Arthur really was. The medieval world had no such worries about the authenticity of Arthur, who probably first appeared in the records as Arthur the War Duke in the ninth-century *Historia Brittonum*, which relates to the history of the Britons.[36] Someone who possibly read it was the eleventh-century writer Geoffrey of Monmouth. When he later wrote *The History of the Kings of Britain*, Geoffrey of Monmouth set in motion an unstoppable Arthurian avalanche. Geoffrey was probably born in Wales, and Arthur was a Briton who fought the Saxons, which made him a natural hero to the Welsh, and furthermore, according to Geoffrey, he never actually died, instead leaving only for the island of Avalon. From the perspective of medieval England this made Arthur effectively Welsh, and his arch enemies the Saxons were, inconveniently, the English themselves. The political problem was that the story suggested he would return to aid the Britons, which was obviously counter to the interests of the English when, for example, they were actually fighting the Welsh during Edward I's reign.[37]

Most Englishmen seemed able to forget that Arthur was a Britannic hero fighting the English, and were able to perform the required mental gymnastics to adopt him as their own. The unavoidable conclusion of Geoffrey's book, however, was that the English were the villains, and some have argued that he did it on purpose. Monmouth drew on a knowledge of Welsh legends, mythology and folk stories, and once his work had gone back to Wales, Welsh versions of Arthur appeared, including in the *Mabinogion* stories.[38] In the twelfth, and especially thirteenth century, within England the Welsh were viewed extraordinarily badly, but the story enjoyed wild popularity despite coming effectively out of Wales. It was during this period of new popularity that another set of stories came out that really pushed the Arthurian tales into a full-blown legend. These spin-offs added the trimmings of swords in stones, Merlin, and Arthur's death, vastly expanding on the original stories. By the late twelfth century, Chrétien de Troyes had written the first narrative romances, specifically books on Lancelot as well as *Perceval, The Story of the Grail*, and the legend of Arthur grew yet more.[39] Even at the time some were sceptical of Arthur's historical basis, and some like William of Newburgh wrote around the time of publication that everything Geoffrey had written about Arthur was nonsense,[40] but almost everyone else was convinced. In France the tales were also a great hit, and parents started to call their children Lancelot and other Arthurian names, a trend which continued for centuries.[41]

That fashion didn't cross the channel despite the Arthur-mania that swept over England, and the fact that, apparently, his body had been found there. Within a suspiciously short time after Chrétien's Arthurian works began circulating, the monks of Glastonbury Abbey were given a suggestion from King Henry II that they should have a look for the tomb of Arthur. Two skeletons were duly dug up, along with a helpful inscription on a lead cross that conveniently identified them as Arthur and Guinevere.[42] The boost this gave to the cult of Arthur also boosted chivalry in England in general, and many knights probably thought of themselves within Arthurian terms. Henry II's cunning plan to prove Arthur was dead was given far less heed in Wales than in England however; indeed, in 1278 Edward I went so far as to rebury the bones to try to show the Welsh that Arthur was not coming back to help them. Edward was not trying to bury the myth though, only the prospect of Arthur's return from Avalon to finish the job he'd started against the Saxon English. Edward and his wife were obsessed with all things Arthur, and Edward staged round table tournaments, including one in 1284 where both the defenders and challengers took up Arthurian roles. Knights taking on such personas of Arthurian characters jousted one at a time with each other in elaborate contests that were more like theatre shows played out on a jousting field. Mounted knights kept up their characters during the evening festivities, and in this way they actually lived the Arthurian romances. The extent to which the stories and myths were embedded into the very fabric of knighthood cannot be understated. The stories might not have all been based on true history, but they influenced how their readers acted, and in that sense they morphed the future behaviour of knights in a self fulfilling prophecy.

Arthurianism peaked in England during the reign of Edward III, when the monarch built a huge Round Table building to house 300 knights. Edward had just instigated the Hundred Years War, and was looking to harness Arthur as a means of binding his elite fighting forces to his cause. He deliberately made an oath to re-establish the Round Table, setting himself up as a new Arthur, in the hope his people would join in enthusiastically. Politically this made sense because Arthur had also happened to be the King of France, the very title which Edward had started the war to gain.

On a practical level too, knights of the royal court could participate in rich fantasy jousts, although the Arthurian element moved the encounters away from warfare, and into the realm of pageantry. One highly suggestive example of how far these jousts had moved into the world of play is a so-called Jousting Letter, designed to be read aloud at court during the festivities. It implies that the king should deliver as many blows as he can, not just in an actual joust, but alone without knights or squires, on a long cold winter night. What this letter is actually doing is suggesting that Edward should enjoy himself with his wife during the night, and is indeed told if he fails in this, he should appear before his queen with linen hanging from his 'little hook'.[43] This sort of innuendo was loved by the noble classes, and gives us a glimpse of a much more vulgar and joyful side of the middle ages than is usually seen. The pervasive influence of Arthur on the upper classes had taken hold early on, but it was the invention of the printing press and Caxton's publication of Malory's *Morte d'Arthur* in the fifteenth century that gave us Arthur as we know him today. Malory included the full list of events and characters, including the Holy Grail and Tristan and Isolde, in a story full of love, conflict, death, loyalty and betrayal. This blockbuster combination of themes, when presented in printed form, meant now the audience was far, far wider than ever before. The knights and their families who had previously poured over richly decorated manuscripts, now read simple undecorated text in printed books created by an early form of mass production. These cheaper books could be found in many medieval book collections, for example Sir John Paston had the 'Death of King Arthur', and Richard II's tutor had the 'book of romances of King Arthur'.

This was not confined to the British Isles in any way however, and in Italy from the early twelve century, Arthurian themes can be seen on a frieze on the archivolt in the cathedral of Modena.[44] In Spain Arthur was more of a novelty, contrasting sharply to England where he was the most important historical figure who had ever lived. De Gamez sardonically noted in the fifteenth century that a number of Merlin's predictions had been false, although he admitted that some in England had been a bit more accurate.[45] Across Europe, both rich and poor people tended to believe that these stories were all true, and from the perspective of the chivalric knight, it mattered not whether they were wrong. Knights took what they wanted to from the stories, and that included models of behaviour. Arthur usually spared the women and children of his enemies, honoured ransoms and tried to rescue his own captured knights, all things we see real knights doing. Fulfilling vows was of critical importance, as was putting chivalry above power and wealth.

In the Alliterative *Morte Arthure* poem, a character described Arthur as someone who worshipped glory rather than wealth.[46] These virtues were there to be emulated by knights from the birth of the stories, right up to and beyond the fifteenth century, and if one wishes to understand the mounted knight, one should read what he did. Not everything in the stories was virtuous of course, and that applies to the most knightly character of all, Lancelot. Indeed from Chrétien's Lancelot onwards, he is a character who is morally in the wrong by actively coveting Guinevere, and in many versions it is they who are responsible for ultimate wrong, the destruction of the Round Table and the death of Arthur. Arthur actually tries to burn Guinevere in some of the romances,[47] although Lancelot partially redeems himself by coming to the rescue. The complexity of the different versions tells us something about the people who read them too; if stories containing complex emotional strands and conflicting themes had been too much for the audience, they would have faded away into obscurity, instead they were being understood and appreciated. The mounted knight, riding across a field on campaign, was not a simple, crude killing machine. Rather he was, certainly by the fourteenth century, a relatively learned man, able to comprehend complex works of literature and apply moral lessons from them. The non-noble man-at-arms was not necessarily any different, especially once the printing press had spread the tales of Arthur across previously less porous social boundaries. Finally, Arthur contributed to the nation as well as the people within it. His myth is perhaps the foundation myth of Britain, and the tone of the stories helped set the tone of the English people. Lancelot betrayed his king, Arthur died and Camelot fell, as before them Rome and Greece had fallen. Even the *Song of Roland* came out of Charlemagne's failed Spanish campaign, and in all these stories, both true and fictional, the English found a glory in adversity and defeat. While this spirit was certainly applicable when England was not doing so well in the Hundred Years War, which of course it also lost, it could be seen again a little later, on the beaches of Dunkirk in 1940.

The Tournament & Jousting

The Tournament was the ultimate display of prowess in the early and high medieval periods, and the vector that spread chivalry across Europe.

This was possible because, rather like Formula 1 roves around the world today, there was a glamorous tournament circuit that meandered its way across parts of Europe. These international gatherings drew in knights who wanted to make either a fortune or name for themselves, which some, such as William Marshal, certainly did. By 1200 the tournament was a feature from England to Germany, and south at least as far as the Pyrenees, and had reached a mature form that would last for a century.[48] David Crouch has described it as the grandfather of all western sports, and certainly a 'pre-modern sport',[49] and it does have a number of parallels to international motor racing, including the cost, risk and extravagance. For the mounted knight, the tournament was fundamental, and the two concepts were linked at their very core, for one needed the other. On a social level, tournaments served as a peacetime outlet for men trained and mentally prepared to kill. The boiling up of energy and boredom when there was no legitimate outlet could have been a problem, but the tournament served as a release. Participants of tournaments still caused plenty of damage on their way to and from the venues, however, not to mention trampling the crops of peasants unlucky enough to live on the sometimes vast playing areas.

Regardless of the pros and cons of the tournaments themselves however, they certainly cultivated fighting skills and spirit among the knightly ranks of Europe, and honed them into elite mounted warriors. Serious knights like Geoffrey de Charny saw tournaments as a proving ground, and a level to reach before moving on to real war.[50] They also spread the ideals of chivalry, and in the early days, nobles on the periphery of France couldn't get enough of the chivalric themes the tournament brought to their doorsteps. As well as being an education in chivalric values, they would have been hugely exciting and addictive in a world much slower paced and quieter than our own. Mounted knights, trained to fight from horseback, wanted to do the thing they existed to do. To show a mastery over an opponent, to take him captive and receive his horse as a ransom would have felt like winning an Olympic medal – as well as coincidentally being financially beneficial. The search for glory and fame were drivers inherent to the knightly class, but on top of this, most knights probably thought that the tournaments were enjoyable. The adrenaline, the discomfort of the armour, the challenge of their horses, the chance to take heavy blows and come out of the other side strong and fighting, not to mention the chance to actually strike other knights, were all reasons why knights flocked in their droves to tournaments. Theirs was not a safe world where almost everyone reached old age, for death visited frequently and without warning even in times of peace. Additionally, within the framework of chivalry, knights were actively supposed to seek out hardships and danger, and what better place than the tournament to do just that. The benefits of doing so included bonding together those who fought alongside each other, and these were strong bonds, especially because tournaments were not much different to battles. Some of these groups fought together later in real wars, such as the Black Prince, John Chandos and James Audley, and their shared experience on the tournament field improved their performances on campaigns.

The knightly class were not the only ones trying to get involved, however. In England, Richard I specified the entry fees for tournaments by social class, but this only went down to landless knights, and there was no provision for the middle classes to participate in the twelfth century.[51] In Germany, fifty years of tournament pedigree was the entry bar, a bar that obviously excluded anyone new whatsoever from joining in.[52] The Sicily Herald also required proof of four lines of noble descent,[53] so tournaments were an elite sport from the very beginning. This never really changed, despite squires eventually being allowed to compete, and non-noble jousts in urban areas springing up in the Low Countries from 1280.

The need to include these checks in the first place seems a lot like insecurity on the part of the upper classes and ruling nobility. Were they worried that those below them were starting to snap at their heels? The rise of the middle classes meant that successful lawyers and merchants could sometimes afford a harness and a horse, enabling their sons to become men-at-arms, and maybe one day, knights. Non-noble troops had always been present at tournaments however, although not taking part – at least they weren't supposed to, but when politically sensitive tournaments took place, occasionally each side brought along large infantry forces for security, and these events could erupt into real pitched battles. This happened in 1274 when the Burgundians supposedly sent in their infantry at the outset, causing a fight that became known as the Little Battle of Chalon.[54] Their enemies, the English, retaliated by sending in their own infantry, who routed the Burgundians and proceeded to cut the girth straps of the enemy knights, in order to cause them to fall to the ground. It is perhaps little wonder that neither kings nor the church stood in the way of the event that eventually replaced the tournament – the joust.

Initially, jousting began as the warm-up to the tournament, for on the evening or morning before the main event, two knights could arrange to joust against each other, one on one.[55] Young knights made up the majority of these encounters because it was a chance to test themselves without risking capture, or hopefully, serious injury. And that enhanced safety was the whole point; the joust was a fair fight, useful for preparing youngsters, both human and equine, for the tournament proper, but it was also a chance to show off and maybe land a job in the retinue of a great lord. This was possible because everyone could see what happened when two knights clashed, the attention was on them alone. This ran in contrast to the main event, where potentially a few thousand knights would clash at once, where, despite heraldry, clearly no one could notice everything that occurred. The joust, therefore, had the potential to be a more crowd-pleasing event because of its simplicity, proximity to the action, and the lower attention span required. We encounter the same problem when trying to promote our tournaments in the modern day, because jousting is simpler and therefore is the audience favourite. William Marshal, however, looked on the development of jousting with disdain, judging those who preferred jousting to tourneying as unmanly, according to his biographer in 1224.[56] Indeed the opinion of the great Marshal here is in line with de Charny, who also favoured the tournament over the joust, and who likely agreed with William's complaint that jousting was softer, lazier and less worthwhile than fighting in the press of the great melee.

Eventually though, the whole day before the tournament was given over to jousting matches, before Arthurian Round Table jousts began to appear in the middle of the thirteenth century and doomed the tournament proper. The sense of individualism that had always hung around knights was ideally suited to the single combat of jousting, and when these factors were wedded to the stories of Arthur, the tournament had a real problem on its hands. It seems that there was no melee in these Arthurian contests, and that the pageantry of the event was the real focus. The tournament maintained a degree of popularity into the fourteenth century, but during the 1340s it died out in England and France,[57] and the spiritual decline of the mounted knight began. The joust, however, went from strength to strength, as did the festivities that went along with it. For the knights taking part they were still useful in terms of horsemanship and career building, but they did little in the way of training for the brutality of war. Safety features such as the tilt barrier,[58] and specialised heavy jousting armour enhanced the safety of the participants even more, and took the experience further and further from the battlefield. Despite these features, the Monk of St Denis wrote that, 'Wise men disapproved of this combat as unreasonable',[59] but presumably the church found jousting much less unreasonable than the tournament. Geoffrey de Charny's famous quote, 'he who does more, is of greater worth',[60] applied to all deeds of arms, and in his hierarchy of exploits, wars and tournaments were ahead of jousting. Jousting on its own wasn't good enough for him, but it was still a lot better than nothing.

In one sense, the rise of jousting and its slow evolution into a less militaristic and more courtly exercise mirrored the role of the mounted knights themselves. More and more they were transformed from knights into gentlemen, and by the 1590s in Spain, although still jousting, the spectacle had changed in nature. In *Del Justador*, Luis Zapata de Chaves explained that jousting was now a royal festival, largely due to the hassle and cost of putting one on. Many jousters borrowed armour, saddles and horses from other people and did not even ride in their own equipment. This unmistakable sign of decline is clear, even when Luis adds that jousting is still the most splendid type of festival.[61] In a bid to always out-do itself, the pageantry of the joust in the later medieval period mushroomed beyond the point of extravagance, but it also served a need in terms of maintaining social cohesion, and keeping society going. One might think the bill for a modern Olympic opening ceremony is overly extravagant too, but at the same time others enjoy the spectacle and think it worthwhile. This comparison is very much applicable to large jousts or other festive occasions across medieval Europe. At the time when a super-rich class developed, there were people who could afford to stage almost anything it was possible to imagine. A Russian oligarch's super yacht today was an expensive jousting pageant in the medieval world. That said, it had a use, even Christine de Pizan wrote that in order to be able to combat the English, the French knights should hold jousts and tournaments two or three times a year, and that the costs should come from public taxation![62]

Orders of Chivalry

The pinnacle that chivalry reached is epitomised by the numerous Orders of Knighthood that were created across medieval Europe. These secular orders, very different from the religious orders of the Templars and Hospitallers, were exclusive clubs of various sizes, idiosyncratic rituals and bemusing names. They were intensely chivalric, and consciously so, and had as members knights who genuinely believed in the ideals the orders represented. As such, they symbolise the spiritual and moral best of knighthood, but also included within them were the seeds for why the age of chivalry could not last.

The first secular order was the Order of the Sash, which likely originated in 1332 in Spain.[63] King Alfonso XI of Castile was having a loyalty problem with his fighting forces, so he created the Order in the hope of securing the faithfulness of those he admitted into it. As such, the Order was filled with the most distinguished and experienced knights he could find, and the focus of those knights was aimed at battles and tournaments. Unfortunately for Alfonso, most of his knights were killed at Najera in 1367, but the political institution that the Order created had worked. Aware of the Spanish concept, Edward III followed suit and created the Order of the Garter in 1344.[64] Their rules included only leaving England with the king's permission and not being allowed to ever fight on opposing sides to another member. Both of these rules, along with the extreme exclusivity of the Order, which had fewer than thirty members, maintained an intensely close cohesion. This group were the leaders of the elite of the elite, in both social and militaristic terms. Ever calculating, Edward III pushed his own claim to the French throne with the Order's motto, 'Shame on him who thinks evil of it'. Indeed, the Order was created to form a core of trusted and competent military leaders who could prosecute Edward III's war in France. Creating a small group of elite knights had distinctly Arthurian overtones too, and this only served to make the Order more glamorous. An Arthurian Round Table tournament was held at Windsor in 1344 that was probably a celebration of the Order, and every knight in England would have craved membership of this group.

The Order of the Garter was more successful than the Order of the Sash, and survived the medieval period intact. This was partly because it was taken so seriously by its members, indeed matters of honour were of paramount importance. When its members behaved in a way which was deemed unsatisfactory, there were stern repercussions. At the Battle of Patay in 1429, an English army under John Talbot and John Fastolf, some 5,000 strong, set up a defensive position on a ridge, effectively in the same dispositions as the English had used at Agincourt. This time, however, the mounted French men-at-arms of the vanguard charged the archers and devastated them. What followed was a reversal of Agincourt, this time 2,000 Englishmen were killed, and a host of important men taken captive, including John Talbot. However, the only knight who had been mounted during the battle was John Fastolf, and once he'd seen clearly that the day was unrecoverable, he saved himself and left the field. The Order of the Garter promptly stripped him of membership on the charge of cowardice, which was, presumably apart from treason, the worst crime a member could commit. It was not until thirteen years later than Fastolf was able to clear his name and get back into the Order, but the accusation of cowardice would continue to dog him.[65]

As the English had originally copied the Spanish, the French then copied the English. The Order of the Star was formed by King John II of France less than ten years after the Order of the Garter had been created. That paragon of French chivalry, Geoffrey de Charny, was heavily involved, and the enterprise had the effective political goal of kicking the English out of France. Critically, one vow that members were required to take was to never retreat in battle. This vow turned out to be rather ill chosen when the first half of the Order were all killed during an ambush in Brittany,[66] before the second half were finished off at Poitiers three years later in 1356. King John II kept his vow to stand firm, and unlike John Fastolf at Patay, he stayed and fought on until he was captured. The very fact that all the members kept their vow shows how deeply chivalry had soaked into them. Death, and even capture, with the potential for financial ruin that it entailed, were infinitely preferably to survival, if survival meant breaking the vow. De Charny, having literally written the book on chivalry, died clutching the sacred war banner of France at Poitiers, fulfilling completely the ideals he had believed in. By his death he showed the sincerity of his written work, an act which means today we can confidently say that for at least some knights, the higher ideals of chivalry were genuinely kept. How far this extended across knightly society we cannot know, but we find some churchmen writing of the folly of chivalry, while others write of the possibility that a Christian knight could be beneficial for mankind.

Unlike in France where it swelled up from the knights themselves, chivalry was very much a top down concept in England, and especially after Edward III created the Order of the Garter, chivalric values trickled down through the nobility from the person of the king. The problem for the Orders of Knighthood were that, however much they believed in the high ideals they espoused, not everyone was inclined to agree. The benchmark they set fed eventually into our view of chivalry today, and this had led many to judge medieval knights as having failed to act well because of how highly that benchmark was placed. This high standard, probably not really realistic when applied to the struggles of war, meant that chivalry had overreached. The birth and maturing of chivalry had added a sense of honour to warfare for those lucky enough to fall under its umbrella, allowing knights to use conflict as a stage to showcase their own personal prowess. The Orders of Knighthood bloomed in the time when missile weapons and paid foot troops started to appear in greater numbers, and also make a difference on the battlefield, which meant paradoxically they were removing honour from the very battlefields where the Orders were adding it. The winds of change were blowing in favour of these professional footsoldiers, and although just a breeze at first, they were starting to make the Orders of Knighthood look slightly old fashioned.

Reality in Practice

The members of knightly orders may have had a fairly good record in terms of following the principles of chivalry, but what about everyone else? Medieval rulers were aware of Saint Augustine's principle of a Just War,[67] but this was discarded or manipulated whenever necessary, for example when Henry V declared war on France. Warfare was a destructive force, especially for the workers in the fields, who frequently found themselves and their property destroyed by the many raids that characterised the period. Ravaging was a relatively risk free way for an army to degrade the future fighting power of an enemy, and as such was a very sensible military strategy. Morally, we take issue with it today, but by no means was this a problem for the medieval aristocrat, and before we judge them too harshly for that short-sightedness, we should recall some much more recent examples of the tactic. Ravaging areas of land was deliberately done in the American Civil War by cavalry forces, and also by Allied strategic bombing in the Second World War, by four-engined strategic bombers. The idea of denying the enemy resources by destroying them was not against the morality of chivalry, and critically it was effective.

Less morally cloudy is the issue of the phenomenon of ransoming captured enemies. Taking prisoners and not selling them into slavery was an important milestone when it appeared in Europe as part of an embryonic code of behaviour. The combining of the idea of sparing enemies, and the church's insistence that Christians could not take each other as slaves, was perhaps the first step on the road to the Geneva Convention. Building on this, there was an idea that ransoms shouldn't bankrupt those having to pay them, and although maybe just pragmatic, it suggests an element of empathy and civility.[68] As with most chivalric subjects, there is another side to the coin, and sometimes captives were not treated as well as they could have been. The Earl of Pembroke was captured at sea in 1372 by the Spanish, and died on the way home three years later due to reasons pertaining to the poor conditions of his captivity.[69] One other knight imprisoned with him, John Hapreden was made by the king of Castile to fight a duel with a pair of African twins. He managed to kill both of them, but setting prisoners to fight each other was not likely to happen in England or France.[70] The Spanish, as well as the Germans, even garnered a reputation of locking up captured knights in order to force higher ransoms.[71] Richard the Lionheart was first imprisoned in reasonable conditions in Germany, but after insulting his captor was weighed down in chains so heavy that he complained a horse would have been rendered immobile by them. Chivalric considerations, it seemed, only went so far when it came to prisoners; indeed the unchivalrous Swiss generally took no prisoners at all.

Better at least can be said of the conduct of Edward III after some of his non-noble servants had been captured in France. In 1360 he helped to free a number of these men, including a young Geoffrey Chaucer. This also shows that if non-nobles worked for a rich enough patron, the ransom system might just extend down to them if they were useful enough.[72] The usual treatment of low-born people at the sharp end of knightly activities was, however, not particularly good. The charge often levelled at knights was that they would bully, exploit and degrade the peasantry, and from a modern view that is absolutely what they did. Even the Black Prince was (accurately) accused of squeezing his lands for money in England, and certainly everyone in the nobility did their best to limit the rights their peasants had. This elitism was a natural consequence of their wealth and martial skills, they naturally thought they were better than those below them, because by the measures of the time, they were. Chivalry helped to maintain this view by putting prowess above piety, and by the measure of prowess, the common man was almost worthless. Medieval illustrated Bibles contain elaborate scenes of the biblical warfare that fill the Old Testament, and knights were probably more drawn to these scenes of cavalry, which looked like them, charging around and disembowelling the enemies of God, than they were to the story of Jesus. Plenty of nobles and monarchs gave alms and addressed the grievances of those on their lands, but on balance, the knightly class were certainly exploitative of the peasants. However, although the ideals of chivalry were intertwined with the fabric of high society, they cannot be entirely blamed for the whole structure of medieval societies.

That structure collapsed in England when the Second Barons' War broke out in the 1260s. It was a bitterly contested war, but when Simon de Montfort's army reached the Sussex town of Lewes, he displayed a surprisingly degree of chivalry. The Waverley Annals describe that, 'they led their troops to the top of a hill overlooking the town of Lewes in which their foes were stationed, and could have overcome their adversaries in their beds, had not chivalrous courtesy forbidden this',[73] and added that if they attacked, 'we would be disgraced'.[74] Simon de Montfort might have wanted to remove the English monarchy, but he wasn't willing to achieve his goal by a sneak attack on a sleeping enemy. In a civil war this restraint has to be admired, but when the tables were turned Simon received none of the chivalric fair play he had himself displayed. The future Edward I had stolen a number of banners from the army of Simon de Montfort's son during an attack at Kenilworth castle, and flew them above his own force as it approached Montfort near Evesham. Seeing the banners in the distant sky, Montfort thought his son had come to save him, but when his army realised the distinctly unchivalrous trick Edward had played, their morale must have taken a heavy hit. Realising he was trapped and doomed, Montfort again followed the path of chivalry, and although he could have fled on his horse, he stood his ground and fought to the death. Edward set the rules of engagement for his side – no prisoners were to be taken. He'd had enough of the civil war and wanted Montfort dead, so he sent out a twelve-man death squad to hunt him down and liquidate him.[75] Probably not the kind of action that would go down in the history of chivalry as a marker of fair play, but also by no means the only medieval death squad sent out to assassinate an enemy.

Montfort was killed by the marcher lord Roger Mortimer, who was on horseback and drove a lance through Montfort's neck. At Evesham, Edward had made a calculated decision, the threat to the crown that he was due to inherit needed to be utterly crushed, and it didn't matter how. Again, here we find success mattered more than the method used to achieve it. The contrasting behaviours and outcomes of Simon de Montfort and Prince Edward show that chivalrous actions were no guarantee of success at all. Montfort's reputation, however, has survived relatively intact, and was good enough for Napoleon to describe him as, 'one of the greatest Englishmen'.[76]

This positive view of an individual certainly did not always apply to knights, or armed men as a whole. Medieval Italian people saw the *condottieri* men-at-arms roving their countryside as robbers, and indeed the difference between a knight who upheld the law, and one who had more in common with the mafia, is only one of intent. This view was probably shared by the people of France who had suffered throughout the Hundred Years War, but as usual there is another side to the story. In the 1420s De Gamez described an attack he and his master, Pero Nino, made on the south coast of England at Portland, which gives us one example of knightly compassion. The usual practice of these amphibious raids was to take anything of value that would fit into their boats, and torch everything else. The French soldiers in their party promptly started to torch Portland, but miraculously, the fires started by the Spanish took no hold because apparently they did not light them willingly. According to De Gamez this divine intervention happened because they felt so badly for the destitute inhabitants of Portland.[77] He added that the knight Pero Nino was gentle to the weak, and therefore Portland was spared destruction. Generally though, the weak were usually not so lucky as those in Portland, and even William Marshal, who is usually held up as being at least proto-chivalric, was quite capable of acting like a common ruffian.[78]

One of the most shameful practices of his time, although not one we know Marshal committed himself, was concerning young bachelor knights. When the two sides in a tournament lined up against each other, sometimes young knights would be doing so for the first time. They represented easy targets for experienced knights, and against the concept of fair play, knights would effectively sell information on who they were to the other side before the action began. Presumably, they then turned a blind eye to their inexperienced teammates when they got battered.[79] The attitude that allowed this kind of behaviour at tournaments ran alongside an opulence and vanity that chivalry seemed nominally to be against. Henry of Grosmont, one of England's greatest knights and prolific tournament enthusiast, warned that jousting and dancing could lead to lechery. He would know, as he also admitted in earlier years to having tried to look as good as possible to impress the ladies at the events.[80]

The fact that one fourteenth-century knight could change so much shows that attitudes were flexible, questioned and as complex as they are today. Despite the negative aspects that tournaments and jousts were known to foster, Geoffrey de Charny rated their participants as deserving of honour, largely because they helped prepare knights and men-at-arms for war. There was a slightly softer side to his advice too, which shines through when he instructs men-at-arms that they should not think badly of men of lower rank, for 'there are many poor men who are of greater worth than the rich'.[81] This sentiment flies in the face of the accusation that knights cared not for the poor; at the very least, Charny recognised that poor people were not necessarily lacking in wealth because they were not good people. Other than guiding the moral compass of his audience, Charny also railed against those who were brave enough to fight, but used their skills and arms in order to rob and kidnap.

There was also criticism when knights employed their efforts in another direction entirely. Still in the fourteenth century, Thomas Walsingham accused the courtiers of Richard II of, 'demonstrating their prowess in the bedroom rather than on the field of battle'.[82] Froissart was less critical than Walsingham when, during a siege, a French squire challenged any English man-at-arms who dared to joust against him, for the love of their ladies. When the French squire was injured, the

English treated his wounds and sent him on his way with some cash, all of which Froissart seemed to approve of.[83] It is relevant to consider Froissart, Charny and others regarding their reliability as sources. They were neither war reporters, sport commentators, nor historians. Froissart often said he used the first-hand accounts of others, so even such a revered source is already second hand. We therefore cannot take everything as literal, nor take the aim of their works at face value. It is perhaps best to see, particularity Froissart, as part-newspaper, part-fable and part-comic book. Despite this, the underlying themes of chivalry probably reflected the reality.

Sometimes the truth needed no embellishment though; in 1437 amid a harsh and snowy winter, a party of Englishmen wrapped in white bedsheets, made a stealthy commando style raid on Pontoise to the Northwest of Paris. They crawled over the frozen moat while comrades disguised as peasants entered the town. Between them they took the town quickly in a lightning attack worthy of a Hollywood film.[84] Although sneaking around in disguise and wearing camouflage might not seem like true chivalric behaviour, it seems again that it didn't matter because it worked. An equally cinema-worthy event occurred at Calais in 1350, when Charny attempted to bribe someone to open a gate and let the French in to the English-held fortifications. However, once a large number of men-at-arms had poured through the opened gate, King Edward III of England, who was aware of the scheme, burst out and caught the French by surprise. The French and Charny pressed the king hard, but broke when they were attacked by the Black Prince.[85] Charny was taken prisoner in an episode that has been argued about ever since as to whether his plan was chivalric or not. Judging by other examples, had it succeeded it is unlikely many would have thought badly of it. Failure was the real dampener of chivalric reputation, and Charny was lucky to have been absent during the French defeat at Crécy, and so avoided any blame for it. He therefore also avoided the accusation as voiced by one chronicler that, 'it was the arrogant ambitions of those knights striving to outshine their fellows in capturing or defeating the king of England that was the cause of their downfall'.[86] Indeed it was absolutely this desire that pushed the French at Crécy onwards with little regard for tactics or patience. By charging into battle piecemeal, they showed their chivalric keenness to engage with the enemy, but by waiting they would also have demonstrated chivalric fortitude, neatly showing the inner contradictions and fluidity of the framework.

French knights are still known as the flower of chivalry for a reason, and the life of Frenchmen Raoul de Gaucourt is one of the best examples of this. He was knighted before the disastrous Battle of Nicopolis in 1396, where he was captured by the Ottomans before being ransomed back home. His luck was better following this episode, and his career was successful until his luck ran out again in 1415, when Henry V of England invaded France. Henry landed and besieged the town of Harfleur, which Gaucourt had entered with reinforcements to try to withstand the imminent attack. With only around 400 fighting men at his disposal, Gaucourt defied Henry and his army of over 10,000 men, and a number of great cannon, for over a month. The delay caused Henry's army to be hit by dysentery and served to badly anger the monarch, who blamed Gaucourt for prolonging matters.

He was quite right too, Gaucourt was an effective soldier and had held Henry up for so long that the English lost thousands of men to illness. When Gaucourt eventually handed Henry the keys to the port, he became an English prisoner. Henry, however, was happy to send Gaucourt off to the Dauphin of France with a message, relying on nothing more than a promise that Gaucourt would turn himself in to English Calais once he'd run his errand. For Henry to send a man who had annoyed him so much off back home, suggests he genuinely believed that Gaucourt would honour that agreement. The French knight, having been released by the English, was now free to arm himself again and go into battle against the hated enemy. Except that he didn't. Gaucourt kept his word, and surrendered himself back to Henry after the Battle of Agincourt.[87] Why would Gaucourt do that, why would he give up his freedom when there was nothing to compel him do to so? The compulsion, of course, was the code of chivalry by which Gaucourt lived – he felt bound by his word, although one wonders if there was ever a flicker of doubt as he walked back towards English-held territory.

This story has a remarkable echo nearly exactly 500 years later, when a British solider was languishing in a German prison during the First World War. Captain Campbell received a letter informing him that his mother was dying, and was subsequently allowed to return home to visit her by the Kaiser himself, on the condition he returned to custody. Captain Campbell went home, said his goodbyes to his mother, and promptly returned to Germany just as Gaucourt had done in the fifteenth century.[88] Gaucourt, however, found himself facing the same choice again. Although he would spend ten years as an English prisoner, Henry felt able to use Gaucourt as a messenger to France on two more occasions, such was the mutual understanding of their code of honour, and both times the Frenchman returned to captivity. Henry eventually allowed almost all of the prisoners taken in the Agincourt campaign to be ransomed, but Gaucourt was only released after Henry's death, so much did the king not want to face him again across a battlefield. The last word in this story belongs to the Frenchman however, who, alongside Joan of Arc, was at the forefront of the series of actions that ejected the English permanently from France.

Both knighthood and chivalry were fickle masters. From failure to success, chivalry could also cover the full spectrum of life and death. On one hand we can find Edward III, full of life, fighting tournaments in disguise, as at Dunstable in 1334 and 1342, where he took part incognito just as Lancelot had done in the romances, no doubt deliberately emulating the hero. But on the other hand, the Italian Salimbene remarked that when Enrico da Pagani was killed, his father's response was, 'I care not; for my son was made a knight and died fighting like a man.'[89] Terse though this seems, chivalry touched every part of the life of those who followed it, they were defined by their relationship to it and how their deeds measured up to the expectations of others. The transience of chivalry was ever present though, and even the normal rules could sometimes be turned upside down. During the Wars of the Roses, it was the nobles who were actively sought out to be killed, sometimes at the hands of death squads sent to hunt them down on battlefields. Lower ranks were often excused and civilians got off lightly,[90] which was a complete reversal of the norms of warfare of the preceding medieval period. This civil war unfolded within an understanding of chivalric behaviour where both sides recognised that those causing the trouble should be the ones dying for it, and that no one benefited from destroying the country. The reality of how chivalry was applied in the medieval world was that it varied hugely across time and territory, and reflected the characters of the knights and men-at-arms who lived by it.

True Meaning

Standards of behaviour and moral codes should not be judged by what came after them, rather they should be judged against what came before. The medieval view of what came before is also a long way from our own concept of history, which means any such judgements are based on a foundation of shifting sands. The spectre of Rome and the chaos of the following period of strife, migration and threat to Christianity, were known through the *Matter of Rome* and *Matter of France*, and these tales and legends gave medieval fighting men the idea that they and their ideals ran back to ancient times. It should also not be forgotten that war was initially a good thing, and this was a legacy that the knight brought with him into the later middle ages, it was never quite shaken off. Chivalry, though, did not come from Rome, in either its mature form, or raw form as a military ethos. Codes of behaviours around armed men and warfare can be found among almost every pre-medieval culture, and form part of a struggle as old as humanity itself to reconcile a (mostly male) human tendency to compete and fight. Humans are certainly not the only species where males fight to achieve dominance, and even chimpanzees are known to go to war.[91]

The act of fighting is traumatic, dangerous, and all consuming, and this bonds together those involved in a way that sets them apart from those members of society who don't fight. The consequence is that those who fought might have thought they were more worthy than those who prayed or worked, for they ran a higher personal risk. In the early days of chivalry, it was more a way of life than an ideological code, and in reality would have been inseparable from the individuals living it. Upon reaching the end of the early medieval period, the mounted warrior's code had a meaning that extended little beyond how to conduct themselves as cavalrymen. However, according to medieval writers, even at this early stage it may have included a duty to protect others. Both De Gamez and Ramon Llull both wrote that the very first knights were chosen by the people, in order to protect them.[92] Although early knights were in all probability not literally chosen by the first people, the meaning behind it is that knights were there to protect them, and their privilege was born from this duty. From this angle, knights were servants of the people in what sounds dimly like an early social contract. When there was no war to demonstrate this ability to protect, knights took part in tournaments, jousting, and other elaborate deeds of arms to showcase themselves. This was not all training or vanity however, and in the same way modern academic professors have to occasionally publish articles and papers to keep their jobs, knights fought publicly so the people could see that they were still up to the task.

This expectation of protection was highlighted by the *chevauchées* in France, when the French nobility were castigated for not coming out and facing the English, not simply from cowardice, but specifically because they were shirking their duty to defend the populace. The resulting shame felt by the knightly class drove their rashness and defined how they approached pivotal battles they went on to lose. It could be viewed that this implicit social contract traded off the wealth and power of the chivalric nobility against the protection from violence they afforded (sometimes) to their peasants. The price the lower classes paid for this was their obedience and poverty, although it is unlikely they always saw it like that. War was the reason that knights and chivalry existed, it was just another fact of life. Honore Bouvet explained that war was ordained by God, and that it had the virtuous aims of gaining peace and tranquillity.[93] If fighting for these reasons, a knight was doing God's work, which in turn meant that their wars were a good thing, and they should be lauded for starting them.[94] This explains why no one in the middle ages was trying to abolish knighthood, an institution that Christ would surely not have endorsed. This murky Christian approval of virtuous war was, in effect, a steppingstone between the old ways, and a new, more peaceful future. By bringing the knightly class along with this change, the church managed to maintain some influence on how knights thought and behaved. While the nobility of Europe often seem to have ignored church calls for a ceasing of fighting against fellow Christians whenever it suited them, the underlying idea of fighting for peace and tranquillity steered the course of chivalry towards ideals of fair play and gentleness.

In the end, telling knights not to fight just didn't work, but telling them they could fight for a righteous cause did. The First Crusade is evidence of that, as is the fact that Henry V put so much effort into insisting that his claim on France was legitimate. Henry's claim to France was tenuous but he wanted everyone to firmly believe in it, so he put great efforts into portraying his aggression as a just war. Henry succeeded spectacularly in this, and both the common soldier and his nobles fully bought into it. It was perhaps the fact that by Henry's time there was a larger noble knightly class, that chivalry had become such a feature of the medieval world. The slow process of the ennoblement of the mounted warrior allowed the flourishing of chivalry by increasing the numbers of men who could be enfranchised into its fold.

This changing nature of the knight expanded their remit from purely fighting, to administration, politics and law giving, and by the fourteenth century, into philosophy and various arts too. Infused with the politeness of the romance stories and courtly poems, a distinctly civilising trend emerged. As the status of the warrior class rose in Europe, the blurring between them and the ruling nobility served to merge both of them together, and enabled a higher degree of social mobility, at least from the twelfth century onwards.[95] In addition, non-noble men-at-arms are explicitly included within Charny's book on chivalry, which therefore meant he thought that non-noble fighting men could be chivalric, even if they were not of noble birth. Indeed Peter de Vinea wrote that, 'nobility is passed on to those in the line of descent, but the dignity of knighthood is not'.[96] Fourteenth-century nobility probably didn't agree with that statement, and they felt under siege from those supposedly below them, those who could now afford to act and dress like them. This is why a rise in the requirement to prove noble ancestry to gain entry to tournaments began to appear. It also maybe shows us another function of chivalry. The continuing elaboration of the rituals and knowledge required to be part of the order of knighthood, had the effect of raising a barrier of entry.

Together with the ever increasing cost of becoming and being a knight, chivalry served to keep out the riff-raff. This was implicit, but did chivalry have any explicit aims? It originally grew organically and without codification, but by the thirteenth century men were thinking about it. According to Ramon Llull's work from the 1280s, *The Book Of The Ordre Of Chyvalry*, 'The office of a knight is to own a castle and horse in order to guard the road.'[97] Additionally, knights should ensure that, 'traitors, thieves and robbers must be persecuted'.[98] This list sounds a lot like the list a modern person might draw up if asked what a knight should be, and shows us that medieval people did actually have those expectations. Llull added that noble virtues were, 'faith, hope, charity, justice, fortitude, loyalty',[99] and that overweight men were not suitable for knighthood. Evidence that Llull's views were widespread was that William Caxton printed his book in the fifteenth century, 200 years after it had been originally written. Furthermore, Caxton complained in his epilogue to the book, 'O ye knygthes of Englond where is the custome and usage of noble chyualry.'[100] Printed during the reign of Richard III, this might be seen as quite a bold move on Caxton's part, but he is clearly making the point that he expected more from the knights of England.

An interesting side effect of chivalry was a partial redemption of woman within knightly circles, because knights were encouraged to extol their virtues, and do anything for them. Ulrich von Liechtenstein, a name picked up and made famous by the film *A Knight's Tale*, was a real thirteenth-century nobleman from Styria.[101] Ulrich wrote an autobiographical work where he jousted his way from Venice to Vienna, breaking over 300 lances on the way, just for the approval of an already married woman.[102] That the woman continued to ignore him afterwards suggests he was wasting his time, but also shows how far a knight might go for the fairer sex, in a world where they were not always viewed positively. Ulrich personified the idea that a knight would fight better if he was in love, a thought that Charny agreed with. We should be careful not to read too much into chivalry's effect on the position of women in society however, and the female Christine de Pizan did not approve of courtly love, instead accusing it of being used as a cover for affairs. Charny might have been more idealised than Christine, but while he believed knights would fight better for the love of a woman, for him chivalry still boiled down to male martial prowess. Prowess was best demonstrated by deeds in war, and the primary aim of chivalry was to create effective fighting men. The more danger and suffering involved, the higher the honour for those men. Charny claimed that a knight's hardships were worse than those suffered by monks who, 'are spared the physical danger and the strenuous efforts of going out onto the field of battle to take up arms, and are also spared the threat of death'.[103] This elevation of knighthood above priesthood in worthiness was a contentious issue, and not one the priesthood necessarily agreed with.

The fact that Charny could write this reinforces how highly praised prowess was, but was this sensible or foolish? The answer can be seen in how the outcomes of the Battle of Poitiers and Agincourt changed western Europe drastically. The battles changed the political landscape, and because war could have this effect, the prowess that won them must be seen as historically important. The earliest forms of chivalry were the skills of the mounted warrior, and those skills were still the core ones Charny wrote about in the fourteenth century. Chivalry may have come to include certain manners and norms of behaviour, as well as an intensely rich cultural backdrop, but the beating heart of it was always riding on a horse in armour and attacking the enemy with a lance.

Chivalry should primarily be understood as meaning the physical and mental training a man and his horse needed to undergo in order to become battle winning. This training produced a very particular mindset, one that had a meaning within chivalry, and would become known hundreds of years later as the cavalier spirit. A certain confidence was required in order to engage in the knightly charge, which naturally spilt over to arrogance, and at its centre was violence of action. This was a similar ethos to that which the eighteenth century Royal Navy developed after it executed Admiral Byng for failing to attack the enemy. A Royal Navy historian described this spirit as, 'a culture of aggressive determination … [which] gave them a steadily mounting psychological ascendancy'.[104] He added that, 'opponents expected to be attacked, and more than half expected to be beaten, so that they went into action with an invisible disadvantage'.[105] This description applies just as well to the aggressive and confident mounted knight as his naval descendants. In addition, the psychological effect of coming up against the Royal Navy also equally applies to the non-knightly enemies that formations of knights faced. A block of mounted knights was a terror weapon. Part of this terror derived from the fact that their focus was on honour and fame, and that knights were not always primarily concerned with surviving a contest. By the time Charny was cut down at Poitiers, he was no longer fighting to win the battle, for that was already lost, he was fighting for the honour of himself, his king, and his chivalry. Knights, as the French often did, wanted to find the hardest place to fight, against the very best enemy they could, and test themselves where the danger was greatest in order to win their fame and honour.

To further the naval link, Pero Nino, on more than one occasion, saw armed men on land from his ship, and for no reason other than to fight them, went ashore to engage. Militarily pointless actions, but perfectly knightly. Pero Nino's actions could very well be judged as rash, but they were described in chivalric terms by De Gamez. This can be contrasted by the Spanish knight Menaguerra, who set great store on restraint, balance and reason.[106] One valid conclusion to draw from this would be that chivalry was not a single concept, and could contain contradictory expectations and aims. On the face of it then, the knight needed to fuse naked aggression with restraint and reason to forge a thinking soldier, able to turn on the violence when needed, and then turn it off to display courtliness at home. It is this gentleness that makes the medieval knight so appealing, precisely because it seems so unlikely. Indeed, the sixteenth-century philosopher Montaigne, who was absolutely no stranger to wearing armour, said of a defeated knight, 'he who does not flinch … looks his enemy in the face with a stern and disdainful countenance … he is killed, not conquered'.[107] In a typically chivalric mix of opposing viewpoints, Montaigne was also the very opposite of a cold-blooded warrior, and in fact during hunts he explicitly avoided seeing the animals being killed because it distressed him so much.[108] Although not necessarily a natural warrior, Montaigne was capable of living up to the role, which was not something that all men managed. Looking back to poor Gilbert Marshal, who was dragged to death by his fiery warhorse, we see a grim example of what happened when the expectations of chivalry were too high. Gilbert's unfortunate end is perhaps the very first recorded example of fatal toxic masculinity, and the blame for it lies with both chivalry itself and the society that made him act against his natural inclinations.

The vanity of knighthood was recognised by the knights themselves – and sometimes rejected, for example by Henry of Grosmont when he left orders for his funeral in 1361, that he wanted 'nothing vain or extravagant'.[109] He also warned against gaudy ceremonial riders in taking part in the funeral, and seems to have wanted a low-key affair. This was a far cry from the excesses of his youth, and the moral direction Henry moved in was due to his religious beliefs, beliefs which were by no means rare. Prowess and piety were then more natural bedfellows than we might have expected. We can turn back to Charny to express this for us when he wrote, 'those who fight well but die in the fray need not fear; they will … enjoy paradise forever'.[110] Charny is effectively reiterating the crusading doctrine, but the emphasis he put on souls and eternity was a universal medieval theme. It was a nagging question for all men-at-arms since their occupation was by nature a threat to their lives, and the most haunting insight into their thoughts is part of the inscription on the tomb of the Black Prince, one that he ordered himself.

> Great riches here I did possess
> Whereof I made great nobleness.
> I had gold, silver, wardrobes and
> Great treasure, horses, houses, land.
>
> But now a caitiff (a captive, or contemptible wretch) poor am I
> Deep in the ground, lo here I lie
> My beauty great is all quite gone,
> My flesh is wasted to the bone.

Death had stalked the Prince's entire life, from the plague to the battlefield, and it is telling that the most renowned knight of his generation saw that in the end, his chivalric achievements mattered little.

Modern Chivalry

Having passed through several centuries since the time of the Black Prince, chivalry has reached the modern era, and the period that most impacted how we see it today was the Victorian era. As the industrial revolution continued to turn people into workers, the individualistic nature of knights of the distant past hit a nerve. The publication of *Ivanhoe*, a rip-roaring story by Walter Scott, put a spotlight on the middle ages and helped to create a new enthusiasm for knights and chivalry. *Ivanhoe* was not terribly bad at portraying chivalry, but the Victorians latched on to the romantic and patriotic elements in particular, and the legacy of this lives on to this day. Between Ivanhoe's heroism, and Don Quixote ridiculously jousting windmills in the seventeenth century, we arrive at the two contrasting faces of chivalry that we recognise today. These two extremes are where our modern clichés originated, and unfortunately both are outliers on the spectrum of historical knighthood. This antiquated view of chivalry was formed in an age containing bolt action rifles and machine guns, and inevitably knights riding around on horses seemed rather quaint in comparison. The allure of the ideals of honour, duty and pride cut through these issues as recently as the Great War, when swathes of the

English gentry were cut down by machine guns as they advanced, their educations and childhoods having been filled with tales of Ivanhoe and King Arthur. Chivalry did not die, but it had drastically changed. Indeed it was changing all the while it was still the central driving force of the nobilities of medieval Europe.

Today the Order of the Garter still exists, knights are still made, and as a culture we value loyalty, generosity and courage. In England, if less so on the continent, martial prowess is still very much admired, and a sense of fair play is seen as quintessentially English. Chivalry, with its perceived idealisation of women, manners, honour and again that sense of fair play, is very much the source of many of the values which are seen as modern and western. The darker side of chivalry manifested itself in greed, vanity and the urge for endless expansion and growth. That it contains so much both good and bad tells us that chivalry really only ever held up a mirror to an individual, or society in general. The single most prevailing result of medieval chivalry to modern life is that concentration on individuality, the focus on fame and glory of the single person was celebrated, and this rise of the individual can be seen as the tournament faded, and was eclipsed by the single combat of the joust. The need to enrich oneself above the interests of the population as a larger entity, unfortunately comes from the oldest parts of medieval chivalry. The reality in modern times is that concerning medieval chivalry, it is not relevant, for wars are no longer fought on horses against mortal enemies wielding lances. It is only relevant within a context of medieval horseback knights and we are now too far removed to try to apply it to ourselves. Chivalry was all encompassing for those who lived within it, and it was a complicated and contradictory subject even then. Being a set of ideals, myths and expectations, it was a very human concept and therefore was never a single definable entity, instead constantly competing with different aspects of its own corpus. Indeed, chivalry can be described as messy. The last word on it, as applicable in the 2020s as it was in the 1020s, is best left to Keen who said that 'chivalry had always been aware that it was at war with a distorted image of itself.'[111]

Chapter Seven

The Rise of Infantry

Pre-Fourteenth-Century Infantry

Heavily armoured infantry has a long heritage indeed, reaching back to the armoured Greek hoplites that defied a global superpower in 490 BC. Then, at the Battle of Marathon, a wall of hoplites annihilated a Persian army of cavalry and infantry, changing the outcome of history.[1] The Greeks fought close together, shield to shield with their comrades, and trusted their lives to the men on either side of them. If only a few men lost their nerve and left their posts, then the result could be the total collapse of the formation, so while the hoplite wall was formidable, it was also fragile. Staying in it therefore required a stable level of morale; for the Greeks this was possible because of a cohesion born of their identity as hoplite warriors within their city state. Fighting was a privilege and a duty, and Greek culture literally drilled this into them, much as happened to the medieval knight. Hoplite training needed to be kept up, for the armour was better worn when the bearer was used to it, and the hoplite wall had to turn, advance and retreat in perfect order to remain intact. These were not peasant levies, they were an advanced military formation made up of those who could afford the required equipment. The great Greek horseman Xenophon wanted cavalry to work with the infantry, and recognised that a combined arms approach was the most effective. He advised that mobile infantry joined in with cavalry attacks to support them, primarily by attacking enemy cavalry.[2] Later Greeks fought in deep formations of infantry armed with long pikes, which in trained hands were formidable, and certainly impervious to a frontal attack from unarmoured ancient cavalry. These phalanxes were a different kind of infantry to the hoplite, and were the blueprint that medieval pikemen would later follow.[3] A third type of ancient heavy infantry was the Roman legionary. These footsoldiers wore sophisticated plate armour in the later parts of the Roman period, and were armed with short stabbing swords. Against cavalry they deployed javelins as spears, and the Greek strategist Arrian suggested that Roman legionaries were to move from four ranks, to eight deep,[4] which would give them the depth to withstand the impact of a charge. The fact that against armies that included armoured *cataphract* cavalry, the Romans doubled the depth of their formation is a testament to the power of ancient cavalry charges.

By the sixth century, Rome had become the Byzantine Empire, and cavalry had become the dominant arm of their army. Infantry units may have switched to a supporting role, but the Byzantine army was still recognisably Roman in organisation. Even though the legions were much reduced in size and offensive abilities, the armies were still Roman in leadership, strategy and education. The psychological impact of the cavalry charge was an important Byzantine tactic, and infantry became a defensive unit from which cavalry could sally forth to launch attacks.[5] Byzantine cavalry was sometimes very heavily armoured too, and this could include the horses, several hundred years before the Christian west emulated them. The regimented nature of the army stood in stark contrast to the Franks, who according to the strategist Maurice, deployed 'according to tribes, their kinship groups, and ties of dependency'.[6] This approach in the sixth century is evidence of the military organisation that would follow right through the medieval period, as soldiers fought for a particular lord or knight, rather than in standardised, professional units. By the eighth century, and facing probing Islamic incursions, the Byzantines were using infantry to hold forts in strategic locations, such as mountain passes and supply depots.[7] Cavalry was used to deal with raiding armies, which could be quite large, but not by trying to bring them to battle. Instead, the very sophisticated Byzantine strategy included using them to wage guerrilla wars, in order to break down the Muslim invaders and defeat them in detail. The empire was hugely competent at this time, and although besieged, it was in respect of its organisation and cavalry usage, ahead of its time.

During the early medieval period, infantry was by and large not well trained,[8] mostly because no one in Europe could afford standing armies. Even if they'd had the resources to, rulers probably also didn't see much need to change this, because they didn't often see what well drilled infantry could do. When they were called up, militias and other low quality infantry had no experience of working in large numbers and formations, and therefore had very limited tactical flexibility. Mounted units could also simply ride away from them, and raid or attack somewhere else. This made them ineffective, which probably acted as a self-fulfilling prophecy to delay the evolution of professional infantry. There were some early professionals in the form of siege engineers and technical experts, but freelance companies of close combat infantry were very rare before the thirteenth century. Units of infantry could be formed earlier than this however, as Richard I of England had done in 1192. During the Third Crusade, he fought his way down the coast of the Holy Land with an army including both spearmen and crossbowmen. Later, as Richard, with a few hundred infantry and just fifty knights, sat in the port of Jaffa, Saladin arrived with 10,000 cavalry to oust him. Richard deployed his troops in front of Jaffa with a line of spearmen protected by shields, and interspersed them with crossbowmen. These crossbowmen had attendants to load weapons for them while they shot, effectively doubling the shooting rate of Richard's army. Additionally, and presumably in a hurry, tent pegs were hammered into the ground in front of the infantry to damage the feet of the incoming horsemen.[9] Saladin's cavalry duly attacked but their arrows didn't do any damage, and the crossbowmen found them easy targets, presumably especially among any horses made lame by the tent pegs. As the Muslims pulled back, and despite being overwhelmingly outnumbered, Richard, along with ten mounted knights (and probably his spearmen), attacked the numerically superior enemy. His horse was killed from under him in a ferocious fight, although Saladin still found time to send a groom with two replacement horses to his enemy in recognition of the English king's valour. This chivalric act is one of the reasons Saladin is seen in knightly terms in the West, and certainly most Christian knights would have done no such thing. However, in the end the Battle of Jaffa proved to be surprisingly one sided, and Saladin's army took heavy casualties in a painful defeat.[10] Richard's armour and that of his horse were described as being covered with arrows like the spines of a hedgehog,[11] such was the arrow storm he withstood. His infantry army, although much smaller than the enemy, had been able to more than hold their own against what should have been a superior force. It may have been 1192, but infantry in a prepared position, and with admittedly above average leadership, had decisively beaten Islamic cavalry. For the next hundred years, infantry rarely lived up to the potential shown under Richard's leadership however, and this is reflected in the scarcity of accounts of them in the records. When searching through primary sources for references to infantry in the thirteenth century, they often appear only when the author wants to record how many of them were recruited or killed in a battle. References to mounted knights fill pages, and although this isn't proof of anything, it does suggest that the authors did not think it important to write about lowly footsoldiers.[12]

This did begin to change however, as the barn-like halls of the twelfth century were replaced by mansions in the thirteenth, the population increased, and wealth was created. These new mansions boasted decorated walls, larger windows, more furnishings than before, and there were more of them being built. Growing economies produce more food, and this meant that more people were able to branch out into other careers, and those included soldiering.[13] As the population in western Europe became denser, the distance between rural communities likewise shrank. This increasing urbanisation meant that it was easier for infantry on the march to reach villages and towns at night, which meant it was easier to stay fed and avoid diseases. In comparison, the vast lands of the steppes and inland Middle East were more sparsely populated, and never moved away from cavalry based armies. In the East, being a cavalryman meant a better chance of surviving the marching part of a campaign, and as a result armies there almost never constituted purely of infantry. However, the higher population density of countries like England, France, Germany and Italy, were much more conducive to those marching on foot.

When footsoldiers are mentioned in sources, they initially appear in the form of mercenaries. Although the Normans took plenty to England in 1066, the French increased their use of infantry mercenaries from the twelfth century onwards.[14] These were more reliable than a peasant levy, who tended to go home at the end of their limited term of service, which was usually only between one and two months. Instead, mercenaries would stick around as long as they were paid, and had the added benefit of being more experienced, well equipped, and actually able to win battles.[15] The French tended to recruit mercenary crossbowmen, especially as their weapons were becoming more powerful from the thirteenth century, by which time a metal stirrup had been added to their crossbows to allow for higher draw weights, and therefore enable greater armour penetrating power. The usefulness of the crossbow was recognised across Europe, and competitions with prizes were held in Italy, the Holy Roman Empire and France.[16] They were the best weapon for defending walled towns and cities too, and thirteenth-century French militia crossbowmen trained in return for tax exemptions.[17] This all moved crossbowmen towards a more professional footing, and in some respect their close-combat counterparts were not too far behind. Urban militias, armed with crossbows or not, were important in northern France and the low countries, but even more so further south, and especially in Italy.[18] These were not just some farmers with spears, but were men from urban environments, and sometimes were as fully armed as genuine men-at-arms.

Thus urbanisation improved the infantry by increasing its number and wealth, which meant better weaponry could be afforded. Additionally, military duty for middle-class urban militias was often seen as a privilege because it marked them out from the poorer town dwellers, and when defending their homes they could be reliable troops. Indeed during the thirteenth century, apart from mercenaries, they were often the only infantry used by the king of France at all.[19] In the Holy Roman Empire, loyalties were more fragmented because power lay with dukes, counts and bishops rather than the emperor,[20] and this had an effect on how infantry developed. Again, they were happy to serve in the defence of their local imperial cities, but were very wary of marching too far away from home. Infantry usually made up a part of any army however, regardless of where in Europe it was recruited, just because they were cheap. Battles were therefore rarely exclusively cavalry affairs, and often leaders deployed their forces with combined arms strategies in mind. These strategies could be complex, and included the use of reserves, flank attacks, digging pits, preparing ambushes and other cunning ruses. At Legano in 1176, militia infantrymen from Milan managed to stop a German cavalry attack and hold it up, which allowed their own knights to launch a charge and gain victory, in a classic example of the use of holding and strike forces.[21]

Infantry Parity

The historian Michael Prestwich has suggested that the challenge to chivalry from the longbow and pike started at the end of the thirteenth century, but glimpses could certainly been seen earlier than that.[22] The Normans, shrewd military operators that they were, had dismounted knights during the Battle of Tinchebrai in 1106, and continued to do so in a number of major battles over the following forty years.[23,24] This should not be a surprise, seeing as Tinchebrai occurred not all that long after the Battle of Hastings in 1066, where one entire army had been dismounted. For the Anglo-Normans then, dismounting to fight was not a revolutionary tactic. It was simply one that was used alongside, or instead of, cavalry attacks, depending on the battlefield situation. On mainland Europe, however, the inclination as we push into the thirteenth century was to fight from horseback, a strategy which for the Imperial army at Bouvines in 1214 included a new combined arms approach. During the battle, a defensive ring created by Imperial infantry held the French cavalry out for a significant period of time. The knights of the Holy Roman Empire were able to sally forth out of this formation, strike the French, then retreat again, numerous times before the French were able to regroup and break the defence.[25] The infantry at Bouvines were armed with a multitude of weapons, but they certainly employed spears and pikes of various lengths to try to keep the knights out. The French knights who had already used up their lances were unable to combat the infantry, and it was knights with new, unbroken lances who were able to defeat them. In the event, the Imperial infantry was not numerous enough to employ a formation sufficiently deep to keep the cavalry out indefinitely, and the lances of the French were long enough to out-range their pedestrian opponents.

Medieval noblemen could read about Greek phalanxes, and would have had an idea what those looked like, and at Bouvines a brief snapshot of the future served as both a reminder and a foretelling. But what was holding medieval infantry back? The eventual French victory at Bouvines is the first clue: knightly lances were almost always longer than spears. If a mounted knight with a long lance could skewer an infantryman, before the infantryman's spear could reach his horse, it didn't matter how well armoured or trained he was, the footsoldier was going down. Then why did it take so long for medieval soldiers to carry full length pikes? If the spear was long enough that it could hit the horse before the knight could strike, then the footsoldier would have the advantage. Of course, the medieval strategist knew this, but the use of pikes comes with a list of downsides. First, being longer than spears they are slightly harder to source, make and transport. Critically, however, because of their length they require a certain level of training, not just to wield effectively, but to not tangle up the pikes of their fellow pikemen. If one pikeman in the middle of the formation goes to lower his pike, but lowers it awkwardly, it will collide with other pikes and scatter them. In high winds the pikes also take more strength to control, and in the chaos and tension of the battlefield, a sudden order to change the direction of the pike block could cause mistakes.

I learnt a passable seventeenth-century pike drill in an afternoon, but I knew that the enemy cavalry was not going to try to charge home when it was put to the test, and no one was shooting at me. That basic level of training needed to be maintained, and practiced with enough comrades that it was meaningful. Additionally and critically, morale also needed to be high enough to stop members of the block fleeing unreasonably early. As with the Greek hoplites, cohesion was everything in a pike block, and if some of its members doubted their fellows would stand fast as the horses thundered towards them, they might see flight as their only chance of survival.

To be reliable as pike infantry then, medieval soldiers had to be semi-professional at least, they couldn't simply be farmers plucked out of their fields at short notice. These factors helped to delay the large scale adoption of pikes, although they crop up time and time again on smaller scales in the fourteenth and fifteenth centuries. Their first famous outing was at the Battle of Courtrai in modern Belgium in 1302.[26] The militias of several Flemish cities formed up before the city of Courtrai, in order to face down the approaching French chivalric army that was attacking it. The Flemish had understood the need for training pikemen, and their militias were both well trained and equipped. Critically, they were also defending themselves, and were also well led. They wore mail armour, steel helmets and were armed with pikes, spears crossbows and *goedendags*.[27] *Goedendags* were a Flemish weapon that was a sort of short spear with a club before the point, a manner of rustic poleaxe that was nonetheless brutally effective.

The Flemish prepared the battlefield, which was already marshy, to make it as dangerous for horses as possible. They emptied rivers of water to make them look passable, dug both ditches and pits, and covered these with branches. Importantly, they then placed their infantry in deep formations, and gave them missile support. Wisely, the French commander Robert of Artois first sent in his own crossbowmen, but they weren't able to cause significant damage to the armoured Flemish infantry. Robert then ordered a full knightly charge, which unfurled with predictable consequences. The bad ground slowed the knights, broke their formations, and caused some horses to fall. Incoming crossbow fire started to cause casualties, and then, unexpectedly for the French, the Fleming infantry did not break as the knights reached them. By that point, the tired horses would not have been charging at full speed, especially on boggy ground, and probably not in one concentrated group either. Instead, they had been defeated before they even charged, and were cut to pieces. The *goedendags* were used to stab them, or brutally club men and horses to death, while the pikes held firm and prevented deep French penetrations. Robert of Artois was killed after sending in his final reserve, and died with around 500 other knights, whose golden spurs were collected up by the victorious Flemings and offered to a church after the battle. In what became known as the Battle of the Golden Spurs as a result, many historians have seen the start of an infantry revolution, and in many senses this is correct.[28] However, the ability of mounted knights to win battles did not suddenly disappear after this battle, indeed they were scoring victories over a hundred years later. What changed after 1302, was that medieval warriors had a contemporary example of how to defeat a chivalric army, although it was based on a very specific set of circumstances. The lesson was that decent infantry on favourable ground, with good leadership, could destroy *any* army.

Bannockburn

This lesson was then famously taught to the English in 1314 by the Scots. A lot had happened in England since 1302, indeed the great Edward I had died, and been succeeded by his significantly less warlike son, Edward II. Despite his comparatively lower interest in war, the younger Edward had sent a large army north to deal with the troublesome Robert the Bruce. Edward I had used a combined arms approach to destroy the Scots at Falkirk nearly twenty years before, and his son probably was expecting, and indeed planning, a repeat performance. This time however, the enemy was not led by the indifferent tactician William Wallace, but the much more formidable Robert the Bruce, who was now also the king of Scotland. Robert had only an infantry army with a few noblemen in support as light cavalry, and these were primarily useful for riding down unprotected English archers. The infantry were armed with an assortment of weapons but the most important was the pike. Robert the Bruce had trained his men in their use in mobile pike units known as *schiltrons*.[29] These could form a defensive hedgehog of pikes on all sides, but critically also had the ability to move. When attempted on a large scale, this was a difficult manoeuvre to pull off safely, and it shows how well drilled the Scots were that they managed it at Bannockburn.

The English army had rushed north to Scotland, 'hence horses, horsemen and infantry were worn out with toil and hunger, and if they did not bear themselves well it was hardly their fault'.[30] The two armies first met at Tor Wood near Stirling Castle, where the Scots ambushed Robert Clifford's English force, killing a number of men. The already questionable morale of the English following their long march was dented by this early defeat, and when combined with the less than perfect leadership it received from Edward II, the English were in real trouble. Before the battle proper began, an incident occurred which famously is described as a joust between Henry de Bohun and Robert the Bruce, in which the Bruce swerved out of the way of de Bohun's lance, before cleaving his head in with his axe. In the chronicle *Vita Edwardi Secundi* however, it is instead written that de Bohun turned his horse away from the Scots in order to get out of the way of the enemy's advance, after which the Bruce hit him with an axe in the back of the head. Whichever version of the story is correct, it was another, literal, blow to English morale. Following this ignominious start, the English left a sensible position, against much advice, and boxed themselves in between rivers and bad ground, sealing their own fate. The *schiltrons* advanced, keeping their discipline while moving, and the English, who couldn't leave the battlefield, were left with no other option than a frontal attack. The flower of English chivalry charged into the Scottish lines, and after a loud impact, both pikes and knights were splintered and broken, according to contemporary accounts of the battle. Interestingly, this suggests very much that the horses charged into the pikes and did not baulk at them, for the impact of beast and pike is the only thing that could have splintered those weapons.

Another nod to the bravery of the English horse is that, according to the *Scalacronica*, the horses were 'bitted' all night.[31] Medieval horse bits were not discomforting to the animals to wear, but over a prolonged period they could rub, and some horses might have struggled to eat with them in. Our normal practice is to only bit our horses five minutes before we need them, in contrast to the English horses who spent an entire night in full battle readiness, who would have had their patience severely tested. Regardless of the night they'd endured they still charged home, but despite their bravery failed to break the Scottish pike formations. During their attempts the Earl of Gloucester, 'once and again penetrated their wedge, and would have been victorious if he had had faithful companions'.[32] Perhaps the Earl thought his dash – or recklessness depending on point of view – would pick up the army and they would follow him to victory? Perhaps if they'd followed him into the hole he'd smashed open, apparently repeatedly, it could have been exploited? We shall never know if the English came much closer to victory than it seems, but even with a forest of pikes against him, the Earl of Gloucester had still got in among them, and out again, more than once. He was eventually killed while his men watched, with the chronicle explicitly stating that almost none of them were killed. This reinforces the suggestion that English morale was low, and some of them were avoiding the fight.

The list of English failings were long at Bannockburn, and almost all were avoidable. Firstly, the English had allowed the Scots to attack them, and secondly, to pen them in on unfavourable ground. For a cavalry-based army this was unforgivable tactical ineptitude. However, contrary to popular belief, Bannockburn was not a failure of English knightly cavalry. Many infantrymen were killed in the English front line too, and they had been unable to break the Scots either. Perhaps critically, the English bowmen had not been able to get into a position to shoot, and they should have been the weapon that defeated the Scots, as they had at Falkirk.[33] The real problem behind all of these failures was leadership, so often the deciding factor in pitched battles, but the chronicles of the time didn't help by heaping the blame onto the knights. The *Vita Edwardi Secundi* asked exasperatedly, 'why do you, who used to conquer knights, flee from mere footmen?'[34]

The English military establishment did certainly learn a lesson from Bannockburn, but it was not the lesson the Scots took from Courtrai. The obvious lesson was the use of pike-armed infantry, which is the one the Scots had employed, but the English had other ideas. The English nobility did not decide that melee infantry, in either the Scottish or Flemish style, was desirable; instead, their doctrinal change was to dismount the cavalry as the default stance for their knights. They had seen that archery could win battles against the Scots, and the logical extension of this was to use the rest of the army to keep the archers safe.[35] Dismounted men-at-arms would do this job well, and the English went on to hone this idea against the Scots, before they exported the tactic to France. Their strategy was based on an adherence to the well known military maxim that the side that defended won – a tactic both the Scots and French usually helped them to employ by willingly attacking them. Longbows proved themselves on multiple occasions, where defensive positions made attacking enemy numbers an irrelevance. So much of armoured fighting is stamina, and the success of the English is in part due to an understanding of this. One overlooked driver of this doctrine was that English armies, both in Scotland, and often in France, were usually outnumbered by their opponents. In such situations they tended, wisely, to fight on the defensive, which meant dismounting from their horses, which were now correctly seen as an offensive weapon by the English. The mounted knight was not obsolete, and was to be a factor in many English victories when they unleashed well timed cavalry charges to destroy their enemies.

Crécy

The first place where the French felt the full force of the new dismounted English way of war was at Crécy in 1346. This battle was yet another example where one side was well led and gained victory. The English picked an advantageous battlefield, and then Edward III deployed dismounted men-at-arms and longbowmen in well defended positions, and waited for the French to attack. While they did this, the French army was streaming in from all directions, clogging the roads and causing terrible traffic jams. As the French army thus swelled, the two sides stood facing each other from sunrise to near sunset without attacking.[36] The French spent that whole day sticking to the maxim than an army should fight on the defensive, but it also might have given the English time to prepare, for they dug pits a foot deep which would hinder both mounted and dismounted attackers.[37] As dark was closing in, the French blinked first, and sent in their Genoese crossbowmen in an attempt to blast the English off their fortified hilltop position.

A story exists that the crossbowmen had allowed their strings to get wet, and therefore suffered a diminished shooting ability, whereas the English longbowmen kept theirs dry and thus won the archery duel. Medieval crossbow strings, however, were waxed,[38] which protected them from the elements, and the professional Genoese troops were unlikely to be so incompetent as the myth suggests. The reality was that the crossbowmen shooting at the English were doing so uphill and in bad light, because the setting sun was in their eyes, and with unknown wind conditions. If the wind was blowing from behind the English lines, it would easily explain why their bolts caused little damage, and why the longbowmen caused hideous causalities among the Genoese. Another factor was that the *pavises*, which are very large shields, that the crossbowmen usually went into battle behind, were stuck somewhere in the traffic jam and were not used in the battle.[39] As a result, it is suspected that the Genoese loosed perhaps two volleys, just to make it look like they'd tried, and then retreated. Seeing the failure of their missile troops, the French cavalry charged. After all, they thought, it was better to close the distance quickly rather than stand around getting hit by arrows. Unfortunately for the French knights (who incidentally rather rudely charged through the retreating crossbowmen), they also charged into a hail of projectiles. Horses were wounded by arrows, and a few stumbled, presumably in part because of the pits that the English had dug. This all happened in fading light, and the French knights in their helms wouldn't have been able to see much on the ground at all. As arrows took an increasing toll on horses, the folly of their plan may have become evident to the knights.

The English also used cannon in a significant volume, which is often overlooked, but French sources do record damage being done by them. This is despite the fact that there is evidence that some chroniclers removed references to guns from their record of the battle because they were unchivalrous instruments.[40] The French horses may not have had huge experience of cannon fire at this date, and they probably did more to scare the horses than the arrows would have. Guns feature in images of the battle too, and Crécy should be remembered for their deployment more than it usually is. The French did battle through to reach the English men-at-arms, and fought a hard battle with the Black Prince's division.

They were defeated, but attacked another fourteen times as more and more French soldiers arrived on the battlefield. The failure of leadership that allowed them to be committed piecemeal is a huge contributing factor to their eventual defeat.

The longbows did cause carnage, but after the first couple of those fifteen attacks, they would have been out of arrows. Instead, it was the dismounted infantry that defeated the assaults one by one, until the early hours of the night when the French retired back to their camp. The French returned to the field on the following morning, at which point the English really would have been out of ammunition. An arrow that has hit *anything* other than earth will probably break, and with the French churning up the ground under their hooves and feet, crushing arrows, it is unlikely that many arrows were recovered to shoot again. The second day of Crécy was therefore a close combat affair, probably punctuated by the loud explosions of the English guns. The redoubtable English men-at-arms defeated the French yet again, but this time they then mounted their horses, and executed a swift counter-attack that shattered the French, killing thousands of them. It was not any single factor that gave the English victory at Crécy, but rather the combination of all arms, and good decisive leadership. In the years following Crécy, the French knights started to dismount on occasion and experiment with the strategy themselves. Like Bannockburn, Crécy was also not the end of the English mounted knight. A group of knights on horseback had made Edward III's choice of battlefield possible in the first place, by making a river crossing at speed, and punching through the French defences on the other side before the battle.[41] This is just one incident that shows the significance attached to dismounted knights should not be exaggerated, especially considering dismounted knights were already a feature of twelfth-century combat.[42]

Poitiers

The mounted knight was still riding high, but the great plague that ravaged Europe in the years after Crécy started to change everything. After the devastation had subsided, the world was different, and armies would be smaller for the rest of the fourteenth century as a result.[43] This was because there was less food available as agriculture had suffered, as well as fewer people from which to recruit armies. Both of these factors meant that war leaders wanted more than ever to take only the best troops with them. Specifically this was because they couldn't afford to pay for men who were of little use, nor find food for them on campaign either.

In 1356, an English army commanded by the Black Prince was chased around France by larger French armies, and eventually cornered near the city of Poitiers. Although he had been trying to evade the superior French forces, the Black Prince found a natural castle, and decided to make a stand atop it. The main feature was a 'hill surrounded by fences and ditches, its slopes being covered in one part by pastureland, thick with bushes, and in another by vineyards and elsewhere by sown crops'.[44] Due to the undergrowth, the English got onto the hill without the French noticing, which shows just how closed in and dense the area was, and it was certainly a far cry from a flat open field. The French became aware of the English dispositions, at the latest when the Black Prince raised his banner, and presumably initially thought better of attacking. However, the Black Prince's standard suddenly looked as if it had disappeared behind the hill – in other words, as if the English were retreating, and the French surged forward. The English, however, had not moved. If the Black Prince did this on purpose, it was a move of military genius, for the French fear of missing out drove them up and onto his prepared position. One source stated that the French pikeman came on first, and were attacked by an English division that had been especially prepared to fend them off.[45] This interesting footnote to the battle suggests that the English had learnt more from Bannockburn than just to dismount, and that they also thought about how to deal with the pikes if they faced them again. Whatever thinking they did clearly worked, because the English division duly defeated the French pikemen.

Meanwhile, English archers attacked the French from out of the way places, above and to the side of them, and used their arrows effectively.[46] Their shooting was probably from quite close range given the terrain, and certainly included flanking fire that would have driven into the more vulnerable areas of the French men-at-arms' armour. Gascon crossbowmen also wrought terrible damage on behalf of the English, and their contribution in this victory has been largely ignored. Critically, however, the marshy ground ruined the French mounted attacks on the archers, where again they had roughly the right plan, but not suitable land over which to execute it. Their prowess and horsemanship should not be neglected, because even with this handicap, their attack was described as having been moderately successful.[47] They did manage to make contact with the English, and possibly gave the rest of the army some small respite from missile fire, but they did not have the impact the French had desired. Indeed, mounted knights charging around vineyards and the hedges of medieval fields, which were far smaller than modern fields, were not exactly in their natural environment. Their failure to smash through the English lines must not be seen as a failure of cavalry, but a failure to use cavalry properly. This can be paralleled in more recent battles, for example the use of tanks within the ruins of Stalingrad during the Second World War made them vulnerable to Russian infantrymen, even armed with the most basic weapons, but this was not a failure of the tank.

While the French in 1356 had, in a way, been forced to try something inadvisable with their cavalry, the English use of mounted knights that eventually followed was masterful. Following their unsuccessful mounted attacks, dismounted French men-at-arms engaged the English in a two-hour struggle, after which they too were defeated. As at Crécy, the English dismounted men-at-arms had shown that a defensive position was difficult to crack. The following French retreat collided with another advancing French division, causing both temporarily to move away from the English. Upon seeing this, the Black Prince thought the French were leaving the field, and ordered 200 Gascon men-at-arms, who were probably the mounted reserve, to ride around the back of the French army and cut off their retreat. As they left, the Black Prince ordered his remaining men-at-arms to mount their warhorses, and prepare for an all out attack. The Black Prince, however, was wrong about the French, and their new division, commanded by King Jean II, absorbed the men who had been retreating from the English, and reformed.

The English were therefore not facing a routing, or even a withdrawing enemy, but a determinedly advancing one. Unexpectedly, a defensive battle had turned into an all out English cavalry charge against an enemy that was still larger – and worse, two thirds of them were fresh. This change in stance from being dug in to full attack mode, represents the incredible flexibility of the English fighting system, as well as the chivalric bravado instilled in their men. This was an attack that was by no means likely to succeed, and was occurring without missile support, and yet the attack was made nonetheless. As the Black Prince charged into the French lines, his Gascon flanking force charged the flank of the French army. The French men-at-arms would have heard the first contact happening in front of them, and then heard the second happening behind them, causing a disorientating effect and spreading uncertainty across their ranks. This was the true power of a flanking assault, and only the most steadfast warriors would not have felt a flicker of panic in their bellies at that moment. Some did panic, and they fled. The English charge carried them into the French lines, and a desperate battle raged around the standard of the French king. Next to the king was the sacred French war banner, the Oriflamme, held by the venerable Geoffrey de Charny. As the melee raged, the English archers and crossbowmen flung themselves into the fight to support their mounted comrades, and eventually the French lines collapsed. Charny was killed, and King Jean II was taken prisoner, a coup for the daring English who had pulled off a monumental victory.

As the dust settled they must have realised that in capturing the king of France, suddenly they might have won the war. And they nearly had. An extremely favourable peace was negotiated as a result of the victory at Poitiers, and with King Jean II in captivity in England, the French found themselves in a dire position. The peace deal was known as the Treaty of Brétigny, and as we previously saw, the number of warhorses in England collapsed in the aftermath of peace. Fighting horses were not the only group to lose out from the peace; fighting infantrymen suddenly found themselves unemployed and out of favour too. The release of high numbers of battle-hardened fighting men from the service of both English and French armies was a problem. By 1361 some had formed up into companies, such as the Great Company,[48] which was filled with soldiers from many nations, but had English leaders. In order to maintain themselves, these companies promptly ravaged France. The French nobility could do little to stop these men who, having put their skills to use in the form of banditry, were now just as much a problem as the official English armies had been. These companies often ended up in Italy in search of employers, becoming some of the famous *condottieri* companies that characterised Italian politics and war in the fourteenth and fifteenth centuries. The Italian Filippo Villani described these young battle-hardened Englishmen in particular as, 'hot and impetuous, used to slaughter and to loot, quick with weapons, careless of safety'.[49] In Italy, mounted men-at-arms were still the dominant battlefield force, and perhaps infantry was still improving, men-at-arms would dismount when appropriate.

The number of knights in England was dropping however, and the proportion of men-at-arms who were not noble was increasing. Before the 1330s, infantry in England was raised by commissions of array and composed of both spearmen and archers,[50] but after the 1330s it tended to be only archers who served. Indentures also started taking over, and this meant that the English military system was taking further modernising steps away from anything resembling feudalism. As recruitment now revolved around daily wage rates, value for money became a driving force of the composition of English armies. Archers, even though mounted for travel, were cheaper than men-at-arms, and as the fifteenth century dawned, the proportion of archers to men-at-arms increased substantially. For example, at the Battle of Agincourt in 1415, Henry V deployed only 1,500 men-at-arms to around 7,000 longbowmen.[51] In a significant departure from the reign of Edward III, he deployed no cavalry. The English were now, and would remain during the medieval period, an army based around the power of infantry.

Elsewhere in Europe the situation was very different, and the mounted knight remained a primary component of armies. The infantry component was changing however, and the fourteenth century had seen increasing levels of professional troops – that is men paid to fight – in all European armies. In Italy this had a foreign complexion, but elsewhere they were more national than not. Militias were still important, and it had long been realised that hordes of unarmoured, unskilled infantry were just useless mouths to feed on campaign. As part of the drive for better infantry, contracts became normal for recruitment, and the line between mercenaries and serving due to an obligation blurred. In the Holy Roman Empire, the Emperor could rely on more modern forms of recruitment in his western lands, but to the east was stuck with older systems of a more feudal nature.[52] Urban troops would defend their own cities, but they wouldn't march out of them, something which helped to keep the Germanic regions fragmented. The fact was, even urban militias across Europe started to get paid, and before long only the very noblest of men served without financial compensation, and even this would change. This professionalisation of infantry is demonstrated by the elite infantry groups that emerged in the fourteenth century, longbowmen in England, crossbowmen in France and Italy, and eventually halberdiers and pikemen in Switzerland.

Not all new infantry types that emerged were successful; in the Hundred Years War after Agincourt, Frenchmen had picked up longbows and started to fight with them, especially those born in the regions which were then allied or loyal to the English.

French archers appeared on both sides during the rest of the war, and sometimes in large numbers. However, the official French attempt to create a body of archers had patchy success at best.[53] The *francs-archers*, were a body of men, one from each parish who was to practice with the bow or crossbow on Sundays and feast days, in order to serve as an archer for the French king. Their name was not due to the fact they were French, but because of the tax exemption their job entitled them to.[54] They were the first real attempt by the French to create an infantry force, and in 1448 an ordinance was proclaimed for their creation. The parallels to the longbowmen of England are there, but the English archers were a significantly more professional group by this time, even as the final stage of their defeat in the Hundred Years War was looming. The French communities who supported the *francs-archers* complained that they were overbearing and costly to equip, and their performance in battle sometimes left a lot to be desired. Indeed, they were a semi-professional military force in a world where the professionals were becoming seriously good at what they did. For example, crossbowmen could reach a level of usefulness for which they were paid half the wage of a knight, and some mercenaries from Brabant during the thirteenth century were considered the 'equal of knights',[55] choosing to fight to the death when they were defeated. Medieval infantry sometimes employed sophisticated tactics too, including field fortifications such as the stakes used at Agincourt, anti-horse pits and wagon lagers as used at Crécy.[56] These measures could be labour intensive, and required tactical nous in order to be put in the right places. When commanders got it wrong, as the English did at Patay, enemy mounted troops could simply go around prepared defensive positions and defeat the infantry, or go and attack another strategic target entirely.

This phase of the middle ages can be labelled as the time of infantry parity. Specifically this is the period of time where professional infantry emerged, and then started to be able to defeat cavalry in large engagements, but also suffered serious reverses. There are, for example, numerous similar cases where cavalry either pursued defeated enemies for great gain, or as at the fourteenth-century Battle of Najera, where cavalry charging at the end of a battle routed the enemy and forced a victory.[57] At Najera, the men-at-arms, 'most gripped their lances with both hands and thrust them as they rode'.[58] What is clear, is that the ideal medieval army in the fourteenth or fifteenth century included infantry, missile troops and mounted men-at-arms. No one arm was in principle superior to the other, and infantry victories can be found from 1192, with Richard the Lionheart's victory at Jaffa, to the steamrollering of the English longbowmen at Verneuil by mounted men-at-arms in 1424. To be prepared for any eventuality, a medieval commander needed infantry who would hold ground, and offensive troops who would win battles if the enemy didn't oblige them by attacking.

The complexity of the relationship between infantry and cavalry success is demonstrated by the Battle of Nicopolis in 1396. That battle is known best for the utter defeat of the Christian mounted knights, even though the battle opened with a successful knightly charge against the Turkish infantry. Interestingly, this fleeting opening victory was made by the cavalry despite a wall of stakes planted in their way.[59] Sometimes the defences to keep the cavalry out were natural, rather than man-made. Perhaps the ultimate natural barrier to cavalry was encountered by the Christian knights who ventured north into the Baltic during the long, roughly 300-year period of the Baltic Crusades. Those knights, the Teutonic knights, never quite got to grips with their elusive pagan opponents, largely because of the unfavourable terrain. Knightly armies struggled to operate over marshy wet ground, and diseases would have been spread by the variety of biting insects that live in such places, affecting both humans and horses. The Lithuanian and Polish peoples who resisted the Christian advance simply avoided facing mounted troops in battles, preferring instead to ambush or avoid them altogether. They used infantry in these encounters, but by avoiding pitched battles they also avoided the need for rigorous training, or the need to main large bodies of professional troops. The ferocity of the resistance put up against the crusaders proves that in these circumstances, even unprofessional infantry could be decisive. In guerrilla wars such as these, knights were as useful as American tanks were in Vietnam; that is locally important, but mostly an expensive irrelevance.

A Change in Perception

The dismounting of noble fighting men in England, following the heyday of the mounted knight between the eleventh and thirteenth centuries, could be seen as a relatively sudden and final event. If one takes evidence firstly from the Battles of Courtrai and Bannockburn, in 1302 and 1314, it may seem that in the space of a decade warfare had changed. By then selecting evidence from Crécy and Agincourt a hundred years later, one would find enough material to back up the assertion that the mounted knight was finished, and that an infantry revolution had indeed taken place. The reality of the rise of infantry is, of course, more convoluted than that, and it is recognised today that if there was a revolution, it did not immediately make the mounted knight obsolete.[60] Indeed, we have seen that English and French mounted knights were still winning battles at Poitiers in 1364, and Patay in 1424, and therefore can conclude that the rise of infantry was a rise to parity rather than supremacy.

The English Wars of the Roses (1455–87) was a conflict fought largely on foot, but even then there was a place for mounted knights. Writing at the time, Philippe Commynes commented that the Earl of Warwick would normally start a battle on his horse but, 'if it was going badly he would make an early escape. This time [at the Battle of Barnet] however he was constrained by his brother … to dismount.'[61] This suggested that Warwick would normally keep himself, and presumably a body of retainers, as a mounted reserve, a practice which was perfectly sensible. Following his brother's advice and dismounting was on this occasion a bad call, as the battle went poorly and he found he was unable to extricate himself. This resulted in him being killed for the lack of a horse. It is an accepted fact that most battles in the Wars of the Roses were fought on foot, but it is interesting to marry up Commynes' comments with the illustrations made at the time, which routinely show cavalry playing a part.[62] It may be that the role of mounted knights in those wars has been understated, or that they were perhaps mostly unleashed in the pursuit of fleeing enemies as Warwick seems to have routinely done. *The Pageant of the birth, life and death of Richard Beauchamp, earl of Warwick, K.G, 1389–1439*,[63] shows the Earl on horseback in battle, which is exactly what Commynes' described him as doing, so perhaps other illustrations of mounted knights are also accurate. One final word on this subject is a reminder that the Wars of the Roses ended with a knightly cavalry charge, into another group of mounted knights. That battle, which took place on the famous fields around Bosworth in 1485, was decided by a cavalry encounter, but despite this, the era of massed English mounted men-at-arms was over.

Across the Channel in France, infantry forces had become part of a new standing army.[64] Roving predatory free companies had been given an ultimatum: join up as the new French army, or be hunted down by the companies that did sign up. This was successful and gave the French King an army to call his own,[65] although this included heavy cavalry as well as the *francs-archers*. These developments were part of a set of maturing military institutions in many countries that reflected the changing face of war. As the fifteenth century neared its end, infantry units had professionalised and increased in number. To grasp the scale of this, we need only to listen to Jean de Bueil, who had fought in the Hundred Years War. He wrote that as of 1471, 'war has become very different. In those days [early fifteenth century] when you had eight or ten thousand men, you reckoned that a very large army: today it is quite another matter.'[66] Armies were recovering their sizes after the Black Death, and de Bueil had noticed it. This was a different situation to Italy, which had largely been at peace in the second half of the fifteenth century, and the Holy Roman Empire which had been steadily expanding. The change in the perception of infantry was, by 1500, almost complete in Europe. The real change however, was not that infantry could be formidable, it was that formidable infantry could be non-noble.

The Swiss

One of the first examples of this were the Swiss halberdiers, who first appear in history at the Battle of Morgarten in 1315.[67] The halberd was for all intents and purposes a poleaxe, and therefore able to take down armoured knights. Critically however, the Swiss put them in the hands of their common soldiers, who were initially not a professional force. Ambushing an Imperial army between a mountain and a marsh, they threw rocks at the enemy horses before taking their riders out with their halberds.[68] The difference between the Scottish pike formations and the Swiss, was that the Swiss tactic persisted and improved. They improved by adding pikemen into their formation, a wise move in order to counter the heavy cavalry that often invaded their lands. The Swiss deployed pikemen when they claimed victory at the Battle of Sempach in 1386,[69] some seventy years later, proving their longevity.

Unlike the Scots, the Swiss retained their independence, and in the process pioneered a new form of warfare. It could more accurately be said that they had rediscovered the use of the pike block, rather than invented it, but they had brought it back and it was back to stay. The Swiss commoner armies had changed the history of Europe, and therefore earned the right to be taken seriously. And indeed they were, the princes of Europe started to hire these useful infantry troops,[70] and they started to appear in all sorts of conflict zones. Hired through contracts, they were cheaper and expendable to employers, both useful in sieges and decisive in the field. Now internationally famous, Swiss halberdiers and pikemen had moved on from ambushing chivalric armies poorly suited to war in the mountains, and had succeeded in exporting their fighting style across the continent. Fighting in blocks with a narrow front but sometimes as deep as fifty ranks, they punched through any infantry in front of them, which usually caused that enemy to rout. Supported by missile troops, this was a combined arms approach that was hard to defeat without artillery. A well placed cannon shot could do a tremendous amount of damage to the Swiss, as could organised missile fire pouring into their dense ranks.

The *Landsknechte*

One of the first armies the Swiss had defeated was from the German speaking areas, and it is unsurprising that it was from this region that a troop type evolved to counter them. The best non-missile counter for a pike block was another pike block, and that is exactly what the *Landsknechte* formations were.[70] Formed in the 1480s as a copy of the Swiss pike blocks, they adopted firearms and promptly dominated European battlefields for over seventy years. Originally a Germanic force, they employed pikes with steely discipline and strategy, winning victories and fame. Eventually the term *Landsknechte* came to refer to their style of fighting rather than their unit, which although evolved, lasted into the eighteenth century.

These infantry units, designed primarily to be able to repulse cavalry, started to change perceptions of cavalry too. Machiavelli himself advised to only use horses for scouting, pursuing and raiding, and specifically warning against using them on battlefields,[71] perhaps because he knew that they would rarely overcome pikemen. Clearly most commanders across Europe did not agree with Machiavelli at the time, however, for they kept fielding heavy cavalry despite his misgivings. They did maintain specialist infantry, who from 1500 onwards were increasingly important. This gradual evolution of infantry from the low skilled levies of the thirteenth century, right up to professional pike formations of 1500, form a military evolution. This period was perhaps also the golden age of medieval close combat, for as the sixteenth century began, the power of firearms started to eclipse those who fought with lance, sword, or indeed pike. When coming up against armies filled with Swiss halberdiers, pikemen and troops who fought how the *Landsknechte* did, mounted knights were finding themselves up against infantry who had their number. They found more and more that professional troops who trusted in both their weapons and their comrades, and crucially weren't going to run away after the initial encounter, were almost unbeatable.

Almost unbeatable is not the same as invincible though, and the mounted man-at-arms was not yet done. Heavily armoured cavalry could get into pike blocks, sometimes smash the corners of the dense formations, but only on rare occasions, break them open entirely. The role of cavalry was not always to try to break Swiss or *Landsknechte* formations however, and from at least 1495 their role on the battlefield was changing. In a landmark victory at the Battle of Lucera in that year, the *condottieri* Camillo Vitelli used a force of light cavalry to defeat a pike army.[72] These light cavalrymen were not heavily armoured, and used bows rather than lances, but managed to destroy their opponents without even having to charge. For the heavily armoured mounted knight, however, this splitting of the function of the cavalry, in effect creating the term cavalry in the first place, was another notable development in their decline. Light cavalry repeatedly demonstrated the ability to win battles from 1495, when as well as at Lucera, light cavalry from the Balkans proved extremely effective at the Battle of Fornovo.[73]

After watershed light cavalry successes such as these, a combined arms approach started to require many more elements than it had a hundred years previously. Now though, light cavalry, artillery and pikemen were all needed, as well as the more traditional heavy cavalry and missile troops. Mounted knights, still clad in armour, now had the job of destroying enemy light cavalry if the opportunity presented itself, but successful frontal assaults against infantry became rarer and rarer. Infantry had cemented itself a place in all armies, but still in the sixteenth century they were very vulnerable on their own. Cavalry and cannon, even with no infantry support, could still counter the new infantry, regardless of how good they were. At the Battle of Marignano in 1515, a French army made up of large artillery batteries and mounted men-at-arms faced up against a large force of Swiss pikemen. Over two days the Swiss advanced into the mouth of the guns, sustaining terrible casualties as cannonballs smashed into their dense formations. Frequently they managed to reach the guns and push the French back, but every time mounted men-at-arms charged them, and smashed into the Swiss, pushing them back to where they had come from. The French king, demonstrating perfect chivalric qualities, joined in these mounted attacks, and although hit three times by pikes he was saved by his armour.[74] At the end of the second day, the battlefield of Marignano was strewn with the corpses of up to 10,000 Swiss, half of their army, and with them the idea that infantry were invincible without support.

Pike and Shot

Blocks of infantry in the sixteenth century could certainly keep out cavalry, but as vividly demonstrated at Marignano, they also made rather nice targets for missile troops, especially as battlefield artillery became more accurate. Personal gunpowder weapons in the hands of infantry were also able to devastate densely packed units of enemy footsoldiers, meaning that the age of pike and shot was able to begin. This age began as early as the end of the fifteenth century, where gunpowder weapons were of limited reliability, but still proved able to defeat traditionally composed armies. The next development was in the 1530s, when the Spanish developed a particularly sophisticated combined arms system known as the *tericos*, or thirds. These were large formations of pikemen, with gunners, and sometimes halberdiers or swordsmen, around or between the pikemen.[75] Each *terico* formed its own arrangement, sometimes a large square, with one *terico* moving in front of two others to form a triangle or *tericos*.[76] Each *terico* therefore supported the others as they advanced, making a flexible system that lasted for over a hundred years. Importantly, the Spanish *tericos* were flanked on both sides by cavalry, and mounted troops were still used to flank enemies to win battles, before finally pursuing fleeing foes.[77] The French clung on to mounted knights longer than the Spanish did, and were slower to adopt the pike and musket, being decades behind them in taking up muskets.[78] As firearms continued to improve throughout the sixteenth century, musketeers needed pikemen less to defend them, and also presented a greater danger to the massed ranks of the pikemen of their opponents. The effective range and power of their guns also increased to the point where armoured cavalry no longer offered a protective benefit over unarmoured cavalry. However, mounted knights were still taking to the field towards the end of the sixteenth century, so while the rise of infantry had not cast them into obsolescence, their number and role had been greatly reduced. The mounted knight had weathered the storm of shot, and (sometimes) avoided the points of the pikes, so what was it that finally drove them to extinction?

Chapter Eight

Dusk of Knighthood

In this chapter we will study the multitude of factors which contributed to the decline of the mounted knight. They had survived the rise of a professional infantry, and instead of being overwhelmed by them, they complemented them. Knights, mounted on horses, wearing armour, and charging their enemies, could be found on the battlefields of Europe throughout the entire sixteenth century, but they did not survive the seventeenth. A simple explanation will not be found, for simplicity is always the enemy of truth. Instead, the noble mounted knight, a medieval institution, faced numerous assaults on his existence, every facet of his identity was challenged. We will see how no one single factor brought him down, but that rather all of them together were an insurmountable problem. First, gunpowder weapons certainly did not remove the armoured knight from the battlefield on their own, although they did challenge his prowess. Second, the knight's very home, his castle, was rendered obsolete by guns and social change. Third, the relationship between knighthood and his warhorse was strained by a decline of military horsemanship, as well as stock levels. Fourth, the solidification of nation states threatened his authority and purpose. Fifth, the urbanisation and democratisation of the world seriously questioned the influence of knights, especially with the growing strength of royal power. Sixth, when the Christian church broke in two and half of Europe switched to a Protestant faith, those knights found their Christian foundation and tradition irreparably cut from them. Finally, the rise of the gentleman pushed back at the very identity of the knight as a fighting man, severing the link between prowess and power. We shall begin with the event that is usually credited with dispatching the knight from the battlefield, the rise of a chemical made from mixing together saltpetre, sulphur, and charcoal. Gunpowder.

A New Terror

> The English guns cast iron balls by means of fire ... They made a noise like thunder and caused much loss in men and horses ... The Genoese were continually hit by the archers and the gunners ... the whole plain was covered by men struck down by arrows and cannon balls.[1]
>
> Giovanni Villani in his Nuova Cronica

The Florentine Giovanni was not describing a seventeenth-century Italian conflict, but the Battle of Crécy in 1346. This battle is known for the presence of cannon in Edward III's army, but it is possible the impact of them has been overshadowed by his bowmen. This has probably happened because the longbowmen were English, and the specialist gunners were foreign mercenaries. Giovanni's is not the only account that mentions the damage caused by the English guns, but the image he gives us of a plain covered by the victims of cannon balls is enduring. The artillery may well have only managed two or three volleys in the fading light of the battle, so if the carnage those wrought was enough to be described alongside that of the arrows of the longbows, then those volleys must have been a terror to behold. The loud and sudden noise was almost certainly a terror to the French horses, especially in what was essentially darkness, and possibly the English ones too, but at least they were safely corralled behind their lines.

The French warhorses of 1346 had been born into a world where gunpowder weapons were by now twenty years old. Guns existed across France in local hands,[2] although it is impossible to know if the French horses had yet been acclimatised to their explosive noise and foul smell. Firearms had truly arrived with a bang by 1346 however, and it is interesting to note that Crécy is also the battle known for introducing the longbow to France. In a very real sense then, the gun had arrived in France *before* the longbow. This little known fact may explain why the longbow was initially afforded very little respect by the French, if they saw that the future was gunpowder, then why give any time to a backward little nation still playing with bows and arrows? The shattering defeat at Crécy showed the arrogance of such an underestimation, but in their general assessment at least, perhaps the French were not all that wrong.

The truth is that the longbow is not as powerful a weapon as the crossbow, has a shorter range, and is far harder to become proficient with. The most important of these facts was the power – crossbows were twice as powerful as the longbow. Longbow arrows record a force of up to around 80 Joules(J), whereas crossbow bolts can range between 100J and 200J.[3] A Joule is a measurement of the transfer of energy, and for context, 55J is required to penetrate 1mm of unhardened mild steel armour head on. This rises to 175J for 2mm armour.[4] Additionally, hardened armour is 50 per cent stronger than unhardened mild steel, and of course armour was also both potentially thicker than that, and angled to deflect missiles. Seen in this light, the French cannot be blamed for sticking with the crossbow, which actually had a chance of defeating the 2mm of armour that was often found on the battlefield. The gunpowder revolution occurred because the penetrating power of black powder weapons was recognised early on. Fifteenth-century handguns could have a rating anywhere from 500J to 1,000J, albeit at point blank range, which meant only the best armour had a chance to save the victim.[5] Lower quality harnesses would be able to do the job at longer ranges, and everything in between was down to what kind of armour a knight could afford – and luck.

Luck was a factor due to the terrible accuracy over distance of early gunpowder weapons, which made them unreliable. Despite this, the upgrade in power from crossbows is not hard to understand, but a grim example is that of the 17-year-old son of veteran knight Sir John Cornwall. His son was an unfortunate young man who during a siege had his head blown off by a gunstone while standing next to his father.[6] The difference in effect from an arrow and a gunstone was thus gruesomely demonstrated to Cornwall, who promptly left the war with a vow to never again fight against other Christians. Even in its early days gunpowder was deadly, but by the sixteenth century, when the English were still using their longbows, in 1592 Humfrey Barwick wrote, 'I never saw any slain outright with an arrow, … but with harqubuze and pistol shot, I have seen several times where 20,000 have been slain outright.'[7] The impact on the body made by arrows was small, more localised, and caused 'relatively little tissue damage'.[8] Getting hit in the stomach by an arrow was far from an instant kill, despite what Hollywood westerns would have us believe, and it likely would not have taken an adrenaline-fuelled man out of a fight. A bullet on the other hand, medieval or otherwise, sends a pressure wave through the tissue and organs around the impact area, and causes vastly more hideous injuries.[9] A single hit from a bullet, however primitive, had a significantly higher chance of removing its target from a battle than an arrow, or even crossbow bolt. Barwick also noted that a musket will kill, 'the armed of proof at ten score yards, the common armour at twenty score, and the unarmed at thirty'.[10] So, by 1592 even the best armour was vulnerable to infantry gunpowder weapons at a range of 180m, and mediocre armour at twice that.

When assessing how effective the armour of the mounted knights was at keeping out firearms, there are a multitude of factors to keep in mind. First, iron armour probably will not stop any hit, but some steel armour had a small chance to deflect a gunshot by its curvature. A rough and fallible generalisation would be that the majority of armour, that worn by most infantry and some men-at-arms, would not be bulletproof during the fourteenth, and first half of the fifteenth century. However, from 1450 Germany joined Italy as a centre of production for good hardened steel, and some of these top quality armours may have provided some protection against firearms. Paradoxically, the heat treating of armour died out on the Continent during the sixteenth century, at the very time when firearms were reaching a true level of effectiveness. It is suggested, and usually refuted, that the softness of unhardened steel is better against bullets because it spreads out some of the energy from the impact.

This is an area where further work is needed, but in the modern solid-lance jousting community, it is no longer common to heat treat visors because treated ones are more brittle and can snap from a direct lance impact. These lances impart a much higher energy than the 200J of a crossbow bolt, and unhardened steel (in thicker layers), seems to keep lances out. This is essentially a modern anecdote, and cannot be taken as evidence of why hardening ceased historically. As medieval steel became cheaper and better made, the arms race between armour and missile weapons simply escalated. From the fifteenth century, however, almost all medieval warriors – but especially those not of noble birth – would have had cause to fear a volley of gunpowder weapons at close range. The second factor was the reliability of firearms, and in this they had a poor start. Even by 1460, cannons were still accidentally exploding and killing those standing too close, which was the cause of death of James II of Scotland during a siege of Roxburgh Castle.[11] Handgunner's weapons frequently misfired, and when they did work, their accuracy was initially more down to luck than judgement. The reloading time of the early guns was also slow,[12] artillery could sometimes manage only a handful of shots per day, which is why at Crécy it is believable that the English guns only fired a few times each. All of these variables improved as technology advanced, but it should be remembered that Crécy happened in 1346, which is before full and optimised plate armour had been developed. Knights did not see fourteenth century gunpowder weapons as a threat to their existence, rather they saw them as a useful tool for sieges, and eventually tried to use them from horseback. In the fifteenth century though, the technology wasn't quite up to it, and it wasn't until the firing mechanism miniaturised, and no longer needed a burning match to light, that the mounted knight started using firearms from his horse.[13]

The adoption of ground-based artillery happened much faster, for example at Beverhoutsveld in 1382, a single volley of 300 guns from the citizens of Ghent caused so much damage to the men of Bruges, that they broke and fled. That the citizens of Ghent could field 300 guns of their own, tells us much about the spread of a weapon that in 1382 was less than fifty years old. Not that it did them much good in the end, for at the Battle of Roosebeke later in the same year, the people of Bruges gained revenge for their defeat. On this occasion, the French cavalry (which was on their side) outflanked the tightly packed defensive infantry formations of the Ghent army, and defeated them, guns or no guns.[14] The success of the new gunpowder weapons was then not necessarily always obvious, or inevitable. Revealingly, in 1390 a Florentine army paid their master of trebuchets more than their master of cannon,[15] and at the Battle of Othée in 1408, Burgundian cavalry attacked, and were victorious, despite the large amount artillery firing against them.[16] The Burgundian knights may have been triumphant, but the castles from which their power was based were starting to look vulnerable.

Henry V had forced Harfleur to surrender after battering it for a relatively short time with only twelve guns, but in 1464 during the Wars of the Roses, Bamburgh Castle became the first large[17] English castle to be taken through the force of artillery. This use of gunpowder weapons had two effects on the core tenet of the mounted knight: his prowess. First, as infantry gunpowder weapons developed into genuinely useful weapons in the fifteenth and sixteenth centuries, they pushed aside the knight's ability to showcase his martial skills as often as he had before. He still could close with an enemy and defeat them, but critically, he could now be killed by a man who had but little training with a fifteenth-century arquebus. This was of course not a new situation, the crossbow could kill a knight from distance already, yet both had coexisted for centuries. The prowess of crossbowmen and arquebusiers were incomparable to the knight and his lifetime of training, and yet they could still strike him down. This was a question for knights to ponder, but gunpowder did not remove them from the battlefield any more than the crossbow had done.

Another issue that would leave a bitter taste in their mouth was the use of siege artillery. The warfare of the mounted knight had been an art form. The control of his horse, his very armour, the manner in which he wielded his lance, all of these were art. Instructions for riding a horse or lowering a lance could be written down, but to learn these skills, one needs to feel them, think about them, and sometimes, trust in instinct. This could not be further from the skills required to manage an artillery piece during a siege. Here the requirements are mathematics, logic, chemistry and accounting, which is rather more a science than an art. Such was the sulphuric taste left in the mouth of the knight watching a siege engineer calculate trajectory, while he and his horse sat watching, wondering when they might next be able to demonstrate their prowess.

The Defeat of Castles, or was it?

By the early fifteenth century, artillery had become reliable enough to break down castle walls, beginning a period where guns had the upper hand, lasting to around 1540. This new dawn was spectacularly heralded by a crescendo of artillery fire, when the famed walls of Constantinople were brought crashing down in 1453. Constantinople's walls had withstood many previous attacks, but this time the Ottoman attackers had brought dozens of large cannon, including one that was 8m long and could fire a 270kg projectile over a mile.[18] With this capability emerging, the home of the mounted knight, his castle, was most definitely under threat.

Artillery didn't immediately make castles obsolete however, and some medieval castles were able to hold out respectably well even against seventeenth-century cannon during the English Civil War.[19] Castles did what they could to adapt to their new situation, gun loops appeared for gunners to shoot out of, artillery towers were built, and over time fortifications became lower, becoming buttressed in front with earth banks to absorb artillery shot. For the smaller castles and keeps of the lower and middling knightly classes, it was another matter entirely, and they were not able to keep serious gunfire out. Handgunners could fire out from these smaller fortifications, but many would not have been large enough to house their own defensive cannon. Not being able to afford gunpowder defences is sometimes put forward as a contributing factor in the decline of the knight, but a closer inspection reveals this not necessarily to be the case.

Edward III and Henry V invested heavily in English gunpowder artillery, which sprung up everywhere for local defence. This was most pronounced around English-held Calais, where a huge quantity of artillery was deployed to ensure the French were kept out.[20] So widespread had guns become, that even English merchants were buying firearms in the fifteenth century to defend their shipping. In fact, by 1486 firearms were already cheap, and Richard Cely was able to purchase eleven serpentines and guns, including ammunition, for just £4, to arm his merchant ship.[21] Revealingly, this amount was enough to buy a fully functional war horse. This simple monetary comparison shows the pressure that the mounted knight was already up against. If a knight's horse, before even thinking of armour, cost the same as ten cannon and handguns, the writing was on the wall. This proliferation of gunpowder weaponry was in evidence during the Wars of the Roses, where artillery made frequent appearances, even popping up being used by private parties around the country. For example, in *The Paston Letters* we find that when the Duke of Norfolk attacked the Pastons' castle at Caistor in 1469, where both sides had guns, one of the defenders was killed, and others hurt by guns and crossbows. The castle itself seems to have suffered most, being 'sore broken with guns'.[22] The castle may not have fallen to cannon in the end, but neither side in the siege were royal forces, and despite it essentially being a local dispute, both were armed to the teeth with an assortment of firearms. Although not present at Caister, the royal arsenal was on occasion deployed in the war, and a number of the guns used to successfully reduce Bamburgh Castle were taken from the Calais garrison. This is not surprising given that the Earl of Warwick was both the Governor of Calais, and the man responsible for taking Bamburgh.[23]

Following the conclusion of the Wars of the Roses, towards the end of the fifteenth century, English noblemen started to build their homes in a more stately, and less military form. This was because the kingdom eventually became more peaceful, and although the English fought in wars in the following century, they usually did so on other people's soil. The sixteenth century in Europe was a much more turbulent period, but the French spent the early part of the century fighting wars in Italy, which meant the home front was as quiet as it was in England. Hence resulting châteaux like Château de Chambord in central France, built between 1519 and 1547. It might have had towers and a moat, but those, along with all the other superficially medieval features, were purely decorative by design. This design was heavily influenced by those in Italy, and labelled as partly renaissance in style, as the world pulled itself away from the medieval era and towards modernity.

Within Italy itself, military construction had taken a different direction. With the French and Holy Roman Empire both fighting in the protracted Italian Wars, fortification was still a priority for the local inhabitants, who were constantly under siege. Even the famed artist Michelangelo sketched out the defences of the gates of Florence when an attack was feared. His drawings show triangular structures optimised for gunpowder warfare, with carefully planned firing positions, resembling the star forts Michelangelo himself would pioneer soon after.[24] From 1530, these star forts started to appear in Italy as their defensive abilities became obvious. The French in particular had brought effective cannon and bombards to the country, and the star forts were the response to their firepower. These forts were low, angled and banked with earth to counter cannon fire. They had wide ditches to delay assaulting infantry, and had bastions positioned so that their cannon could fire along the ditches if enemy infantry got too close. From above these fortifications look like strange geometric shapes, jagged edges sometimes bordered with watery moats, but when manned with enough artillery, they were a very difficult proposition for attackers. Their reduced profile, compared to tall medieval castles, meant they were much smaller targets for artillery, and as a result these forts essentially replaced the military function of castles.

Cities and urban areas tended to be the ones which had such defensive works built around them, and for the mounted knight this was the beginning of a cultural change which saw them losing their status as defenders of the countryside. After all, a knight's job was to defend his land from his castle, and raise troops from that area, or at least the money to pay for some. In this sense, the obsolescence of the knight's home was actually caused because it no longer needed to be a centre for troop recruitment, and the fact that warfare had shifted away from the lands that had been the birthplace of the castle.

In England and France, conflict ravaged up and down the country far less after the end of the Wars of the Roses than during the Hundred Years War, and as a result, small military fortifications simply weren't needed, and as they also cost astronomical sums of money to build, the nobility had little incentive to build or maintain them any longer. The castle was first and foremost an instrument of war; as wars became less frequent and siege artillery continued to improve, the importance of castles diminished. The paradox is that despite the rise of infantry, and the lessening importance of the medieval castle in the sixteenth century, the mounted man-at-arms did not find his services were likewise no longer needed. Instead, pitched battles raged across southern Europe, in which swift-moving cavalry were indispensable. The failure of the Swiss pikemen to attack the French guns at Marignano in 1515 had been very much instigated by the repeated charges of the French men-at-arms, whose horses had attacked the pikemen and beaten them. The victorious French king said that, 'no one in future will be able to say that cavalry are of no more use'.[25] A statement which does of course suggest that some were already questioning it.

Having a fast-moving armoured fist, therefore, was still a requirement in the sixteenth century, even in the age of cannon, infantry, and fortification. These fortifications had caught up with gunpowder weapons, and as a consequence sieges became longer and longer; for example, the siege of Ostend went on from 1601 to 1604.[26] The legacy of the traditional medieval castle was not forgotten however, and in the Low Countries the nobility were interested enough to bother to classify their fortifications. To do this, in the Province of Utrecht in around 1610, a register was drawn up of true ancient castles, which were built before 1400, castles of around 200 years of age, and then everything more recent. To belong to the Knightly Order in Utrecht in 1536, one had to have a castle, and that castle had to comply with strict standards – for example having a moat.[27] The defensive abilities of castles had been tested by artillery, and superseded by forts, but what the Utrecht register shows is that they still held a power in the imagination of people, even when the mounted knight had ceased to use them as operational bases. In the end, castles were successful in their primary intended purpose, to delay attacking forces, but after they were no longer required, they simply changed. They morphed slowly, over centuries, into stately homes instead.

The Last Knight

Maximilian I, The Holy Roman Emperor (1459–1519) is also sometimes known as 'The Last Knight'. In his youth he wore the most ornate armour the western world has ever seen, Gothic armour waspishly tight around his waist, and decorated with jaw-dropping metalworking skills. He was a patron of various arts, especially the art of armour. He even deployed armour for political and diplomatic aims, by giving potential allies harnesses of armour as gifts. Henry VIII of England was given a helmet with horns and a pair of spectacles on it, with a face made to resemble Maximilian's own. However odd this may seem, the English king was thrilled with the gift from a man he rather idolised, and even inducted the Emperor into the Order of the Garter.[28] Maximilian courted chivalric association, and took part in elaborate jousts and tournaments designed to put across a certain image of himself to his people. His full-on propaganda campaign is perhaps best encapsulated by what was inscribed into a triumphal chariot made for him, 'What the sun is in the heavens, the Emperor is on Earth.'[29] His armour and horsemanship were used to create the image of the perfect medieval ruler, but importantly Maximilian wasn't all talk and no substance. Before he had been the Emperor, and when only twenty years old, he formed an army to claim an inheritance he thought rightfully his. His goal was nothing less than the Duchy of Burgundy. At Guingate in 1479, Maximilian formed his army into two pike squares facing a French army that was standing in his way. Unlike the French, Maximilian could see which way the winds of change were blowing, and did something no one expected. He got down from his horse, picked up a pike, and joined one of his infantry squares.[30] He ordered a couple of hundred of his nobles to do the same, and fighting in the front rank, led his army to victory.

The Last Knight he may have been, but Maximilian saw no chivalric contradiction in dismounting when appropriate. His court, filled with jousting, horsemanship, arts and science, was a true chivalric court and, although he wasn't the literal Last Knight, his efforts and patronage pushed chivalry to its final peak.[31] Not long after Maximilian's death, an Ottoman army invaded Hungary, and in 1526 faced one of the last chivalric armies in Europe. The Hungarian army consisted of heavily armoured mounted knights and men-at-arms, and wouldn't have looked out of place a hundred years earlier. The only sixteenth-century upgrade was that they had fifty cannon, primed and facing the Ottomans. The Ottomans, however, marched into Hungary with a modern army, filled with musketeers and with an artillery train that boasted up to 200 cannon. They met at the Battle of Mohacs where the Hungarian heavy cavalry charged across the plain and defeated bodies of Muslim cavalry as their forefather's had done for 400 years.[32] However, this was no longer enough to win battles, and the chivalric army was promptly shot to pieces. The Ottomans knew that large volumes of firearm infantry could pour fire into an enemy, at least one who did not counter them, and overwhelmed by firepower, the Hungarians were defeated.

The increasing Ottoman presence in Europe, as symbolised by Mohacs, was changing its character as well as its borders. In a breakdown of Christianity that included Protestants fighting Catholics, even Christian states seemed willing to ally with the Islamic Ottomans. In 1543, the French allied with them in order to capture Nice in Italy, with troops from both taking part.[33] This happened because King Francis I of France hated the Christian Duke of Savoy more than he cared about the threat the Ottomans posed to his own religion. The spirit of collaboration that launched the First Crusade was a distant memory indeed. The following year in 1544, the Battle of Ceresole in Italy showed how far European military thought had come, and also what position the mounted knight still held in combat. In the north west of Italy, a French army containing a core of Swiss pikemen fought a bitter battle against a Hapsburg army featuring a large *Landsknechte* force. When these two pike formations clashed in the middle of the battlefield, the carnage was terrible. The French had innovated by putting musketeers in their second rank behind the front rank of pikes, and had given them the order to fire a volley at point-blank range. As they reached the enemy, the delight in their cunning plan may have evaporated when they saw that the second rank of the *Landsknechtes* comprised of pistol-wielding troops, who therefore were using exactly the same plan. Both sides closed, both sides paused, and then both sides fired a terrible volley into the massed ranks opposite them. The result was that the front rank of both pike formations was utterly wiped out, with no advantage given to either side.

As the Swiss and *Landsknechtes* fought out a battle of attrition following this devastating volley, two cavalry actions occurred that would be decisive. To the north, the majority of the French heavy cavalry attacked, but was defeated by, the Hapsburg army, despite breaking a corner of their formation. However, a group of French knights and men-at-arms, fewer than a hundred in strength, charged the flank of the *Landsknechtes* fighting the Swiss, and ruptured their cohesion. Despite the French only having eighty horsemen to face 7,000 pikemen, the cavalry didn't just disrupt the pike formation, they broke it.[34] A desperately small group of mounted men-at-arms created a victory for the French in the face of well disciplined pike infantry, even though it had its own integrated firearms support. The mounted knight might have been feeling social, financial and technological pressures, but he was not done yet.

The Knight's Horse

Despite some successes on the battlefield, the mounted knight in the sixteenth century was under pressure. The strong currents of change which were transforming Europe would not stop, and they would also fundamentally change the type of horse that knights would ride. In another of the contradictions that collect around the knight, the new horse would be the most chivalric yet, and yet utterly unsuitable for the battlefield. This change can be illustrated by the evolution of horsemanship within the Tudor court in England, especially during the reign of Henry VIII.

What comes to mind when one thinks of Henry VIII, at least after his wives, is jousting. As the heir to the throne, his father had not allowed him to joust for fear of his death, but like many young people forbidden something, this only made him want it more. Once he was king, a young and athletic Henry VIII became a keen and competent jouster, using any opportunity he could to show the world what kind of man he was. His royal jousts were a far cry from the early medieval tournament fields however; no longer would bands of knights clash in tournaments on the boundaries of two territories, jousting was a matter of state. This did not signal a decline of its popularity or importance, and in 1511 Henry VIII spent almost twice as much on one tournament than he did on a 900-ton warship.[35] These huge occasions demanded a spectacle, producing lavish spending on what can only be described as sumptuous luxury. For example, £1,000 (over £600,000 today) was spent on costumes for everyone involved in one tournament, including horses bardings.[36]

The knightly practice of jousting had been subsumed by pageantry and theatre, but it hadn't gone away, and the horses and armour involved were still the same. Even during Elizabeth I's reign in the second half of the century, jousting retained a prized place at the court. The practice, however, became even more localised around the monarch, and private individuals increasingly took on the burden of paying for jousting.[37] Elizabeth had a political use for the knightly sport, it gave her the ability to project an image of manly power by her proximity to it, and played a small part in maintaining her authority. Even after Elizabeth's death, a jousting arena with 12,000 spectators was planned in 1622, and although never built, it shows that enthusiasm for the sport persisted.[38] Neither Henry VIII nor his successors had issues with waning popularity, he was able to lay on extravagant jousting events for himself. He also, perhaps surprisingly, had enough horses. Considering the English army by then had a tradition of fighting on foot, Tudor England was still described as the kingdom of the horse by foreign observers.[39] One cause of this was a shift in the ranking given to the various types of knightly horses. When De Gamez had listed those as being horses for war, jousting and the parade,[40] he would probably have put their importance in that order.

During the early sixteenth century however, with the Renaissance in full swing, it is not surprising that there was a change in this ranking. The parade horse, although seen in medieval art and mentioned as far back as Xenophon, had been in the back seat, but now was raised to greatness. As early as 1517, Henry VIII himself was said to have performed, 'marvellous feats',[41] in between jousting courses where he made horses, 'jump and execute other arts of horsemanship'.[42] The definition of horsemanship had changed. The jumps and other acts that Henry was performing were of the sort now labelled as Classical Dressage, and not genuine battlefield moves. This signalled the moment by which horsemanship in itself had finally become courtly, and detached from the battlefield. This new courtly riding, that is precise, elegant and sometimes explosive dressage movements, became exceedingly popular across Europe, with Sir Thomas Elyot proclaiming in 1531 that horsemanship was 'the most honourable exercise'[43] that one could practice. Henry VIII himself was a pupil of Robert Alexander, a follower of Federico Grisone,[44] who had founded a riding academy in Naples in 1532, and published *The Rules of Riding* in 1550. This work spread across the courts of Europe just as fast as the Arthurian romances had done, and was hugely influential. Men of knightly status read this work, as well as the others that followed from other riding masters, and applied them to their own horses. The art of dressage was now fashionable, and the art of war was the casualty. This helps to explain the contradiction between the perceived importance of horses and horsemanship in England, versus the lack of English heavy cavalry serving Henry VIII.

Thomas Bedingfield, who in 1584 complained that, 'the Gentlemen of this land have studied to make horses more for pleasure than service',[45] clearly understood the issue. By the time he was writing, we can clearly see that the knights of England were throwing their energy into the new horsemanship, a discipline that was potentially harder to master than riding in war, but had no martial application. The horses trained for the jumps could be more sensitive and higher maintenance than those suitable for campaigns, and once trained, far too valuable to risk in war. The mounted knight might still be mounted, but by the end of the sixteenth century he was probably spending more time on his parade horse than his jousting horse, let alone his warhorse. Tudor horsemanship within the nobility was therefore primarily concerned with reaching these high levels of courtly horsemanship, skills which are preserved in modern times by the Spanish Riding School of Vienna in Europe, and by some displays at Bolsover Castle in England.

I have had the honour to ride in these displays, performing the school jumps to an audience at Bolsover Castle. While I will never be as good as Henry VIII when he performed his jumps, they are so enjoyable I can appreciate why he wanted to show them to the world. The seventeenth-century occupant of Bolsover Castle, one William Cavendish, represents the height of courtly horsemanship in England. However, his stud was sold by the Puritans in 1644 when he and his royalist allies were defeated in the English Civil War. Cavendish was a knight who led mounted troops on the battlefield, but was ultimately bested by lower-born Parliamentarian rivals mounted on their more basically trained horses. Although some of these cavalrymen in the English Civil War were actually armoured, this was now not common, and the mounted knight had by the 1640s, *almost* fully vacated the battlefield. The horses still used on those battlefields were not the highly schooled dressage horses of the court, or even the well trained knightly war horses. What happened to those?

Warhorses

Despite the repeated assertion that the English knight had dismounted by the fifteenth century, the fact is that the nobility still kept up the skills of fighting from horseback. The defeat of Richard III's final knightly charge at Bosworth is significant in that it was a mounted charge. The new king wanted to keep them too, and the victor of Bosworth, now Henry VII, went as far as to ban the export of warhorses in 1495. This probably was less about stopping good English stock being sold to foreigners, and more about keeping decent native horses in the country in the first place. The issue Henry VII had was that English royal stud numbers, from a height of forty in around 1350, never get above five after 1410.[46] Henry VIII inherited this shortfall, and continually imported horses in one strategy to make up for it, as well as enacting laws in the 1530s on breeding methods.[47] The knights of the realm may have still been riding horses trained for war, but their numbers were comparatively small,[48] and as such the actual demand for warhorses was low. This was a sure sign of the decline of the old horse-based culture, the culture that harked back to the martial chivalry of the tournament and William Marshal.

In the Tudor knight's horse we see another example of knighthood changing and yet staying the same. Prowess on horseback was still a key requirement, but now it was displayed in the riding houses of England, rather than on the battlefields of Europe. Incidentally, the fact that it was European battlefields where the English knight demonstrated his prowess for much of the entire medieval period, should be analysed. When we earlier saw Henry II's reluctance to ship his lesser knights overseas, that the fact England was an island was influencing how it waged war. The cost of transporting horses to France was high, shipping was usually scarce, and extra men were better to have than extra warhorses. Special shipping was also needed because horses couldn't simply be walked into the cargo hold of a ship, and be expected to walk out again unscathed after a voyage. These sea voyages were notoriously risky for horses too, and specialist shipping or not, some would die on even a calm trip. Storms were a terrifying risk, and horses were lost in high quantities when they hit.

The cost of equine shipping meant that waging war in France was significantly more expensive for the English than the French. One temporary solution to the problem was to buy horses upon reaching France, which was possible in the fourteenth century, but in the fifteenth it seems to have been harder. Likewise, it was more an option in the south of France than the north, which had lower stocks of horses available.[49] This geographical feature of the middle ages may not have killed off the English warhorse, but it was yet another pressure on it, and means we have to look to mainland Europe to see how warhorses were faring. The Spanish too were feeling financial pressures in their wars in the sixteenth century. In 1536, Spanish Captain Diego de Salazer complained that Spanish knights were taking four horses to the battlefield each, ride only one, and still often perform badly. The German knights, he said, only took one horse in total, and were therefore not using up huge resources which could be employed elsewhere.[50] Despite this acknowledgement of financial pressures, mounted knights were still fighting across the continent, and it is the French enemies of the Spanish who give us perhaps the finest example of how mounted knights were still a force to be feared.

An Officer of Light Cavalry

The Wars of Religion in France spanned the final forty years of the sixteenth century, and were a set of conflicts pitting the Catholic French, with their Spanish allies, against the Protestant factions of Europe, who were supporting King Henry of Navarre. In this internationalised civil war, it was Henry of Navarre who would be victorious, becoming King Henry IV of France, who both utilised and modernised the mounted knight. Henry IV realised that mounted troops could fulfil a number of roles, and unusually he led his armies from the front, a fact which even some on his own side thought was somewhat foolish and old fashioned. Henry IV's personal bravery and prowess give him a better claim than others to being The Last Knight, even if his enemies described him derogatorily as, 'an officer of light cavalry'.[51] Henry IV would have the last laugh, and at the same time was able to prove that chivalry could still flicker on the battlefields of Europe.

Henry IV recognised the mobility of mounted firearm infantry, but also perfected the use of heavy shock cavalry. Being chronically underfunded, Henry IV relied on his lower nobility fighting for little or no pay, and the fact they did speaks much for the conviction of religious feeling, as well as his personal leadership. For example, among his somewhat ragtag army, one of his noblemen complained that although he had a fine Arab horse, his only armour was a cuirass.[52] Perhaps spurred on by his scarce cavalry resources, Henry perfected better ways to use them. He dispensed with the long thin line of the classic knightly charge, and replaced it with deeper blocks of men-at-arms, armed with swords and pistols. This would be an effective combination once deep within an enemy army, the men-at-arms able to blast and slash away at close quarters. This was a recognition that the lance was sometimes not the most devastating weapon on the battlefield, but also of the fact that enemy infantry was now usually deployed in so many ranks, that a full charge would not break them straight away. Although this new formation wasn't Henry IV's idea, his insistence they closed with the enemy, preferably getting in and among them, was rarer.

Other earlier users of the pistol-armed formation had, instead of charging home, rode up to the enemy and ridden around in a large circle, discharging their pistols on their way round. Due to the low technological sophistication of these weapons, however, these so-called 'caracole' tactics were usually a waste of time. During the French wars, Henry IV's heavily armoured sword and pistol troops frequently came up against lance-wielding Catholic cavalry, and found that they could beat them. Their deep ranks could punch through the single rank of their enemies, and by maintaining good order they could then finish off the fragmented enemy. The ability to draw several pistols, and rapidly shoot at enemy knights at close range was critical to Henry IV's success. In close combat their pistols would penetrate an awful lot of the armour that got in their way, and quickly too, certainly much more quickly than a lancer could finish the same opponent off.

Gunpowder wasn't ending the dominance of the mounted man-at-arms, it was making him more powerful. At the battle of Ivry in 1590, Henry IV's massed ranks of armoured cavalry annihilated the Catholic army, killing thousands while sustaining only small losses themselves. This was done by the armoured men-at-arms, but Henry also perfected the use of light cavalry, and separated their role from the knights, which allowed both categories of cavalry to do their respective jobs better. Henry's armies were sometimes entirely mounted, allowing him to outmanoeuvre, and then outfight the larger, more unwieldy armies of the Catholics. Having the ability to bring up arquebusiers to a critical point because they were on horseback, allowed him to support the attacks of his men-at-arms too. Yet again we find an example where a combined-arms approach is successful when combined with good leadership. Although his armies had many more men-at-arms than noble knights, both served in his cavalry and both wore plenty of armour. They may have left their lances hanging over their fireplaces when they went to war, but the knights were still mounted, and at the end of the sixteenth century they were still winning wars and allowing kings to be crowned.

For the losing side, change came too, but not quite as quickly. In 1582, one Spaniard argued that his heavy cavalry was useful as 'bastion' in a defensive stance, and that they should still train with the sword and lance and be skilled at charging into the enemy.[53] Old ways die hard, partly because sometimes the knightly charge with lance still worked, but by 1600 this was becoming rarer. Importantly, even Henry IV's deep formation wielding swords and pistols still needed warhorses nimble enough to be able to cope with the tactic, as well as the noise and smoke of the firearms. Back at the Battle of Ivry, we find some 7,000 warhorses involved in one location, and so the systems to breed, train, and maintain them were therefore still in place, just ten years before the seventeenth century.

The knight's horse had undergone a radical process of change from 1500 to 1600, but the warhorse was still very much present. Rather, the knight had started to focus on his other horses, his courtly horses, and split his time between the two. Increasingly in England this led to the nobility concentrating very much more on their riding houses than their jousting tilt yards, but in Europe the warhorse was still a formidable weapon of war. It was also still being ridden by armoured knights. The warhorse was the aspect of knighthood that actually survived the middle ages most intact, and although continuously changing, was still a major part of armies in 1914. The difference between the warhorse of 1514, and 1914, was who was riding them.

The Man-at-Arms

The sixteenth century could legitimately be called the century of the man-at-arms, but they had been a presence even on the early medieval battlefield. The Norman cavalry who ascended the hill at Hastings could equally be called men-at-arms as knights, and armoured mounted troops are a continuing medieval feature. By the fourteenth century, the armies of Edward I and Edward III had at least three men-at-arms to each knight,[54] but by the early fifteenth century we see that the proportion of men-at-arms had risen still further. For example, in a muster roll after Agincourt for the Harfleur garrison, we find 300 men at arms, of which just thirty were knights, lords or barons.[55] This is a rate of nine men-at-arms for each knight, and by the 1430s the number of knights available in total was down to a few hundred. Compared to the 1,500 knights estimated to have existed in 1300, this was a heavy drop, and a decrease made up for by men-at-arms.[56]

The fifteenth century was a maturing period for men-at-arms; that is, those men who could afford the horse, armour and weapons required in order to fight as armoured cavalrymen. They proved they could fight as effectively as their noble counterparts, but largely slip under the radar concerning the medieval military landscape. Social mobility within medieval society increased along with the trend for urban living, a mobility that was stronger for those who fought. The son of a tradesman or official could purchase enough equipment to serve as an archer, and if fortunate enough, could come out of a lucrative campaign with the funds to upgrade to a man-at-arms. Their pay would then be higher, and so was their chance of capturing a prisoner, whose ransom could be a life-changing sum. Therefore, it was possible for a man of initially modest means to move up the ranks to become an armoured cavalryman, riding alongside knights into battle. This route also bypassed the education and training undertaken by the nobility, for a veteran archer who had been slowly buying armour would be familiar with riding in it, as well as the ways of war.

The manner in which these men were recruited also had an impact, and the fourteenth century saw the English move to an indenture system of contracts for military forces, which was a significant move towards a modern professional army. The move towards smaller forces than had been fielded in the thirteenth century also points to the understanding that training and experience meant more than numbers. Even Squires were allowed to participate in tournaments for the first time during the century, and with class boundaries blurring considerably, non-noble men-at-arms were in demand and rising in status. Towards the end of the fourteenth century, fewer than 10 per cent of men-at-arms in English armies were actual knights, and it has to be recognised that knights were already acting as an officer class.[57] Men-at-arms into the fifteenth century were as effective as actual knights on the field, but not anywhere near as expensive to produce or pay, partly because all men mustered with their own equipment.

The trend of removing pieces of armour and serving in units of lighter cavalry made them cheaper too, and we can see an example of a demi-lancer, that is a man-at-arms with only partial armour, in a famous woodcut by Albrecht Dürer in 1495. The rise of light cavalry was fuelled by the men-at-arms who manned these units, as most knights would serve in heavy cavalry. This combination of light cavalry, and what became known as heavy cavalry, would be the constituent parts of cavalry as a whole, a concept which persisted through the renaissance period. This means that the warhorse and armour, of the mounted knight survived within the concept of the man-at-arms, as he became the cavalryman of the seventeenth and eighteenth centuries. Therefore, the martial prowess of the knight was a mantle that was taken up by this non-noble colleague, and it was not his knightly abilities on the battlefield that led to his ultimate fall.

Power

The authority wielded by knights stemmed from their enduring ability to control battlefields as well as their local lands. The strongest example of this local power was in the Anglo-Norman period, where the Dukes of Normandy were nearly as powerful as the French kings to whom they were supposedly subordinate. We saw earlier that such a climate, one containing many powerful men in the form of the knightly class, flourished to fill a power vacuum above them. Kings of the period were acutely aware that they did not have the personal authority to fully control their knights and nobles – not all of the time at least – but over the following 600 years this changed. The middle ages can be seen as an age where power coalesced, merging multiple areas of smaller territories into larger ones. This solidification of kingdoms, most apparent in France, was also a solidification of power. With the crown spreading its sphere of influence, someone had to lose out, and that was the nobility. One indicator of this is that France contained eighty large noble fiefdoms in 1480, but by 1530 there were only forty.[58] As kings increased their royal power, nobles became less critical to the running of the state, and instead became a threat to it. Fourteenth-century armies were raised by nobles because they saw it as their duty, and these forces were the foundation of military expeditions, but by the sixteenth century, kings were raising armies themselves.

In 1439 Charles VII of France created a number of ordinances,[59] effectively authoritative orders, that reformed the French military landscape. All commands were to be allocated by the king, civilians were prohibited to be attacked, and no longer would armies live off the land. Instead a tax would be levied against the nation to pay for a single royal army and its provisions. This meant no more pillaging of the French countryside by mercenary companies, or the French armies themselves for that matter. As with all programs of change, Charles VII's reforms didn't go well to begin with as some nobles ignored it, others even joined an armed rebellion which lasted for a whole summer. This approach of funding an army through tax was maintained in the Truce of Tours in the 1440s, which bound the English forces in France to do the same.[60] This was a major modernising step, by stopping armies living off the land it went a long way towards protecting non-combatants from becoming collateral damage, although it was not an instant solution.

In 1445, Charles VII continued his policy of reform, and created a standing army made up from fifteen captains, who each commanded a company of 100 lances each. A lance was the most basic medieval unit, whose constitution varied greatly, and did not mean one man armed with a lance. In the fourteenth century for example, an English lance as used by mercenaries in Italy was defined as two men-at-arms and a page, who would help them arm and act as an assistant.[61] The French lance as specified in the 1440s, however, consisted of 'one man-at-arms, two archers, and three armed attendants'.[62] Therefore, the French companies comprising 100 lances, was actually made up of 600 armed men. These fifteen companies had to be mustered and reviewed periodically to ensure compliance with the ordinances, and these companies were stationed around the country, providing the French with a defence network. The number of companies in this standing army increased over time, partly because of how popular they were. After the 1445 ordinance in particular, the minor nobility of France joined up in droves so that they could benefit from the good rates of pay on offer. One consequence of this was that the price of good horses in France shot up as the nobility rearmed themselves in order to meet the entry requirements.[63] The gentlemen of France effectively needed good jobs. This also tells us something of the financial state of the minor nobility in the mid-fifteenth century. If they needed to swap their time for a salary, then they must have had financial pressures. The mounted knight in France was not training because it was his duty and privilege to do so, but because he needed the money, and the army was now the best employer around.

Clearly not a man to leave a job half done, Charles VII went even further in 1448. He decreed that for every area of fifty to eighty households, one man-at-arms or crossbowman had to be available to the army. This cunningly enfranchised towns and villages, by sending men from them to all corners of France in service, and in a small way binding those population centres to the state. This was a sort of reserve army to be mustered as and when required, but before we judge it as an unprofessional bunch of reservists, we should remember that this was the army that kicked the English out of France for good. Following this victory, the French engaged in yet more organisational changes to shore up their new kingdom, but the most important theme across all the ordinances for the mounted knight, was that the job of mustering soldiers had been taken away from them.[64] This reduction in their role would have implicitly taken power away from their class. For centuries, the primary job of the knight living in his castle had been to protect his lands, which meant protecting them with the soldiers he could muster himself. The king of France had moved in on this, and replaced the nobility as the defenders of the people. One driver of this was reliability. When a king relied on nobles to raise troops, it had often been the case that some didn't turn up, and others mustered with inadequate numbers in order to save their own cash.

Even worse was when kings and nobles fell out, as the English did on a spectacular scale in the Wars of the Roses, in which case the nobles ended up fighting against the king. Charles VII probably had these problems in mind when he decided it was best if only he could raise armies in his kingdom. This creation of standing armies is linked to the rise of so called 'nation states', an important step on the road to modernity, and a concept made possible by the solidification of territory that was well advanced in the fifteenth century. However, the French did not necessarily get there first, and 'the first European rulers to build a standing were actually the Ottoman sultans.[65] Similarly, Poland from 1466 is described as being 'one of the early modern nation-states', after it managed to defeat the Teutonic knights and began carving out a national identity.[66] The losers in this trend were not confined to the knightly class and, 'by the end of the sixteenth century, the Hanseatic League of trading cities had effectively relinquished its international role to nation-state rivals'.[67] The Hanseatic League was a confederation of merchants spread across northern and central Europe, a hugely wealthy and influential entity, but not one that could stand up to the new nation states. The states of France, England and Spain also had to stand up to each other, and by the sixteenth century this meant raising larger and larger armies.

Knights and recruitment systems of a feudal flavour couldn't raise enough troops to meet the demand, and this was another driving factor behind the program of changes enacted by Charles VII in France. While nation states in their full form were still in their childhood in the fifteenth and sixteenth centuries, the process of their forming included an increase in bureaucracy which also served to remove power from the mounted knight. These bureaucracies were administered by professionals who could be called civil servants, and they implemented tax systems, legal codes, and organised the enforcement of them.[68] These were functions that knights had been performing for a thousand years, and the loss of them was yet more chipping away at their responsibilities and power. In

England it was even worse; the institution of parliament held additional powers, serving to centralise power and move it another step away from knights in their rural castles.[69] If things were already looking bad for the power of the English knightly class, there was perhaps an even greater existential problem. The fact that parliaments granted taxation requests from the monarch, meant that a good case had to be made in order for the members of parliament to acquiesce. It was not in their interest to finance a poorly thought-out war, not when the taxation raised would also come partly out of their own pockets. It was for war that most requests for taxes were needed, and war remained the primary function of the knights. Having a parliament served to limit wars, which limited the need for knights, as well as the potential profit that could be made from them. It also reduced the scope for mounted knights to demonstrate their prowess, and together all these factors give the impression of a social group under the most severe pressure. With their stage shrinking, the cast of knights who kept up their martial skills likewise withered.[70]

The Gentleman

In his fourteenth-century *Canterbury Tales*, Geoffrey Chaucer, who tellingly introduces his knight first, describes him as a 'gentil knyght'.[71] By the time of William Shakespeare, the term 'gentleman' was widespread, and he wrote a play entitled *The Two Gentlemen of Verona* towards the end of the sixteenth century. In the centuries between Chaucer and Shakespeare, the knight morphed slowly into the gentleman, his very character changed and he became something slightly removed from his older medieval self. The same, yet different. The shift from knight to gentlemen was one of purpose, a slide away from war being the reason of existence, to an optional and temporary occupation. One threat to martial usefulness materialised in the 1520s, when some mounted knights adopted wheel-lock pistols. These were pistols that no longer needed matches to fire, which made them viable on horseback, and as a result, knights started to leave their lances at home.

The early ineffectiveness of these pistols threatened to kill off the mounted knight because they did very little damage at all. So pointless they appeared to be, that the philosopher Montaigne wanted to throw away the wheel-lock entirely, and go back to the sword.[72] This was a low level crisis of usefulness, and the mounted knights' experimentation with various weapons during the sixteenth century was part of that self doubt. Knights were getting off their horses and joining the infantry as officers, as Maximilian I had done at Guingate, and in the Spanish army they were already being referred to as captains. The volume of true knights was dropping off, leaving almost only the true nobility of kingdoms as genuinely knightly. This simply served to reinforce the status of the knight as an officer, especially once their powers of recruitment and local administration had been subsumed by the state.

The leaders of armies in the sixteenth century didn't have to lead mounted charges from the front any longer, despite the exploits of the French King Henry IV, and they didn't even have to demonstrate personal prowess in battle. Leadership started to rely less on personal charisma and leading by example, and more on logistics, planning, calculation and diplomacy. Commanders now had to place cannon, calculate trajectories and organise ever more complicated logistics.[73] This change in the nature of required leadership skills, necessarily changed the nature of the men who displayed them. In one sense this move towards science represented the emotional shift from a style of warfare that some could see as romantic, to an industrial killing-scape. The romances of Arthur's splendid court had no place among the acrid cannon smoke, smoke that also served to obscure most genuine displays of heroism. Hard pressed on every side by an encroaching modern world, the knight as a primarily fighting man found himself squeezed out of history. Knights had always been officers, commanding groups of other knights or men-at-arms, but they had also lowered their lances and smashed into the enemy at the head of their troops. At Agincourt, they had stood in the front rank and fought with poleaxes and knives, yet a hundred years later this requirement had faded away.

In 1528, Baldassare Castiglione wrote *The Book of the Courtier*, a work more aimed at gentlemen than knights. Within its pages heroes were still classical but now also contemporary, and a disdain for the unsophisticated middle ages was being born. Reputation within its pages is everything, actual reality means nothing at all. There is no romance in *The Book of the Courtier*, it advocates doing whatever is required to get what you want. If you read it alongside Charny's work on chivalry, the differences jump out. Charny's focus on great deeds, even if no one knows about them, might have found approval with Aristotle and his concept of Virtue, whereas Castiglione would judge it naive and pointless. The sense of individualism that chivalry fostered is, however, still alive and kicking in *The Book of the Courtier*, and the courtier, or gentleman, is truly a man out for himself.

It is perhaps unsurprising that such an outlook originated in Italy, the country of Machiavelli and mercenaries, but in 1528 there is still an acceptance that a courtier needed martial skills. Castiglione recommended that men still learnt to fight, and while it was only just another skill, he wrote that, 'I would have our Courtier a perfect horsemen in every kind of seat … understanding horses and what pertains to riding.'[74] A courtier the Italian gentleman may have been, but the DNA of the mounted knight was still within him. Externally this DNA was becoming less visible however, and the heraldry that once announced the arrival of a knight on the field of battle was dying out.

The Swiss used perhaps the first national banners in Europe to identify their armies from 1339,[75] and by the Thirty Years War, there were few banners displaying the identity of individual knights on show. The state had muscled in here too, and now national banners flew above advancing troops instead of the banner of the noblemen leading them. Troops were by this time part of standing armies, armies within which the individual mattered little. Men of knightly rank were still there, but their identity now didn't matter, and no one was going to save their life to gain a ransom. Even though he may have been mounted, and sometimes still armoured, the officers of the knightly class were not, in themselves, knights. They had been consumed by the very nations their prowess had helped to forge, and their character changed internally by the progress of the world. Knights had become gentlemen first, and officers of the military second. There was, however, one lingering legacy of the medieval knight that lived through and past the renaissance. A notion of chivalry, that ever-changing mix of ideas, persisted and outlasted the knight himself. The perfect example of this progression is that of British General Charles Hay, who at the Battle of Fontenoy in 1745, asked his opponents, 'Gentlemen of France, perhaps you would care to fire first?'[76] This ultimate sense of fair play was alive in the eighteenth century, and indeed gentlemen of that age still lived by a code of honour, a code that really was just chivalry in new clothes. The mounted knight was gone, but how did a part of his identity outlive him?

Chivalry

The mounted knights who rode into battle during the sixteenth century still lived by a code of chivalry. They still rode horses, trained with weapons and jousted. Jousting, however, had became more of a pageant, more thematic and allegorical as the decades drifted by. Henry VIII promoted jousting, and so did Elizabeth I, but during both reigns the activity was limited to the most noble participants, or at least the ones nearest court.[77] These jousts were no training for war, and were perhaps a little hollow when viewed from the perspective of an active soldier. Some mounted games lived on; in Spain, games involving teams throwing canes at each other's shields continued,[78] and bull running and fighting became a spectacle, but the tournament was gone. The tournament had been the great dissipater of chivalric ideals, and without it, or any new chivalric literature, there was nothing left to preach the cause.

The legends of Arthur, and all the other medieval heroes, were no longer useful analogues to the wars, politics and mindsets of the sixteenth century, they were now just stories. No knights actively tried to live up to Sir Gwain or Sir Lancelot, and that key element of prowess in war, that Charny had tried so hard to impress on everyone, was much faded. Even in what was probably the most blatantly chivalric event of the sixteenth century, the disconnect between chivalry and reality seeped through. The magnificent spectacle that was the Field of the Cloth of Gold, an event that was a no-expense-spared carousel of jousting, foot combat, archery, pomp, ceremony and colossal showing off. However, what Henry VIII and Francis I of France were really doing in 1520 was acting out the past they wanted to live in. The armour technology involved, for example, was so advanced that it could cover the entire body and lose no mobility. However, outside of the maze of pavilions and the exclusive guest list, the real world was one of pike blocks and the acrid smoke of gunfire.

The Field of the Cloth of Gold was a re-enactment, and no different to Edward III's generation acting out episodes from the classical past. Both are examples of the elite trying to bolster their legitimacy by claiming links to the traditional past. It is perhaps fitting that the French won the mounted portion of the competitions at the Field of the Cloth of Gold, and Henry even lost a wrestling match with the French king. In a sign of the decline of chivalry, even the alliance that the event existed to arrange only lasted about a year. Indeed, jousting itself in England would not last another century. King James I's eldest son, Prince Henry, had been keen on the sport, but after he died in 1612, it fizzled out. With few opportunities to display prowess in war, and none whatsoever in tournaments, Charny's chivalry was looking decidedly threadbare. By the sixteenth century, only jousting was keeping the idea alive, and that only for a few noblemen.

Losing Faith

The final straw for his version of chivalry was the loss of the last fundamental piece of Charny's vision, religion. To fourteenth-century knights who aspired to the higher ideals of chivalry, their faith was an inseparable part of it. Except, of course, faith could be removed from knighthood, and the emergence of Protestantism in Europe cut the knightly community in half. No more would knights from across Christendom unite to face a common enemy, instead Catholic and Protestant nations would nearly destroy each other in the various European Wars of Religion.[79] Knights on opposing sides of the divide were less inclined to ransom each other, and terrible atrocities were committed on both sides. Additionally, the traditional trappings of chivalry had somewhat of a Catholic tinge to them, and this was an issue for knights in Protestant countries. As the historian Maurice Keen suggested, chivalry can be seen to have lost touch with religion.[80] This disconnect appears to leave us with nothing of chivalry left, but that is not quite the case.

The printing press had acted to spread the stories of chivalry to a wide audience, and the values it promoted hung in the imagination. For example, honour as a value stuck so hard that gentlemen duelled each other over it for the next few hundred years. These one-on-one combats were jousts by definition, a practice that was very much rooted in the medieval past. It is no accident that it was among gentlemen that duelling occurred; it was an upper-class phenomenon, often between men who had served, or were still serving, in the military. They lived by a code of behaviours, rules and standards that governed how they should act, in much the same way as chivalry had governed the mounted knight. Of course, the code that the eighteenth-century gentleman followed was not distinct from chivalry – it was chivalry. It had lost many facets and changed radically, but it was still the ethos under which the noble class, at least the male half, lived. Military service was the career path of many gentlemen, and Montaigne's assertion that the 'essential life for one of the nobility in France is the life of a soldier', remained true until perhaps after the First World War.[81] Even in that ghastly conflict we can see the ghost of chivalry past, we can see it in the quiet actions of the common men who went into battle when they knew it was futile, but did so anyway because it was their duty. Charny would have been proud.

The Fallen Knight

The mounted knight was not blasted out of his saddle by firearms or longbows, his was a slow withdrawal and fragmentation that took place over the course of over 200 years. The concept of knighthood was born out of a world looking for order, stability and safety, when everything in it was uncertain, violent and hard. They became, through force of arms, responsible for the physical protection of their people, alongside the church which looked after their spiritual safety. This was a fractious partnership, but it allowed Christianity to survive and spread. However, this success allowed progress, both technological and social, to drag the world forwards, and away from the one which needed knights to look after it. Knights, of course, were not perfect instruments of justice and peace, they caused as much trouble as they averted, and Europe began to look for better ways to look after itself. The solution was found by the most senior knights themselves, the kings who consolidated power and took it away from the noblemen below them.

The cavalry aspect of their military function was taken up by non noble men-at-arms, so they fell back on making up an officer corps, a role they'd had since the beginning. This was in itself not an existential problem for the mounted knight, what was being questioned in the sixteenth century was the need for such a high maintenance noble class at all. Perhaps the critical thing that ended the dominance of the knight in politics was that idea, an idea that had already been alive in the fifteenth century. Humanism originated in Italy, but had already spread as far as some of the more learned of the nobility in England. It was in 1516 that Thomas More first published Utopia, and it should be noted that Thomas More was for a period the High Chancellor of England under Henry VIII.

The exact contents and meaning of Utopia are not as important as the kind of thinking that it shows was happening across Europe. Intelligent people were entertaining thoughts about how societies should be organised, with aims including fairness, and sometimes even the notion that private property was immoral. The very social structures that had to exist underneath the knights to support them was being questioned, and the authority that once had been assumed, was slowly chipped away. For radicals who entertained such thoughts, the notion of a knightly class became absurd.

The absurdity of knighthood is most famously explored in Don Quixote, the second part of which was published in 1615. The author, Miguel de Cervantes, was a veteran soldier, and knew his subject well. The book follows the adventures of a nobleman who loses his mind after reading too many chivalric romances, and embarks on a mission to restore chivalry to Spain. However, this final quest of chivalry is in vain, and the nobleman ends up jousting against a windmill, and losing his lance in its sail.[82] Cervantes wrote a work that captured the end of the knight, a romantic image battered and savaged by the modern world, labelled as naive and foolish. But likeable. It is a tragedy and a comedy, a masterpiece of literature which reminds us that the past was both good and bad, much like the mounted knight himself. The concept of chivalry still suffers in the shadow of Cervantes' windmill sails, much as the decline of the mounted knight is obscured by the gun smoke that is assumed to have finished him. In the end, however, the knight was simply a man of an earlier time. A time when strongmen were needed, and when people were more or less accepting of the social contract that resulted. The mounted knight did not therefore fall, he merely faded into history.

Chapter Nine

Rebirth of the Mounted Knight

Eglinton

In 1838, 150 Victorian gentlemen met to discuss the idea of holding a joust, the first for 200 years. Among their number were earls, viscounts, captains, counts and the odd prince. A suitable cast to attempt their goal perhaps, but many of them dropped out as soon as the required investment in both cost and time and had become clear.[1] Their plan was to train fifty jousting horses, and then to conduct a huge tournament, with the aim of reviving a sense of chivalry in the country. This was a typically Victorian scheme, though an extremely ambitious one. The Victorians knew how to train warhorses; the massed cavalry charges of the Battle of Waterloo just over twenty years earlier were not old memories, and the Charge of the Light Brigade had not yet happened. Considering their success in training horses to charge into heavy cannon and small arms fire, it is somewhat surprising that in the event, they only successfully managed to train thirteen.[2] This 25 per cent success rate is low for men who were no strangers to horses or combat, but does serve to highlight how taxing jousting can be for some horses and trainers. Some horses take to it quickly, whereas others can take a year of careful work to get them there; it is probable that some of these horses were therefore rushed.

The so-called Eglinton Tournament of 1839 went ahead, and to start with was a chaotic affair. It was a rain-affected event where the participants just about managed to conduct their joust on the second day. Their exploits were looked down on by those in politics who wanted to distance the crown from power, and felt threatened by the historic links between chivalry and royalty.[3] However, the vast number of spectators who turned up to watch is almost unbelievable; 100,000 people made the journey to Eglinton in Scotland[4] to watch the spectacle, and despite the rain they were not disappointed. This Victorian attempt to bring back the mounted knight, even for only a pageant, was a flickering of light in the darkness of the memory of the medieval knight.

Remounting the Knight

Today, in a rural Northamptonshire village in central England, there is a horse riding school. If you visit in the evenings you will find children being taught to ride, but this is no ordinary riding school. Two boys are riding in the small indoor school, one is on a Spanish horse, and both are wielding training swords. These children are not learning to ride so that they can take part in showjumping, or score highly in a dressage test, they want to be knights. This aspiration is not merely a boyish game, it is one that they could genuinely achieve. At least in the sense of riding in armour, and breaking lances on other knights that is, for this riding school is a centre dedicated to the restoration of historical riding in England.

Outside of the riding house where the boys clash swords, there are some gentle rolling hills dotted with grazing horses. Atop the highest hill is a flat area with a unique riding arena. It is a long, thin rectangle, and the riding surface means that horses can ride there regardless of how wet the surrounding grass may be. Running along the middle of this rectangular arena, is a 6ft high fence. It is a tilt rail, the barrier used to separate jousting horses in the fifteenth and sixteenth centuries. This arena is known as the tilt yard, and is where new jousters can hone their skills, learning the arts of riding in armour, and the lowering of the lance. A flat area of grass sits alongside the tilt yard, and this area is used to practice thirteenth-century tournaments. Knights in mail armour, and riding *caparison*-clad warhorses, joust against each other with no tilt rail, breaking lances on each other's shields and heads. This humble piece of grass is where martial horsemanship is truly tested, for riding an excited warhorse in a straight line to joust out in the open, safely, is a feat of prowess. Once shattered lances have been discarded, steel swords are then drawn, and a swirling melee begins. Energetic horses circle and push into each other while their riders exchange heavy blows, causing their victim's ears to ring. New visitors who are unaware of these goings on watch quietly, not always sure what to make of it, unsure how they should react. One source of this hesitation is an unfamiliarity with the mounted knight, and medieval history in general.

To make inroads into this unfamiliarity is one of the main goals of the company that runs the riding school, as well as the people in the community that work with it. This company is called Historic Equitation and is run by Dominic Sewell. Dominic was one of two armoured riders who escorted the coffin containing Richard III's remains through the city of Leicester in 2015. Riding in front of England's last Plantagenet King, the pair of knights gave the thousands who lined the streets a fleeting glimpse of what Richard III looked like on his last day alive. Many of those people would never have seen the shining metal of a knight in motion, let alone two horses wearing barding and metal *chamfron's* on their heads. The two mounted knights, only a few metres away from a real medieval king, were bridging the gap of history. This visceral demonstration, of sight and sound, is one reason why the effort to revive the mounted knight is worthwhile. However, amid the spectacle and emotion of that day, how many of the audience wondered where those knights came from, where their armour came from, and how a modern person could end up encased in armour and riding a horse?

One answer to how one can emulate those two knights can be found at Dominic's company. Historic Equitation is responsible for conducting authentic jousting events across the country every summer, and also acts as a hub for those interested in historical riding in the United Kingdom. As a part of this, horse owners and historical enthusiasts bring their own horses to Historic Equitation on clinic days, to further their riding and combat skills, as well as meet other like-minded individuals. In this way the knowledge of the past, as best we know it, is finding a new and eager audience. The political and social role of the knight cannot be replicated in modern times, but his mounted skills can. These purely martial skills are ones we can study, experiment with, and try to understand. Importantly, the awareness of this possibility is one that is gaining ground, the very concept that one can learn to ride as a knight is spreading. Both group and individual lessons are open to all, an approach that hopefully will aid the revival of the mounted knight still further. This revival of the spirit of the mounted knight, through the attempt to recreate his martial skills, is not an easy process, and to complete the full journey requires commitments in both time and money. Learning to ride from scratch will absorb much of both, but the undertaking is a worthwhile one and can be beneficial physically and mentally.

Medieval knights started riding at an early age, and that is undoubtedly an advantage in modern times, but it is never too late to start. Beginning to ride only when I was nearly thirty, I first began weekly riding lessons with Dominic at Historic Equitation. However, due to a lack of natural ability, it eventually became clear that weekly lessons were not frequent enough. This was an issue if I intended to take riding seriously, a problem compounded by living an hour away from the stable yard. This moment of realisation coincided with the great March of 2016, which was organised to commemorate the 950th anniversary of the Battle of Hastings. A small group of re-enactors travelled on foot and horseback from York to Battle Abbey in Sussex, a route of well over 250 miles. This journey was to follow in the footsteps of King Harold as he made his way to confront the Normans, having just defeated the Vikings at the Battle of Stamford Bridge. This march took three weeks, a time high on mileage and low on sleep, and ended with the mighty Battle of Hastings re-enactment on a chilly October weekend. Being part of a Norman cavalry charge on the very field where England was lost and won in 1066 was special, as well as a valuable learning experience.

Battles are the most chaotic thing you can do on a horse, and planning them can only go so far. There is no room for hesitation, perfectionism or reflection. When a group of horses charges, the ground really does shake, horses snort, and clumps of mud and grass fly up into your eyes. Some horses want to race, some hesitate and end up being squeezed out of formation, and a lucky few don't think anything of it. Each individual rider faces their own unique challenge, but the shared one is to stay in formation, stay as safe as possible, and complete the job. Even just staying in formation on excited horses takes practice, not to mention balance. Riding knee to knee while wearing shields and holding spears is inherently problematic. A neighbour can disrupt you, their spear can poke your horse's leg, causing it to jump, or their legs can entangle with your own, and I have nearly had my leg dislocated when a neighbour's horse shot off forwards, nearly taking my knee with it. However, getting through the discomfort that battlefields entail is rewarding, because the experience can improve the relationship between rider and horse. Getting through it is not an individual act, but a partnership of man and animal, and one that teaches lessons on horsemanship that cannot be learnt in a riding arena.

The immersive experience of the March had told me that I wanted to work with horses, but the battle itself told me that I needed to. Having decided that, and needing more time in the saddle than I was getting, I moved house to ten minutes from the yard, and was then able to ride every day. The real accelerating moment for me came when Dominic rather generously gave me a horse to ride each day, and I have done so ever since. Indeed this book was an unexpected consequence of that moment, because it was this path, full of luck and largesse, that allowed me to joust and to join the international community of historical riders.

Looking the Part

In order to present an accurate impression of a mounted knight, a great deal of research must be done, and a wide range of skills applied and drawn on. Medieval saddles were made out of wood, works of art in themselves, and had to fit both the horse and rider. Each horse's back is different, and getting the saddle wrong can cause damage to them, so this skill is as important as it is rare. These saddles must also fit the rider, an important consideration when they are wearing plate armour, which serves to make the rider bigger and interact with the saddle in unique ways. Luckily for us, there are talented makers of saddles in Europe who create wonderful war saddles, because to ride like a knight we must sit atop the horse like a knight. The distinctive long-legged riding style of the medieval knight is possible because of the shape of the saddles and is not at all possible when using modern saddles. Saddle makers are therefore a critical part of a group of exceptionally skilled craftspeople, whose dedication helps to allow the mounted knight to come back to life. Secondly, once the horse is dressed with their saddle, the prospective knight requires some armour. This is the biggest single expense, but also the most important, considering that it is the only thing standing between the jouster's face, and the end of a lance.

Over the past few decades, the knowledge and skills required to sculpt safe and aesthetically accurate fifteenth-century armour have been developed. Scattered across the world there are a small number of talented armours who can produce hardened, and at the same time highly decorated, armour. These armours can also survive hits from solid pine lances that are tipped with metal lance-heads, making their profession a pressured one, on which lives literally depend. The numbers of these armourers is increasing, as is the quality of their work. Some, for example, are now capable of intricate *pointillé* decoration, that is patterns made up of small dots punched into the metal, a technique over 500 years old. Others are gilding parts of armour with gold, an expensive process that, as in the middle ages, only the richest patrons can afford. This level of quality extends to the steel of the armour itself, and the hardening process some armourers are skilled in. Our steel is of a better quality than the medieval armourer had the luxury of using, it is of a significantly more consistent and reliable chemical make up. This makes modern armour safer than historical armour, especially as technology has made the hardening process likewise more reliable.

Armourers have understood how their medieval forefathers made armour work; that is, how to make them protective as well as flexible. They have noticed how, in some places, two plates of metal are not riveted together in the normal way. Sometimes the hole on one plate, instead of being a circle for the rivet to pass through, is elongated, allowing the rivet to slide up and down the hole. These 'sliding rivets' mean that two pieces of metal can be solidly connected, and yet still move independently from each other. This simple but ingenious system means that the armour is that little bit more flexible than it otherwise would be. The weight and complex shapes of different pieces of armour have also been understood, and modern armour can be of a comparable thickness and weight to the pieces they are trying to copy. In the quest for authenticity, those who commission armour sometimes copy a whole harness from either an effigy, manuscript, or painting. For example, my harness is based on a knight from southern Germany called Eberhard von Kirchberg, who died in the 1470s, and whose effigy is in the former Benedictine abbey church in Wiblingen near Ulm. That armourers are now able to produce functional armour that looks and weighs the same as those they are copying, means those who wear it can start to be confident that they are feeling the same thing as their medieval ancestors did. This is a very important step, because it allows us to understand a small part of what being a mounted knight meant. If we wore armour made out of titanium or plastic, or that was shaped differently to real armour, we would have no affinity to the medieval mounted knight.

In accurate armour, we can experience the weight of it as they might have, feel the heat building up on a hot day, and start to make educated theories on what the medieval mounted knight could and could not do. For example, we know for a fact that knights in full harness could mount their horses themselves, although it is vastly easier to do so with help. They could run, fall over and get back up again, crawl on the ground, and climb ladders. Less easy is walking up and down steps in helms with no visors, and that is something usually attempted slowly and with great care. Armour can be borne with relatively minor discomfort if it is worn enough, a sentiment we previously saw more than one medieval writer note, and wearing it often is part of the journey of understanding the medieval knight. The stories of these knights sleeping in their armour, or at least the majority of it, are believable based on our experience, and one can certainly spend a day in the saddle while armed.

These small steps towards understanding the knight extend to fighting in armour too. For foot combat and swordsmanship, groups of people around the world study the medieval fight manuals, trying to understand and replicate the moves described and depicted in them. This discipline is known as Historical European Martial Arts (HEMA). Mostly engaging in foot combat, these practitioners are keeping alive the techniques of the dismounted knight, and some of them will fight in full harness and with steel poleaxes. Some fighters rely on technique and strategy, while others leverage strength and aggression instead, and perhaps such a variety of approaches could also be found on the medieval battlefield.

HEMA has a large footprint in Europe and is growing in the United Kingdom, however practising it on horseback is extremely rare on the English side of the Channel. Rare perhaps, but not quite absent. Mounted HEMA is what we primarily do, and jousting and the melee form a part of that. The use of weapons on horseback is the easier part, it is riding the horse well enough to get close enough to use them that is the challenge. To be able to ride a horse close enough to an opponent to stab them with a sword before turning on the spot and chasing after them requires substantial dressage skills. This is what dressage was for, and forms the building block of the horsemanship of the mounted knight. Learning to ride dressage movements while wearing armour should not be overly daunting if done slowly and steadily. Indeed, for those who go deeper into the rabbit hole of historical mounted combat, their endeavour quickly becomes more about the horse than their own skill with swords or lances. Relatively speaking, riding a horse along a fifteenth-century tilt rail, and then using a lance to joust, is not a difficult riding exercise, providing someone has given you a trained horse to do it with. If that horse is not interested in the activity, and canters along quite happily, taking no notice of the lances breaking above it, then one can joust with no dressage knowledge. However, when it comes to jousting horses who are excited by the activity, or training new ones to the exercise, then being a rider is not sufficient, one must be a horseman (or horsewoman). Experts in practical historical riding are not usually occasional riders, and furthermore they are often embedded in the lifestyle that owning horses entails. It is no coincidence that perhaps the two greatest proponents of the modern jousting scene in Europe, Dominic Sewell and Arne Koets, are also able to perform classical dressage to the highest level.

Horsemanship

At our home in rural Northamptonshire, the indoor riding school is almost the same size as the rather special Riding House at Bolsover Castle in Derbyshire. The Riding House in Bolsover is the spiritual home of English dressage, and was the residence of William Cavendish, the Duke of Newcastle, during the seventeenth century. William Cavendish wrote a work on horsemanship that still holds up today; sensitive to the horse, it included many movements that we today would recognise as dressage. Cavendish was a more humane trainer of horses than could be expected of his era, indeed he advocated gentle rewards for horses and, like Xenophon, warned against anger and violent punishments. The most spectacular outcome of his training methods was that his horses could perform the 'airs above the ground', the so-called school jumps. These can be seen at the famous Spanish Riding School in Vienna today, and include a movement where a highly trained horse would lift his front end off the ground, and balance for a while on his hind legs. Some of these horses would leap forwards from this position, and the most explosive would kick both of their legs out behind in the *capriole*, or 'leap of the goat'. These movements teach the rider how to sit well in the saddle, for you either learn it or fall off, but are not usually ridden by inexperienced riders.

We are fortunate to have been able to perform these exercises and leaps in the Riding House at Bolsover Castle, which is a privilege beyond words for all involved. After our demonstrations we speak to the audience, who are frequently surprised that anything like our demonstrations still exist, and amazed at the abilities of the horses. When we explain that by showing their ability in the Riding House, renaissance gentlemen were by proxy showing their ability to rule, everything falls into place. It is simply impossible to bully or lie to a horse in order to make it rise up on its legs, and then hop in the air for you. The sixteenth-century horses that did this, first had to understand the request that their riders made of them, and once they had, the gentleman would have proven his capacity for patience, empathy and prowess as a trainer. Second, the horses, even if they understood the request, had to be willing partners in the movement. A horse will not perform something so hard if it does not want to, they are simply too big and too strong to be pushed around for long. The gentleman who succeeded in this showed that he had learnt to work with his horse, engage in cooperation and invest time in gaining familiarity with his partner. These skills are all equally useful for a civil servant, a general, or a king. Once our spectators understand this, the whole display becomes full of meaning.

The dressage lessons imparted by Cavendish also equip us to train horses for war today. Warhorses need to move sideways the instant we ask them to, just as the dressage horse does. They also need to bend their bodies in the direction we need them to, again, just as the dressage horse does. The tight circles of a pirouette, undertaken in canter, are central to mounted combat, and also an important part of modern dressage. After all, to circle round behind one's opponent is always the best strategy to defeat them. These principles of horsemanship can take years to learn, and a lifetime to acquire the ability to actually train the horses. It is this aspect, the training of warhorses, that has taken over the lives of some of those who started out merely with an interest in jousting. Endless days are spent exercising horses to build their strength and understanding of the requests we put to them. Weeks can be spent slowly riding a horse in more and more armour, until it is either strong enough to not notice it, or confident enough to not to be wary of it. Each horse is different, and it is training each horse in the best way suited for its own personality, that we find horsemanship. It is also perhaps one way in which we come close to the medieval mounted knight. They spent unending time with their horses, and lived in a world where these animals were everywhere. To understand the mounted knight, one must therefore understand the living being that made up half of that war machine. It is because of this that many members of the community are heavily focused on the horse.

Some of these people are committed academically, and are making strides in researching the world of the medieval horse. For example, Mike Canfor, who has conducted excellent research into the feeding practices of medieval horses, including illuminating the commonplace, and surprisingly sensible, medieval phenomenon of horse bread. Horse bread was often made out of pea flour and various beans, making it probably quite healthy for the animals, as well as being very convenient to transport, which would have been an important consideration for the mounted knight.[5] This interest in historical research, widespread among the historical jousting community, has cultivated an urge to 'get it right'. In our public events we wish to represent the mounted knight as he truly was, with the right saddles, the right armour, and use them in the right way. With regards to fifteenth-century jousting, this means showing the audience how it was done at the time.

The aim of the joust was to break a lance on your opponent, and in some scoring systems, different points were awarded for hitting certain areas, such as the shield, helm, arm or body. A surviving score sheet from 1584 shows a tally of courses run versus lances broken, and no further details, which is an indication that scoring was fluid and always changing.[6] The primary target area for most jousts of peace was the shield. Known as a *targe*, it gave us the word 'target', with the 'et' meaning small. This shield, strapped over the heart and left arm of a knight, was where most knights would aim to strike, and these shields were often curved and ribbed in order to catch the lance-heads, encouraging the lances to break. This target area simulated where a knight should aim in a joust of war, or indeed actual war, where he had the most chance of doing damage to his opponent. To the left of the shield, some of a knight's body is visible as a target, but this would have been a lower scoring area due to the greater angle of strikes there, and their resulting minimal usefulness of it in war. The highest points score to be awarded are given to breaks of the lance to the head. Helms are generally designed, for obvious reasons, to deflect incoming blows, and as a result it is very difficult to actually break the lance on them. When a lance hits anywhere but then skids off without breaking, this is called an *ataint*, and usually scores no points, which is especially common with helm hits. This scoring system necessarily then includes deliberate blows to heads, and is one way to separate other types of public jousting displays from historical ones.

Also, you may have noticed that no mention has been made of knights being knocked off horses. Unhorsing an opponent did not happen on every hit, or even all that often. The medieval saddles used for jousting, with their high backs, make falling off the horse actually quite difficult. It can happen after particularly powerful hits, but when it does, it is often so explosive and so violent, it is obviously not choreographed. The benefit of falling off a horse in armour, something I haven't yet experienced, is that it acts as a roll cage, or an exoskeleton, and provides considerable protection to its wearer.

But what does jousting feel like? The answer depends entirely on the horse under you. On a steady and experienced mount, the jouster only has to deal with the inconvenience of their armour. The restricted vision of armour has the effect of inducing mild claustrophobia in some new riders, especially when an uncertainty creeps in, and the realisation that they cannot get out of their armour surfaces. This is similar to scuba diving in caves, where if a problem with air supply occurs, matters can become dangerous exceedingly quickly. If you can scuba dive calmly, you can probably cope with wearing armour. Reduced visibility is something you can become accustomed to, but it can be troublesome when jousting an excited horse. Horses can enjoy jousting so much that they become overexcited. One example of how this manifests, is when a horse looks down the tilt rail, is so excited that it can't hold itself back, and charges down it. This is a problem because jousting requires two horses to meet each other along the tilt rail, and here our excited horse has not waited for his opponent to be ready, and made his rider look rather silly. Solving this problem is where horsemanship and equestrian tact come into play. The first thing the jouster might try, could be to point his horses away from the tilt rail until his opponent is ready, therefore avoiding the trigger that previously caused his horse to become overexcited and charge. This however adds a new problem, in that by pointing his horse away from the tilt rail to keep it calm, the jouster himself cannot now see when his opponent is ready. The jouster, now blind to the situation, then relies on his ground crew to shout up to him when it is time to turn and charge. This element of teamwork is likely to be unnoticed by spectators, but adds a layer of skill and patience to both the jouster and his assistant on the ground.

Overexcitement is not the only issue we can face while jousting, sometimes the horses are too intelligent for their own good. The horse I usually joust, Charlie, learnt to recognise what it felt like when a lance was pressed into my hand. Once Charlie had learnt this, every time he felt the lance lock in, he started to bounce around on the spot expecting to joust, which made my job a lot more difficult. The only way to resolve this was to dissociate the act of me taking a lance, with the act of jousting, which Charlie finds tremendously exciting. The method I employed was patience and repetition. I would stand with Charlie at the end of the tilt rail atop the grassy hill at Historic Equitation, pick the lance up and down, but never joust. It took weeks for him to start to ignore me taking a lance, but we were able to overcome the issue calmly and quietly. It is these hidden activities, challenges, and tactics that add layers of complexity to what can on the surface look like a simple exercise.

It is precisely because of the variation of horses and their reactions to jousting that it is not suitable for a truly competitive scoring system in modern times. First, any emphasis on scoring encourages jousters to try too hard to hit their targets, an attitude that increases the chances of dangerous low blows. Second, a mediocre jouster on a brilliant horse will probably always beat a fantastic horseman on a fiery new one. If jousting was ever to become formalised, at say, the Olympics, perhaps the scoring system should treat it as a performance art, in the same way that gymnastics is. Horses could be graded on their difficulty level, and jousters scored on their ability to control them, and the elegance of the riding, rather than purely where their lances strike. This returns us to the main goal of a jouster, which is actually to provide a target for his opponent. This shade of chivalry is unique among martial arts, because in a large sense, the two jousters are not really competing against each other. What their opponent does with their lance will, usually, have no bearing on what you do with yours. As long as the opposing horse is close enough to the tilt rail to be hit, everything else is down to the individual jouster. This is why offering yourself as a target is the real aim of the game. For example, when the jouster Lisa Dixon sustained an injury to her right arm during a joust, she found herself unable to lower her lance safely. Had point-scoring been her focus, she would have continued on for a while, chanced her injured arm, and tried to break a few more lances. However, because for her the horses always come first, she instead declined to lower her lance at all, so that there was no chance of her hitting one accidentally. She also declined to retire, because even though she could no longer score any points, she wanted to continue, to enable the other jousters to hit her. This is the perfect example of 'being a target', a very chivalric intention that once again puts the horse at the very heart of the enterprise.

The first priority then, is to ride well enough to be that target, and only secondly to hit the opponent, and this is the order in which we try to work to today. Riding is indeed a more difficult skill to master than basic weapons training, and is the discipline which needs to be mastered first for anyone who wishes to follow the path of the mounted knight. The lance comes last. When we come to the lances, the reality again is more complex than it initially seems. The primary concern for those using a lance in the joust is not to score points, but to keep their lance away from their opponent's horse. Allowing a lance to drop so low that it bounces off the top of the tilt rail will incur penalties, and most likely a stern warning. Horses were injured relatively frequently in medieval jousts, but in the modern age this must be completely avoided. The lance therefore must be kept vertical as much as possible, and only lowered at the last possible moment. This lowering technique means that by the time the lance is low enough to strike, the head of the opposing horse has already ridden past it. One therefore does not begin the jousting course with the lance already aiming at their target, as this causes injuries to horses. The lowering of the lance is a skill that takes time to build into muscle memory, and the spinning *quintain* exists in order to help with this process. The point of the lance should in fact only be low enough to strike the target at the exact moment it connects with it, before and after it should be above the target. This is a skill of pin-point accuracy that takes time to perfect, as well as a certain level of strength. Getting this technique right is an important part of the art of jousting, but using the right lances is important too.

Accurate lances were the final piece to be added to modern historical jousting, and the one which had the most dramatic impact. The number of men and women who are both capable and willing to wield a long lance made of pine, tipped with a steel lance-head, lock it into an *arret*, and then joust, are low. Jousting with these so-called 'solid lances' is rare, mildly dangerous, and almost the only way a modern person can experience something *exactly* as the medieval mounted knight did. When solid lances break they do not shatter, rather they crack or snap, sending out a sonic boom which sounds like a gunshot. The steel lance-heads can bite into helms, collapsing the less well made ones, and if they get in between pieces of plate armour, they can injure. That visceral experience is the same as Geoffrey de Charny or Henry VIII felt when they jousted, and for those who do it, they can claim some small understanding into the mindset of the mounted knight. That is what the historical riding school in the middle of England is trying to keep alive, it is keeping open the possibility that a committed enough individual can reach the point where they joust with these lances, and in doing so make a small connection with our martial past. Efforts to expand this link include teaching the younger generation to ride, but also in pushing the boundaries of modern jousting. Recently we have been able to stage a number of thirteenth-century tournaments, events where multiple riders joust at the same time in the same space, with no tilt barrier. We have done this with six jousters only, because that is approximately the number of people who can do it, and even then two had to be brought over from Europe. We did succeed in fighting with lances and swords in a very small space, in a contest which was swirling, chaotic and a microcosm of a medieval tournament. These modern tournaments require more participants in order to grow, and maybe one day we can produce an event which has the scale of an early medieval tournament. This will take a great deal of effort and time, so we should ask, is it worth it?

The physical process of learning to ride in a historical manner, wearing armour without complaint and wielding the weapons of a knight, is a humbling one. Learning to ride is never instant, and will teach any overly proud student that they do not know everything, and cannot do everything perfectly. They must look at their weaknesses in order to improve, and as such must perform an introspection that modern life seldom affords. Committing enough time to see results also encourages long term work towards a goal, which in the end will yield more satisfying results than anything that is easy. Learning to work with a horse, rather than simply to use a horse, will also teach a respect for the animal that can only improve a person. On top of this, the more obvious positives of fitness and spending time outside are beneficial, but those who look deeper into the subject matter have even more to gain.

The knight is an emotive figure, one who is of interest and value today because of the range of human experience which he encompassed. From the most extreme violence, desperation or brutality, we can contrast to their courage, strength and brilliance. Not to mention their literary, social and philosophical pursuits, where although some knights such as Jean de Beuil might have looked forward to hearing the screams of his enemies, they also produced works of undoubted genius such as the Canterbury Tales. This spectrum of knightly behaviour puts it all on display, and allows us to decide what we think is good and bad. We can learn from them, from their constructive and destructive deeds, their various examples of redemption and failure. They are a sounding board for morals, and their history can teach us much that can be applied today. We can conclude that one individual can be complex and contradictory, fall on hard times and rise again. For example, in Geoffrey de Charny's death at Poitiers, we cannot help but find virtue in how he stuck to his beliefs despite the consequences. Likewise, the early demise of the Black Prince and the words he placed on his tomb warn us of the fragility of life, words which should serve to render those humble who contemplate them. The mounted knight has far more to offer us than tales of victorious battles and heroic deeds. In our modern world we can learn from his example, and strive to connect with the medieval world by studying and recreating him as best we can. He may have risen and faded away for a time, and although centuries divide us, in his modern rebirth the mounted knight is still very much alive.

Notes

Introduction
1. *A concise Anglo-Saxon dictionary*, John Richard Clark Hall (Swan Sonnenschein & Company, 1894), 58
2. *Dictionary of the English and German and German and English Languages: Volume 2*, Newton Ivory Lucas (C. Shunemann, 1868), 1019
3. For a detailed and fascinating Muslim view of the crusade, see *An Arab-Syrian Gentleman and Warrior in the Period of the Crusade*, Usamah Ibn Munqidh, trans Philip K. Hitti (Columbia University Press, 2000)
4. *The Unconquered Knight A Chronicle of the Deeds of Don Pero Niño, Count of Buelna, by His Standard-bearer Gutierre Diaz de Gamez (1431–1449) Translated and Selected from El Vitorial by Joan Evan*, Joan Evans (G. Routledge & sons Limited, 1928), 2
5. *Thomas Hoccleve, The Regiment of Princes*, Edited by Charles R. Blyth (Medieval Institute Publications, Kalamazoo, Michigan,1999), 870
6. Skeletal remains, mostly famously from Towton and Visby, show old wounds existed in those who died, see *Wounds and Wound Repair in Medieval Culture*, Kelly DeVries and Larissa Tracy (Brill, 2015), 204

Chapter 1 – Dawn of Knighthood
1. Really a very long time ago, see *The Domestic Horse: The Origins, Development and Management of Its Behaviour*, S.M. McDonald (Cambridge University Press, 2005), 6–9
2. *The Horse, the Wheel, and Language: How Bronze-Age Riders from the Eurasian Steppes Shaped the Modern World*, David W. Anthony (Princeton University Press, 2010)
3. *Religions of the World: A Comprehensive Encyclopedia of Beliefs and Practices, 2nd Edition* [6 Volumes], J. Gordon Melton and Martin Baumann (ABC-CLIO, 2010), 1412
4. *Cavalry: The History of Mounted Combat*, John Ellis (Pen & Sword, 2004), 9
5. *Tutankhamun's Armies: Battle and Conquest During Ancient Egypt's Late Eighteenth Dynasty*, John Coleman Darnell and Colleen Manassa (Wiley, 2007), 177
6. In ancient Athens the third of three classes were specifically called the hippeis class which can be translated as knights, see *Ancient Greek Horsemanship*, J.K. Anderson (University of California Press, 1961), 128
7. A translation of *Nimrud Letter 89* mentioned ninety-seven cavalry horses and 161 cavalrymen in a list of troops, see the article *The Assyrian Army in Zamua* by J.N. Postgate in the journal *Iraq, Volume 62* (British Institute for the Study of Iraq, 2000), 90
8. Ellis, 11
9. *The Cavalry General*, Xenophon (Public Domain Book), VIII
10. For other types of Alexander's cavalry see *The Macedonian Empire: The Era of Warfare Under Philip II and Alexander the Great, 359–323 B.C*, James R. Ashley (McFarland Incorporated, 2004), 34–35
11. *The Cavalry of the Roman Republic*, Jeremiah B. McCall (Taylor & Francis, 2005), 4

12. *Romans at War: The Roman Military in the Republic and Empire*, Simon Elliot (Casemate, 2020), 60
13. *FERHENGA BIRÛSKÎ Kurmanji – English Dictionary Volume One: A – L*, Michael L. Chyet (Transnational Press, 2020), 24
14. See *Sasanid Soldiers in Early Muslim Society: The Origins of 'Ayyārān and Futuwwa*, Mohsen Zakeri (Harrassowitz Verlag, 1995)
15. *Knights in Azerbaijan: Article 2*, Sabuhi Ahmadov (IRS-AZ)
16. *Sports and Games of the Ancients*, Steve Craig (Greenwood Press, 2002), 158
17. Тревер К.В. Очерки по истории и культуре Кавказской Албании (IV в до н.э. – VIII в н.э.). М.- Л., 1959. Aka *Essays on the history and culture of Caucasian Albania*, Trever, Kamilla Vasilievna (USSR Academy of Sciences, 1959)
18. For Clovis and the early Franks see *Essays on the Early Franks*, Ernst Taayke (Barkhuis, 2003)
19. *Merovingian Military Organization 481–751*, Bernard S. Bachrach (University of Minnesota Press, 1972), 4
20. Although we can see that even in the nineteenth century the phrase 'Dark Ages' was being challenged, *The Quarterly Review 1896*, G.W. Prothoro etc (John Murray, 2018), 445
21. See the article *Military Organization in Aquitaine under the Early Carolingians* in the Journal Speculum, Vol. 49, Bernard S. Bachrach (The University of Chicago Press, 1974), 9
22. For full details of Merovingian campaigns see Bachrach, 1972
23. See *The History of the Franks*, Gregory of Tours, Translated by Lewis Thorpe (Penguin Books Ltd, 1974)
24. *The World of the Huns, Studies in Their History and Culture*, J. Maenchen-Helfen, Otto Maenchen-Helfen, Otto Helfen (University of California Press, 1973), 203
25. The Battle of Vouillé, see *The Battle of Vouillé, 507 CE*, Ralph W. Mathisen, Danuta Shanzer (De Gruyter, 2012), 30
26. Bachrach, 136 and the article *Procopius, Agathias and the Frankish Military* by Bernard S. Bachrach in the journal *Speculum* (The University of Chicago Press, 1970), 439
27. Again see article *ibid*, 439
28. *Early Carolingian Warfare: Prelude to Empire*, Bernard S. Bachrach (University of Pennsylvania Press Incorporated, 2011), 179
29. Gregory of Tours, 290
30. *The Cambridge Medieval History, Volumes 1 – 5*, J.B. Bury (Plantagenet Publishing, 1911), Chapter V, 3 and also *Medieval Technology and Social Change*, White, pp.3–4
31. *Translations and Reprints from the Original Sources of European history*, Translated by C.D. Munro (University of Pennsylvania Press, 1900), Vol VI, No. 5, 11–12
32. *Charlemagne*, translated P.D. King (P.D. King, 1987),260–266
33. *Historie des fils de Louis le Pieux*, Nithard, trans P. Lauer (Paris, 1926), 110–112s
34. *Mercenaries to Conquerors: Norman Warfare in the Eleventh and Twelfth-Century Mediterranean*, Paul Brown (Pen & Sword, 2016), 11
35. *The Carolingian Army and the Struggle Against the Vikings*, Simon Coupland (article in Viator, 2004), 62
36. Images are available online, Württembergische Landesbibliothek Stuttgart
37. *Western Warfare In The Age Of The Crusades, 1000–1300*, John France (Taylor & Francis, 2020), 41
38. Specifically mines at Hartz, see *The Metallurgy of Silver and Lead: A Description of the Ores; Their Assay and Treatment, and Valuable Constituents*, Robert H. Lamborn (C. Lockwood, 1878), 5

39. For Charles the Simple see *The Capetians: Kings of France 987–1328*, Jim Bradbury (Bloomsbury Publishing, 2007), 32–34
40. *Norman Rule in Normandy, 911–1144*, Mark S. Hagger (Boydell, 2017), 269
41. *Norsemen in the Viking Age*, Eric Christiansen (Wiley, 2008), 175
42. *Beowulf: The Fight at Finnsburh*, Kevin Crossley-Holland, Heather O'Donoghue, (OUP Oxford, 1999), 35
43. and
44. *Beowulf: Facing Page Translation – Second Edition*, Edited by R.M. Luizza (Broadview Press, 2012), 117
45. For a standard version of the now outdated trope, see *Saxon Shakedown*, Mike Noakes (Artemis Publishers, 2012), 51
46. For the Saxons in England see *The Anglo-Saxons: A History of the Beginnings of England*, Marc Morris (Random House, 2021)
47. *Law and Order in Anglo-Saxon England*, Thomas Benedict Lambert and Tom Lambert (Oxford University Press, 2017), 144 or Eadgar *II, 1,1*
48. *History of the English Landed Interest: Its Customs, Laws and Agriculture*, Russell Montague Garnier (Sonnenschein, 1892), 112
49. *The Ideal of Men Dying with the Lord in the Germania and in The Battle of Maldon*, Rosemary Woolf (Anglo-Saxon England 5, 1976), 63
50. *Anglo-Saxon England: Volume 32*, Michael Lapidge (Cambridge University Press, 2004), 55
51. *The Horned Moses in Medieval Art and Thought*, Ruth Mellinkoff (Wipf & Stock Publishers, 1997), 43
52. *Anglo-Saxon England: Volume 35*, Malcolm Godden (Cambridge University Press, 2008), 141
53. See *Encyclopedia of Norse and Germanic Folklore, Mythology, and Magic*, Claude Lecouteux (Inner Traditions/Bear, 2016)
54. *Charlemagne*, Roger Collins (University of Toronto Press, 1998), 55
55. *Bede's Ecclesiastical History*, ed. B. Colgrave and R.A.B. Mynors (Oxford, 1969), 429
56. *Maxims I*, trans S.A.J. Bradley, (University of York: Everyman's Library, 1982), Maxim I, 58
57. For one example see the *Winchester Manuscript (A) 937* as found within *The Anglo-Saxon Chronicle*, ed Michael Swanton (Routledge, 1998), 108
58. See *The Laws of King Athelstan 924–939 A.D.* where it states that horses should not be sold overseas, just gifted, which suggests an interest in maintaining English horse stock
59. See *The Return of the Vikings: The Battle of Maldon 991*, Donald Scragg (History Press, 2006)
60. *The Battle of Maldon: War and Peace in Tenth-Century England*, Mark Atherton (Bloomsbury Academic, 2020), 33
61. See chapter 1 in *Medieval Technology and Social Change*, Lynn Townsend White (Oxford University Press, 1964)
62. See *Cataphracts: Knights of the Ancient Eastern Empires*, Eric B. Anderson (Pen & Sword, 2016)
63. *AN EXPERIMENTAL INVESTIGATION OF LATE MEDIEVAL COMBAT WITH THE COUCHED LANCE*, Alan Williams, David Edge & Tobias Capwell (Journal of the Arms *and Armour Society, www.academia.edu, 2016)*
64. *An Anglo-Saxon Dictionary*, Joseph Bosworth (Clarendon Press, 1882), 920

Chapter 2 – The Norman Era
1. Hagger, 2017, 46
2. Ibid, chapters 1 and 2
3. *The Age of Robert Guiscard Southern Italy and the Northern Conquest*, Graham Loud (Taylor & Francis, 2014), 82
4. *Anglo-Norman Studies XXVII Proceedings of the Battle Conference 2004*, ed John Gillingham (The Boydell Press, 2005), 97–98
5. *The Norman Conquest of Southern Italy and Sicily*, Gordon S. Brown (McFarland Incorporated, 2015)
6. *Norman Campaigns in the Balkans, 1081–1108*, Georgios Theotokis (Boydell Press, 2014)
7. Ibid, 133
8. *The Normans*, Marjorie Chibnall (Wiley, 2008), 128
9. *Royal Succession and the Growth of Political Stability in Ninth-Century Wessex*, Richard Abels (Boydell & Brewer, 2003)
10. *Northwest Europe in the Early Middle Ages, C. AD 600–1150: A Comparative Archaeology*, Christopher Loveluck (Cambridge University Press, 2013), 222
11. Medieval Military Technology, Kelly DeVries (University of Toronto Press, 2003), 204
12. *The Verdict of Battle: The Law of Victory and the Making of Modern War*, James Q. Whitman (Harvard University Press, 2012), 2
13. *Castles, Battles, and Bombs: How Economics Explains Military History*, Jurgen Brauer and Hubert van Tuyll (University of Chicago Press, 2008), 75
14. *Conquest: The English Kingdom of France 1417–1450*, Juliet Barker (Harvard University Press, 2012), 382
15. The Book of the Deeds of Arms and of Chivalry, Christine de Pizan, 1400s trans Summer Willard (The Pennsylvania State University Press, 1999)
16. *English Castles: Volume 22*, Reginald Allen Brown (Batsford, 1962)
17. *Medieval Castles (Greenwood Guides to Historic Events of the Medieval World)*, Marilyn Stoksad (Greenwood Press, 2005), 1
18. They also did not necessarily sever ties to their original family, see M*edieval Monks and Their World: Ideas and Realities: Studies in Honor of Richard Sullivan*, Amy Livingstone, David Blanks & Michael Frassetto (Brill, 2019), 98
19. See page 1 of the account of *The Battle of Hastings*, William of Poitiers in *England: The Autobiography:2,000 Years of English History by Those Who Saw it Happen*, John Lewis-Sempel (Penguin Books Ltd, 2006)
20. The Normans had performed the feigned retreat in 1053 at the Battle of Saint Aubin, see *Die Schlact von Hastings*, Wilhelm Spatz (Kraus Reprint, 1965), 61–62
21. *The Battle of Hastings*, R. Allen Brown (PBC 3, 1980), 1–21
22. The *Stavelot Triptych* resides at the Morgan Library & Museum in New York, and despite its diminutive size, its intricacy is remarkable
23. The peculiar hunched nature of the shoulders of the charging knights is actual reminiscent of the act of tightening the grip on the lance at the moment of impact as practised today. If the lance is tight into the body for a whole charge, the result will be an inaccurate strike as the lance will move up and down with the canter of the horse
24. *Mercenaries in Medieval and Renaissance Europe*, Janin Hunt & Ursula Carlson (McFarland Incorporated, 2014), 64
25. *Reflections on Law and Armed Conflicts*, Professor Colonel G.I.A.D Draper OBE (Kluwer Law International, 1998), 30
26. Ibid
27. *The Norman Conquest*, Marc Morris (Penguin Random House, 2013), 320

28. Ibid, 319–320
29. *Henry II: A Medieval Soldier at War, 1147–1189*, John D. Hosler (Brill, 2007), 105
30. Brown, 1980, 16
31. *A Short History of England*, R.J.A. White (Cambridge University Press, 1967), 50
32. *The Formation of the English Social Structure: Freedom, Knights, and Gentry, 1066–1300*, in the journal *Speculum*, Jean Scammell (University of Chicago Press, 1993), 11
33. Ibid
34. See Chapter 'The Assize of Arms (1181)' starting on page 106 within *England in the Early Middle Ages*, Derek Baker (Boydell & Brewer, 1995)
35. *The Composition of Anglo-Norman Armies*, in the journal *Speculum*, John Beeler (University of Chicago Press, 1965)
36. As demonstrated by the increase in hiring soldiers rather than mustering just from duty, Ibid, 408
37. For a standing army in the Marches and the creation of a 'military buffer zone' see *The Medieval March of Wales: The Creation and Perception of a Frontier, 1066–1283*, Max Liberman Cambridge University Press, 2010), 10
38. For how Orderic Vitalis viewed matters, see Morris, 2013, 207
39. *The Deeds of Louis the Fat*, trans R. Cusimano and J. Moorhead (Washington DC, 1992), 8
40. When Odo of Bayeux rebelled against William II, son of the conqueror, and was defeated, he and many others returned to the fold rather than be put to death.
41. *Matilda: Wife of the Conqueror, First Queen of England*, Tracy Borman (Vintage Books, 2012), 154
42. *Courtly Culture and Courtly Style in the Anglo-Norman World* in journal *Albion: A Quarterly Journal Concerned with British Studies*, C. Warren Hollister (The North American Conference on British Studies, 1988), 9–11
43. This meeting was described as a 'firm peace and serene friendship', which could include homage but could be something closer to a peace treaty. See *Capetian France 987–1328*, Elizabeth M. Hallam (Taylor & Francis, 2014), 126
44. See Hallam, 2014
45. *Henry I*, C. Warren Hollister (Yale University Press, 2003), 221–223
46. Hallam, 2014, 178
47. Ibid, 13
48. *Princes and Territories in Medieval Germany*, Benjamin Arnold (Cambridge University Press, 2004), 13–14
49. See *The Battle of Lechfeld and Its Aftermath, August 955: The End of the Age of Migrations in the Latin West*, Charles R. Bowlus (Taylor & Francis 2016)
50. *Progress and Problems in Medieval England*, Edward Miller, Richard Britnell & John Hatcher (Cambridge University Press, 2002), 96
51. *Textiles and the Medieval Economy: Production, Trade and Consumption of Textiles, 8th–16th Centuries*, Angela Ling Huang (Oxbow Books, 2015), 127
52. Italy was very different to North France or England, but it is not as if there were no landowning noblemen living outside of urban centres who could maintain private armies. As Maurice Keen suggests these men were no strangers to chivalry in the twelfth century, see *Chivalry*, Maurice Keen (Yale University Press, 2005), 37–40
53. The Duke of Romagna, Cesare Borgia claimed he could recruit one man per house in two days, see *An Unlikely Prince: the Life and Times of Machiavelli*, Niccolo Capponi (Da Capo, 2010), 119
54. *Logistics of Warfare in the Age of the Crusades*, John H. Pryor (Ashgate, 2002), 214
55. *Banking, Trade and Industry: Europe, America and Asia from the Thirteenth to the Twentieth Century*, Sheldon Dick & Alice Teichova (Cambridge University Press, 1997)

56. *The Business of War: Military Enterprise and Military Revolution in Early Modern Europe*, David Parrott (Cambridge University Press, 2012), 43
57. *Medieval Armies and Weapons in Western Europe*, Jean-Denis G.G. Lepage (McFarland Incorporated, 2014), 236
58. *The Official Horse Breeds Standards Guide*, F. Lynghaug (Voyageur Press, 209), 128
59. *The Medieval Warhorse*, R.H.C. Davis (Thames and Hudson, 1989), 49–50
60. For the Reconquista see Chapter 2, *Reconquest and Crusade in Medieval Spain*, Joseph F. O'Callaghan (University of Pennsylvania Press, 2013)
61. Specifically when El Cid defeated a Christian army at the Battle of Morella, see *The Quest for El Cid*, Richard A. Fletcher (Alfred A. Knopf, 1989), 138–39
62. It is interesting to look at the Spanish word *hidalgo*, which translated to 'son' and suggests an inheritance of status. Essentially they are the lower, often knightly, nobility. See *Spain in the Middle Ages: From Frontier to Empire, 1000–1500*, Angus MacKay (Macmillan Education UK, 1977), 47–48

Chapter 3 – The Crusades

1. *The First Crusade: The Call from the East*, Peter Frankopan (Harvard University Press, 2012), 33
2. The Pope specifically set the crusade as something apart and above inter-Christian warfare. See *The First Crusade: A New History*, Thomas Asbridge (Oxford University Press, 2005), 36
3. Bongars, *Gesta Dei per Francos*, translated in *A Source Book for Medieval History*, Oliver J. Thatcher, and Edgar Holmes McNeal, (New York: Charles Scribner's Sons, 1905), 382
4. According to Marcus Bull, knights were both inspired by the church and also supported it themselves. *Knightly Piety and the Lay Response to the First Crusade: The Limousin and Gascony, c. 970 – c. 1130,* Marcus Bull (Oxford: Clarendon Press, 1993), 285
5. With hundreds of people too, far too large a group to be sneaking around the Holy Land unnoticed. This was also only one of a number of eleventh-century mass pilgrimages. *Byzantines and Crusaders in Non-Greek Sources, 1025–1204*, Mary Whitby, (OUP/ British Academy, 2007), 5. Also see Hallam, 1997, 26–27
6. See the section on Peter the Hermit in *Historia Hierosolymitanae expeditionis*, Albert of Aachen, twelfth century. Available not in Latin here: https://sourcebooks.fordham.edu/source/albert-cde.asp (Last accessed 25/08/2021)
7. Following the destruction of the church of the Holy Sepulchre by al-Hakim in ad 1009, Pope Sergius IV proclaimed that all Italians should send a fleet to reclaim the tomb of Christ, in language that mentioned the last judgement. Whether this document is genuine is a matter for debate, but the Christian world was nonetheless outraged by the destruction of a holy site. Hallam, 1997, 25
8. Jonathan Riley-Smith noted that 'earthly glory' had to be a motivation for some knights because of their upbringing and their culture, which would actively encourage anything that promoted that earthly glory. *The First Crusade and the Idea of Crusading*, Jonathan Riley-Smith (University of Pennsylvania Press Inc, 1986), 41
9. *The Social Structure of the First Crusade*, Connor Kostick (Brill, 2008), 171
10. Folbertus, miles egregius de castello Bullon ortus'. See *The Crusader Kingdom of Jerusalem*, Alan V. Murray (Prosopograhica et Genealogica, 2000), 195
11. *Le Jouvencel*, Jean le Bueil, edited L. Lecestre and C. Favre as translated in *Laws of War in the Late Middle Ages*, Maurice Keen (Routledge, 1965), 3
12. This was critical because it removed the greatest military threat in the area, Sultan Kilij Arslan and paved the way for negotiation. *The New Concise History of the Crusades*, Thomas F. Madden (Rowan & Littlefield, 2005), 24

13. Raymond of Aguilers was so overcome when the lance was discovered that he kissed the point even as the excavation continued. Possibly he did this in order to distract onlookers from what might have been very fresh looking earth. *Holy Warriors: A Modern History of the Crusades*, Jonathan Phillips (Random House, 2012), 19
14. See *The Chanson d'Antioche: an Old French account of the First Crusade*, trans Susan B. Edgington, Carol Sweetenham (Farnham: Ashgate, 2011)
15. The fact that one knight gave his protection to a group of Muslims who has sought refuge in the Temple of the Lord, only to return and find them massacred, speaks of the bloodbath that occurred. Kostick, 264
16. For a full discussion see *Victory in the East*, John France (Cambridge University Press, 1996), 122–142
17. After Antioch, those who had plundered the city and the fleeing enemy army went straight to Caesarea and Homs to buy Arab horses. Kostick, 185
18. This was Frederick II and the work was called *De Arte Venandi cum Avibus*, or in English *On The Art of Hunting with Birds*
19. The fog of war possibly decided the matter however, as a few hundred Fatimid horsemen apparently thought the battle was won and rode off to Jaffa. *The Crusaders in the East: A Brief History of the Wars of Islam with the Latins in Syria During the Twelfth and Thirteenth Centuries*, W.B. Stevenson, (Cambridge University Press, 2012), 45
20. *Historia Hierosolymitana*, Fulcheri Carnotensis (aka Fulcher of Chartres), 1095–1127, Henrich Hagenmeyer Translation (Carl Winters Universitatsbuchhandlung Heidelburg, 1913), 414
21. *A History of the Expedition to Jerusalem 1095–1127*, Fulcher of Chartres, (translated Francis Rita Ryan, edited Harold S. Fink, University of Tennessee Press, 1969), bk. III, ch. XVIII.4, 242
22. For a detailed look see *Turkish Myth and Muslim Symbol: The Battle of Manzikert*, Carole Hillenbrand (Edinburgh University Press, 2007)
23. *Famous Battles of the Medieval Period*, Chris McNab (Cavendish Square Publishing LLC, 2017), 24
24. Regarded as the prince of Antioch, see *The creation of the principality of Antioch, 1098–1130*, Thomas S. Asbridge (Boydell Press, 2000), 139–146
25. *The Crusader States and Their Neighbours*, Nicholas Morton (Oxford University Press, 2020), 232–223
26. For an in depth discussion of the battle, see *Journal of Medieval History*, Volume XI, Edited by Clifford J. Rogers, Kelly DeVries, John France (Boydell Press, 2013), 95–106
27. The King of Jerusalem had actually asked Reynald to make amends for his crime, for he had by this attack broken a personal truce with Saladin the previous year, but Reynald rudely refused. *The Leper King and His Heirs, Baldwin IV and the Crusader Kingdom of Jerusalem*, Bernard Hamilton (Cambridge University Press, 2005), 225
28. Hallam, 1997, 157
29. Waspish contemporary sources blamed Balian's Greek wife for him leaving the field because she had corrupted him, whereas realistically he was simply being pragmatic. 'The holiness of that forsaken place': The Purpose of Sin in the *Itinerarium Peregrinorum et Gesta Regis Ricardi*. in the journal, *Studies in Philology*, Stefan Vander Elst (Studies in Philology, University of North Carolina Press, 2019), 200
30. *Rare and Excellent History of Saladin by Baha al-Din Ibvn Shaddad*, D.S. Richards (Farnham: Ashgate, 2002), 146
31. Richard's ordering of the killing of potentially more than 2,000 prisoners happened because Saladin did not keep his side of the agreement of the surrender of Acre. Saladin may have been testing Richard, and if he was, Richard showed himself to be

implacable and immune to manipulation. Gruesome and abhorrent the act itself may have been, it sent a message to Saladin that he was up against a fearsome opponent. See *The Chronicles and Memorials of Richard I (Itinerarium peregrinorum et gesta regis Ricardi)* Volume 1, 1864, London, XXII

32. See this translation of the Rule itself: *The Rule of the Templars, The French Text of the Rule of the Order of the Knights Templar,* Translated by Judith Mary Upton-Ward (Boydell Press, 1997)
33. For more details see chapters 5 and 6, *The Templars,* Dan Jones (Head of Zeus, 2017)
34. *Saladin's Hattin Letter in The Horns of Hattin,* Melville and Lyons (Jerusalem, 1992), 211
35. Saladin also set a ransom figure for the whole population of Jerusalem's people, some 20,000 people, but the church and religious orders only gave enough to free 7,000 of those. Saladin's brother, al-Adil was so appalled that he begged Saladin to free a thousand of those abandoned souls, which his elder brother agreed to. See *A History of the Crusades, Volume 2,* Steven Runciman (Penguin, 1987), 466
36. For details on this abject failure, see *The Seventh Crusade, 1244–1254, Sources and Documents,* Edited by Peter Jackson (Taylor & Francis, 2020)
37. For anyone unsure whether the Templars were occultist or anything else, see *The Templars,* Dan Jones (Head of Zeus, 2017)
38. To understand the history of the Teutonic Knights, see *The Teutonic Knights, A Military History,* William L. Urban (Greenhill, 2003)
39. To look in more depth at the Mamluks, see *Templar Knight Vs Mamluk Warrior, 1218–50,* David Campbell (Bloomsbury Publishing, 2015)

Chapter 4 – The Mounted Knight
1. More or less the whole of *A Knight's Own Book of Chivalry,* Geoffroi de Charny, trans Richard E. Kaeuper & Elspeth Kennedy (University of Pennsylvania Press Inc, 2013)
2. Bennet, 2009, 86
3. Ancient Sparta is the obvious extreme example
4. *Charlemagne and Louis the Pious,* Thomas F.X. Noble (Pennsylvania State University, 2009), 199
5. For the influence that Vegetius had on the medieval commander, see *The De Re Militari of Vegetius,* Christopher Allmand (Cambridge University Press, 2011)
6. Written in normal French this work was also important because of the reach it had, see Coopland, 1949
7. *Honore Bouvet, the Tree of Battles, and the Literature of War in Fourteenth-Century France,* Nicholas A.R. Wright (PHD, Edinburgh, 1972), 12
8. Henry V's order has elsewhere been translated as meaning English boys are not to be taken onto campaign, but a careful reading of the source confirms it is taking about prisoners of war. *History of the Battle of Agincourt,* Nicholas Nicolas (London, 1832), Appendix VIII, 37
9. *Selected Sermons of Hugh Latimer,* A Chester (Charlottesville, 1968), 67
10. For an in depth look at the use of logic in medieval language, see *Humanism and Education in Medieval and Renaissance Italy,* Robert Black (Cambridge University Press, 2001), 70
11. The *Annales Lamberti* Chronicle, from as early as 1075 complained that it was the lack of physical fitness in the peasant population that meant nobles didn't bother recruiting them as warriors, see *History of Sport and Physical Activity,* ed James G. Thompson & Ronald A. Smith (Daniel Smith, 1991), 92
12. See *Lord of the Pyrenees: Gaston Fébus, Count of Foix (1331–1391),* Richard Vernier (Boydell Press, 2008)

13. *Hunting in the Middle Ages*, in the journal *Speculum*, Henry L Savage (University of Chicago, 1933), 31
14. See, *Medieval Hunting*, Richard Almond (History Press, 2011)
15. *Knight: The Medieval Warrior's Unofficial Manual*, Michael Prestwich (Thames & Hudson, 2010), 172
16. *Gentry Culture in Late-medieval England*, Alison Truelove & Raluca Radulescu (Manchester University Press, 2020), 77
17. Crouch, 2005
18. *Henry III: The Rise to Power and Personal Rule, 1207–1258*, David Carpenter (Yale University Press, 2020), 242
19. Fallows, 2010, 272–273
20. Crouch, 2005, 93
21. When riding in a melee, unless it has degenerated into a stationary brawl (which would have happened) there is a certain distance, like a buffer zone, around each horse. This is partly because no knight wants to break his kneecap against his opponents, but it means that if someone makes a move to steal your reins, you will see their hand move towards your horse. At which point a swift sword strike to their hand or arm will remove the problem swiftly.
22. They could also last for days, see Crouch, 2005, 124
23. Ibid, 126
24. *The Unconquered Knight*, Gutierre Diaz de Gamez, Translated by Joan Evans (Boydell & Brewer, 2004), 2 142
25. Ibid
26. Normally one of the two knights notices the other and veers away, but historically collisions certainly happened, and they would have been painful for man and horse.
27. De Gamez & Evans, 2004, 142
28. Fallows, 2010, 92
29. Ibid, 399–502
30. From as early as 1280 onwards the joust overtook the grand tournament as the main event, until by the fifteenth century when largely only the joust remained. See Crouch, 2005, 124
31. See *Recueil des actes des comtes de Pontieu (1026–1279)*, ed Clovis Brunel (Paris, 1930), VII, 8–9
32. *Medieval Knighthood V*, ed Ruth Harvey & Stephen Church (Boydell Press, 1995), 96
33. *Saladin and the Fall of the Kingdom of Jerusalem*, Stanley Lane-Poole (Putnam, 1898), 356–357
34. *The Knight on His Quest: Symbolic Patterns of Transition in Sir Gawain and the Green Knight*, Piotr Sadowski (University of Delaware Press, 1996), 220
35. *William Marshal*, David Crouch (Taylor & Francis, 2016), 30
36. See *L' Ordene de Chevalerie*, Anonomous (BiblioLife, 2013)
37. *The Book of the Order of Chivalry*, Alfred T.P. Byles (Routledge Taylor & Francis Group, 2010), 85
38. Ibid, XXII
39. *Richard III in the North*, M.J. Trow (Pen & Sword, 2020), 53
40. *Chronicles of England, France and Spain and the Surrounding Countries, by Sir John Froissart, Translated from the French Editions with Variations and Additions from Many Celebrated MSS*, by Thomas Johnes, Esq. (William Smith, 1848), CHAPTER CXXIX
41. Interestingly this was a Portuguese king knighting his own knights, but he also offered to knight a group of Englishmen, but they declined his offer. See *Chronicles of England, France, Spain, and the Adjoining Countries: From the Latter Part of the Reign of Edward*

II to the Coronation of Henry IV, Jean Froissart, translated Thomas Johnes (Routledge, 1874), 119
42. *Livro Da Ensinanca De Bem Cavalgar Toda Sella, Duarte I, king of Portugal, 1391–1438*, ed Joseph Piel, trans J.L. Forgeng (Livraria Bertrand, 2010), 65
43. *A Chronicle of the first thirteen Years of the Reign of King Edward IV*, ed J Halliwell (Camden Soc, 1839), 39
44. Similar quotes abound from Dr Tobias Capwell who is the world's foremost authority on armour and perhaps the greatest living proponent of the idea that medieval armour was art and should be treated as such. For a deeper insight into armour or jousting see any of his books which are all written from the perspective of someone who has had years of practical experience. Experience I have felt physically when he has broken lances on me! For this quotation see https://theartssociety.org/arts-news-features/become-instant-expert-art-armour Last accessed on 06/09/2021.
45. Hans Talhoffer is perhaps the most famous author, but there were many others, including Paulus Kal, who for example described how it was possible to use a lance to parry an incoming lance strike in such situations. In his fifteenth century *Paulus Kal Fechtbuch*, a diagram shows a knight with reins looped around his arm and holding his lance with two hands. This defence turns into attack as once the enemy's lance has been pushed aside, the two-handed lance can be brought back to bare on the now defenceless opponent. Medieval warfare could be extremely technical for those who had the time to work on their technique.
46. Gamez & Evans, 2004, 196
47. Excalibur can be traced back to a Welsh legend from the tenth century where it was a sword with magical powers. See *Mythological Swords*, Rocky Pendergrass (Lulu.com, 2015), 29–31
48. France, 2020, 35
49. Hitti, 2000, 129
50. Crouch, 2005, 99
51. Fallows, 2010, 390
52. Specifically Claude Blair in his work *European Armour, c.106 – -c.1700*, Claude Blair (London, 1958), 157–158
53. Hitti, 2000, 90
54. *Crusading and Warfare in the Middle Ages: Realities and Representations, Essays in Honour of John France*, Edited by Simon John and Nicholas Morton (Routledge Taylor & Francis Group, 2016), 24
55. *The Legend of Bouvines: War, Religion and Culture in the Middle Ages*, by Georges Duby, trans Catherine Tihanyi (University of California Press, 1990), 203 (Song XI)
56. If you visit Temple Church in London, where the great William Marshall is buried, you can also find an effigy of his third son, Gilbert Marshall. He was killed in a tournament in 1241 and under his right arm, beneath his surcoat, you can just about make out some flat armour and the buckles down his side that fastened them. This armour is either a leather breastplate or metal coat of plates. A coat of plates is a sleeveless vest made of linen that has a series of square or rectangular plates riveted onto it. This vest is potentially open down both sides, and has buckles to close it around the body of the knight and keep it as tight as possible. At the fall of Acre in 1291, William of Beaujeu is mentioned as being pierced by a javelin under his armpit where the plates of his armour left a gap. This reinforces the assertion that high ranking knights in the thirteenth century were wearing coats of plates in battle. In appearance, the coat of plates resembles modern body armour but is thinner, although the weight is comparable.

57. *Deeds of Arms*, Steven Muhlberger (The Chivalry Bookshelf, 2005), 191
58. Fallows, 2010, 35
59. Ibid
60. *The Battle of Agincourt: Sources and Interpretations*, Anne Curry (Boydell Press, 2000), 359
61. *Some Neglected Fights Between Crécy and Poitiers*, T. Tout (EHR, 1905), 726–730
62. *The Medieval Archer*, Jim Bradbury (Boydell Press, 1998), 55
63. *The Collected Papers of Thomas Frederick Tout*, Thomas Fredrick Tout (Manchester University Press, 1932), 230
64. The Italian men-at-arms at Verneuil were the heavy tanks of their day, and the armour designed for them reflected this fact. An Italian harness could be more than 10kg heavier than a German armour made for the same man. As English knights had fought largely on foot during the Wars of the Roses, in the middle of the fifteenth century their armour adapted accordingly and their style is separate to either the Italian or German. For details on English Armour see *Armour of the English Knight 1400–1450*, Tobias Capwell (Thomas Del Mar, 2015) and *Armour of the English Knight 1450–1500*, Tobias Capwell (Thomas Del Mar, 2021). If you wish to see just how ornate German fifteenth-century armour became, the best way is to visit the Wallace Collection in London to see their Gothic German harness, called A21, sitting atop a fully armoured horse. Another stellar collection of armour at the Kunsthistorisches Museum in Vienna shows armour made by a superstar of the period, Lorenz Helmschmid. This Germanic armour consists of fluted plates with copper alloy edging that is incredibly ornate and has the appearance of gold. The German style of armour favoured lightness and freedom of movement over protection, in comparison to the Italian approach which focused on protection and often plainer decoration.
65. *The Ambraser Codex by Master Hans Talhoffer*, Hugh T. Knight (Lulu.com, 2008), 2
66. f, 30
67. Ibid
68. Fallows, 2010, 367
69. Of course the line between church and state was blurred to the extreme in the middle ages, just consider a king who went on crusade.
70. *Society at War: The Experience of England and France During the Hundred Years War*, C.T. Allmand (Boydell Press, 1998), 32–33
71. Barker, 2012, 32–33
72. Evans, 1928, 36
73. Ibid, 38
74. Ibid
75. www.famaleonis.com/inventory-sforza-manatarms.asp Last accessed on 06/09/2021
76. *Works of Geoffrey Chaucer*, Edited by F.N. Robinson (Boston: Houghton Mifflin, 1957), A 66
77. *Chaucer and War*, John H. Pratt (University Press of America, 2000), 104
78. Hence the imposition of *The Penitential Code of Ermenfrid* we saw being inflicted on the victorious Normans following the Norman Conquest in chapter three, significantly levelled in 1050, *after* the harrying.
79. Keen, 1965, 181
80. Willard, 1999, 172
81. *Jean de Bueil: Le Jouvencel*, ed Craig Taylor & James H.M. Taylor (Boydell Press, 2020), 175
82. Barker, 2005, 305
83. Another knight who had his helmet shattered, presumably from repetitive blows, was hit in the head with a hammer and fell from his horse in agony. The fate of this knight

Notes 245

and Rodolfo Gonzaga show just how vulnerable the face was in war. See *Diara de Bello Carolino (Diary of the Caroline War)*, trans Dorothy M. Schullian (Frederick Ungar, 1967)

Chapter 5 – The Knight's Horse
1. *Miscellaneous Publications*, Ministry of Agriculture and Fisheries (H.M. Stationary Office, 1927), 8
2. *Like Engend'ring Like: Heredity and Animal Breeding in Early Modern England*, Nicholas Russell (Cambridge University Press, 2007), 62
3. Historical horse size is a notoriously difficult problem, but a full discussion can be found here, wherein the conclusion is that the medieval horse averages between 14 hands and 15 hands. This fits in with our modern experience of riding in armour, horses of around, or just over, 15 hands are more than capable of performing dressage movements while carrying a fully armoured rider. *The Medieval Horse and Its Equipment, C.1150 – c.1450*, John Clark (Boydell Press, 2004), 22–30
4. *Diagnosis and Management of Lameness in the Horse*, Michael W. Ross & Sue J. Dyson (Elsevier Health Sciences, 2010), 1068
5. *A New Method, and Extraordinary Invention, to Dress Horses, and Work Them According to Nature*, William Cavendish (Creative Media Partners LLC, 2018), 78
6. When you need to turn quickly to avoid an emerging danger, manoeuvrability suddenly becomes very important!
7. Clark, 2004, 23
8. Ibid, 25
9. *Icelanders in the Viking Age: The People of the Sagas*, William R. Short (McFarland Publishers Incorporated, 2010), 154
10. The Statue of Marcus Aurelius in Rome from the second century suggests his horse was perhaps 14 hands (142cm) tall. The Greeks also imported heavier horses from the east which can be seen on stone carvings at Xanthos, and judging by the height of the human next to one of them, they could be almost 15 hands. These carvings also show the Greeks working the horse in hand (the person is on the ground rather than riding) as we do today.
11. *Knights and Warhorses: Military Service and the English Aristocracy Under Edward III*, Andrew Ayton (Boydell Press, 1994), 63
12. *History and Heraldry, 1254–1310*, Neil Denholm-Young (Oxford, 1965), 20
13. *Knights and Esquires: The Gloucestershire Gentry in the Fourteenth Century*, Nigel Saul (Clarendon Press, 1981), 37–47
14. Ayton, 1994, 47
15. *Medieval Warfare: A History*, Maurice Keen (OUP Oxford, 1999), 191
16. *The Cartulary of Shrewsbury Abbey*, The Abbey of St. Peter and St Paul (National Library of Wales, 1975), 34–42
17. *The Beast Within: Animals in the Middle Ages*, Joyce E. Salisbury (Taylor & Francis, 2012), 23
18. Sweetenham, 2011, 187
19. Ayton, 1994, 48
20. Salisbury, 2012, 23
21. Ayton, 1994, 67
22. Evans, 1928, 41
23. Piel and Forgeng, 2010, 6
24. Ibid, 9
25. Ibid, 11
26. Fallows, 2010, 339

27. Specifically the *traver*, or haunches-in movement.
28. *A treatise upon horsemanship*, Francois de la Gueiriniere, trans William Frazer (1801), 39
29. *Le Cheval vivant*, Léon Battista Alberti (1430s) (Les Belles Lettres, 1999), 12
30. The Latin manuscript can be viewed on the Yale University website
31. *Hippiatria sive Marescalia*, Lorenzo Rusio (Parigi, Christianum Wechelum, 1532)
32. Ibid, own translation from Latin. Having seen other translations specify a rod of hot iron be applied to the rear of the horse, I suspected that this seemed unlikely. A heated staff of hazel wood is not as cruel as a heated iron bar, but it still leaves something to be desired in terms of animal welfare.
33. *Anglo-Saxon Farms and Farming*, Debby Banham & Rosamond Firth (Oxford University Press, 2014), 79–82
34. For what happens when breeding is not selective, we can note the example of the medieval Welsh Powys horse, as described by Gerald of Wales. In 1166, after infusions of stock from Spain, the Powys was a prestigious, much sought-after breed, purchased by kings like Henry II. In the late thirteenth century, however, probably as a result of frequent, indiscriminate breeding with feral mares, the breed was mostly remarkable for its predominantly dun colouring and the fact that its price was only 37 per cent as high as that of other breeds.
35. *Anglo-Saxon Wills*, Dorothy Whitelock (Cambridge University Press, 2011), 61
36. *Burton Abbey Twelfth Century Surveys*, ed C.G.O. Bridgeman (William Salt Arch. Soc, 1916), 212 and 228
37. *Rotuli Litterarum Clausarum* in Turri londinensi asservati: *1224–1227*, ed Sir Thomas Duffus Hardy (G. Eyre and A. Spottiswoode, 1844), 150
38. *L'Histoire Guillaume le Marechal*, trans Paul Meyer, 1891–1901, II, 2933–5
39. Davis, 1989, 63
40. *Order and Innovation in the Middle Ages*, Bruce McNab & Teofilo F. Ruiz (Princeton University Press, 2015), 182
41. Davis, 1989, 65
42. Carpenter, 2020, 242. Also see the original Matthew Paris manuscript via the British Library, *Historia Anglorum, Chronica majora, Part III; Continuation of Chronica maiora*, Matthew Paris (St Albans, 1250–1259), Royal 14 C VII
43. Davis, 1989, 86
44. Ibid, 87
45. Ibid
46. Ibid, 88–97
47. I was part of a team that rode and walked on foot from York to Battle Abbey, over three weeks, in a recreation of King Harold's march towards Hastings in 1066. The horses kept up a constant pace for 300 miles and those walking had no option but to keep up. The humans walking suffered blistered feet and aches until they acclimatised, but no horse ever looked tired or sore at any point.
48. *Discours politiques et militaire*, edited F.E. Sutcliffe (Geneve: Droz, 1967), 211
49. For an example from Edward I's reign see *The Oxford Encyclopedia of Medieval Warfare and Military Technology, Volume 1*, Clifford J. Rogers (Oxford University Press, 2010), 221
50. *The Road to Crécy: The English Invasion of France, 1346*, Marilyn Livingstone et al (Pearson/Longman, 2005), 52
51. Ibid
52. *The Hundred Years War (part II): Different Vistas*, L. J. Andrew Villalon, Donald J. Kagay (Brill, 2008), 113

53. *The patterns of war through the eighteenth century*, Larry H. Addington (Indiana University Press, 1990), 64
54. The horse, Charlie, is a British bred Lipizzaner of poor confirmation and twenty years of age. He has a main occupation of a jousting horse, and frequently trains carrying armour. He is therefore a good parallel for a medieval warhorse, if perhaps potentially an inch taller than would be ideal, standing at 15.2 hands, although not naturally built for it. The distance of 110m was used because that was the length of the field available.
55. *The Rise of the Centaurs: The Origin of Horsemanship. The Untold Story*, Bjarke Rink (AuthorHouse, 2013), 215
56. For a diagram of a Roman saddle and further explanation, see *The Roman Cavalry*, Karen R. Dixon & Path Southern (Taylor & Francis, 2013), 74
57. For a good example of saddle-steels, see the sixteenth-century saddle at the Wallace Collection in London, which weighs nearly 15kg. See *Masterpieces of European Arms and Armour in the Wallace Collection*, Tobias Capwell (The Wallace Collection, 2011), 110–111
58. See the fifteenth-century Bohemian saddle made out of bone at the Met Museum in New York.
59. Duby, 1990, 202
60. For a good diagram of horse armour, see *Armour and Weapons*, Charles Ffoulkes (Outlook Verlag, 2020), 67
61. Down from twelve oxen in the eighth century to two oxen in the sixteenth. See *The Knight and the Blast Furnace: A History of the Metallurgy of Armour in the Middle Ages & the Early Modern Period*, Alan R. Williams (Brill, 2003), 43
62. Fallows, 2010, 243
63. The horse whom I conducted the speed test on, Charlie, walks noticeably slower when carrying me in armour than without, contrasting with his equal galloping speed armoured and without.
64. Clark, 2004, 94
65. Spikes can be seen on the shoes of the horse on the famous Westminster Psalter of the knight, Royal MS 2 A XXII, f, 220
66. *Breaking and Riding*, James Fillis (Xenophon Press LLC, 2018), 5. Modern horse owners with young horses should read this book.
67. For example, one mare used for jousting was in its paddock at a St George's Day event, when a man in a dragon suit walked past her on his way to perform. She rushed towards it and squared up to the dragon, and had they not been separated by a fence, I have no doubt she would have performed St George's duty for him.
68. For a fair view of stallions, see *The Natural Stallion: His Behaviour, Management and Training*, Lesley Skipper (Black Tent Publications, 2010)
69. See all of Hitti, 2000
70. If a person stands in the middle of our arena with a sword and walks normally over to me on my horse, he will ignore them. If they stride over with an aggressive stance, even without a weapon, he most certainly knows what that means, and will try to get out of the way.
71. An army of Alfonso IV was described as having a thousand mounted troops, but an unspecified number of infantry. See *Journal of Medieval Military History Volume X*, ed Clifford J. Rogers, Kelly DeVries & John France (Boydell Press, 2012), 97
72. Ayton, 1994, 49–83
73. If an average fourteenth century horse was worth £5 it would today be worth £3,000. To compare, the cost of a Javelin anti-tank missile in 2021 is around £49,000. In this respect, horses were (sadly) positively expendable.

74. Ayton, 1994, 256
75. Ibid, 62
76. Hitti, 2000, 127
77. Ibid, 126
78. Ibid, 127
79. For example at the siege of Rouen in 1418, see *A History of the Late Medieval Siege, 1200–1500*, Peter Fraser Purton (Boydell & Brewer, 2009), 253
80. Williams, 2003, 43
81. For an example, see *The Black Prince and the Grande Chevauchée of 1355*, Mollie M. Madden (Boydell Press, 2018)
82. Although it can take only a few minutes to put on a harness, a man-at-arms would have to be near it, and have someone to help him with the upper portions for it to be useful.
83. Barker, 2012, 63–64
84. *Henry the Young King, 1155–1183*, Matthew Strickland (Yale University Press, 2016), 247
85. *The Last Years of the Teutonic Knights, Lithuania, Poland and the Teutonic Order*, William Urban (Pen & Sword, 2018), 121
86. Duby, 1990, 193
87. Ibid, 207
88. Hallam, 1997, 302–303
89. Perhaps only three or four, which a charge of knights would have likely broken through. See *Historical Dictionary of Late Medieval England, 1272–1485*, Ronald H. Fritze & Ann E. Faulkner (Greenwood Press, 2002), 22
90. Or perhaps slightly deeper formations of four to eight were common, which may have been enough to absorb a charge. The reality is that the disposition of medieval armies was varied and not easily subject to generalisations. *European Warfare, 1350–1750*, ed D.J.B. Trim & Frank Tallet (Cambridge University Press, 2010), 206
91. For a full discussion of the role of the mounted knight at Verneuil, see the section: *II. The Role of the Lombard Cavalry* in *Medieval Warfare 1300–1450*, ed Kelly DeVries (Taylor & Francis, 2017)
92. Barker, 2012, 122–123
93. Ibid, 218
94. *Charles the Bold, The Last Valois Duke of Burgundy*, Richard Vaughan & Werner Paravincini (Boydell Press, 2002), 209–210
95. *Horse Behaviour Explained*, Margrit Zeitler-Feicht (CRC Press, 2003), 73
96. *Journal of the United States Cavalry Association*, ed Lieutenant Colonel Ezra B. Fuller (United States Cavalry Association, 1917), 262
97. Ibid
98. Ibid
99. Clark, 2004, 173
100. *'Tails' of Masculinity: Knights, Clerics, and the Mutilation of Horses in Medieval England*, from the journal *Speculum*, Andrew G. Miller (University of Chicago Press, 2013), 959
101. Ibid, 976
102. Ibid, 991–995
103. Ibid, 975
104. *The Oxford Handbook of the French Revolution*, ed David Andress (Oxford University Press, 2015), 386
105. Fallows, 2010, 367
106. *'Svá lýkr hér hverju hestaðingi': Sports and Games in Icelandic Saga Literature*, in the journal *Scandinavian Studies*, John D. Martin (University of Illinois Press, 2003), 27

107. *The complete essays of Montaigne*, Michel de Montaigne, trans Donald Murdoch Frame (Stanford University Press, 1958), 269

Chapter 6 – Age of Chivalry
1. Not just loyalty, but a solider who by himself was timid can, when in a group, act like an entirely different man. See *Psychology and the Solider*, F.C. Bartlett (Cambridge University Press, 2014), 92
2. *Weapons and Fighting Techniques of the Medieval Warrior 1000–1500 AD*, Martin Dougherty (Chartwell Books, 2008), 74
3. *The Life and Campaigns of the Black Prince*, Richard Barber (Boydell Press, 2002), 124
4. *The Lettered Knight*, Martin Aurell, Jean-Charles Khalifa & Jeremy Price (Central European University Press, 2017), 50
5. *The British Military Journal, Volume 1* (John Carpenter, 1840), 136
6. Duby, 1990, 60 and *Agincourt*, Juliet Barker (Abacus, 2007), 159
7. *Introduction to Medieval Europe, 300–1500*, Wim Blockmans & Peter Hoppenbrouwers (Taylor & Francis, 2014), 101
8. See *Arminius the Liberator, Myth and Ideology*, Martin M. Winkler (Oxford University Press, 2016)
9. *The Chivalric Turn*, David Crouch (Oxford University Press, 2019), 68
10. *William Marshal, Knight Errant, Baron, and Regent of England*, Sidney Painter (Johns Hopkins Press, 1933), 289
11. *Knighthood, War and Chivalry*, David Crouch (Longman, 2002), 164
12. There were Peace of God councils almost every year from 989 to 1038, which does rather suggest that they weren't working, see *The Peace of God*, Richard Landes & Thomas Head (Cornell University Press, 2018), 261–262
13. Ibid, 9
14. Although partly out of self interest, because if a knight allowed his peasants to be killed, he was going to have a problem financially, see *Growing up in the Middle Ages*, Paul B. Newman (McFarland Incorporated, 2015), 236
15. Geoffrey de Charny never mentions the Templars in his book, and although that cannot be taken as evidence, he did at least not choose to hold them up as the finest example of chivalry, see Kaeuper & Kennedy, 2013, 19
16. For an early example, where crusaders claimed the protection of the Virgin Mary, see *Chivalry and Exploration, 1298–1630*, Jennifer R. Goodman (Boydell Press, 1998), 110
17. For what is complex subject, see all of, *Women in Medieval Western European Culture*, Linda E. Mitchell (Taylor & Francis, 2012)
18. A trend started by Henry III who was a very pious king, *The Shrine of Our Lady of Walsingham*, J.C. Dickinson (University Press, 1991), 17
19. *Aquinas, Political Writings*, R. W. Dyson, Raymond Geuss & Quentin Skinner (Posts and Telecommunications Press, 2002), 242
20. *Life in a Medieval Castle*, Gary L. Blackwood (Lucent Books, 2000), 62
21. Crouch, 2005, 71
22. *Medieval Chivalry*, Richard W. Kaeuper (Cambridge University Press, 2016), 274
23. *Studying Late Medieval History*, Cindy Wood (Taylor & Francis, 2019), 159
24. Keen, 2005, 102
25. *The Chivalric Biography of Boucicaut, Jean II Le Meingre*, Jane H.M. Taylor (Boydell Press, 2016), 30–31
26. See all of *The Flower of Chivalry, Bertrand Du Guesclin and the Hundred Years War*, Richard Vernier (D.S. Brewer, 2007)
27. Keen, 2005, 111–113

28. *Term Paper Resource Guide to Medieval History*, Jean S. Hamm (Greenwood, 2010), 88
29. Although there are differing versions of what Taillefer actually did, for a good list see the end note in *The Exploitations of Medieval Romance*, Ivana Djordjevic & Judith Elizabeth Weiss (D.S. Brewer, 2010), 58
30. *History of the Middle Ages, 284–1500*, Sidney Painter (Macmillian Education Limited, 1963), 451
31. For an example of this, the thirteenth-century *Questre del Saint Graal*, was an attempt by a churchman to make work on religion look like one on chivalry, *Rethinking Chivalry and Courtly Love*, Jennifer G. Wollock (ABC-CLIO, 2011), 97
32. Crouch, 2019, 61
33. *War, Justice, and Public Order: England and France in the Later Middle Ages*, Richard W. Kaeuper (Oxford University Press,1988), 186
34. *Global Convulsions*, Winston A. Van Horne (Sate University of New York Press, 1997), 94–95
35. Saul, 1995, 20
36. *The Historia Brittonum*, Nennius Hibernicus & William Gunn (Arch, 1819), 35
37. *A Great and Terrible King, Edward I and the Forging of Britain*, Marc Morris (Windmill Books, 2009), 166–169
38. See *The Mabinogion*, Jeffrey Gantz (Penguin Books Ltd, 1976)
39. Chrétien's works were still being copied up until around 1350, which is a sign of his impact in a world before the printing press, *A Companion to Chrétien de Troyes*, Norris J. Lacy (Boydell & Brewer, 2008), 215
40. Morris, 2009, 166
41. This is painfully visible in the number of Lancelots, Gwains and others who were killed at Agincourt, see *Monstrelet: Enguerrand de Monstrelet*, La Chronique d'Enguerran de Monstrelet, ed L. Douet d'Arcq (Société de l'Histoire de France, 1859), vol. iii, iii, 114–18
42. Morris, 2009, 162–164
43. See (fol.96 De Calengis Pacis) Or Challenge of Peace. EUL MS183 Judith Letter. Taken from *CHIVALRIC GAMES AT THE COURT OF EDWARD III: THE JOUSTING LETTERS OF EUL MS 183*, *Medium Ævum, vol 87 No 2*, Philip E. Bennett, Sarah Cartenter and Louise Gardiner (Society for the Study of Medieval Languages and Literature, 2018)
44. Keen, 2005, 40
45. Evans, 1928, 23
46. *The Alliterative Morte Arthure*, Karl Heinz Goller (D.S. Brewer, 1981), 125
47. Ibid, 42
48. Crouch, 2005, 10
49. Ibid, 12. Crouch makes the grandfather comment in the 2006 edition of the same book.
50. Kaeuper & Kennedy, 2013, 50
51. *Richard I*, John Gillingham (Yale University Press, 1999), 278
52. *Geschichte der Heraldik*, G. A. Seyler (Nuremburg, 1985), 48–49
53. *Parties medites de l'oeuvre de Sicile Heraut*, ed Ferdinand Roland (Societe des Bibliophiles Belges de Mons 22, 1867), 72–78
54. Crouch, 2005, 127
55. To joust simply means to fight one against one, it does not by definition have to involve horses.
56. Crouch, 2005, 116
57. Ibid, 130

58. The tilt barrier is the fence that separates both jousting horses, introduced probably in Spain around 1420, but only reaching England later. It had the effect of lowering the difficulty level of jousting, I would go so far as to say that a decent rider can joust along a tilt, but only a horseman or horsewoman can joust 'at large' in the open.
59. Muhlberger, 2005, 223
60. Kaeuper & Kennedy, 1996, 87
61. Fallows, 2010, 386–387
62. *The 'Livre de la Paix'*, ed C. Willard (The Hague, 1954), 134
63. *Edward III's Round Table at Windsor*, Julian Munby, Richard Barber & Richard Brown (Boydell Press, 2008), 145
64. Ibid, 80–82
65. Barker, 2012, 123
66. *The Perfect King, The Life of Edward III, Father of the English Nation*, Ian Mortimer (Random House, 2010), 301
67. See *The Just War Tradition, An Introduction*, J. Daryl Charles & David D. Corey (Intercollegiate Studies Institute (ORD), 2014)
68. *Chivalry and the Ideals of Knighthood in France During the Hundred Years War*, Craig Taylor (Cambridge University Press, 2013), 206
69. Hastings, John, Thirteenth Earl of Pembroke *(1347–1375)*, R. Ian Jack *(ODNB, online edition, 2008)*
70. *Historia Anglicana*, ed H.T. Riley (R.S, 1863), Vol.I 319n
71. Jean-Denis, 2014, 125
72. *Chaucer, Life Records*, M. Crow and C. Olsen (Oxford, 1966), 23–25
73. *The Waverley Annals in vol II of Annales Monastici*, H.R. Luard (Rolls Series 1864–9). Also see Hallam, 1995, 97
74. Ibid
75. Morris, 2010, 68
76. *Napoleon's Notes on English History made on the Eve of the French Revolution, illustrated from Contemporary Historians and referenced from the findings of Later Research by Henry Foljambe Hall* (New York: E. P. Dutton & Co., 1905), 56
77. De Gamez, 2004, 120
78. See all of Crouch, 2016
79. Crouch, 2005, 70
80. *Le Livre des seyntz medicines: The Unpublished Devotional Treatise of Henry of Lancaster*, S.J. Arnold (Anglo-Norman Text Society, 1940)
81. Kaeuper & Kennedy, 1996, 129
82. *The Saint Albans Chronicle*. The Chronica Maiora of Thomas Walsingham, ed John Taylor, Wendy Childs, & Leslie Watkiss (Clarendon Press, 2003), 11
83. *Chroniques*, ed Luce et al (Renouard for the Société de l'Histoire de France, 1869–1875), IX: 272–279
84. Barker, 2012, 257–258
85. Barber, 2002, 90–91
86. Hallam, 1997, 248
87. The only way to understand the whole of Gaucourt's story is to read all of *Agincourt*, Juliet Barker (Abacus, 2007)
88. *British Prisoners of War in First World War Germany*, Oliver Wilkinson (Cambridge University Press, 2017), 46
89. Keen, 2005, 40
90. *The Wars of the Roses*, A.J. Pollard (Macmillian Education Limited, 2017), 84
91. There was a four year long conflict known as the 'The Gombe Chimpanzee War' which was observed in the 1970s. This is the tip of the iceberg, see Chapter 2, 'Nationalism

and Animals', *The Routledge Companion to Animal-Human History*, ed Hilda Kean & Philip Howell (Taylor & Francis, 2018)
92. Muhlberger, 2005, 13
93. Coopland, 1949, 125
94. Muhlberger, 2005, 13
95. As demonstrated by the rise of Thomas Beckett from the son of a petty knight to one of the highest offices in Christendom in 1162.
96. Seyler, 1985, 183
97. *The Book of the Order of Chivalry / Llibre de L'Ordre de Cavalleria / Libro de la Orden de Caballería – Ramon Llull, 1274–1276*, trans Antonio Cortijo Ocana (John Benjamins Publishing Company, 2015) (ebook), 87
98. Ibid
99. Ibid, 107
100. Byles, 2010, 122
101. Styria was parts of southern Austria and northern Slovenia.
102. *Service of Ladies, An Autobiography*, Ulrich von Liechtenstein, trans John Wesley Thomas (Boydell Press, 2004)
103. Kaeuper & Kennedy, 2013, 166–167
104. *The Command of the Ocean: A Naval History of Britain, Volume 2, 1649–1815*, N.A.M Roger (Allen Lane, 2004), 272
105. Ibid
106. Fallows, 2010, 169
107. *Essays of Montaigne*, Michel de Montaigne, trans James Hain Friswell (Sampson Low, Son, & Marsten, 1869), 146
108. Ibid, 223
109. *Shaping the Nation, England 1360–1461*, Gerald Harriss (Clarendon Press, 2005), 122
110. Kaeuper & Kennedy, 2013, 96
111. Keen, 2005, 234

Chapter 7 – The Rise of Infantry
1. See *Persian Fire, The First World Empire, Battle for the West*, Tom Holland (Abacus, 2006)
2. *The Cavalry General*, Xenophon (Public Domain Book), V
3. See the chapter, 'The Legacy of the Hellenistic Pike-Phalanx' in *An Invincible Beast, Understanding the Hellenistic Pike Phalanx in Action*, Christopher Matthew (Pen & Sword Books, 2015)
4. *A Companion to the Roman Army*, Paul Erdkamp (Wiley, 2011), 262
5. *Journal of Medieval History*, Volume XII, Edited by Clifford J. Rogers, Kelly DeVries, John France (Boydell Press, 2014), 128
6. Maurice in the *Strategicon*, sixth century. See Bennet, 2009, 58
7. *Procopius on Soldiers and Military Institutions in the Sixth-Century Roman Empire*, Conor Whatley (Brill, 2021), 147
8. *The Circle of War in the Middle Ages*, Donald Kagay (Boydell Press, 1999), 52
9. Standing on a tent peg while moving quickly could actually damage the foot of a horse fatally, and certainly render it lame and unable to move quickly.
10. Stevenson, 2012, 285
11. Ibid
12. Even in Wales, were one would expect poorer infantry to make up a large part of armies, they are missing from records and stories. *War and Society in Medieval Wales 633–1283*, Sean Davies (University of Wales Press, 2014), 10–11

13. Hallam, 1997, 161
14. Hallam, 2014, 128, 208
15. Hunt & Carlson, 138
16. *Archery and Crossbow Guilds in Medieval Flanders 1300–1500*, Laura Crombie (Boydell Press, 2016), 160
17. Ibid, 30
18. *The Routledge Companion to Medieval Warfare*, Jim Bradbury (Taylor & Francis, 2004), 277–278
19. Medieval Warfare Sourcebook, Volume I, David Nicolle (Arms and Armour Press, 1996), 108
20. Bradbury, 2004, 159
21. Nicolle, 1996, 219
22. Bennet, 2009, 161
23. Capwell, 2015, 10 and also
24. Bradbury, 2004, 153
25. Duby, 1990, 201
26. *The Battle of the Golden Spurs (Courtrai, 11 July 1302)*, J.F. Verbruggen (Boydell Press, 2002)
27. Ibid, 81
28. *Journal of Medieval Military History*, Clifford J. Rogers & Kelly DeVries (Boydell & Brewer, 2010), 172
29. *Bannockburn, Battle for Liberty*, John Sadler (Pen & Sword Military, 2008), 47
30. *The Life of Edward the Second*, trans Noel Denholm-Young (London, 1957), 89
31. *Scalacronica: The Reigns of Edward I, Edward II and Edward III*, Sir Thomas Gray & Sir Herbert Maxwell (Leopold Classic Library, 1992), 55
32. Denholm-Young, 1975, 52
33. Bradbury, 1998, 86
34. Denholm-Young, 1975, 54
35. *Infantry Warfare in the Early Fourteenth Century, Discipline, Tactics, and Technology*, Kelly DeVries (Boydell Press, 1996), 126
36. Hallam, 1997, 246
37. Ibid
38. *The Longbow*, Mike Loades (Bloomsbury Publishing, 2003), 39
39. *The Medieval Way of War*, Gregory I. Halfond (Taylor & Francis, 2016), 312
40. *Artillery, An Illustrated History of Its Impact*, Jess Kinard (ABC-CLIO, 2007), 57
41. *Jean Froissart, Chronicles*, trans Geoffrey Brereton (Penguin Books, 1978), 80–81
42. Bradbury, 1998, 57
43. *The Cambridge History of Warfare*, Geoffrey Parker (Cambridge University Press, 2020), 94
44. Hallam, 1997, 268
45. Ibid, 270
46. Ibid
47. Ibid
48. *Hawkwood, Diabolical Englishman*, Frances Stonor Saunders (Faber and Faber Limited, 2004), 30
49. *The English Traveler to Italy*, George R. Parks (Stanford, 1954), 392
50. *The Encyclopedia of War*, Gordon Martel (Wiley, 2012), 100
51. *At Agincourt, A Tale of the White Hoods of Paris*, G.A. Hentry (Fireship Press, 2011), 288
52. Nicolle, 1996, 170
53. *Understanding the Middle Ages*, Harald Kleinschmidt (Boydell Press, 2003), 183

54. Allmand, 1998, 55
55. Hunt & Carlson, 2014, 9
56. Even more sophisticated than the English lager were the early fifteenth-century Hussites from Bohemia. Their entire strategy was based around war wagons, which they used to encircle enemy foot troops, before attacking them from all sides from the safety of their wagons.
57. Bennet, 2009, 173
58. Hallam, 1997, 292
59. *The Bondage and Travels of Johann Schiltberger*, trans J. Buchan Telfer (Hakluyt Society, 1879), series 1, no.58
60. See the Infantry Revolution section in *The Military Revolution Debate*, Clifford J. Rogers (Avalon Publishing, 1995)
61. *Memoirs. The Reign of Louix XI, 1461–83*, Michael Jones (Hammondsworth, 1972), 195
62. *The Wars of the Roses*, Anthony Goodman (Taylor & Francis, 2017), 179
63. *The Pageant of the birth, life and death of Richard Beauchamp, earl of Warwick, K.G, 1389–1439*, ed Viscount Dillion & W. H. St John Hope (London, 1914)
64. *The Training and Socializing of Military Personnel*, Peter Karsten (Garland Pub, 1998), 17
65. *Outlines of Medieval History*, Charles William Previte-Orton (Biblo and Tannen, 1965), Chapter XI, Section I
66. *Le Jouvencel*, Jean de Beuil, ed Favre and Lecestre (Paris, 1887), I, cclxxxi. Alternatively, quoted by *War and Chivalry*, Malcolm Vale (Duckworth, 1981), 148–149
67. Bradbury, 2004, 244
68. *The halberd and other European polearms, 1300–1650*, George Aaron Snook (Museum Restoration Service, 1998), 25
69. *A Global Chronology of Conflict*, Spencer Tucker (ABC-CLIO, 2010), 314
70. *Expansions, Competition and Conquest in Europe Since the Bronze Age*, Axel Kristinsson (ReykjavíkurAkademían, 2010), 256
71. *Machiavelli, Volume 1*, Allen H. Gilbert (Duke University Press, 1965), 375
72. *The Art of War in Italy 1494–1529, Prince Consort Prize Essay 1920*, Frederick Lewis Taylor (Cambridge University Press, 2010), 70
73. Ibid, 72
74. *Francis I*, R.J. Knecht (Cambridge University Press, 1984), 46
75. *The Later Thirty Years War*, William P. Guthrie (Greenwood Press, 2003), 17–18
76. *The Irish in the Spanish Armies in the Seventeenth Century*, Eduardo de Mesa (Boydell Press, 2014), 81
77. *The state in early modern France*, James B. Collins (Cambridge University Press, 1995), 64
78. *The Quest for Peace, Three Moral Traditions in Western Cultural History*, James Turner Johnson (Princeton University Press, 2017), 136

Chapter 8 – Dusk of Knighthood
1. Extract from *Crécy 1346: Triumph of the longbow* by David Nicolle © 2000 Osprey Publishing www.ospreypublishing.com, 65
2. *Gunpowder Weaponry and the Rise of the Early Modern State*, in the journal *War in History* volume 5, Kelly DeVries (Sage publications Inc, 1998), 130
3. Williams, 2003, 945
4. Ibid, 928
5. Ibid, 945

6. Barker, 2012, 43
7. *A briefe discourse, concerning the force and effect of all manual weapons of fire*, Humfrey Barwick, 1592, 7th Discourse, 14. Can be viewed online at ProQuest, or published by EEBO Editions, ProQuest in 2010
8. *Health and Wellness in the Renaissance and Enlightenment*, Joseph P. Byrne (ABC-CLIO, 2013), 190
9. Ibid, 190–191
10. Barwick, 1592, 5th Discourse, 10
11. *Encyclopedia of the Wars of the Roses*, John A. Wagner & Edward Wagner (ABC-CLIO, 2001), 136
12. Lepage, 2014, 255
13. As early as the fifteenth century in fact, although the increase in use of pistols from horseback was a gradual process. See *Use of Firearms and Their Control*, Anil Kumar Sinha (Mittal Publications, 1991), 11
14. Bennet, 2009, 185
15. Ibid, 197
16. *The Artillery of the Dukes of Burgundy, 1363–1477*, Kay Douglas Smith, Robert Douglas Smith, Kelly DeVries (Boydell Press, 2005), 77–78
17. The smaller castle at Thorpe Waterville was probably taken with guns in 1461. It had been ordered to be besieged by Edward IV, who sent a 'joyner' to the castle at Thorpe Waterville with three artillery pieces. It fell quickly. Purton, 2009, 300
18. *Medieval Maritime Warfare*, Charles D. Stanton (Pen and Sword Maritime, 2015), 290
19. Scarborough Castle managed to hold out for five whole months in 1645. See *A Place of Great Importance: Scarborough in the Civil Wars*, J. Binns (Carnegie, 1996)
20. *The Defence of Calais and the Development of Gunpowder Weaponry in England in the Late Fifteenth Century* in the journal *War in History* volume 7, David Grummit (Sage Publications inc, 2000)
21. Ibid, 254
22. *The Paston Letters*, ed Norman Davis (Oxford World's Classics, 2008), 184
23. Grummit, 2000, 259–260
24. *Study of Fortification for the Porta al Prato of* Ognissanti, by Michelangelo Buonarroti, 1529–1530
25. Ellis, 2004, 79
26. Tucker, 2010, 559
27. *The Quest for an Appropriate Past in Literature, Art and Architecture*, ed Karl A.E. Enenkel & Konrad A. Ottenheym (Brill, 2018), 337
28. *The History of the Most Noble Order of the Garter*, Elias Ashmole (A. Bell, 1715), 382–383
29. *Ceremonial Entries in Early Modern Europe*, ed Anna Maria Testaverde, J. R. Mulryne & Maria Ines Aliverti (Taylor & Francis, 2016), Figure 9.1
30. Rogers, 2010, 198
31. *Shining Armour: Emperor Maximilian, Chivalry, and War*, Larry Silver (Art Institute of Chicago Museum Studies, 1985), 61–85
32. *From Nicopolis to Mohács*, Tamas Palosfalvi (Brill, 2018), 441–442
33. See *Allies with the Infidel, The Ottoman and French Alliance in the Sixteenth Century*, Christine Isom-Verhaaren (I.B. Tauris, 2011)
34. *A History of the Art of War in the Sixteenth Century*, Charles Oman (Papamoa Press, 2018), 237
35. *Tudor and Jacobean Tournaments*, Alan Young (George Philip, 1987), 23
36. The Public Record Office, London, E. 36/217, fols. 77–88. See L.P., II ii, 1510
37. Young, 1987, 30

38. Ibid, 74
39. *Horses in Early Modern England: For Service, for Pleasure, for Power,* Joan Thirsk (Stenton Lecture, Reading, 1978), xi
40. De Gamez & Evans, 2004, 41
41. *Four Years at the Court of Henry VII,* Sebastian Guistinian Brown, volume II, trans Rawdon Brown, (London,1854), 102
42. Ibid, but also see Young, 1987, 68
43. *The Boke Named the Governour,* Sir Thomas Elyot (London, 1531); For more information, see *Becoming Centaur: Eighteenth-Century Masculinity and English Horsemanship,* Monica Mattfeld (Pennsylvania State University Press, 2017), 1
44. Young, 1987, 68
45. *The Art of Riding,* Thomas Bedingfield (London, 1584). Additionally see, *Horse and Man in Early Modern England,* Peter Edwards (London: Continuum, 2007), 82
46. *Statutes of the Realm,* volume ii, 518 and also see, Davis, 1989, 87
47. Young, 1987, 68
48. There were maybe only 5,000 gentlemen in 1558, and only some of these were knights. The other groups within the total were esquires and smaller gentry. *Encyclopedia of Tudor England, vol 1,* John A. Wagner & Susan Walters Schmid (ABC-CLIO, 2012), 499
49. *Shipping the Medieval Military,* Craig Lambert (Boydell Press, 2011), 96–97
50. *Tratado de Re Militari,* Diego de Salazar, ed Eva Botella Ordinas (Ministerio de Defensa, 2000), 162
51. *All the King's Horsemen': The Equestrian Army of Henri IV, 1585–1598,* Ronald S. Love (The Sixteenth Century Journal, 1991), 511–512
52. *Memoirs,* Jacques Pape, in Michaud et Poujoulat, 11:499
53. *Dialogos militares,* Garcia de Palacio, sols. 56R and 56rv
54. Only 15 per cent of Edward I's men-at-arms in 1297 were knights, and this ratio increases to 25 per cent in Edward III's campaigns. See Ayton, 1994, 228
55. Barker, 2007, 216
56. Ayton, 1994, 228
57. *Indentured Retinues and English Expeditions to France,* J. W. Sherborne (Oxford University Press, 1964), 718–746
58. *A History of France, 1460–1560,* David Potter (Macmillan Education limited, 1995), 110
59. *Medieval France,* Arthur Augustus Tilley (Cambridge University Press, 2020), 159–160
60. Barker, 2012, 330–331
61. DeVries, 2017, 136–137
62. *Enduring Controversies in Military History: Critical Analyses and Context, Volume 1,* Spencer C. Tucker (ABC-CLIO, 2017), 146
63. *Memoires,* La Marche, ed Buchon (Paris, 1854), 407–408
64. *Early modern Europe, 1450–1789,* Merry E. Wiesner-Hanks (Cambridge University Press, 2006), 95
65. *Global Political Cities,* Kent E. Calder (Brookings Institution Press, 2021), 85
66. Ibid, 34
67. Calder, 2021, 34
68. For civil servants, see *Literature and Learning in the English Civil Service in the Fourteenth Century,* in the journal *Speculum,* Thomas Frederick Tout (University of Chicago Press, 1929)
69. Calder, 2021, 89
70. Ibid, 91

71. *Chaucer's Knight's Tale*, Monica E. McAlpine (University of Toronto Press, 1991), 56
72. *The Essays of Michael Seigneur de Montaigne*, trans Charles Cotton (Alex Murray & Son, 1870), 190
73. For the varied items required to be sourced for gunpowder weapons, see *Journal of Medieval Military History, Volume IX: Soldiers, Weapons and Armies in the Fifteenth Century*, Adrian R. Bell & Anne Curry (Boydell & Brewer, 2011), 187
74. *The Book of the Courtier*, Baldassarre Castiglione (Dover Publications, 2003), 30
75. *The Age of Wars of Religion, 1000–1650 An Encyclopedia of Global Warfare and Civilization, Volume 1*, Cathal J. Nolan (Greenwood Press, 2006), 298
76. *Military Quotations, Stirring Words of War and Peace*, Ray Hamilton (Summersdale Publishing Limited, 2012), 94
77. Note the case of the non-noble Zinzan family, who were frequently able to joust in the late sixteenth century, possibly because they were actually joust trainers. Young, 1987, 69
78. Fallows, 2010, 506
79. Most of the wars included in this umbrella had little to do with religion, but the fact remains that there was split within Christianity and the sides taken were often split down religious lines.
80. Keen, 2005, 250
81. Ibid, 249
82. *Don Quixote*, Miguel de Cervantes, trans Edith Grossman (Vintage, 2005)

Chapter 9 – The Rebirth of the Mounted Knight
1. *The Knight and the Umbrella: An Account of the Eglinton Tournament, 1839*, Ian Anstruther (Geoffrey Bles Ltd, 1963), 133
2. Young, 1987, 187
3. *Sir John Tenniel, Aspects of His Work*, Roger Simpson & John Tenniel (Fairleigh Dickinson University Press, 1994), 96
4. Ibid
5. www.mikecanfor.com/feed
6. Young, 1987, 48–49

Bibliography

Abels, Richard, Royal Succession and the Growth of Political Stability in Ninth-Century Wessex (Boydell & Brewer, 2003)
Addington, Larry H., The patterns of war through the eighteenth century (Indiana University Press, 1990)
Ahmadov, Sabuhi, Knights in Azerbaijan: Article 2 (IRS-AZ)
Alberti, Léon Battista, Le Cheval vivant (1430s) (Les Belles Lettres, 1999)
Allmand, Christopher, Society at War: The Experience of England and France During the Hundred Years War (Boydell Press, 1998)
Allmand, Christopher, The De Re Militari of Vegetius (Cambridge University Press, 2011)
Almond, Richard, Medieval Hunting (History Press, 2011)
Anderson, Eric B., Cataphracts: Knights of the Ancient Eastern Empires (Pen & Sword, 2016)
Anderson, J.K., Ancient Greek Horsemanship (University of California Press, 1961)
Andress, David (ed), The Oxford Handbook of the French Revolution (Oxford University Press, 2015)
Anonymous, L' Ordene de Chevalerie (BiblioLife, 2013)
Anstruther, Ian, The Knight and the Umbrella: An Account of the Eglinton Tournament, 1839 (Geoffrey Bles Ltd, 1963)
Anthony, David W., The Horse, the Wheel, and Language: How Bronze-Age Riders from the Eurasian Steppes Shaped the Modern World (Princeton University Press, 2010)
Arnold, Benjamin, Princes and Territories in Medieval Germany (Cambridge University Press, 2004)
Arnold, S.J, Le Livre des seyntz medicines: The Unpublished Devotional Treatise of Henry of Lancaster (Anglo-Norman Text Society, 1940)
Asbridge, Thomas, The creation of the principality of Antioch, 1098–1130 (Boydell Press, 2000)
Asbridge, Thomas, The First Crusade: A New History (Oxford University Press, 2005)
Ashley, James R., The Macedonian Empire: The Era of Warfare Under Philip II and Alexander the Great, 359–323 B.C (McFarland Incorporated, 2004)
Ashmole, Elias., The History of the Most Noble Order of the Garter (A. Bell, 1715)
Atherton, Mark, The Battle of Maldon: War and Peace in Tenth-Century England(Bloomsbury Academic, 2020)
Aurell, Martin et al, The Lettered Knight (Central European University Press, 2017)
Ayton, Andrew, Knights and Warhorses, Military Service and the English Aristocracy Under Edward III (The Boydell Press, Woodbridge, 1994)
Bachrach, Bernard S., Early Carolingian Warfare: Prelude to Empire (University of Pennsylvania Press Incorporated, 2011)
Merovingian Military Organization 481–751 (University of Minnesota Press, 1972)
Bachrach, Bernard S., Military Organization in Aquitaine under the Early Carolingians in the Journal Speculum, Vol. 49 (The University of Chicago Press, 1974)

Bachrach, Bernard S., Procopius, Agathias and the Frankish Military, in the journal Speculum (The University of Chicago Press, 1970)
Baker, Derek, England in the Early Middle Ages (Boydell & Brewer, 1995)
Banham, Debby and Rosamond Firth, Anglo-Saxon Farms and Farming (Oxford University Press, 2014)
Barber, Richard, The Life and Campaigns of the Black Prince (Boydell Press, 2002)
Barber, Richard, The Reign of Chivalry (St Martin's Press Inc, 1980)
Barker, Juliet, Agincourt (Abacus, 2007)
Barker, Juliet, Conquest, The English Kingdom of France 1417–1450 (Harvard University Press, 2012)
Bartlett, F.C., Psychology and the Solider (Cambridge University Press, 2014)
Barwick, Humfrey, A briefe discourse, concerning the force and effect of all manual weapons of fire (ProQuest, EEBO Editions, 2010)
Beckett, Ian Frederick William, Britain's Part-Time Soldiers: The Amateur Military Tradition: 1558–1945 (Pen & Sword Military, 2011)
Bedingfield, Thomas, The Art of Riding (London, 1584)
Beeler, John, The Composition of Anglo-Norman Armies, in the journal Speculum (University of Chicago Press, 1965)
Bell, Adrian R. and Anne Curry, Medieval Military History, Volume IX: Soldiers, Weapons and Armies in the Fifteenth Century (Boydell & Brewer, 2011)
Bennet, Matthew (ed), The Medieval World at War (Thames & Hudson Ltd, 2009)
Bennett, Philip E. et al, CHIVALRIC GAMES AT THE COURT OF EDWARD III: THE JOUSTING LETTERS OF EUL MS 183, Medium Ævum, vol 87 No 2 (Society for the Study of Medieval Languages and Literature, 2018)
Bentley, Samuel, Excerpta historica: Or Illustrations of English History (London, 1831)
Bernstein, David J., The Mystery of the Bayeux Tapestry (Weidenfeld and Nicolson London, 1986)
Black, Robert, Humanism and Education in Medieval and Renaissance Italy (Cambridge University Press, 2001)
Binns, J., A Place of Great Importance: Scarborough in the Civil Wars (Carnegie, 1996)
Blackwood, Gary L., Life in a Medieval Castle (Lucent Books, 2000)
Blair, Claude, European Armour, c.1066–c.1700 (London, 1958)
Blockmans, Wim and Peter Hoppenbrouwers, Introduction to Medieval Europe, 300–1500 (Taylor & Francis, 2014)
Blyth, Charles R. (ed), Thomas Hoccleve, The Regiment of Princes (Medieval Institute Publications, Kalamazoo, Michigan,1999)
Borman, Tracy, Matilda: Wife of the Conqueror, First Queen of England (Vintage Books, 2012)
Bosworth, Joseph, An Anglo-Saxon Dictionary (Clarendon Press, 1882)
Bovet, Honoré, trans G.W. Coopland, The Tree of Battles (Liverpool: Liverpool University Press, 1949)
Bowlus, Charles R., The Battle of Lechfeld and Its Aftermath, August 955: The End of the Age of Migrations in the Latin West (Taylor & Francis 2016)
Bradbury, Jim, The Capetians: Kings of France 987–1328 (Bloomsbury Publishing, 2007)
Bradbury, Jim, The Medieval Archer (Boydell Press, 1998)
Bradbury, Jim, The Routledge Companion to Medieval Warfare (Taylor & Francis, 2004)
Bradley, S.A J. (trans), Maxims I (University of York: Everyman's Library, 1982)
Brauer, Jurgen and van Tuyll, Hubert, Castles, Battles, and Bombs: How Economics Explains Military History (University of Chicago Press, 2008)
Brerton, Geoffrey (trans), Jean Froissart, Chronicles (Penguin Books, 1978)

Bridgeman, C.G.O. (ed), Burton Abbey Twelfth Century Surveys (William Salt Arch. Soc, 1916)
Brown, Rawdon (trans), Four Years at the Court of Henry VII, Sebastian Guistinian Brown, volume II (London,1854)
Brown, Gordon S., The Norman Conquest of Southern Italy and Sicily (McFarland Incorporated, 2015)
Brown, Paul, Mercenaries to Conquerors: Norman Warfare in the Eleventh and Twelfth-Century Mediterranean (Pen & Sword, 2016)
Brown, Reginald Allen, English Castles: Volume 22 (Batsford, 1962)
Brown, Reginald Allen, The Battle of Hastings (PBC 3, 1980)
Brunel, Clovis (ed), Recueil des actes des comtes de Pontieu (1026–1279) (Paris, 1930)
Bull, Marcus, Knightly Piety and the Lay Response to the First Crusade: The Limousin and Gascony, c. 970 – c. 1130 (Oxford: Clarendon Press, 1993)
Bury, J.B., The Cambridge Medieval History, Volumes 1 – 5 (Plantagenet Publishing, 1911)
Byles, Alfred T.P., The Book of the Order of Chivalry (Routledge Taylor & Francis Group, 2010)
Byrne, Joseph P., Health and Wellness in the Renaissance and Enlightenment (ABC-CLIO, 2013)
Calder, Kent E., Global Political Cities (Brookings Institution Press, 2021)
Campbell, David, Templar Knight Vs Mamluk Warrior, 1218–50 (Bloomsbury Publishing, 2015)
Carpenter, David, Henry III: The Rise to Power and Personal Rule, 1207–1258 (Yale University Press, 2020)
Capponi, Niccolo, An Unlikely Prince: the Life and Times of Machiavelli (Da Capo, 2010)
Capwell, Tobias, Armour of the English Knight 1400–1450 (Thomas Del Mar Ltd, 2015)
Capwell, Tobias, Armour of the English Knight 1450–1500 (Thomas Del Mar, 2021)
Capwell, Tobias, Masterpieces of European Arms and Armour in the Wallace Collection (The Wallace Collection, 2011)
Castiglione, Baldassarre, The Book of the Courtier (Dover Publications, 2003)
Cavendish, William, A New Method and Extraordinary Invention to dress horses and work them according to Nature (London, 1667)
Cavendish, William, A New Method, and Extraordinary Invention, to Dress Horses, and Work Them According to Nature (Creative Media Partners LLC, 2018)
Charles, J. Daryl and David D. Corey, The Just War Tradition, An Introduction (Intercollegiate Studies Institute (ORD), 2014)
Chester, A., Selected Sermons of Hugh Latimer (Charlottesville, 1968)
Chibnall, Marjorie, The Normans (Wiley, 2008)
Christiansen, Eric, Norsemen in the Viking Age (Wiley, 2008)
Chyet, Michael L., FERHENGA BIRÛSKÎ Kurmanji – English Dictionary Volume One: A – L (Transnational Press, 2020)
Clark, John, The Medieval Horse and Its Equipment, C.1150 – c.1450 (Boydell Press, 2004)
Colgrave, B and Mynors, R.A.B. (ed), Bede's Ecclesiastical History (Oxford, 1969)
Collins, James B., The state in early modern France (Cambridge University Press, 1995)
Collins, Roger Charlemagne (University of Toronto Press, 1998)
Cotton, Charles (trans), The Essays of Michael Seigneur de Montaigne (Alex Murray & Son, 1870)
Coupland, Simon, The Carolingian Army and the Struggle Against the Vikings (Viator, 2004)
Craig, Steve, Sports and Games of the Ancients (Greenwood Press, 2002)
Crombie, Laura, Archery and Crossbow Guilds in Medieval Flanders 1300–1500 (Boydell Press, 2016)

Crossley-Holland, Kevin and O'Donoghue, Heather, Beowulf: The Fight at Finnsburh (OUP Oxford, 1999)
Crouch, David, Knighthood, War and Chivalry (Longman, 2002)
Crouch, David, The Chivalric Turn (Oxford University Press, 2019)
Crouch, David, Tournament (Hambledon and London, 2005)
Crouch, David, William Marshal (Taylor & Francis, 2016)
Crow, M. and C. Olsen, Chaucer, Life Records (Oxford, 1966)
Curry, Anne, The Battle of Agincourt: Sources and Interpretations (Boydell Press, 2000)
Cusimano, R. and Moorhead, J. (trans), The Deeds of Louis the Fat (Washington DC, 1992)
Darnell, John Coleman and Manassa, Colleen, Tutankhamun's Armies: Battle and Conquest During Ancient Egypt's Late Eighteenth Dynasty (Wiley, 2007)
Davis, Norman (ed), The Paston Letters (Oxford World's Classics, 2008)
Davis, R.H.C., The Medieval Warhorse (Thames and Hudson Ltd, 1989)
Davies, Sean, War and Society in Medieval Wales 633–1283 (University of Wales Press, 2014)
Delbruck, Hans, History of the Art of War, IV: The Dawn of Modern Warfare (University of Nebraska Press, 1985)
Denholm-Young, Neil, History and Heraldry, 1254–1310 (Oxford, 1965)
Denholm-Young, Noel (trans), The Life of Edward the Second (London, 1957)
Dent, Anthony, The Horse: Through Fifty Centuries of Civilization (Phaidon Press Limited, 1974)
DeVries, Kelly, Gunpowder Weaponry and the Rise of the Early Modern State, in the journal War in History, volume 5 (Sage Publications Inc, 1998)
DeVries, Kelly, Medieval Military Technology (University of Toronto Press, 2003)
DeVries, Kelly, Infantry Warfare in the Early Fourteenth Century, Discipline, Tactics, and Technology (Boydell Press, 1996)
DeVries, Kelly, The Role of the Lombard Cavalry in Medieval Warfare 1300–1450 (Taylor & Francis, 2017)
DeVries, Kelly and Tracy, Larissa, Wounds and Wound Repair in Medieval Culture (Brill, 2015)
de Cervantes, Miguel, trans Edith Grossman Don Quixote (Vintage, 2005)
de Mesa, Eduardo, The Irish in the Spanish Armies in the Seventeenth Century (Boydell Press, 2014)
de Pizan, Christine, trans Summer Willard, The Book of the Deeds of Arms and of Chivalry (The Pennsylvania State University Press, 1999)
de Riquer, Martin, Caballeros Andantes Españoles (Madrid: Editorial Espasa-Calpe, 1967)
de Salazar, Diego, ed Eva Botella Ordinas, Tratado de Re Militari (Ministerio de Defensa, 2000)
de Vinsauf, Geoffrey, Anonymous translation, Itinerarium Regis Ricardi (Publications Medieval Latin Series, Cambridge, Ontario, 2001)
Dick, Sheldon and Teichova, Alice, Banking, Trade and Industry: Europe, America and Asia from the Thirteenth to the Twentieth Century (Cambridge University Press, 1997)
Dickinson, J.C., The Shrine of Our Lady of Walsingham (University Press, 1991)
Dixon, Karen R. and Path Southern, The Roman Cavalry (Taylor & Francis, 2013)
Djordjevic, Ivana and Judith Elizabeth Weiss, The Exploitations of Medieval Romance (D.S. Brewer, 2010)
Dougherty, Martin, Weapons and Fighting Techniques of the Medieval Warrior 1000–1500AD (Chartwell Books, 2008)
Draper OBE, Professor Colonel G.I.A.D, Reflections on Law and Armed Conflicts (Kluwer Law International, 1998)

Duby, Georges and trans Catherine Tihanyi, The Legend of Bouvines: War, Religion and Culture in the Middle Ages (University of California Press, 1990)

Dyson, R.W. et al, Aquinas, Political Writings (Posts and Telecommunications Press, 2002)

d'Arcq, L. Douet (ed), Monstrelet: Enguerrand de Monstrelet, La Chronique d'Enguerran de Monstrelet (Société de l'Histoire de France, 1859)

Edgington, Susan B. (trans), The Chanson d'Antioche: an Old French account of the First Crusade (Farnham: Ashgate, 2011)

Edwards, Peter, Horse and Man in Early Modern England (London: Continuum, 2007)

Elliot, Simon, Romans at War: The Roman Military in the Republic and Empire (Casemate, 2020)

Ellis, John, Cavalry: The History of Mounted Combat (Pen & Sword, 2004)

Elst, Stefan Vander, 'The holiness of that forsaken place': The Purpose of Sin in the Itinerarium Peregrinorum et Gesta Regis Ricardi (Studies in Philology, University of North Carolina Press, 2019)

Elyot, Sir Thomas, The Boke Named the Governour (London, 1531)

Enenkel, Karl A.E. and Konrad A. Ottenheym (ed), The Quest for an Appropriate Past in Literature, Art and Architecture (Brill, 2018)

Erdkamp, Paul, A Companion to the Roman Army (Wiley, 2011)

Evans, Joan (trans), The Unconquered Knight, Gutierre Diaz de Gamez (Boydell & Brewer, 2004)

Evans, Joan (trans), The Unconquered Knight A Chronicle of the Deeds of Don Pero Niño, Count of Buelna, by His Standard-bearer Gutierre Diaz de Gamez (1431–1449) (G. Routledge & sons Limited, 1928)

Fallows, Noel, Jousting in Medieval and Renaissance Iberia (The Boydell Press, 2010)

Ffoulkes, Charles, Armour and Weapons (Outlook Verlag, 2020)

Fillis, James, Breaking and Riding (Xenophon Press LLC, 2018)

Fink, Harold S.A. (ed), Ryan, Francis Rita (trans), History of the Expedition to Jerusalem 1095–1127 (University of Tennessee Press, 1969)

Fleming, R., Rural Elites and Urban Communities in Late-Saxon England (Past and Present, 1993)

Fletcher, Richard A., The Quest for El Cid (Alfred A. Knopf, 1989)

France, John, Western Warfare In The Age Of The Crusades, 1000–1300 (Taylor & Francis, 2020)

France, John, Victory in the East (Cambridge University Press, 1996)

Frankopan, Peter, The First Crusade: The Call from the East (Harvard University Press, 2012)

Fritze, Ronald H. and Ann E. Faulkner Historical Dictionary of Late Medieval England, 1272–1485 (Greenwood Press, 2002)

Fuller, Lieutenant Colonel Ezra B. (ed), Journal of the United States Cavalry Association (United States Cavalry Association, 1917)

Gantz, Jeffrey, The Mabinogion (Penguin Books Ltd, 1976)

Garnier, Russell Montague, History of the English Landed Interest: Its Customs, Laws and Agriculture (Sonnenschein, 1892)

Gilbert, Allen H, Machiavelli, Volume 1 (Duke University Press, 1965)

Gillingham, John (ed), Anglo-Norman Studies XXVII Proceedings of the Battle Conference 2004 (The Boydell Press, 2005)

Gillingham, John Richard I (Yale University Press, 1999)

Godden, Malcolm, Anglo-Saxon England: Volume 35 (Cambridge University Press, 2008)

Goller, Karl Heinz The Alliterative Morte Arthure (D.S. Brewer, 1981)

Gonzaga, Paulo Gaviao, A History of the Horse, Volume 1: The Iberian Horse from Ice Age to Antiquity (J.A. Allen, 2004)

Goodman, Anthony, The Wars of the Roses (Taylor & Francis, 2017)
Goodman, Anthony, The Wars of the Roses The Soldiers' Experience (Tempus Publishing Ltd, 2005)
Goodman, Jennifer R., Chivalry and Exploration, 1298–1630 (Boydell Press, 1998)
Gray, Sir Thomas & Sir Herbert Maxwell, Scalacronica: The Reigns of Edward I, Edward II and Edward III (Leopold Classic Library, 1992)
Grummit, David, The Defence of Calais and the Development of Gunpowder Weaponry in England in the Late Fifteenth Century, War in History Journal (Sage Publications Inc, 2000)
Gueiriniere, Francois de la, trans William Frazer, A treatise upon horsemanship (1801)
Guthrie, William P., The Later Thirty Years War (Greenwood Press, 2003)
Hagger, Mark S., Norman Rule in Normandy, 911–1144 (Boydell, 2017)
Halfond, Gregory I., The Medieval Way of War (Taylor & Francis, 2016)
Hall, John Richard Clark, A concise Anglo-Saxon dictionary (Swan Sonnenschein & Company, 1894)
Hall, Henry Foljambe, Napoleon's Notes on English History made on the Eve of the French Revolution, illustrated from Contemporary Historians and referenced from the findings of Later Research by Henry Foljambe Hall (New York: E.P. Dutton & Co., 1905)
Hallam, Elizabeth, Capetian France 987–1328 (Taylor & Francis, 2014)
Hallam, Elizabeth, Chronicles of the Age of Chivalry (Tiger Books International Plc, 1995)
Hallam, Elizabeth, Chronicles of the Crusades Eye Witness Accounts of the Wars Between Christianity and Islam (Bramley Books, 1997)
Halliwell, J. (ed) A Chronicle of the first thirteen Years of the Reign of King Edward IV (Camden Soc, 1839)
Hamilton, Bernard, The Leper King and His Heirs, Baldwin IV and the Crusader Kingdom of Jerusalem (Cambridge University Press, 2005)
Hamilton, Ray, Military Quotations, Stirring Words of War and Peace (Summersdale Publishing Limited, 2012)
Hamm, Jean S., Term Paper Resource Guide to Medieval History (Greenwood, 2010)
Hardy, T. (ed), Rotuli Litterarum Clausarum in turri Londinensi asservati 1204–1227 (London, 1844)
Harriss, Gerald, Shaping the Nation, England 1360–1461 (Clarendon Press, 2005)
Harvey, Ruth and Stephen Church (ed), Medieval Knighthood V (Boydell Press, 1995)
Hentry, G.A., At Agincourt, A Tale of the White Hoods of Paris (Fireship Press, 2011)
Hibernicus, Nennius and William Gunn, The Historia Brittonum (Arch, 1819)
Hillenbrand, Carole, Turkish Myth and Muslim Symbol: The Battle of Manzikert (Edinburgh University Press, 2007)
Hitti, Philip K. (trans), An Arab-Syrian Gentleman and Warrior in the Period of the Crusade, Usamah Ibn Munqidh (Columbia University Press, 2000)
Holland, Tom, Persian Fire, The First World Empire, Battle for the West (Abacus, 2006)
Hollister, Warren, Anglo-Saxon Military Institutions on the Eve of the Norman Conquest, Oxford: Clarendon Press, 1962)
Hollister, Warren, Courtly Culture and Courtly Style in the Anglo-Norman World in journal Albion: A Quarterly Journal Concerned with British Studies (The North American Conference on British Studies, 1988)
Hollister, Warren, Henry I (Yale University Press, 2003)
Hosler, John D., Henry II: A Medieval Soldier at War, 1147–1189 (Brill, 2007)
Huang, Angela Ling, Textiles and the Medieval Economy: Production, Trade and Consumption of Textiles, 8th-16th Centuries (Oxbow Books, 2015)
Hunt, Janin and Carlson, Ursula, Mercenaries in Medieval and Renaissance Europe (McFarland Incorporated, 2014)

Hyland, Ann, The Medieval Warhorse from Byzantium to the Crusades (Alan Sutton Publishing Limited, 1994)
Isom-Verhaaren, Christine, Allies with the Infidel, The Ottoman and French Alliance in the Sixteenth Century (I.B. Tauris, 2011)
Jack, R. Ian, Hastings, John, Thirteenth Earl of Pembroke (1347–1375) (ODNB, online edition, 2008)
Jackson, Peter, (ed), The Seventh Crusade, 1244–1254, Sources and Documents (Taylor & Francis, 2020)
Jankovich, Miklos, They Rode into Europe (George G. Harrap & Co. Ltd, 1971)
John, Simon, (ed) and Nicholas Morton, Crusading and Warfare in the Middle Ages: Realities and Representations, Essays in Honour of John France (Routledge Taylor & Francis Group, 2016)
Johnes, Thomas Esq, Chronicles of England, France, Spain, and the Adjoining Countries: From the Latter Part of the Reign of Edward II to the Coronation of Henry IV (Routledge, 1874)
Johnes, Thomas Esq, Chronicles of England, France and Spain and the Surrounding Countries, by Sir John Froissart, Translated from the French Editions with Variations and Additions from Many Celebrated MSS (William Smith, 1848)
Johnson, James Turner, The Quest for Peace, Three Moral Traditions in Western Cultural History (Princeton University Press, 2017)
Jones, Dan, The Templars (Head of Zeus, 2017)
Jones, Michael, Memoirs. The Reign of Louix XI, 1461–83 (Hammondsworth, 1972)
Kaeuper, Richard W., Chivalry and Violence in Medieval Europe (Oxford University Press, 2001)
Kaeuper, Richard W., Medieval Chivalry (Cambridge University Press, 2016)
Kaeuper, Richard W., War, Justice, and Public Order: England and France in the Later Middle Ages (Oxford University Press,1988)
Kaeuper, Richard W. and Kennedy, Elspeth, A Knight's Own Book of Chivalry (University of Pennsylvania Press Inc, 2013)
Kagay, Donald, The Circle of War in the Middle Ages (Boydell Press, 1999)
Karsten, Peter, The Training and Socializing of Military Personnel (Garland Pub, 1998)
Kean, Hilda and Philip Howell (ed), The Routledge Companion to Animal-Human History (Taylor & Francis, 2018)
Keen, Maurice, Chivalry (Yale University Press, 2005)
Keen, Maurice, Laws of War in the Late Middle Ages (Routledge, 1965)
Keen, Maurice, Medieval Warfare: A History (OUP Oxford, 1999)
Kinard, Jess, Artillery, An Illustrated History of Its Impact (ABC-CLIO, 2007)
King, P.D. (trans), Charlemagne (P.D. King, 1987)
Kleinschmidt, Harald, Understanding the Middle Ages (Boydell Press, 2003)
Knecht, R.J., Francis I (Cambridge University Press, 1984)
Knight, Hugh T., The Ambraser Codex by Master Hans Talhoffer (Lulu.com, 2008)
Kostick, Connor, The Social Structure of the First Crusade (Brill, 2008)
Kristinsson, Axel, Expansions, Competition and Conquest in Europe Since the Bronze Age (ReykjavíkurAkademían, 2010)
La Marche, ed Buchon, Memoires (Paris, 1854)
Lacy, Norris J., A Companion to Chrétien de Troyes (Boydell & Brewer, 2008)
Lambert, Craig, Shipping the Medieval Military (Boydell Press, 2011)
Lambert, Thomas Benedict, Law and Order in Anglo-Saxon England (Oxford University Press, 2017)
Lamborn, Robert H., The Metallurgy of Silver and Lead: A Description of the Ores; Their Assay and Treatment, and Valuable Constituents (C. Lockwood, 1878)

Landes, Richard & Thomas Head, The Peace of God (Cornell University Press, 2018)
Lane-Poole, Stanley, Saladin and the Fall of the Kingdom of Jerusalem (Putnam, 1898)
Lapidge, Michael, Anglo-Saxon England: Volume 32 (Cambridge University Press, 2004)
Lauer, P., (trans), Historie des fils de Louis le Pieux, Nithard (Paris, 1926)
Lecestre and Farve (ed), Le Jouvencel, Jean de Beuil (Paris, 1887)
Lecouteux, Claude, Encyclopedia of Norse and Germanic Folklore, Mythology, and Magic (Inner Traditions/Bear, 2016)
Lewis-Sempel, John, England: The Autobiography:2,000 Years of English History by Those Who Saw it Happen (Penguin Books Ltd, 2006)
Liberman, Max, The Medieval March of Wales: The Creation and Perception of a Frontier, 1066–1283 (Cambridge University Press, 2010)
Livingstone, Marilyn et al, The Road to Crécy: The English Invasion of France, 1346 (Pearson/Longman, 2005)
Livingstone, Amy et al, Their World: Ideas and Realities: Studies in Honor of Richard Sullivan (Brill, 2019)
Lepage, Jean-Denis G.G., Medieval Armies and Weapons in Western Europe (McFarland Incorporated, 2014)
Loades, Mike, The Longbow (Bloomsbury Publishing, 2003)
Loud, Graham, The Age of Robert Guiscard Southern Italy and the Northern Conquest (Taylor & Francis, 2014)
Love, Ronald S., All the King's Horsemen': The Equestrian Army of Henri IV, 1585–1598 (The Sixteenth Century Journal, 1991)
Loveluck, Christopher, Northwest Europe in the Early Middle Ages, C.AD 600–1150: A Comparative Archaeology (Cambridge University Press, 2013)
Luard, H.R., The Waverley Annals in vol II of Annales Monastici (Rolls Series 1864–9)
Lucas, Newton Ivory, Dictionary of the English and German and German and English Languages: Volume 2 (C. Shunemann, 1868)
Luce, (ed), Chroniques (Renouard for the Société de l'Histoire de France, 1869–1875)
Luders, A et al, Statutes of the Realm (1101–1713) (London, 1810–1828)
Luizza, R.M. (ed), Beowulf: Facing Page Translation – Second Edition (Broadview Press, 2012)
Lynghaug, F., The Official Horse Breeds Standards Guide (Voyageur Press, 209)
MacKay, Angus, Spain in the Middle Ages: From Frontier to Empire, 1000–1500 (Macmillian Education UK, 1977)
Madden, Mollie M., The Black Prince and the Grande Chevauchée of 1355 (Boydell Press, 2018)
Madden, Thomas F., The New Concise History of the Crusades (Rowan & Littlefield, 2005)
Maenchen-Helfen, Otto, The World of the Huns, Studies in Their History and Culture (University of California Press, 1973)
Martel, Gordon, The Encyclopedia of War (Wiley, 2012)
Martin, John D., 'Svá lýkr hér hverju hestaðingi': Sports and Games in Icelandic Saga Literature, in the journal Scandinavian Studies (University of Illinois Press, 2003)
Mathisen, Ralph W. and Shanzer, Danuta, The Battle of Vouillé, 507 CE (De Gruyter, 2012)
Mattfeld, Monica, Becoming Centaur: Eighteenth-Century Masculinity and English Horsemanship (Pennsylvania State University Press, 2017)
Matthew, Christopher, An Invincible Beast, Understanding the Hellenistic Pike Phalanx in Action (Pen & Sword Books, 2015)
Melton, J. Gordon and Baumann, Martin, Religions of the World: A Comprehensive Encyclopedia of Beliefs and Practices, 2nd Edition [6 Volumes] (ABC-CLIO, 2010)

Melville and Lyons, Saladin's Hattin Letter in The Horns of Hattin (Jerusalem, 1992)
Meyer, Paul (trans), L'Histoire Guillaume le Marechal (1891–1901)
McAlpine, Monica E., Chaucer's Knight's Tale (University of Toronto Press, 1991)
McCall, Jeremiah B., The Cavalry of the Roman Republic (Taylor & Francis, 2005)
McDonald, S.M., The Domestic Horse: The Origins, Development and Management of Its Behaviour (Cambridge University Press, 2005)
McNab, Bruce and Teofilo F. Ruiz, Order and Innovation in the Middle Ages (Princeton University Press, 2015)
McNab, Chris, Famous Battles of the Medieval Period (Cavendish Square Publishing LLC, 2017)
Mellinkoff, Ruth, The Horned Moses in Medieval Art and Thought (Wipf & Stock Publishers, 1997)
Meyer, Paul (translator), L'Histoire Guillaume le Marechal (Paris, 1891–1901)
Miller, Andrew G, 'Tails' of Masculinity: Knights, Clerics, and the Mutilation of Horses in Medieval England, from the journal Speculum (University of Chicago Press, 2013)
Miller, Edward et al, Progress and Problems in Medieval England (Cambridge University Press, 2002)
Ministry of Agriculture and Fisheries, Miscellaneous Publications (H.M. Stationary Office, 1927)
Mitchell, Linda E., Women in Medieval Western European Culture (Taylor & Francis, 2012)
Molyneaux, G., The Formation of the English Kingdom in the Tenth Century (Oxford, 2015)
Montaigne, Michel de, trans Donald Murdoch Frame, The complete essays of Montaigne (Stanford University Press, 1958)
Montaigne, Michel de, trans James Hain Friswell, Essays of Montaigne (Sampson Low, Son, & Marsten, 1869)
Morris, Marc, A Great and Terrible King, Edward I and the Forging of Britain (Windmill Books, 2009)
Morris, Marc, The Anglo-Saxons: A History of the Beginnings of England (Random House, 2021)
Morris, Marc, The Norman Conquest (Penguin Random House, 2013)
Mortimer, Ian, The Perfect King, The Life of Edward III, Father of the English Nation (Random House, 2010)
Morton, Nicholas, Crusader States and Their Neighbours (Oxford University Press, 2020)
Muhlberger, Steven, Deeds of Arms (The Chivalry Bookshelf, 2005)
Munby, Julian et al, Edward III's Round Table at Windsor (Boydell Press, 2008)
Munro, C.D. (trans), Translations and Reprints from the Original Sources of European history (University of Pennsylvania Press, 1900)
Murray, Alan V., The Crusader Kingdom of Jerusalem (Prosopograhica et Genealogica, 2000)
Newark Timothy, Medieval Warfare (Jupiter Books (London) Limited, 1988)
Newman, Paul B., Growing up in the Middle Ages (McFarland Incorporated, 2015)
Nicolas, Nicholas, History of the Battle of Agincourt (London, 1832)
Nicolle, David, Crécy 1346: Triumph of the longbow (Osprey, 2000)
Nicolle, David, Hungary and the fall of Eastern Europe, 1000–1568 (Osprey, 1998)
Nicolle, David, Medieval Warfare Source Book. Volume I: Warfare in Western Christendom (BCA, 1996)
Noakes, Mike, Saxon Shakedown (Artemis Publishers, 2012)
Noble, Thomas F.X., Charlemagne and Louis the Pious (Pennsylvania State University, 2009)

Nolan, Cathal J., The Age of Wars of Religion, 1000–1650 An Encyclopedia of Global Warfare and Civilization, Volume 1 (Greenwood Press, 2006)
Ocana, Antonio Cortijo (trans), The Book of the Order of Chivalry / Llibre de L'Ordre de Cavalleria / Libro de la Orden de Caballería – Ramon Llull, 1274–1276 (John Benjamins Publishing Company, 2015) (ebook)
Oman, Charles, A History of the Art of War in the Sixteenth Century (Papamoa Press, 2018)
O'Callaghan, Joseph F., Reconquest and Crusade in Medieval Spain (University of Pennsylvania Press, 2013)
Painter, Sidney, History of the Middle Ages, 284–1500 (Macmillian Education Limited, 1963)
Painter, Sidney, William Marshal, Knight Errant, Baron, and Regent of England (Johns Hopkins Press, 1933)
Palosfalvi, Tamas, From Nicopolis to Mohács (Brill, 2018)
Paris, Matthew, Historia Anglorum, Chronica majora, Part III; Continuation of Chronica maiora (St Albans, 1250–1259)
Parker, Geoffrey, The Cambridge History of Warfare (Cambridge University Press, 2020)
Parks, George R., The English Traveler to Italy (Stanford, 1954)
Parrott, David, The Business of War: Military Enterprise and Military Revolution in Early Modern Europe (Cambridge University Press, 2012)
Pendergrass, Rocky, Mythological Swords (Lulu.com, 2015)
Phillips, Jonathan, Holy Warriors: A Modern History of the Crusades (Random House, 2012)
Piel, Joseph (ed) and trans J.L. Forgeng, Livro Da Ensinanca De Bem Cavalgar Toda Sella, Duarte I, king of Portugal, 1391–1438 (Livraria Bertrand, 2010)
Pollard, A.J., The Wars of the Roses (Macmillian Education Limited, 2017)
Postgate, J.N., The Assyrian Army in Zamua, in the journal Iraq, Volume 62 (British Institute for the Study of Iraq, 2000)
Potter, David, A History of France, 1460–1560 (Macmillan Education limited, 1995)
Pratt, John H, Chaucer and War (University Press of America, 2000)
Preston, Richard et al, Men in Arms: A History of Warfare and Its Interrelationships with Western Society (New York: Frederick A. Praeger, 1956)
Prestwich, Michael, Knight: The Medieval Warrior's Unofficial Manual (Thames & Hudson, 2010)
Previte-Orton, Charles William Outlines of Medieval History (Biblo and Tannen, 1965)
Prothoro, G.W. et al, The Quarterly Review 1896 (John Murray, 2018)
Pryor, John H., Logistics of Warfare in the Age of the Crusades (Ashgate, 2002)
Purton, Peter Fraser, A History of the Late Medieval Siege, 1200–1500 (Boydell & Brewer, 2009)
Rees, Una, The Cartulary of Shrewsbury Abbey (Aberystwyth, 1975)
Richards, D.S., Rare and Excellent History of Saladin by Baha al-Din Ibvn Shaddad (Farnham: Ashgate, 2002)
Riley, H.T. (ed), Historia Anglicana (R.S, 1863)
Riley-Smith, Jonathan, The First Crusade and the Idea of Crusading (University of Pennsylvania Press Inc, 1986)
Rink, Bjarke, The Rise of the Centaurs: The Origin of Horsemanship. The Untold Story (AuthorHouse, 2013)
Robertson, Howard (trans), The Song of Roland (London, 1972)
Robinson, F.N. (ed), Works of Geoffrey Chaucer (Boston: Houghton Mifflin, 1957)
Roger, N.A.M., The Command of the Ocean: A Naval History of Britain, Volume 2, 1649–1815 (Allen Lane, 2004)

Rogers, Clifford J. et al, Journal of Medieval History, Volume VIII (Boydell Press, 2010)
Rogers, Clifford J. et al, Journal of Medieval History, Volume X (Boydell Press, 2012)
Rogers, Clifford J. et al, Journal of Medieval History, Volume XI (Boydell Press, 2013)
Rogers, Clifford J. et al, Journal of Medieval History, Volume XII (Boydell Press, 2014)
Rogers, Clifford J. The Military Revolution Debate (Avalon Publishing, 1995)
Rogers, Clifford J. The Oxford Encyclopedia of Medieval Warfare and Military Technology, Volume 1 (Oxford University Press, 2010)
Roland, Ferdinand (ed), Parties medites de l'oeuvre de Sicile Heraut (Societe des Bibliophiles Belges de Mons 22, 1867)
Ross, Michael W. and Sue J. Dyson, Diagnosis and Management of Lameness in the Horse (Elsevier Health Sciences, 2010)
Runciman, Steven, A History of the Crusades, Volume 2 (Penguin, 1987)
Runciman, Steven, A History of the Crusades Volume III (Cambridge University Press, 1987)
Rusio, Lorenzo, Hippiatria sive Marescalia (Parigi, Christianum Wechelum, 1532)
Russell, Nicholas, Engend'ring Like: Heredity and Animal Breeding in Early Modern England (Cambridge University Press, 2007)
Sadler, John, Bannockburn, Battle for Liberty (Pen & Sword Military, 2008)
Sadowski, Piotr, The Knight on His Quest: Symbolic Patterns of Transition in Sir Gawain and the Green Knight (University of Delaware Press, 1996)
Salisbury, Joyce E., The Beast Within: Animals in the Middle Ages (Taylor & Francis, 2012)
Saul, Nigel, Age of Chivalry, Art and Society in Late Medieval England (Brockhampton Press, 1995)
Saul, Nigel, Knights and Esquires: The Gloucestershire Gentry in the Fourteenth Century (Clarendon Press, 1981)
Saunders, Frances Stonor Hawkwood, Diabolical Englishman (Faber and Faber Limited, 2004)
Savage, Henry L., Hunting in the Middle Ages, in the journal Speculum (University of Chicago, 1933)
Scammell, Jean, The Formation of the English Social Structure: Freedom, Knights, and Gentry, 1066–1300, in the journal Speculum (University of Chicago Press, 1993)
Schullian, Dorothy M. (trans), Diara de Bello Carolino (Diary of the Caroline War) (Frederick Ungar, 1967)
Scragg, Donald, The Return of the Vikings: The Battle of Maldon 991 (History Press, 2006)
Seyler, G.A., Geschichte der Heraldik (Nuremburg, 1985)
Sherborne, J.W., Indentured Retinues and English Expeditions to France (Oxford University Press, 1964)
Short, William R., Icelanders in the Viking Age: The People of the Sagas (McFarland Publishers Incorporated, 2010)
Silver, Larry, Shining Armour: Emperor Maximilian, Chivalry, and War (Art Institute of Chicago Museum Studies, 1985)
Simpson, Roger and John Tenniel, Sir John Tenniel, Aspects of His Work (Fairleigh Dickinson University Press, 1994)
Sinha, Anil Kumar, Use of Firearms and Their Control (Mittal Publications, 1991)
Skipper, Lesley, The Natural Stallion: His Behaviour, Management and Training (Black Tent Publications, 2010)
Smith, Kay Douglas, et al, The Artillery of the Dukes of Burgundy, 1363–1477 (Boydell Press, 2005)

Bibliography 269

Snook, George Aaron, The halberd and other European polearms, 1300–1650 (Museum Restoration Service, 1998)
Spatz, Wilhelm, Die Schlact von Hastings (Kraus Reprint, 1965)
Stanton, Charles D., Medieval Maritime Warfare (Pen and Sword Maritime, 2015)
Stevenson, W.B., The Crusaders in the East (Cambridge University Press, 1907)
Stevenson, W.B., The Crusaders in the East: A Brief History of the Wars of Islam with the Latins in Syria During the Twelfth and Thirteenth Centuries (Cambridge University Press, 2012)
Stoksad, Marilyn, Medieval Castles (Greenwood Guides to Historic Events of the Medieval World) (Greenwood Press, 2005
Strickland, Matthew, Henry the Young King, 1155–1183 (Yale University Press, 2016)
Sutcliffe, F.E. (ed), Discours politiques et militaire (Geneve: Droz, 1967)
Swanton, Michael (ed), The Anglo-Saxon Chronicle (Routledge, 1998)
van, Winston A Horne Global Convulsions (Sate University of New York Press, 1997)
von Liechtenstein, Ulrich, trans J.W. Thomas, The Service of Ladies (UK: Boydell & Brewer Ltd, 2004)
Taayke, Ernst, Essays on the Early Franks (Barkhuis, 2003)
Taylor, Craig, Chivalry and the Ideals of Knighthood in France During the Hundred Years War (Cambridge University Press, 2013)
Taylor, Craig and H.M. Taylor (ed), Jean de Bueil: Le Jouvencel (Boydell Press, 2020)
Taylor, Frederick Lewis, The Art of War in Italy 1494–1529, Prince Consort Prize Essay 1920 (Cambridge University Press, 2010)
Taylor, Jane H.M, The Chivalric Biography of Boucicaut, Jean II Le Meingre (Boydell Press, 2016)
Taylor, John (ed) et al, The Saint Albans Chronicle. The Chronica Maiora of Thomas Walsingham (Clarendon Press, 2003)
Telfer, J. Buchan (trans), The Bondage and Travels of Johann Schiltberger (Hakluyt Society, 1879)
Testaverde, Anna Maria et al, Ceremonial Entries in Early Modern Europe (Taylor & Francis, 2016)
Thatcher, Oliver J., A Source Book for Medieval History (New York: Charles Scribner's Sons, 1905)
The Abbey of St Peter and St Paul, The Cartulary of Shrewsbury Abbey (National Library of Wales, 1975)
Theotokis, Georgios, Norman Campaigns in the Balkans, 1081–1108 (Boydell Press, 2014)
Thirsk, Joan, Horses in Early Modern England: For Service, for Pleasure, for Power (Stenton Lecture, Reading, 1978)
Thompson, James G. (ed), History of Sport and Physical Activity (Daniel Smith, 1991)
Thorpe, Lewis (trans),The History of the Franks, Gregory of Tours (Penguin Books Ltd, 1974)
Tilley, Arthur Augustus, Medieval France (Cambridge University Press, 2020)
Tout, Thomas, Literature and Learning in the English Civil Service in the Fourteenth Century, in the journal Speculum (University of Chicago Press, 1929)
Tout, Thomas, Some Neglected Fights Between Crécy and Poitiers (EHR, 1905)
Tout, Thomas, The Collected Papers of Thomas Frederick Tout (Manchester University Press, 1932)
Trim, D.J.B and Frank Tallet (ed), European Warfare, 1350–1750 (Cambridge University Press, 2010)
Trow, M.J., Richard III in the North (Pen & Sword, 2020)
Truelove, Alison and Raluca Radulescu, Gentry Culture in Late-medieval England (Manchester University Press, 2020)

Tucker, Spencer, A Global Chronology of Conflict (ABC-CLIO, 2010)
Tucker, Spencer, Enduring Controversies in Military History: Critical Analyses and Context, Volume 1 (ABC-CLIO, 2017)
Urban, William L., The Last Years of the Teutonic Knights, Lithuania, Poland and the Teutonic Order (Pen & Sword, 2018)
Urban, William L., The Teutonic Knights, A Military History (Greenhill, 2003)
Upton-Ward, Judith Mary (trans), The Rule of the Templars, The French Text of the Rule of the Order of the Knights Templar (Boydell Press, 1997)
Vale, Malcolm, War and Chivalry (Duckworth, 1981)
Various, The British Military Journal, Volume 1 (John Carpenter, 1840)
Vasilievna, Trever Kamilla, Essays on the history and culture of Caucasian Albania (USSR Academy of Sciences, 1959)
Vaughan, Richard and Werner Paravincini, Charles the Bold, The Last Valois Duke of Burgundy (Boydell Press, 2002)
Verbruggen, J.F., The Battle of the Golden Spurs (Courtrai, 11 July 1302) (Boydell Press, 2002)
Vernier, Richard, Lord of the Pyrenees: Gaston Fébus, Count of Foix (1331–1391) (Boydell Press, 2008)
Vernier, Richard, The Flower of Chivalry, Bertrand Du Guesclin and the Hundred Years War (D.S Brewer, 2007)
Villalon, L.J. Andrew and Donald J. Kagay, The Hundred Years War (part II): Different Vistas (Brill, 2008)
Viscount Dillion, The Pageant of the birth, life and death of Richard Beauchamp, earl of Warwick, K.G, 1389–1439 (London, 1914)
Wagner, John A. and Edward Wagner, Encyclopedia of the Wars of the Roses (ABC-CLIO, 2001)
Wagner, John A. and Susan Walters Schmid, Encyclopedia of Tudor England, vol 1 (ABC-CLIO, 2012)
Whatley, Conor, Procopius on Soldiers and Military Institutions in the Sixth-Century Roman Empire (Brill, 2021)
Whitby, Mary, Byzantines and Crusaders in Non-Greek Sources, 1025–1204 (OUP/British Academy, 2007)
White, Lynn Townsend, Medieval Technology and Social Change (Oxford University Press, 1964)
White, R.J A., A Short History of England (Cambridge University Press, 1967)
Whitelock, Dorothy, Anglo-Saxon Wills (Cambridge University Press, 2011)
Whitman, James Q, The Verdict of Battle: The Law of Victory and the Making of Modern War (Harvard University Press, 2012)
Wiesner-Hanks, Merry E., Early modern Europe, 1450–1789 (Cambridge University Press, 2006)
Wilkinson, Oliver, British Prisoners of War in First World War Germany (Cambridge University Press, 2017)
Willard, C. (ed), The 'Livre de la Paix' (The Hague, 1954)
Willard, Summer (trans), The Book of the Deeds of Arms and of Chivalry, Christine de Pizan (The Pennsylvania State University Press, 1999)
Williams, Alan and Edge, David and Capwell, Tobias, AN EXPERIMENTAL INVESTIGATION OF LATE MEDIEVAL COMBAT WITH THE COUCHED LANCE (Journal of the Arms and Armour Society, www.academia.edu, 2016)
Williams, Alan, The Knight and the Blast Furnace: A History of the Metallurgy of Armour in the Middle Ages & the Early Modern Period (Brill, 2003)

Bibliography 271

Winkler, Martin M., Arminius the Liberator, Myth and Ideology (Oxford University Press, 2016)
Wollock, Jennifer G., Rethinking Chivalry and Courtly Love (ABC-CLIO, 2011)
Wood, Cindy, Studying Late Medieval History (Taylor & Francis, 2019)
Woolf, Rosemary, The Ideal of Men Dying with the Lord in the Germania and in The Battle of Maldon (Anglo-Saxon England 5, 1976)
Wright, Nicholas A.R., Honore Bouvet, the Tree of Battles, and the Literature of War in Fourteenth-Century France (PHD, Edinburgh, 1972)
Xenophon, The Cavalry General (Public Domain Book)
Young, Alan, Tudor and Jacobean Tournaments (George Philip, 1987)
Zakeri, Mohsen, Sasanid Soldiers in Early Muslim Society: The Origins of 'Ayyārān and Futuwwa (Harrassowitz Verlag, 1995)
Zeitler-Feicht, Margrit, Horse Behaviour Explained (CRC Press, 2003)

Index

Aberlemno Stone 16
Acre 56–57, 62–64
Alexander the Great 3, 133, 134
Alexius I Comnenus 40
Antioch 45–47
Antioche, Chanson d' 45, 97
Aquitaine 8, 33
Aristotle 2, 134, 214
armour
   arming doublet 91–92
   chainmail, see mail
   coat of plates 83
   cuirass 92, 205
   frogmouth 81
   greathelm 72, 82–83, 119
   shield 17, 27, 36–37, 80, 110, 228
artillery 187, 190–199
arret de lance 80, 84, 232
Arthur, mythical king of Britain 79, 137–146, 213, 215
Assize of Arms 30

Baldwin, king of Jerusalem 48–49
Baldwin II, king of Jerusalem 52–54, 59, 119
Baltic Crusades 64, 182
battle of
   Agincourt 17, 84–86, 147, 180–183
   al-Sannabra 51
   Andernach 11
   Ardres 86
   Arsuf 57, 62–63
   Artah 51
   Azaz 52
   Bannockburn 171–174
   Barnet 183
   Bosra 52

Bouvines 81, 111, 120, 169
Ceresole 199
Chalon 143
Courtrai 170–173
Crecy 17, 77, 153, 174–176, 190–193
Cresson 54, 61
Dorylaeum 44
Evesham 150–151
Falkirk 96, 171, 173
Field of Blood 52
Fontenoy 214
Fornovo 93, 187
Gaugamela 3
Grandson 121
Hab 52, 119
Harran 50
Hastings 17–19, 25–28, 37, 121, 135
Hattin 53–56, 59–62
Ivry 206
Jaffa 166, 182
Kadesh 1
Lechfeld 34
Lincoln 130
Lucera 186–187
Lewes 150
Manzikert 50
Marathon 164
Marignano 187, 197
Morlaix 86
Mauron 86
Mohacs 199
Montgisard 53
Morlaix 86
Najera 137, 146, 182
Nicopolis 120, 154, 182
Othee 193
Patay 85, 120, 147, 181, 183

Index 273

Poitiers 103, 134, 147, 176–179
Ramla, first 48
Ramla, second 49
Rimini 8
Roncevaux Pass 135
Roosebeke 193
San Romano 78, 114
Sarmin 51
Sempach 185
Somme 115
Stamford Bridge 17, 222
Tannenburg 120
Teutoburg Forest 129
Tinchebrai 169
Verneuil 86, 112, 120, 182
Waterloo 114, 124, 219
Yibneh 49
Baybars 63–64
Bayeux Tapestry 18, 25–28, 79, 95, 110
Bede, venerable 16
Bedingfield, Thomas 202
Beowulf 13–14
Black Prince 77, 116, 150, 153, 162, 175–179
Bohun, Henry de 172
Boucicaut 71, 86–87, 120, 134
Bouvet, Honore 157
bridle 13, 15, 46, 59, 98, 111
brothers-in-arms 87–88
Bruce, Robert, king of Scots 171–172
bullfighting 36, 96, 98
Burgundy 143, 193, 198
Byzantines 8–9, 40, 44, 50–51, 165

caparison 47, 67, 110, 116–117
Caesar 133–135
Calais 153, 195–196
cannons 121, 154, 176, 187, 190–197
Canterbury Tales 90, 212, 233
captives 31–32, 75–76, 91, 142, 147, 149
Carolingian Dynasty 9–11, 16, 33, 135
Castiglione, B 213–214
castles 22–25, 43, 63, 194–198
cataphract 19, 165
Cavendish, William 95, 202–203, 226–227

Caxton, William 76, 140, 159
ceremony of knighthood 75–77, 109, 215
chainmail, see mail
Chandos, John 143
chariots 1–2
chamfron 111–112, 116, 221
Charlemagne 11, 69, 135, 141
Charles VII, king of France 209–211
Charles the Bold, duke of Burgundy 121
Charles the Simple, King of France 12–13
Charny, Geoffrey de 68–69, 133, 142–147, 152–153, 159–161, 179, 213, 215–217, 233
Chaucer, Geoffrey 29, 90, 149, 212
chevauchée 118, 157
crinet 111–112
Christianity 6, 42, 59–60, 130–133, 156, 199, 217
Clermont 39
Clovis, king of the Franks 6, 8
condottieri 35, 89, 151, 179, 186
Constantinople 40, 43, 194
courtesy 32, 136, 150
cnight 4, 14, 29
Crusades 39–67, 97, 131–133

Damietta 63
De Beuil, Jean 43, 91, 184, 233
De La Noue, Francois 105
Dennis, St 145
Don Quixote 162, 218
Domesday Book 29
Duarte, King of Portugal 98–99

Edward I, king of England 42, 64, 73, 102–103, 139, 150–151
Edward II, king of England 171–172
Edward III, king of England 77, 103, 115, 139–140, 146–149, 153, 155, 190
Eglinton Joust 219–220
El Cid 36, 90
Elizabeth I, queen of England 201, 215
equites 3–4

Fastolf, John 147
Fatimids 48–49
fencing 86, 93

Field of the Cloth of Gold 215
Florence 34, 196
Foix, Gaston, count of 70
fortification 22–25, 195–197
francs-archers 181, 184
France, Matter of 135, 156
Froissart, Jean 152–153
furusiyya 66

Garter, order of the 76, 146–148, 163, 198
Gaucourt, Raoul de 154–155
Germany 14–16, 33–35, 49, 63, 125, 129, 143, 185, 192
Ghulam 47
Glastonbury 139
Gloucester, earl of 173
grapper 80
Grosmont, Henry of, duke 152, 161
Guesclin, Bertrand du 134
Guinevere, Queen 139, 141
gunpowder 187–198, 206

Hanseatic League 211
Harold II, King of England 17–18, 26–29, 75, 121, 222
Hawking 21
Hawkwood, John 29
heaven 39, 46
Henry II, king of England 30, 139, 203
Henry II, king of France
Henry III, king of England 130
Henry IV, king of England
Henry IV, king of France 204–206
Henry V, king of England 69, 88, 91, 148, 154–158, 180, 193
Henry VI, king of England
Henry VII, king of England
Henry VIII, king of England 198, 200–203, 215
heraldry 5, 144, 214
Hoccleve, Thomas ix, x
Holy Land 39–67, 79, 87, 132, 166
Holy Roman Empire 33–34, 168–169, 180, 196
horsemanship 2, 70–75, 101, 124, 127, 145, 198–203, 226–229

horse
 archery 7, 34, 44–45, 50–57
 chapter 94–126
 care 1–2, 68, 100–101
 Italian 102–103, 112
 psychology 113
 shoes 113
 size 15, 94–95
 Spanish 36, 95–97, 102, 122–123, 202
 speed 106–108, 230
 type 96–98
 value 96–97, 102
 vulnerability 116–117
Hospitaller Knights 54, 57–64, 132, 146
Hundred Years War 23, 86, 118, 139, 141, 151, 181
Hungary 199
hunting 21, 70–71, 123, 128

Ibelin, Balian of 55
Ibn Khaldun 90
infantry 163–188
Islam 36, 165–166
Italy 8, 22, 33–35, 89, 102, 168, 179–184, 196–199, 214

Jerusalem 39, 41–66, 124
Joan of Arc 155
John, king of England 102, 130
John II, king of France 147
jousting 19, 37, 71–81, 97–98, 139–145, 192, 200–202, 215–218, 219
Just War 65, 148, 157

Kenilworth 150
knighthood
 ceremony 75–77
 decline 189–218
 education 66–71, 87–88
 origins 1–20

La Hire 121
lance
 couching 25–28, 80
 power 19
Lancelot 137–141, 215

Index   275

Landsknechte 185–186, 199–200
Latimer, William 69
laws of war 69
Liechtenstein, Ulrich von 159
Lithuania 64, 182
Llull, Ramon 76, 156, 158–159
Louis, king of France 33, 57
love 136, 140, 152, 159

Malory, Sir Thomas 140
mail 16, 20, 26, 36, 45, 57, 67, 72, 79–83, 110–111, 117
Mamluks 53, 63–64, 66
Mappa Mundi 41
Marshal, Gilbert 72, 102–103, 161
Marshal, William 76, 102
Maximilian I, Emperor 198–199, 213
mélee 48, 61, 97, 106, 114, 144, 174, 220, 225
mercenaries 28, 30, 35, 53, 89–90, 167–168, 180–181, 190, 209–210, 214
   Genoese crossbowmen 175, 190
Merovingian Dynasty 6–11
men-at-arms viii, 23–24, 31, 152–153, 158, 161–162, 174–184, 205–212
money 2, 12, 35, 88, 150, 180, 197
Michelangelo 196
Milan 34, 89, 168
militia 6–7, 35, 75, 165, 168, 170, 180
ministeriales 34
Molyneux, Nicholas 88
Monmouth, Geoffrey of 138
Montaigne, M. de 125, 161, 212, 217
Montfort, Simon de 150–151
muster 2, 7, 10, 207–208, 210–211

Naples 202
Navarre 204
Newburgh, William of 138
Nino, Pero ix, 9, 74, 78–79, 88, 117, 151, 160
nobility 11–12, 29, 71, 129, 157–158, 205–217
Nogent, Guibert de 43
Normans 21–38
Normandy 13, 17–18, 21–22, 31–33, 209

Orderic Vitalis 27, 32
orders of chivalry 146–148
Oriflamme 179
Ottoman Turks 40–54, 154, 199, 211

Paris, Matthew 103
Paston family 140, 195
pay 2, 14, 28, 32, 69, 78, 103, 207, 210
Peace of God 131
peasants 29, 41, 43, 70, 82, 131, 150
Penitential Code of Ermenfrid 28
Persians 162
pistols 191, 200, 205–206, 212
Pizan, Christine de 24, 69, 90, 145, 159
plague 103, 117, 176, 184
Poitiers, William of 26–27
Poland 182, 211
Popes 22, 39–40, 42, 56, 65–66, 132, 133
Ponthieu, Guy of 75
Prowess 68, 127–130, 134–135, 150, 159–160, 216

quintain 231

ransoms 12, 31–32, 72, 88, 149, 155, 207
religion 130–133, 204–205
Renaissance 196, 201, 208, 214
Repton Stone 16
retinues 6, 8, 64, 85, 93, 116, 119, 144
Richard I, king of England 42, 56–63, 129, 143, 149, 166–167, 182
Richard II, king of England 140, 152
Richard III, king of England 76, 159, 203, 221
Robert Curthose 31, 42
Roland 135, 136, 141
Rollo 12–13
Roman army 4
Roman legacy 6, 34
Rome, Matter of 133–135, 156
Roman saddle 19–20
romance literature 133–141
Roses, Wars of the 155, 183–184, 195–196, 197, 211
Round Table 137, 139, 141, 144

saddles 14, 19–20, 59, 95, 99, 107, 108–109, 229
Saladin 42, 48, 53–58, 62, 75, 76, 166
Sassanid Empire 4–5
Saxons 13–18, 24–28, 36–38
Saxon Chronicle 16
Scalacronica 172
Shakespeare, William 212
Sicily 13, 21, 40, 102
siege of
  Antioch 45
  Harfleur 154, 193
  Melun 88
  Ostend 197
  Roxburgh 193
siege techniques 23, 193, 197
Song of Roland 135, 136, 141
Spain, Iberia 35–36, 39–40, 96, 102, 135, 145, 146, 215, 218
spurs 66, 75–76, 77, 98–99, 101, 171
squires 87–88, 143, 208
Stavelot Triptych 27
stirrup 19–20, 103, 108
surcoat 67
Swiss infantry 121, 149, 184–187, 197, 199, 200, 214
sword's symbolism 75–76, 78–79

Tacitus 14
Talhoffer, Hans 86
Templar Knights 53–64, 132, 146
tericos 188
Teutonic Knights 63–64, 182, 211
Thegn 13–14
tilt-rail 37, 74, 145, 220, 226, 229
tournament 71–75, 141–145
Tower of London 25
Treaty of Brétigny 103, 179
Troyes, Chretien de 138
Truce of God 131
turcopoles 53
Turks 41, 43–45, 60, 90, 120

Uccello, Paolo 78
Urban II, Pope 39–40, 65, 66, 132
Usamah Ibn Munqidh 81, 114, 116
Utopia 217–218

Vegetius 69, 100
Venice 34, 159
Vienna 159, 202, 226
Viking 12–13, 14, 17, 21, 65, 95, 222
Villani, Filippo 179
Villami, Giovanni 190
Virgin Mary 132
vows 140, 147

Wars of the Roses 155, 183–184, 195–196, 197, 211
Warwick, Earl of 183–184, 196
weapons
  arrows 44, 45, 47, 50, 51, 55, 61, 66, 85, 106–107, 117, 166, 175–177, 190–191
  axes/poleaxes 87, 172, 184, 213, 225
  crossbows 35, 57, 58, 88, 106–107, 166–168, 175, 177, 181, 191–195
  knives 213
  goedendags 170
  guns 175–176, 187–188, 190–198
  halberds 181, 184–188
  lances 19, 25–26, 79–84, 107, 220, 230–232
  longbows 85–86, 106–107, 112, 168, 174–176, 181, 182, 190–191
  pikes 164, 168–173, 177, 185–188, 197–200
  sword 42, 70, 75, 78–79, 88, 93, 128, 205, 206, 212, 220, 225
West Franica 11–13, 22, 131
William I, King of England 18, 22, 24, 27, 28–31, 32, 90, 109
women 5, 71, 132, 136, 137, 159, 163

Xenophon 2, 100, 164, 201, 226

York, duke of 70